6/03

CONFRONTING THE WAR MACHINE

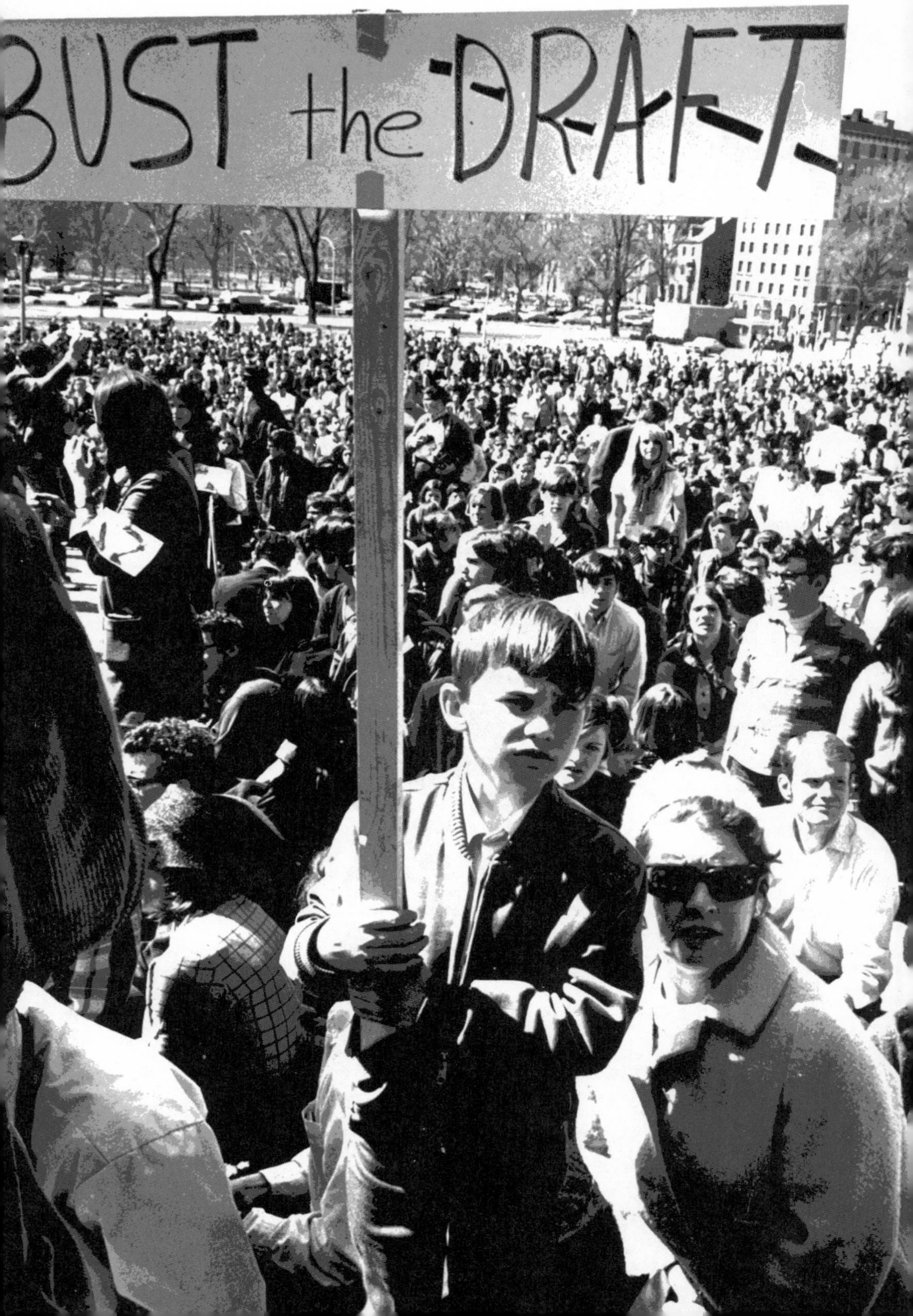
BUST the DRAFT

CONFRONTING THE WAR MACHINE

DRAFT RESISTANCE DURING THE VIETNAM WAR

Michael S. Foley

The University of North Carolina Press

Chapel Hill and London

© 2003 The University of North Carolina Press
All rights reserved
Manufactured in the United States of America
Set in Charter and Campaign types by Keystone Typesetting, Inc.
The paper in this book meets the guidelines for permanence and
durability of the Committee on Production Guidelines for Book
Longevity of the Council on Library Resources.

Library of Congress Cataloging-in-Publication Data
Foley, Michael S.
Confronting the war machine : draft resistance during the Vietnam War / Michael S. Foley.
   p. cm.
Includes bibliographical references and index.
ISBN 0-8078-2767-3 (cloth: alk. paper)
ISBN 0-8078-5436-0 (pbk.: alk. paper)
1. Vietnamese Conflict, 1961–1975—Draft resisters—United States. 2. Vietnamese Conflict,
1961–1975—Protest movements—United States. I. Title.
DS559.8.D7 F65 2003
959.704'38—dc21   2002010967

cloth   07 06 05 04 03   5 4 3 2 1
paper   07 06 05 04 03   5 4 3 2 1

Phil Ochs, "Draft Dodger Rag," © Barricade Music, Inc.
Reprinted by permission of Meegan Lee Ochs.

Portions of Chapter 6 appeared earlier, in somewhat different form, in Michael S.
Foley, " 'The Point of Ultimate Indignity' or a 'Beloved Community': The Draft Resistance
Movement and New Left Gender Dynamics," in *The New Left Revisited*, ed. Paul Buhle and
John McMillian (Philadelphia: Temple University Press, 2003) (reprinted by permission).

Portions of Chapter 8 and 9 appeared earlier, in somewhat different form, in Michael S.
Foley, "Sanctuary!: A Bridge between Civilian and GI Dissent," in *The Companion to the
Vietnam War*, ed. Robert Buzzanco and Marilyn Young (Boston: Blackwell, 2002)
(reprinted by permission).

Portions of Chapter 8 also appeared earlier, in somewhat different form, in Michael S.
Foley, "Confronting the Johnson Administration at War: The Trial of Dr. Spock and the Use
of the Courtroom to Effect Political Change," *Peace & Change* (January 2003) (reprinted
by permission of Blackwell Publishers).

FOR EMMA

CONTENTS

A section of illustrations follows page 204

PREFACE

My kind of loyalty was loyalty to one's country,
not to its institutions or its officeholders.
—Mark Twain, A Connecticut Yankee at King Arthur's Court, *1898*

On September 11, 2001, as this book neared completion, terrorists attacked the city in which I live and work, thus amputating its skyline and killing thousands of the world's citizens. In a matter of weeks, the United States mobilized for an unprecedented distant war against a nearly invisible foe, executed primarily from the skies above Afghanistan. In time, the rolling sea of American flags that buoyed New York in the aftermath of the attack grew weathered and tattered, and the city's residents—like the rest of America— gradually allowed themselves to be distracted from international affairs by sporting events and the insipid situation comedies and reality-based shows that litter American television programming. But half a world away, thousands of Afghan civilians with no such luxury of distraction are caught in the crossfire of an expanding "war without end." As I write, it seems clear that the war will soon spread to other countries in the Middle East and Asia.

Since the start of this "new kind of war," I have been asked many times, particularly by students, about the possibility of a military draft, what form it would take, how it would work, and if one could resist it or beat it. At this writing, it no longer seems hasty to discuss a new draft. Although the United States military is well-equipped with a substantial all-volunteer force and particularly reliant on air power, on December 20, 2001, Congressmen Nick Smith (R-Michigan) and Curt Weldon (R-Pennsylvania) introduced the Universal Military Training and Service Act of 2001 (H.R. 3598) in the House of Representatives. As the new war expands on multiple fronts, and the president and vice president tell the American people to prepare for the long haul, we can no longer dismiss the possibility of a revived draft.

If Congress and administration policy makers do ultimately call for a new draft, one would hope that the Selective Service would apply the lessons of the Vietnam War–era draft and ensure that any new system of conscription be administered more fairly across all segments of society (as it stands, the all-volunteer force is nearly as disproportionately poor, working class, and minority as the draft-fed military of the Vietnam era). Of course, the government also may have learned from the Vietnam War experience that the draft makes a useful target for opponents of a war; without thousands of people defying the draft and confronting the government through direct action, antiwar protest is much easier to ignore. So far, what little protest that has occurred has been dismissed by the administration and the press.

This raises another point about the current political environment to which this book speaks: the parallels between the calls for unity and patriotism that dominate American life today with similar calls in the 1960s. Today's climate, in many ways intolerant of alternative voices or dissenting opinions, is very much reminiscent of the early days of the Vietnam War when self-styled patriots not only shouted down dissent but sometimes beat it out of people. The mainstream media fanned the flames of division by focusing on the most extreme, outlandish acts of protest carried out by very few while ignoring the more thoughtful expressions of opposition voiced by many. The same is true today. Just as it did in 1967, for example (see Chapter Four), the *Boston Globe* recently ran a front-page photograph of a lone protester burning an American flag on the campus of the University of Massachusetts. We never see front-page photographs of thoughtful protesters standing at a microphone, speaking to a crowd.

And so dissent is demonized again. Resistance and confrontation are demonized. But we would do well to recall that the history of American freedom is not a tale of a people united by certain durable ideals, marching as one toward some promised land of a better society. Rather, as historian Eric Foner has remarked in a recent column, it is "a story of countless disagreements and battles in which victories sometimes prove temporary and retrogression often follows progress." At its best, America has always tolerated—and, indeed, thrived on—deliberation, discussion, and disagreement. At its worst, often during wartime, various administrations have crushed that natural democratic impulse by limiting civil liberties, expanding police powers, and encouraging intolerance for alternative views. It is an ugly phenomenon and it should be resisted.

As I hope this book makes clear, in a republic such as ours, questioning war is a perfectly valid act of citizenship. Unity for unity's sake is best left to nations led by totalitarian regimes.

M. S. F.
New York City
February 2002

ACKNOWLEDGMENTS

I have incurred the debt of a great many people in the course of doing the research for and writing of this book. First, and foremost, I cannot overstate the importance of everyone who participated in this study by sitting for an interview or completing the questionnaire. Those who agreed to interviews often welcomed me, a stranger, into their homes and their offices; they often fed me in their own kitchens when I overstayed my welcome, or took me out for a meal. Most important, they told me the stories that are at the center of this book. Not only would this project have been impossible to complete without their cooperation, it would have been impossible to begin. Their hospitality and generosity were unanticipated bonuses. I only regret that I could not interview everyone I contacted and that so many of the stories told to me could not be included without extending the length of this book considerably.

I am grateful to those who helped me with all phases of preparing the questionnaire. My sociologist friends, Carrie Yodanis, Sean Lauer, and Barrie Thorne, provided essential advice on conceptualizing and writing the questionnaire itself. Doug McAdam, whose book on Mississippi Freedom Summer inspired me to use a survey in this project, offered encouragement and important tips on administering the questionnaire through alumni offices. Howard Zinn and Michael Ferber endorsed the survey in a letter that several respondents credited with moving them to complete it. David Clennon underwrote the cost of copying and mailing more than 300 questionnaires with a generous grant, administered through the Gunst-Wilcox fund at the University of New Hampshire. My parents, Bill and Judy Foley, mailed most of the questionnaires for me as I ran off to California to conduct interviews. Most important, I thank the 185 people who returned completed surveys; their cooperation has proven indispensable.

Finding former draft resisters and other activists thirty years after the fact proved difficult, and I am immensely grateful to the following people for helping me to locate others (I apologize if I leave anyone out): Michael Ferber, Howard Zinn, Barrie Thorne, Noam Chomsky, Ray Mungo, Peter Simon, Alex Jack, Connie Field, Neil Robertson, Bill Hunt, Michael Colpitts, Joel Kugelmass, Roxanne Dunbar-Ortiz, Sue Katz, Charles Fisher, Saul Slapikoff, Louis Kampf, Hilde Hein, Shawn Donovan, Ellen DuBois, Rob Chalfen, Ramsey Clark, Mark Mostow, Penney Kurland Lagos, and James Carroll.

I owe an additional measure of gratitude to James Carroll for publishing a timely column on the Boston draft resistance movement in his weekly *Boston Globe* column. At the end of the piece, he asked readers to contact me with information that might be useful to this project. My phone rang for days and immediately gave my research a much-needed boost.

One of the people who called in response to the Carroll piece was Alex Jack, who, it turned out, kept six large archival boxes of papers in his basement all these years. Little did I know how well draft resisters and their comrades understood their moment in history; eighteen different draft resistance activists gave me access to their personal private collections: Bill Bischoff, Rev. Jack Bishop, Fred Bird, Rev. John Boyles, Rob Chalfen, Michael Colpitts, Michael Ferber (papers now at Swarthmore College Peace Collection), Charles Fisher (papers now at Swarthmore), Dick Hughes, James Hunt, Alex Jack, Chick Marston, Jim Oestereich, Dave Satz, Bob Shapiro, John Sisson, Nan Stone, and Michael Zigmond. I owe special thanks to Deborah Jelmberg and Ellen Ford for providing access to and copies of a scrapbook chronicling Chick Marston's experience, and to Charles Fisher for sharing his unpublished manuscript on the Boston Draft Resistance Group. All of these collections have proven indispensable to my research. In addition, Stanley Moss at the Arlington Street Church went above and beyond the call of duty in making records from the church available to me. Finally, Wendy Chmielewski at the Swarthmore College Peace Collection and archivists at Michigan State University, Syracuse University, the Lyndon Johnson Presidential Library, and the Nixon Presidential Materials Staff at the National Archives (Archives II) gave essential assistance, too.

The Department of History at the University of New Hampshire, where this project originated as a doctoral dissertation, is home to an uncommonly nurturing group of historians, and I received excellent feedback on work-in-progress from faculty and fellow students. In particular, graduate school colleagues Bill Jordan, Beth Nichols, Gretchen Adams, David Chapin, Scott Hancock, and Dave Cecere helped me to refine ideas and smooth the rough edges. Graduate director Jeff Bolster consistently offered cogent advice on structure, organization, and the rewards and pitfalls of writing a narrative. As everyone who has had the privilege to work with him knows, Jeff never fails to dispense wise counsel from his tiny office (or while standing in the history department's corridors)—balanced with the right mixture of cheerleading and pitchforking.

Harvard Sitkoff, my mentor and dissertation adviser, has been exceptionally supportive of this project since the day we first discussed it. He always encouraged me when I needed reassurance, challenged me when I thought I knew everything, and applauded me when I earned it. Through it all, he gave me the breathing room to think for myself, make my own mistakes (and learn from them), and shape the dissertation into its final form. When he went to Ireland on a Fulbright, he diligently read chapters and provided valuable feedback. And long after the dissertation's completion, he is always there when I need him for advice of the scholarly kind and otherwise. I cannot thank him enough.

A host of others at UNH and beyond read complete drafts at various stages. I am grateful to Lucy Salyer, Janet Polasky, Bill Harris, Michael Ferber, Steve Russell, Kurk Dorsey, Bill Hunt, Ian Lekus, Christian Appy, and Melvin Small. Each read respective drafts closely and made excellent suggestions for preparation of the manuscript for publication. Ellen DuBois, Barbara Tischler, and Wini Breines offered thoughtful critiques and direction on my interpretation of gender dynamics in the draft resistance movement. Michael Ferber warrants special mention for getting me involved in the subject of draft resistance in the first place. His visit to Harvard Sitkoff's course on Vietnam in 1994 inspired me to investigate draft resistance further and led to a unique relationship in which Michael has played the parts of historical source, adviser, and, most of all, good friend. He even helped to get me to the airport on time for my trip to the Johnson Library in Texas when my car broke down.

The History Department and the Graduate School at the University of New Hampshire assisted me financially with graduate assistantships, summer research fellowships, and several small grants that paid for trips to Michigan and California, and the purchase of a tape recorder and transcriber. In addition, I thank the Lyndon Johnson Library Foundation for the Moody Grant that made travel to Austin possible. I also benefited from the hospitality of friends and family who gave me places to stay when I traveled to do research: Erin Foley and Bob Mocharnuk in Los Angeles; Penny Blair in San Francisco; Pam Gubuan and Bobby Robinowitz in New York; Katie Porter in Washington, D.C.; and, more recently, Tony Foley and Heather Horton on return trips to New England.

Katie Porter, an undergraduate at the University of New Hampshire when this project was still in the dissertation stage, provided essential research assistance and gave the first complete draft a thorough proofreading. And Corley Kenna, another former UNH student now in a position of influence on Capitol Hill, has provided critical help with Library of Congress requests.

At a time when the nation's press photographic heritage is held hostage by huge media conglomerates that charge exorbitant fees for permission to reprint images, I have had the good fortune to encounter people of conscience in my hunt for this book's images. In particular, my heartfelt thanks to Peter Simon, Bob Hohler, Jim Oestereich, Rob Chalfen, Tom Rothschild, and Fred Bird for providing photographs at no charge. (Interested readers should see Peter Simon's wonderful book of photography, *I and Eye: Pictures of My Generation*, available through his website, PeterSimon.com.) In addition, where charges had to be incurred, Aaron Schmidt of the Print Department at the Boston Public Library did yeoman's work in finding photos in the *Boston Herald Traveler* collection and charged humane fees for their use. Likewise, John Cronin, the *Boston Herald* librarian, gave me the run of the *Boston Record American* photograph files and also chose to charge modest fees for the photos I have selected. Even with this special treatment, however, the total cost for this book's photographs proved far beyond my reach. I am, therefore, grateful for the financial assistance of two benefactors whose last-minute financial support made the publication of most of the images in this book possible: my father, Bill Foley, and Dean David Podell and the Research Foundation at the College of Staten Island. And thanks, too, to Warrick Bell, who digitized several photographs from contact sheets and made the management of the various digital formats in which some of the photographs arrived possible.

I was fortunate to be recruited to the University of North Carolina Press by Lewis Bateman, who showed tremendous confidence in the project from the start. Following Lew's departure, David Perry and Mark Simpson-Vos have offered steadfast support and encouragement while putting up with my missed deadlines. And Mary Caviness, copyeditor extraordinaire, saved me from being painfully repetitive in dozens of places and helped sharpen my prose. All of this assistance notwithstanding, I alone am responsible for any remaining errors of omission or commission.

And in the important category of more general support, I owe thanks to many other people. I am deeply grateful, for example, to Maria Foley for her support of this project over a number of years. My parents warrant further mention for instilling in me a love of history and an interest in social justice. There is something about growing up in an Irish American family full of storytellers—amateur historians all—that I'm sure channeled me into this profession (even after my first miserable career). Thanks, too, to Charlie Hattman for making a long hot summer of revisions in Philadelphia more tolerable by dragging me out to see Nate Wiley and the Crowd Pleasers every week at Bob and Barbara's. Now, in New York, Kathryn Dale makes sure I don't lose sight of the value of good music, good enchiladas, and good company. And my colleagues in the History Department at the College of Staten Island have welcomed me into a stimulating intellectual environment where they have set high standards as teachers and scholars, but even higher ones as colleagues.

Finally, this book is dedicated to Emma, who is far too young to be interested in draft resistance or the Vietnam War but who I hope will one day understand that it is acceptable, and indeed, "American," to resist illegitimate authority. Of course, the legitimate authority of her mother and father is another issue.

ABBREVIATIONS

ACLU	American Civil Liberties Union
AFSC	American Friends Service Committee
AWOL	Absent without Leave
BAFGOPI	Boston Area Faculty Group on Public Issues
BDRG	Boston Draft Resistance Group
BU	Boston University
BUF	Black United Front
CARS	Concord Area Resistance Summer
CCEWV	Cambridge Committee to End the War in Vietnam
CCV	Committee of Concern for Vietnam
CIA	Central Intelligence Agency
CLUM	Civil Liberties Union of Massachusetts
CNVA	Committee for Non-Violent Action
CO	Conscientious Objector
DOD	Department of Defense
FBI	Federal Bureau of Investigation
IWW	Industrial Workers of the World
LBJ	Lyndon Baines Johnson
MIRV	Multiple Independent Reentry Vehicle
MIT	Massachusetts Institute of Technology
NER	New England Resistance
PL	Progressive Labor Party
SANE	Committee for a Sane Nuclear Policy
SNCC	Student Non-Violent Coordinating Committee
SSS	Selective Service System
SVN	South Vietnam

CONFRONTING THE WAR MACHINE

Nothing can bring you peace but yourself. Nothing can bring you peace but the triumph of principles.
—*Ralph Waldo Emerson,* Self-Reliance, *1841*

A significant number of young Americans have decided they must refuse military service in Vietnam, even if the consequence will be their imprisonment. . . . If this country does not listen to their testimony, if it simply scorns them as "draft dodgers" or proceeds to impose legal penalties, then there will occur, among other disastrous consequences, a terrible alienation between generations that could only damage our hopes for a new upsurge of social progress in the U.S.
—*"Students & the Draft,"* Dissent, *May–June 1968*

What do you think—that all people of this country can say whether or not they want to go to war? You couldn't get a decent war off the ground that way.
—*Archie Bunker,* All in the Family, *1974*

BOURGEOIS VOUS N'AVEZ RIEN COMPRIS
—Student Poster, Paris, June 1968

INTRODUCTION
DRAFT RESISTANCE IN AMERICAN MEMORY

*The love of Americans for their country is not an indulgent, it is
an exacting and chastising love; they cannot tolerate its defects.*
—Jacques Maritain, Reflections on America, *1958*

On October 18, 1997, about three dozen men and women gathered in
the same church in which they had, thirty years earlier, confronted their
nation's government during wartime. Seated in a large circle, they went
around, one after another, summarizing their lives since their activist days
in Boston's draft resistance movement. At first they agreed to keep the
reports to five minutes each, but gradually they stretched to fifteen and
twenty minutes. As they looked across the circle at one another, and
through the mist of three decades of memory, they spoke of careers and
family, but few dwelled very long on the years since 1970 or so; instead,
most focused on the draft resistance years themselves and the few years
after. It became increasingly clear that while most had a general sense of
how they had all come *to* draft resistance, they knew very little about how
they each had experienced those years, or how their respective antiwar
stories had concluded.

The former draft resistance activists who came to the Arlington Street
Church that day no doubt got more out of this group discussion—which
lasted several hours and continued over a Vietnamese dinner—than they
did from the next day's more formal Sunday service that acknowledged the
work they had done in attempting to end the American war in Vietnam.
Though the church service produced several moving moments, the few
activists who participated in it spoke primarily to the current congregation,
as if to pass on a chapter of family history. On the previous day, however,
those in the larger group spoke only to each other, and the range of stories
varied in ways that surprised even themselves.

For example, Larry Etscovitz, who had been enrolled as a junior at
Boston University in 1967, described his persistent regret that he had not

followed through with his resistance all the way to prison. After agonizing over the war for more than two years, and finally turning in his draft card as part of an organized movement against the draft and the war, his draft board reclassified him I-A, draft eligible. When he went to the Boston Army Base for his pre-induction physical and did not cooperate, however, the officers let him leave. They did not have him arrested, and the government did not attempt to prosecute. He never knew why. Later, his draft board reclassified him with a draft deferment. In retrospect, he saw that the system had made it easy for him, at a time when he had never been so scared, to take a way out. Sheepishly, now, he told the others he wished he had gone to prison.

Similarly, David Clennon, who disrupted his studies at the Yale Drama School when he resisted the draft, recounted his ambivalence on the day of the big draft card turn-in at the Arlington Street Church and on the damage his resistance did to his relationship with his father. When his draft board finally tried to call him for induction more than a year after he turned in his draft card, Clennon applied for conscientious objector status; the board rejected the idea outright. Recognizing by then that the movement had lost confidence in its strategy of flooding the courts and filling the jails, and at the same time more acutely doubting his ability to withstand more than two years of prison, he succeeded in getting a psychological deferment. Thirty years later, Clennon characterized this act to his peers as "a copout."

The way such confessions were made, conveying a genuine sense of shame, elicited an immediate response from the others present, who, like a big brother offering reassurance to a younger sibling, made it clear that the community did not judge them harshly. Going to prison, someone mentioned, did not stop the war. That these men even harbored such feelings so many years later, however, came as news to most of the group.

In fact, no one in attendance had gone to prison, though most had welcomed the idea. Some, like Alex Jack, one of Boston's main draft resistance organizers, had been interviewed by the Federal Bureau of Investigation (FBI) and fully expected to be prosecuted, but heard nothing. As a student at the Boston University School of Theology, Jack had been one of the original founders of the New England Resistance (NER)—the primary sponsor of Boston's draft card turn-ins—and a key movement strategist. Although Boston University later expelled him for Resistance work on campus, his draft board never reclassified him and the Justice Department never indicted him. He later speculated that the government must have decided that it would be more trouble than it was worth to go after a movement "leader."

As Nan Stone, another key organizer, noted, women could not be prosecuted for draft resistance, per se, because they were not subject to the draft. Nevertheless, Stone, who also had been a student at the BU School of Theology, did everything possible to assume the same level of risk as the men, and constantly had to push the men in the movement for the opportunity to do so. And at a time when women in social movements were so often restricted to support roles, Stone also had to fight for more responsibility throughout her tenure with the New England Resistance. As she told the group, she came to the women's movement directly from this experience in draft resistance. When she spoke to the parishioners at the Arlington Street Church the next day, she noted that it marked the first time that she had been invited to speak on the same platform with the men of the movement. Certainly, the men who were involved in the day-to-day operations of the draft resistance organizations knew something of the way women felt as a result of such treatment, but for others around the room, Stone's account came as another revelation.

So, too, did Harvard professor Hilary Putnam's report of his experience in the draft resistance movement. One of the century's most influential philosophers, Putnam had organized faculty and students against the war as early as 1965. Later, in 1967 and 1968, he accepted draft cards from resisters at all of Boston's major draft card turn-ins. By the spring of 1968, however, he joined many opponents of the war in the Progressive Labor Party (PL), a doctrinaire Maoist organization that many activists later blamed for destroying the New Left and some strains of the antiwar movement. Thirty years later, Putnam told the reunion that he had made a mistake in joining PL. He had been impressed with the organization's commitment to building alliances and the members' willingness to try to organize from within the army, but he later grew alienated from the undemocratic, browbeating tactics they used to command unity among their ranks.

Not all of the stories told at the reunion were new to those in attendance. Michael Ferber, another of the original founders of the Boston movement, for example, required little time to tell his story because, unlike the other resisters', his had been so public. The government did indict Ferber, in part for delivering a sermon at the Arlington Street Church draft card turn-in on October 16, 1967, but they put him on trial with the noted pediatrician Benjamin Spock, the Yale chaplain William Sloane Coffin Jr., and two other older advisers. The trial, set in Boston, became a cause célèbre in 1968 and resulted in convictions for four of the men, including Ferber. A year later, an appeals court overturned the convictions, and Ferber eventually drifted back to his graduate studies at Harvard.

Today, library shelves groan under the weight of books about the Vietnam War, including scores of memoirs written by politicians and veterans, so if most of these reunion stories were unfamiliar to the people who participated in this movement, the day's discussion of such varied experiences and emotions certainly would have surprised most Americans who know anything about the Vietnam War era. And if more draft resistance alumni had been able to attend, the stories of defiance and accommodation, of alienation and support from friends and family, of FBI visits, of induction calls, of demonstrations, and of prison would have been even more varied. The reality is that American collective memory about both the war and opposition to it has long been too simplistic, and draft resistance may be one of the least understood phenomena of the period. To paraphrase historian Robert Buzzanco, thirty years have passed since the United States withdrew its forces from Southeast Asia, and still Americans believe lies about the Vietnam War. Thanks to the examples of several high-profile draft "dodgers"-turned-politicians, the public's distinction between draft evaders and draft resisters is imperceptible; anyone who violated a draft law, it seems, was and is a draft dodger. And draft dodgers, it follows, were disloyal and un-American. That draft resistance may have been an important strain of the antiwar movement, or that it even influenced government policy, does not come up for consideration. That draft resisters may have broken the law as an act of patriotism seems inconceivable.[1]

To date, historians have not done enough to investigate and understand the experience of draft resisters and their movement. In fact, draft resistance has been virtually forgotten or, at best, understated by historians of the antiwar movement,[2] the 1960s, and the New Left. Todd Gitlin's influential history/memoir called *The Sixties*, for example, describes draft resistance as just one of the "varieties of antiwar experience." Likewise, Terry Anderson's popular book, *The Movement and the Sixties*, devotes approximately 2 of its 423 pages to draft resistance.[3] Even the many books on the events of 1968 contain few references to draft resistance, which is most puzzling given the amount of space the subject occupied in big-city newspapers across the country that year, especially from January to July.[4] Furthermore, critics of the sixties generation or of the antiwar movement emphasize the most militant factions of the New Left and the civil rights movement and, consequently, pay no attention to draft resistance.[5] By the time descriptions of the antiwar movement filter down to surveys about the 1960s and to college textbooks, then, the history of draft resistance is often absent or inaccurate. To the extent that some textbooks or syntheses on the 1960s discuss the draft and the protest against it, the emphasis inevitably centers on draft card burning or draft evasion, neither of which, as this book shows, was at all synonymous with draft resistance.[6]

Finally, the situation is made worse by several books that examine the experience of men who evaded the draft, either by emigrating to Canada or by pulling off some ploy that got them rejected by the Selective Service, but use the term "resister" to describe men who, by draft resistance standards, *dodged* the draft. The blurring of this distinction annoys former draft resisters who today find themselves stressing the difference whenever they talk about it. Part of the reason they chose to resist the draft derived from the unfairness of the Selective Service System, the machinery of which provided "safety valves" that channeled potential troublemakers or recalcitrants out of the system while it required others to take their places on the battlefield. To accept one of the deferments that marked a man ineligible for service or even to leave the country was viewed by resisters as tantamount to letting the system win. The confusion of "draft resister" and "draft dodger" labels has become so frustrating that one draft resistance leader has said on several occasions (only partially in jest) that when he dies, his epitaph should read, "I Didn't Dodge, I Resisted."[7]

The extent of the general public's misunderstanding of draft resistance during the Vietnam War became obvious almost immediately when I began six years of research for this book. I soon grew used to being reminded of the controversial and misunderstood nature of the historical events described here. When people asked about the project, almost inevitably they interpreted it as a study of draft "dodgers," they made comments about Bill Clinton, Dan Quayle, or George W. Bush, and they sometimes wondered aloud why I would be interested in such people. Others understood quite well the difference between draft resistance and draft dodging but still could barely contain their contempt. For example, in the course of explaining the process for requesting certain papers in a collection at the Lyndon Johnson Presidential Library, one archivist smiled and used the name "Idiots against the Draft" as an example of an organization that might have some letters in President Johnson's correspondence files.

The most hostile reactions, however, came from people I never met. In the course of trying to locate hundreds of former draft resistance move-

ment participants, I often used Internet sites with the nation's phone listings. Frequently, however, I could not determine if a person who had the
same name as a former activist was the person I sought. Often I could not
narrow my search down to fewer than seven or eight people, all of whom
had the same name. Consequently, on a case-by-case basis, I sometimes
decided to send an introductory letter to, say, seven people named John
Doe to inquire if any of them were the John Doe who had participated in
the draft resistance movement in Boston. If I sent seven letters, of course, it
meant that at least six—and maybe all seven—were going to the wrong
people and so I tried to make it clear in the opening paragraph of each
letter that I was not sure if I had sent the letter to the right person.

In most cases, I received very courteous (what I would call "neutral")
responses to my inquiries either by phone call, by e-mail, or by letter.[8] Most
of these communications were made simply to inform me that I had not
found the correct person. One of those was from a man who called me
directly because he feared he might not receive an expected government
security clearance if his name could be found somewhere out there, even
erroneously, on a document identifying him as a draft resister.

At the same time, however, another ten individuals called or wrote to
express their disapproval of draft resistance and, sometimes, their disapproval of the project. In spite of my attempts to make it clear that I did not
know if I was writing to the correct person, some recipients interpreted my
letter as some kind of *accusation* that they were draft resisters or that they
were somehow on an official list of American draft resisters. "Please insure
that my name and address is not on your list. I would hate to be in any way
associated with this group," wrote one man. Another scribbled, "I have
never participated in any draft card turn-in ceremony. I [*sic*] never been to
Boston. How my name got in your file, I don't know. Please remove it! I
have serviced [*sic*] my country. And proud of it and I was not drafted. I
enlisted." Several, it turned out, were veterans of World War II, the Korean
War, and the Vietnam War, and they made sure to express their pride in
having served their country and their "disdain" for those who did not. In a
letter to the president of my university, one former marine demanded that
his name be removed from the records I cited and urged the president to
caution her faculty "to be more thorough in their efforts to communicate
with 'possible participants' especially with such a controversial subject as
'draft resistance.'"

Some phone calls and letters were particularly vituperative. One man
called to tell me that his middle initial was different from the man I sought

but concluded the conversation by saying his namesake "ought to be shot, that's what I say." Another wrote, "I was shocked to receive your letter wondering if I was one of the contemptible scum you are trying to locate. I served twenty-two years in the Army, and you are free to do your research due to the efforts of people like me. I find it hard to imagine that someone would attempt to develop a history of a group of self-centered 'useful fools,' to quote Lenin." Another veteran wrote that he believed civil disobedience to be a "synonym for anarchy" and that he regarded draft resisters, including, he said, "our draft-doging [sic] president," as cowards. He went on to criticize the "army of second-guessers who simply can't comprehend the magnitude of the Soviet Menace to our way of life," and especially to the United States. "It is so easy for the cloistered PhD," he wrote, "to ruminate over the way it should have been with present knowledge. It is quite another thing to have been there, and been fully informed on what the Reds would have done to all of us, had they been able to do the job."

This is a pretty unscientific sampling of public opinion, but given the failure of historians to properly chronicle the draft resistance movement, its ideals, and its impact on its participants and the government, it is not surprising that these Americans characterized draft resisters as they did. Draft resisters, the writers and callers suggested, were "cowards," "self-centered," and, by not serving their country, disloyal and unpatriotic. Indeed, Lawrence Baskir and William Strauss, two analysts of the Vietnam War–era draft, asserted in 1978 that "the most severe punishment suffered by draft resisters . . . has been the condemnation and misunderstanding of their fellow citizens." True forgiveness, they wrote, could not come from any government amnesty program but "only from understanding."[9] Today, a lack of understanding regarding draft resisters persists.

One goal of this book is to provide a basis for that understanding by exploring the contested notions of morality, citizenship, and freedom that fueled the draft resistance movement during its brief but influential history, while also being attentive to the day-to-day experiences of the draft resisters themselves. The stories told here dismantle the popular misperceptions of the citizens who confronted the war machine and restore the draft resistance movement to its rightful place as the leading edge of opposition to the war in 1967 and 1968. In short, I argue that draft resisters were the antiwar movement's equivalent to the civil rights movement's Freedom Riders and lunch-counter sit-in participants; today, Americans regard those dissenters as heroes while they view draft resisters as selfish, cowardly, and traitorous.

Yet the draft resistance movement targeted a system of conscription that, by 1967, few Americans would defend as fair and equitable. The stories of Muhammad Ali's and Bill Clinton's encounters with the draft are useful in demonstrating the system's inequities. In April 1960, when he turned eighteen, Ali (still known as Cassius Clay) registered for the draft just as every other draft-age man in Louisville, Kentucky, did through Selective Service Local Board 47. In March 1962, Local Board 47 reclassified Ali 1-A, eligible to be drafted. Two years later, just weeks before he won the heavyweight boxing title from Sonny Liston, he failed the pre-induction mental examinations. Ali scored in the sixteenth percentile, far below the thirtieth percentile score required to pass. A second mental test proved that Ali did not fake the first exam, and he soon received a classification of 1-Y, not qualified for service. The publicity that followed his deferment humiliated Ali. "I said I was the greatest," he told reporters, "not the smartest."[10] In early 1966, as the demand for troops increased with the escalation of the war in Southeast Asia, however, the U.S. Army lowered its standards on the mental examination to make anyone with a score in the fifteenth percentile or better eligible for the draft. In February, Ali's local draft board reclassified him 1-A. The heavyweight champ could not understand it and, in frustration, uttered the words heard around the world: "Man, I ain't got no quarrel with them Vietcong." The media and the public recoiled; by the time he refused induction over a year later, he had become so controversial that some state boxing commissions moved to bar closed-circuit broadcasts of his fights. Although the retired judge who heard his appeal recommended that the appeals board grant Ali conscientious objector status— based on his membership in the Nation of Islam—by fall 1966, Ali's case had become politicized and the board rejected the appeal. Ali refused induction and did not fight again until 1971, when the Supreme Court finally ruled in his favor. He gave up the best years of his athletic career to make a point.[11]

The apparently arbitrary manner in which Ali's case had been handled by the Selective Service was not unique. As draft calls soared, it grew increasingly obvious that the men being called to serve in this war came primarily from minority and working-class homes and were often under-educated or close to illiterate. Where, for instance, were the white professional athletes? Unlike the World War II system, this draft called few national celebrities. Elvis Presley answered the call of the armed forces in the late 1950s during a period of relative peace. In 1966, George Hamilton, the handsome Hollywood actor who was then dating one of President Johnson's daughters, escaped conscription by claiming his mother needed him to care for her. But famous, wealthy, white men were not the only safe ones; more glaring were the millions of college and graduate students who held deferments while those who could not go to college faced the draft.

Bill Clinton, a young Arkansan studying at Georgetown University, benefited from just such a deferment. As an undergraduate, the future president dodged the draft the same way millions of other college men did: legally. As part of its program of "manpower channeling," the Selective Service maintained its peacetime system of deferments for vocations deemed to be in the "national interest." Students in college, they assumed, were being educated for the future benefit of the nation, whereas gas station attendants and construction workers were not. Like thousands of other men who graduated from college in the middle of the war (1966), Clinton "pyramided" a graduate school deferment on top of his undergraduate one. Before graduate deferments were eliminated in 1968, registrants could conceivably use this tactic until they reached the age of twenty-six, when they were much less likely to be drafted. Clinton came along too late to adopt a similar strategy; in the middle of his Rhodes scholarship at Oxford University, Congress eliminated graduate deferments. Despite the example of the draft resistance movement and his Rhodes scholar roommate, who chose to accept prison over induction, Clinton manipulated the system as well as he could. After receiving an induction notice in May 1969, he sought and gained acceptance into an advanced Reserve Officer Training Corps (ROTC) program at the University of Arkansas Law School. This move successfully pushed him out of the 1-A pool into the 1-D classification for reserves and kept him from being inducted. Clinton held that deferment until late October, when he reneged on his ROTC commitment and asked to be reclassified as 1-A. By that time, President Nixon had changed draft regulations to allow graduate students who were called to finish the entire school year (which meant Clinton would be safe until July 1970) and was strongly hinting that a random selection process would soon begin. When the Selective Service held its first draft lottery on December 1, 1969, Clinton's number was so high (311), he knew he would never be called.[12]

Bill Clinton's Selective Service saga is important not simply because he is now seen (along with Dan Quayle and George W. Bush, among others) as one of the nation's best-known draft dodgers, but because it illustrates how the draft, which so efficiently marched some men off to war, could be so easily subverted and ignored by others. In New York City and Cleveland, Ohio, thirty-eight fathers and sons were arrested for paying up to $5,000 for false papers used to get deferments. One New York draft board official was convicted of selling deferments and exemptions for as much as $30,000.[13] The parallels with the Civil War–era practice of buying substitutes to fight on one's behalf are obvious. As unscrupulous parents bought bogus medical records to keep their sons out of Vietnam, working-class men vanished from their neighborhoods and landed in Southeast Asia. The same could be said of the forty to fifty thousand draft-age men who emigrated to Canada, Sweden, Mexico, and other countries. Asylum in these places cost money and resulted in someone else bearing the burden of fighting in Vietnam. Most important, students who wrote annual checks to their university's bursar's office not only paid their tuition but ensured that other draft-age men—in effect, substitutes—took their places in the army.

At its heart, draft resistance turned on this question: What could a man do when his country expected him to participate in a system of conscription that sent some of his fellow citizens to fight in a war he regarded as immoral and illegal yet protected him? It was a complicated dilemma of conscience versus obligation. Those who, like Bill Clinton, opposed the war but manipulated the system to evade service in Vietnam, served neither their conscience nor their sense of obligation. James Fallows is another case in point. A few years after the war ended, Fallows, a Harvard graduate and today a high-profile journalist and former editor for *U.S. News & World Report*, wrote about the sense of guilt he felt for evading the draft. On the day of his pre-induction physical, Fallows and all of the other registrants from Harvard and Cambridge arrived at the Boston Army Base with letters from doctors and psychiatrists that would keep them from being drafted. In the weeks leading up to the physical, Fallows dropped his weight to 120 pounds, making him virtually useless to the army. Meanwhile, as the Harvard men were being processed, a busload of strapping working-class kids from Chelsea arrived. Fallows quickly realized that they knew nothing about draft loopholes. On that day, the middle-class kids escaped the draft as the Chelsea boys went off to serve in the army.[14]

During wartime, political scientist Michael Shafer has argued, the obligation of citizenship is not merely to serve. "It is," he writes, "an obligation to active involvement whether in pursuit of policy or protest against it." Those who opposed the war but accepted the Selective Service System and their privileged places within it, Shafer charges, did not fulfill their responsibilities as citizens. Two other men were drafted into the armed forces instead of Bill Clinton and James Fallows. They may have served in Vietnam. They may have died there. Draft resisters cannot claim to have prevented other men from being drafted in their stead, but they can take some comfort in knowing that their actions fully exemplified their opposition to the war. In the end, the Selective Service moved to a more equitable lottery system (though some deferments remained), and in time, an all-volunteer force replaced conscription altogether. Even so, if as many draft-age men resisted the draft as opposed the war, the war effort might have crumbled before 1968.[15]

The point of making this distinction between resisters and dodgers is not, however, to pass judgment on either. Instead, it is to make clear that during the Vietnam War, the Johnson and Nixon administrations dishonored a generation of men by making them decide between 1) fighting in a war regarded by many as immoral and illegal, 2) going to prison, or 3) evading both the war and prison. To this day, those choices haunt many of that generation and, I would argue, contribute significantly to the cynicism so many Americans have come to share about the faithfulness of their government.

The virtual omission of draft resistance from the historical accounts of the Vietnam War is a manifestation of the period's still nagging effect on American culture and memory. The irony is that while most Americans— across the political spectrum—regard the war as a disaster (or a "tragedy" or a "mistake"), most Americans also regard those who sought to end the war as equally worthy of contempt. Those who tried to end a villainous war are themselves seen as villains.[16]

The stories told in this book complicate such simplistic characterizations. The experience of the draft resistance community in Boston, one of the cities where it was strongest, reminds us that an expanded definition of citizenship is possible and, indeed, derives from well-worn American traditions of dissent. In particular, the emphasis on obedience to one's conscience over allegiance to one's government has roots that reach as far back as the abolitionist movement and more directly to Henry David Thoreau. The movement made frequent references to twentieth-century peace heroes such as Mohandas Gandhi, Albert Camus, and Martin Luther King Jr., but draft resistance organizers quoted no one as often as they did Thoreau.

Resisters and their supporters acted on the premise that when the nation's government sets illegal or immoral policy, citizens are obligated to disagree with those policies, to disobey them if necessary, and to accept the legally prescribed punishment. But while they emphasized dissent and civil disobedience to one's government as a necessary duty of citizenship, critics of the movement charged it with being unpatriotic; they likened refusal to answer the government's call to service to an act of disloyalty. Perhaps in no other part of the antiwar movement did the battle over citizenship and patriotism grow so intense. In this debate, however, the draft resistance movement took a page from the civil rights movement, which had, after all, produced citizens who, despite repeated jailings, were counted among America's finest in the 1960s.

The draft resistance movement that emerged in Boston and across the country in 1967 and 1968 raised the stakes for both the rest of the antiwar movement and for the Johnson administration. "From Protest to Resistance" became the slogan that gained popularity throughout the antiwar movement in 1967, but it might have been more accurately phrased "From Protest to Confrontation," for the draft resisters' strategy constituted an open challenge to the administration to prosecute them for violation of draft laws in hopes that the system would break under the weight of so many court cases. More important, draft resistance activists possessed a moral clarity that fueled a kind of impatient citizenship. By late 1967, when thousands of men and women, young and old, gravitated to draft resistance, their minds were made up: the war in Vietnam was not only illegal and immoral but "obscene." They had studied Vietnamese history and culture and believed the United States had upset an indigenous drive for independence led by Ho Chi Minh and had established a puppet government in South Vietnam. In creating and perpetuating the conflict in Vietnam, draft resistance activists reasoned, American forces killed thousands of noncombatants and did incalculable damage to the rural countryside. In short, the war offended them in every possible way.

The impatience and urgency that drove these activists did not betray a lack of deliberation, however; rather, it reflected a realization among people who had protested this war legally for a long time that going to teach-ins, picketing Dow Chemical (the manufacturer of napalm) and ROTC, and boarding buses bound for marches in Washington or New York no longer seemed useful. Those events occurred only periodically and could not sustain an ongoing grass-roots effort to oppose the war. Draft resistance, on the other hand, mobilized the local antiwar community to take positive action against the administration and against the war in ways that marches and teach-ins could not.

This book focuses on draft resistance in Boston, though, in many ways, of course, the city is unique. First, there is the long heritage of disobeying authority that dates to before the Revolution and that resurfaced especially during the antebellum period, when Boston led the nation's movement to abolish slavery. One draft resistance activist later emphasized the importance of Boston's history to draft resistance when he said, "You could just *feel* it. There was something in the bricks." In addition, the religious tradition in Boston made it atypical among other draft resistance communities. Across most of the country, the location for draft card turn-ins and other public events mattered little, but in Boston they often took place in churches, where the actions of draft resisters appeared more solemn. Finally, the concentration of colleges and universities in Boston also meant that more than 100,000 students lived within a very small area, thus providing a ready-made base for protest.

In spite of these uncommon characteristics, Boston makes sense as the focus of this analysis for several reasons. First, although the Resistance grew to over seventy-five chapters across the country, the New England Resistance, centered primarily in Boston, quickly became the largest single chapter. The Boston branch published the national newsletter and later a national newspaper called *The Resistance*. Indeed, a March 1968 issue of the *Resistance* characterized the New England Resistance as the country's "coordinating center for the movement."[17] In addition, several United States Supreme Court decisions evolved out of Boston draft cases, and the widely followed trial of Dr. Benjamin Spock, the famed pediatrician, and his four codefendants for conspiracy to aid and abet draft resistance took place in Boston in 1968. By 1969, the city had become so clearly identified with draft resistance that when the Rolling Stones performed at the Boston Garden, Mick Jagger strutted out onto the stage in a tight long-sleeve T-shirt emblazoned with a hand-painted omega symbol, the mark of the Resistance, on his chest.[18] Although Resistance groups in Philadelphia, New York, Chicago, Madison, the Bay Area, and elsewhere also thrived and, in some cases, outlasted their New England counterpart, Boston led the way through the movement's most effective period.

More than thirty years have passed since the heyday of Vietnam War–era draft resistance and until now it has gone almost forgotten. This book argues that the Resistance is worth remembering. Although their numbers never amounted to a significant portion of the American population, draft resistance activists dominated the antiwar movement at a time when Johnson administration policy in Vietnam approached a crisis state. Like so many nonviolent American dissenters before them, their clear-eyed interpretation of the problem (in this case, the war) fueled an intense urgency to act. Draft resisters and their allies, like the abolitionists and the young civil rights activists, pushed their movement toward confronting their own government and demanding an end to the violence of war. Draft resisters were, as their critics charged, radicals, but they were home-grown radicals who, despite their faults, represented long-standing American traditions of dissent. This is, therefore, a story about veterans of the Vietnam War: civilian veterans who tried to reclaim American hearts and minds from the culture of the military-industrial complex that permeated American life in the late 1960s.

TOWARD A MOVEMENT

1 A LITTLE BAND OF BOLD PIONEERS

A common and natural result of an undue respect for law is, that you may see a file of soldiers, colonel, captain, corporal, privates, powder-monkeys and all, marching in admirable order over hill and dale to the wars, against their wills, aye, against their common sense and consciences, which makes it very steep marching indeed, and produces a palpitation of the heart. They have no doubt that it is a damnable business in which they are concerned; they are all peaceably inclined. Now, what are they? Men at all? or small moveable forts and magazines at the service of some unscrupulous man in power? . . .

The mass of men serve the State thus, not as men mainly, but as machines, with their bodies. . . . A very few, as heroes, patriots, martyrs, reformers in the great sense, and *men*, serve the State with their consciences also, and so necessarily resist it for the most part; and they are commonly treated by it as enemies.

—Henry David Thoreau, "On the Duty of Civil Disobedience" (1848)

In times of war, pacifists often get mugged. On March 31, 1966, a handful of Bostonians learned this lesson the hard way. Despite the raw spring weather, hundreds of people gathered in the early morning shadow of the South Boston District Courthouse all because they had heard something offensive on the radio. Or maybe someone else had heard it. Certainly, the man in a dark suit holding a motion picture camera at the front of the throng had heard it. And so, too, the few other men who, similarly dressed, tried to blend in with the crowd. They were not altogether successful in this, but the larger group didn't seem to mind. Most in the crowd were high school students; nearly all were residents of Southie and probably could spot a government man as well as anyone. In any case, the multitude anxiously waited for the "cowards" and "commies" to make their appearance on the steps of the grand old building—a "natural stage" for the first act in what would become a three-year-long morality play.

A few minutes before the appointed hour of 9:00 A.M., Gary Hicks and Suzanne Williams of the Boston Committee for Non-Violent Action (CNVA) stepped off a city bus near the courthouse. Several reporters approached and asked what they knew about the draft card burnings planned for that morning. "What draft card burnings?" Hicks replied. He later recalled thinking, "This is the penalty for not having a phone in my house." Indeed, he soon learned that four of his CNVA colleagues had publicized their intent to burn their draft cards on the courthouse steps that morning but had been unable to reach him to see if he wanted to join them. The large crowd he soon saw immediately made sense.

Soon after Hicks and Williams arrived at the courthouse, other CNVA members—there were now eleven young men and women in all—approached, filed by the edge of the crowd, and silently climbed the steps of the courthouse. Their physical appearance no doubt surprised some in the crowd. The men in the group had short haircuts and wore suits and ties. The women wore neat-looking dresses and, like some of the men, also were clad in overcoats to beat the chill. These were not the bearded beatniks that some in the Southie crowd expected.

Four of the men—David O'Brien, John Phillips, David Reed, and David Benson—stood in the middle of the group and, as they had promised in their press release, produced their draft cards. The other members of their group looked on as a reporter asked David O'Brien if the group received funding or other support from the Soviet Union. For several minutes, O'Brien attempted to respond as the crowd, now numbering more than 250, drew nearer and grew louder, shouting, "cowards!" and calling the four "yellow!" The smaller group's clean-cut appearance, if it had affected the crowd earlier, no longer mattered.

David Reed silently pulled out a small portable gas burner and ignited it. Each of the men then held his Selective Service document to the fire, corner first, and watched as the orange flame grew larger and brighter. Amid the sudden, unmistakable expressions of hostility from the mob—some were now yelling "Shoot them!" and "Kill them!"—John Phillips began to speak: "I am a pacifist," he said. "I do what I believe as an individual.

I believe in the law but when the law violates my conscience. . . ." He did not finish. Just then a gang of about seventy-five high school boys broke from the rest of the crowd and rushed up the steps.

The eleven pacifists had little opportunity to brace themselves for the attack, and seven of them went down quickly. As the mob punched and kicked them, most of the victims tried to cover their faces; others, consistent with their training in nonviolence, went limp and fell to the steps as the youths stomped on their backs. Someone repeatedly slapped eighteen-year-old Suzanne Williams in the face. David Benson clung to the cold steel rail that bisected the steps while at least four young men pounded him at once. Phillips later remembered: "I saw one person going down in front of me so I grabbed him and . . . pulled him around so he could be pushed into the courthouse." Three government agents who had infiltrated the crowd to witness the card burning (two from the FBI and one from the army's Criminal Investigation Division) were knocked down as they attempted to guide the pacifists up the stairs away from the mob and into the building. Their actions may have saved some of the victims' lives. As some of the high schoolers ran into the courthouse chasing two of their quarry, FBI agent Thomas McInerney pulled David O'Brien through the door and ran with him through the lobby to the janitor's room some seventy-five feet from the front entrance. Inside the room, which was equipped with a camera and tape recorder, O'Brien nervously lit a cigarette while McInerney quizzed him on whether or not he had burned his draft card. John Phillips was not so lucky. Before anyone could prevent it, a fist—sharpened by a class ring— slammed into the side of his nose, breaking it. As he staggered into the courthouse, blood spilled from his face.[1]

The police at last arrived as the melee wound down, but they arrested no one. They sealed the entrance to the building, scattered the crowd, and took Phillips to the hospital; Williams accompanied him. Inside the courthouse, a young woman, holding the hand of her toddler, approached one of the mob's victims and apologized on behalf of the community of South Boston, saying the assailants were not representative of the people who lived there.[2] Outside the building, however, a police officer told one reporter, "Anyone foolish enough to commit such an unpatriotic gesture in South Boston can only expect what these people got."[3] Nearby, state representative James F. Condon commented that "this wouldn't have happened if these were South Boston boys; our boys are patriotic."[4] Activists in the incipient draft resistance movement came to expect this kind of reception in 1966.

In the public outcry that followed the attacks, opinions were sharply divided. For the next month, Boston's public officials, newspaper editors, and residents debated and discussed the meaning of draft card burning as a method of protest and the appropriate responses to it. Because the timing of the event coincided with a month-long strike that had shut down Boston's three daily newspapers, many of the city's residents awoke two days later to read a front-page editorial on the subject in the Manchester, New Hampshire, paper, which was trying to make inroads in the Boston market during the strike. William Loeb, the publisher of the *Union-Leader*, one of the most conservative and stridently anticommunist papers in the country, called the card burners "Anti-American 'kooks'" who had not only "thumbed their nose deliberately and spat in the face of American patriotism" but also insulted "our soldiers fighting in Viet Nam." Their assailants, according to Loeb, responded with "the type of natural patriotic reaction that they SHOULD have had." In fact, he said, "there were probably millions of Americans all over the United States who said to themselves: 'Give them another one for me.'"[5]

Few people who sympathized with the attackers would go as far as Loeb in their characterizations of those involved, yet they did see the issue in terms of loyalty and disloyalty, patriotism and traitorous behavior. In a letter to the *Boston Globe* (which began printing again on April 8), one woman complained about the paper's criticism of the South Boston mob: "There is something drastically wrong," she wrote, "when our country's defenders are condemned and vilified" for beating up draft card burners who "most likely provoked the attack in the first place."[6] Another young woman argued that the South Boston students "could not have reacted in any other way in order to preserve the American image of red-blooded patriotism." The demonstrators, she said, "were asking for trouble," and those who assaulted them "showed their love for America by not standing by apathetically while their government's dignity and authority was being desecrated" by a "defiant, selfish minority." "They are heroes," she finished.[7] The *Globe* also printed a letter from an army private stationed in Vietnam: "It's difficult to suppress the feeling I have for Boston and this patriotic display," he said. "It is indeed gratifying to know that the draft card burners who aren't men enough to face the responsibilities and hazards of defending their country . . . now face a hazard they didn't bargain for—outraged, patriotic citizens."[8]

In contrast, those who criticized the South Boston mob did not view the event as a question of patriotism or loyalty but of freedom, morality, and especially legality. For instance, although the editors of the *Boston Globe* referred to the card burners as "misguided" and suggested that "few will support or justify" their actions, they condemned even more harshly "those who took the law into their own hands" as "more criminal" because "it could have amounted to murder." Such lawlessness, they said, and the subsequent blaming of the pacifists for "inciting riot" (as one city councilor charged) came "straight from the handbook of the Southern segregationist."[9] Others agreed but were more generous to the pacifists. One letter writer believed that those "who had their heads cracked recently probably know far more about the concept of freedom and care far more about what America is and is becoming than all the punks who attacked them."[10] Still others suggested that the "bullies" were deluding themselves because they could not "face the possibility that the war in Viet Nam might be both immoral and futile, and the consequent thought that those who have given their lives there may have done so in vain." More than that, another argued, the private who wrote so glowingly of the beating proved that even GIs knew that rather than fighting for "freedom and democracy" they were "defending the right to beat to the ground, with no fear of arrest, anyone with whose opinions they disagreed."[11]

Although Boston's newspaper editors printed such opinions in relatively equal numbers for each side of the debate, other indications made obvious the ongoing hostility that early draft resisters faced. One week after the incident at the courthouse, a group of ministers calling themselves the Clergy Group for the Right to Dissent sponsored a march to protest the treatment of the draft card burners and the complete lack of police protection. Estimates vary, but somewhere between 175 and 300 people marched to the Boston Common from two different starting points: the South Boston District Courthouse and the Arlington Street Church in the Back Bay. Although the police department, stung by criticism of its absence a week earlier, provided 150 officers (some on horseback and motorcycles) to escort the two groups, it could not keep counterdemonstrators from confronting the marchers. From apartment windows in South Boston, several residents pelted the marchers with eggs, occasionally missing and hitting a police officer. People on the sidewalks threw things, too, and yelled "coward" and "maggot" as the demonstrators walked by. One heckler walked up to the group with a live chicken and broke its neck in a less-than-subtle warning; he then followed the group with the dead animal dangling from the end of a stick. The marchers made it to the Common safely and, thanks to the police presence, held a small rally without incident. Later, Mayor

John Collins told the press that he would continue to take measures to ensure greater police presence at such events, noting that "precisely because any protest against U.S. foreign policy in Viet Nam is unpopular among some of the citizens of Metropolitan Boston, it is even more urgent to protect this right."[12]

These events of March and April 1966 came as something of a shock to the city of Boston. The protest in Southie, along with a few others the week before, constituted some of the earliest demonstrations against the war in Vietnam—and certainly the first public challenge to the draft—that the city had seen. The mob response also took counterdemonstrating to a new, more frightening level, thus mirroring the reaction that so many social movements experience in their formative stages. More important, however, the public's perception of these events as articulated in letters to the editor and comments made on the street quickly established the terms of debate that people not only in Boston, but across the country, would settle upon in evaluating draft resisters. Despite the great lengths to which the resisters went to appeal to the public's sense of morality, its sense of justice, and its sense of tradition (as exemplified by figures such as Thoreau) in the coming years, resisters constantly found themselves accused of disloyalty and of being unpatriotic. Even in early 1968, when draft resistance became a national movement unto itself, and draft card burnings were being discouraged in favor of draft card turn-ins held in churches, the words "draft resister" conjured up images of flaming cards that, like the Stars and Stripes afire, caused many Americans to cringe. Those images persist to this day.

More important, the nascent draft resistance of 1966 and the reaction to it also inaugurated other important trends that later extended into the subsequently much wider resistance movement, or at times set precedents that proved instrumental in the way organizers shaped the later movement. For Gandhian pacifists, the act of civil disobedience—burning one's draft card—served both as an act of moral witness and as a vehicle for confronting the government. Unlike stereotypical draft "dodgers" who sought ways to protect themselves from the draft by fleeing or making themselves ineligible through some act of subterfuge, resisters openly defied the law and awaited the state's punishment. They were impatient, no longer satisfied with marching and attending demonstrations. Likewise, they possessed a certain moral clarity that made evading the draft unconscionable and, at the same time, drove them to fight the administration and the

Selective Service System. In their challenge to the draft and to the policy makers responsible for America's presence in Vietnam, these protesters highlighted the problem of the individual's place in a civil society in a way that few others in the antiwar movement could. For them, individual dissent was not inconsistent with good citizenship.

But moral witness had its shortcomings, too. Particularly because it seemed to be carried out primarily by children of privilege—white, middle- and upper-class college students—the act of resistance took on an air of condescension for some working-class observers. Although draft resisters successfully sought to expose the inequities of the Selective Service System, the same system that sent a disproportionate number of working-class and minority men to fight in Vietnam for much of the war, the draft resistance movement never attracted significant numbers of men from those groups to join in severing their ties to the draft.

Finally, this first confrontation with the government led the Department of Justice, through its efficient handling of early draft violators' cases, to unwittingly encourage the formation of a broader movement against the draft. Although the early resisters, so few in number anyway, never attempted wide-ranging recruitment efforts aimed at bogging down the courts and filling jails with enough potential draftees to hamper the operations of the draft, the speedy work of prosecutors and the federal courts in dispatching the first burners and returners to prison made that notion seem possible. The later draft resistance movement of 1967 and 1968 fully expected mass arrests and imprisonment thanks to the example set by the first draft resisters and the Department of Justice in 1966.

Indeed, the government seemed well prepared to penalize those who resisted fulfilling roles that men their age had ostensibly performed in earlier wars. And since the majority of the population in April 1966 continued to approve of Lyndon Johnson's management of the war in Vietnam, the administration expected popular support for prosecuting draft violators.[13] Those Americans old enough to remember the Second World War and Korea had grown used to a peacetime draft and at the outset, it seemed, viewed Vietnam as the younger generation's turn to go and do what those before them had done. As Joseph, the main character in Saul Bellow's first novel, *Dangling Man*, who was waiting to be drafted, might have said, the sixties was an "era of hardboiled-dom." The first Vietnam-era draft resisters, beaten and bloodied in the city that liked to call itself "the cradle of Liberty," could understand Joseph's assertion that "most serious matters are closed to the hard-boiled. They are unpracticed in introspection, and therefore badly equipped to deal with opponents whom they cannot shoot like big game or outdo in daring."[14]

SONS OF LIBERTY? 1740–1966

Since the American Revolution, of course, Boston has had a reputation as a hotbed of protest and resistance to unjustifiable authority. Given the events that took place long before and long after the Sons of Liberty dumped tea into the harbor, its legacy is, in fact, fairly mixed. In the eighteenth century, impressment of local sailors for the king's navy became such a threat to the city that, despite the encouragement of several ministers to take up arms against the Catholic French to the north, Bostonians often armed themselves against ship captains suspected of pressing men into service. In 1741, for example, a mob of 300 men wielding "axes, clubs and cutlasses" terrorized the commander of the man-of-war *Astrea* when they suspected that he planned to sweep the city's docks for men. Such mob assaults on ships' officers and the government officials who backed them became commonplace and no doubt laid the foundation for the protests against the Stamp Act in 1765. At that time, a mob of forty to fifty tradesmen burst into the stamp distributor's home and destroyed everything in it. Twelve days later, the crowd chased Chief Justice (and future provincial governor) Thomas Hutchinson and his family out of their dining room and proceeded to loot and gut their home before razing it completely. Surely, by 1773, the nighttime dumping of 342 casks of tea into Boston Harbor should not have surprised anyone.[15]

In the nineteenth century, Bostonians took pride in their revolutionary heritage and invoked it in other campaigns to right injustice. In nearby Concord, Henry David Thoreau went to jail rather than pay taxes that he knew were subsidizing the Mexican War. In an essay that influenced few of his contemporaries but profoundly inspired twentieth-century proponents of civil disobedience from Mohandas K. Gandhi to Martin Luther King Jr., Thoreau wrote: "Under a government which imprisons any unjustly [e.g., fugitive slaves, Mexican prisoners], the true place for a just man is also a prison." One hundred and twenty years later, draft resisters would be inspired by such rhetoric: "A minority is powerless while it conforms to the majority . . . but it is irresistible when it clogs by its whole weight. If the alternative is to keep all just men in prison, or give up war and slavery, the State will not hesitate which to choose. If a thousand men were not to pay their tax-bills this year, that would not be a violent and bloody measure, as it would be to pay them, and enable the State to commit violence and shed innocent blood."[16] Thoreau was the nagging conscience of his fellow citizens and set the example that obedience to one's moral principles took precedence over allegiance to one's government.

Soon after the end of the Mexican War, following passage of the Fugitive Slave Act of 1850, abolitionists in Boston took their protests to a new level as they planned to prevent fugitive slaves from being recaptured in their city and, failing this, to prevent their transport back to the South. In February 1851, a mob rushed through the doors of the courthouse in Court Square seeking a captured fugitive slave named Shadrach. When they emerged with him on their shoulders and quickly spirited him out of harm's way to Canada, Theodore Parker, one of several abolitionist ministers on the Boston Committee of Vigilance, described the mob's action as "the noblest deed done in Boston since the destruction of the tea in 1773." James Brewer Stewart tells us that resistance to authority was in the air: "Antislavery politicians of all shadings were openly opposing federal authority, debating the limits of peaceful dissent, and exploring the imperatives of forcible resistance." Indeed, in May 1854, following a failed attempt by abolitionists to free another fugitive slave, Anthony Burns, from jail, Bostonians shrouded many of the city's buildings in black as officials escorted Burns to the ship that took him south.[17]

By the first half of the twentieth century, however, Boston's history of resisting authority mostly seemed a distant memory. The city's campaigns to root out all manner of vice led to book bannings that made famous the phrase "Banned in Boston." During the Red raids that followed the Great War, Department of Justice agents and local police arrested six hundred alleged communists ("in most instances," one judge later said, "perfectly quiet and harmless working people"), handcuffed them in pairs, and paraded them through Boston's streets, where the masses of citizens who witnessed the spectacle jeered and taunted them.[18] Certainly the city experienced its share of conflict rooted in ethnic tensions, and the demonstrations against the government that condemned Sacco and Vanzetti to death seemed to recapture the city's radical past, but after World War II, even Boston's place as home to numerous colleges and universities and its reputation as a liberal, free-thinking town did not insulate it from the same kind of Cold War conformist attitudes that affected the rest of the country. The city sent John F. Kennedy, a committed cold warrior, to the White House and soon after helped elect his like-minded youngest brother, Ted, to fill his vacant Senate seat.

Like most Americans, Bostonians were fervently anticommunist and supported Kennedy's policies in Laos and South Vietnam as essential to holding back the spread of the Red menace. In 1965, when Kennedy's successor, Lyndon Johnson, took steps to escalate American involvement in Vietnam, few Americans protested. Even in July, when Johnson made the decision to use the draft rather than the reserves to increase military manpower, few balked. Nationally, 63 percent of Americans continued to favor the draft against only 13 percent who opposed it. There is little indication that the people of Boston felt any different, even though the doubling of draft calls soon began to affect more and more families.[19]

In fact, when early opponents to the war first attempted a march and rally on the Boston Common (as part of the International Days of Protest) on October 16, 1965, they received very little serious consideration from the media and counterdemonstrators easily broke up their meeting. The day before the march, the *Boston Globe* ran an article by Gordon Hall, an apparent expert "observer and reporter of extremist movements," that suggested that the scheduled march and demonstration would be dominated by communists. Hall noted that of the fourteen sponsoring organizations, all but ten were "tightly knit permanent organizations of left-wing persuasion" and that even when apparently benign organizations such as the Cambridge Committee to End the War in Vietnam (CCEWV) (the primary sponsor) "are not the actual creations and front groups of the extreme Left, they are custom tailored for infiltration and control by extremists." Hall argued that "their paper-maché structure and general informality are no match for the militancy, and superior organization of the extremist." He offered no evidence that militants were, in fact, taking over the CCEWV but quoted Young Socialist Alliance memos that urged members to become active in the antiwar movement. Readers of the *Globe*, then, most likely viewed the march not as a legitimate expression of opposition to the escalating war made by concerned citizens but instead as a communist front.[20]

Things only got worse for the demonstrators on the day of the march. A total of 3,000 people had assembled at three separate locations—the Cambridge Common, the Massachusetts Institute of Technology (MIT) administration building on Massachusetts Avenue ("Mass. Ave.," to locals), and Boston University's Marsh Plaza on Commonwealth Avenue ("Comm. Ave." to locals)—before marching to Boston Common, where they met at the Parkman Bandstand. At the Mass. Ave. bridge, where the three groups joined for the final leg of the march, six Harvard freshman held a banner that read, "We Support LBJ in Viet Nam." The six followed the marchers to the Common, where they joined another group, numbering 300, the core of which were members of the conservative student group Young Americans for Freedom; they waited until the marchers settled in front of the bandstand and the speakers took their seats before making their move. This smaller crowd, made up largely of students who came from Boston University, Harvard, MIT, Northeastern University, Boston College, and Emerson College, then pushed their way through the demonstrators until they positioned themselves directly in front of the platform. To the relief of the speakers, fifty police patrolmen had already posted themselves at the bandstand, with six men guarding the steps. The counterprotesters carried signs that said "Stay in Viet Nam," "Draft the Pinkos," "Drop the Bombs," and "Send the Draft Dodgers to Viet Nam." Seeing the signs, the antiwar marchers began to chant, "We want peace in Vietnam. We want peace," only to have the counterdemonstrators respond with "We want victory in Vietnam. We want victory." Russell Johnson of the American Friends Service Committee (AFSC) attempted to speak, but he could outshout the insurgents only briefly. State representative Irving Fishman from Newton and MIT linguistics professor Noam Chomsky could not match Johnson's performance, and police ended the rally before it turned violent. Chomsky later remembered that he "wasn't unhappy that there was a large contingent of police, who didn't like what we were saying . . . but didn't want to see people murdered on the Common."[21]

The placard urging that draft "dodgers" be sent to Vietnam must have seemed incongruous to many protesters in attendance because, at that point, very few people had dared to challenge the draft as a method of protesting the war. Indeed, after *Life* magazine published a photograph of Catholic Worker Chris Kearns burning his draft card on July 29, 1965, Congress quickly passed a law making draft card destruction punishable by up to five years in prison and a $10,000 fine. After that, antiwar activism had been largely limited to marches and rallies. But on the same day that the counterprotesters broke up the Boston Common rally, David Miller, another Catholic Worker from Syracuse, stood on a platform in Manhattan and said, "I believe the napalming of villages is an immoral act." As he held his draft card aloft, he declared, "I hope this will be a significant political act, so here goes," and set his card on fire.[22] Miller was the first person to challenge the new law against card burning, and his picture ran on the front pages of newspapers across the country. In reaction, the senior senator from Massachusetts, Republican Leverett Saltonstall, urged support for the men serving in Vietnam "who are exposed to danger," not "those who are trying to avoid their duty to their country." Clearly, he had missed Miller's point. As evidenced by his easy submission to arrest, trial, and imprisonment, Miller did not try to "avoid" anything; rather, he intended to set an example for others who viewed the war as immoral and who believed it was their duty as citizens to disobey any laws that perpetuated that immorality. Saltonstall could only say, "We want freedom of speech, but we want patriotism," too.[23]

In Boston, public officials dismissed the protesters and reaffirmed their support for U.S. policy. "Those who question the U.S. policy," said Ted Kennedy, "ought to be just as quick to condemn the terrorist activities of the Viet Cong, such as assassination and kidnaping." Governor Volpe said, "Let those misguided individuals who protest our actions in South Vietnam know that the frontiers of freedom do not stop at the territorial limits of the United States of America. They extend around the world, to all people of all races, customs and beliefs." State representative Patrick W. Nee stood in Park Square a few days after the protests and distributed 2,000 bumper stickers with the message, "We Support Our Boys in Viet Nam." "The way they were snapped up by motorists," he said, "shows how the real Americans feel." Truly, it was a time of hardboiled-dom.[24]

Interestingly, college students seemed to be the most outspoken critics of the antiwar protesters. In an early example during the war of one deriding the appearance of those with whom one disagrees, one of the Harvard freshman who held the "We Support LBJ in Viet Nam" banner remarked that the idea to carry the sign came about because he "wanted people to know that all students aren't unwashed beatniks." Meanwhile, at Boston University, members of the Young Republicans and the Young Democrats collected 6,000 student signatures for a petition pledging support to Johnson's Vietnam policy and presented them to Assistant Secretary of State William P. Bundy. (At the time, BU had only 8,000 day students and a total enrollment of 15,000.)[25]

The protesters had their defenders, too, but they were few and found themselves most often defending the marchers from charges that they were communists (as they had been called by several congressmen and senators). Howard Zinn, an associate professor of government at Boston University, decried the name calling, saying that the student "radicals" were a "new breed," one without "commitment to any other country" or "fixed loyalties to any dogma." In a *Globe* opinion piece, he wrote that although the student protesters believed that "the Communists will use any means to gain their ends," they also concluded, after seeing "American planes bombing Vietnamese villages, and Marines throwing grenades down tunnels in which crouch helpless women and children," that the United States would do the same. "Force and deception," he said, "are found on all sides," and then he quoted Randolph Bourne, who, at the outbreak of the Great War, warned that in times of war, "the mass of the people, through some spiritual alchemy, become convinced that they have willed and executed the deed themselves." Soon, Bourne argued, they "allow themselves to be regimented, coerced . . . and turned into a solid manufactory of destruction" toward any other people targeted by the government. Zinn defended the protesters as uncommon in their ability to resist this tendency.[26]

Like Zinn, most supporters of the protesters tried to focus attention on what they perceived to be the immoral nature of the war by invoking examples from an earlier generation. In a letter to the *Globe*, one of these people wrote: "We really should humbly remember that Hitler's and Tojo's obedient, patriotic, brave soldiers were considered murderers by us because of their government's stand. . . . Those who demonstrate for peace want a firm, defensible basis for this war. Please give them your patience, tolerance, and consideration." Another person, a potential draft resister, wrote: "The Nuremberg Trials established that it was the responsibility of each individual to refuse to participate in any activity which violated moral standards." For that reason, he said, he would have to refuse induction if he were called. Echoing Thoreau, he said: "I hold allegiance to one thing higher than the government of the United States, and that is my own conscience."[27]

In the fall of 1965, such appeals to conscience persuaded few. Another Gallup Poll indicated that 58 percent of Americans believed that there was "a lot" of communist involvement in Vietnam protests, another 20 percent believed there was "some," and only 4 percent believed there was none "at all." It was a lonely time to oppose the war. On Veteran's Day, over 300,000 people turned out on the streets of Boston's Back Bay to see the longest parade (it lasted 2½ hours) the city had held in twenty-seven years. Mayor John Collins and eleven servicemen who had been wounded in Vietnam led the procession of 17,000 marchers. According to one reporter, "pro–Viet Nam fervor infused" the day.[28]

Disagreements within the budding antiwar movement over tactics further limited its effectiveness. Mainstream New Left groups planned more marches and teach-ins but shied away from draft noncompliance as a tactic, fearing such direct confrontation with the federal government. At the national convention of Students for a Democratic Society (SDS) held in June in Kewadin, Michigan, the organization decided that attacks on the draft were too radical and instead chose to focus on "stopping the seventh war from now." Activists in the National Coordinating Committee to End the War in Vietnam thought draft resistance would undermine other antiwar work and allow the administration "to convince everybody that our main objective is to be a bunch of professional draft-dodgers." A small group of individuals disagreed with these assessments. Emboldened by David Miller's public defiance, a crowd of 1,500 sympathizers, including nationally known figures such as Dorothy Day of the Catholic Worker movement and A. J. Muste of the Fellowship of Reconciliation, turned out in New York's Union Square in November to watch five pacifists burn their cards. Although someone with a fire extinguisher "bolted from the crowd and doused the pacifists and their cards," they managed to burn them anyway.[29] More and more, radical pacifists began to see the draft as the ideal point of entry for protesting the war.

PACIFISTS' PROGRESS, 1957–1966

A newly formed branch of the CNVA can be credited for initiating what became the draft resistance movement in Boston. Members of several pacifist organizations had come together to form the original CNVA in 1957 as a way "to go beyond words" in protesting the escalating nuclear arms race. On August 6, the twelfth anniversary of the bombing of Hiroshima, eleven members were arrested for trespassing at a nuclear test site at Camp Mercury, Nevada, seventy miles west of Las Vegas. After a quick trial resulting in convictions and suspended sentences, they went back to the entrance of the test site to pray. There they saw the giant mushroom cloud of the blast, and it convinced them that they "could never rest while such forces of evil were loose in God's world." The following year, several CNVA members led by Albert Bigelow, a former World War II naval officer, attempted to sail a thirty-foot ketch named *The Golden Rule* into an American hydrogen bomb test site at the Eniwetok atoll in the Marshall Islands. They were twice intercepted by the Coast Guard and, after the second attempt, spent sixty days in jail in Honolulu. The events garnered national headlines, and the *Boston Herald Traveler* characterized the mission as "Thoreau-esque."[30]

In 1960, Bradford Lyttle, the son of a Unitarian minister and a pacifist-Socialist mother, established the New England CNVA in Groton, Connecticut, and pushed the organization toward a more confrontational "obstructionist" approach to protest. As historian James Tracy has described it, this move showed "that radical pacifists privileged individual cathartic action over pragmatic efficacy," a practice that would later prove significant in Boston. In Groton, CNVA activists focused their attention on protesting the manufacture of the navy's most powerful weapon: the Polaris nuclear submarine. Each time the shipbuilders launched a new Polaris, CNVA activists rowed their boats and paddled their canoes out into the Thames River in a symbolic attempt to block the sub. One person actually managed to swim out to a sub and climb aboard the hull as if to demonstrate his willingness to sacrifice his own body for peace. On land, occasional violence broke out: In the first week of its operation someone shattered all of the windows in the CNVA office. Later, an angry shipyard worker punched Lyttle and knocked him out as he distributed leaflets.[31]

By 1965, the New England CNVA had moved to Voluntown, Connecticut, where members continued to plan submarine protests, demonstrations at the Sikorski helicopter plant in Stratford, and peace marches, including one from Quebec to Guantanamo in 1963. Their activities were well known within pacifist circles; in fact, membership tended to overlap among groups such as the CNVA, the War Resisters League, the Workshop in Nonviolence (later WIN magazine), the Fellowship of Reconciliation, and the AFSC. In time, the CNVA's work drew the attention of two Boston University students, John Phillips and David O'Brien. Both were members of the War Resisters League and had been active in BU Students for Peace (and O'Brien had marched with civil rights leaders from Selma to Montgomery in his first year at BU), but they were looking for an opportunity to make a more powerful personal commitment to ending the war in Vietnam. They spent much of their free time participating in CNVA-sponsored demonstrations and at the farm in Voluntown, where they received permission to form a Boston branch of the organization in January 1966.[32]

For Phillips and O'Brien, much of the CNVA's attraction lay in the "spiritual underpinnings" of Lyttle's Gandhian pacifism and the CNVA's utopian vision of operating as an alternative society within a society. According to Phillips, compared to the "reactive" nature of many antiwar groups, the CNVA focused on building a new society. He felt "the presence of God" all through that time. "You couldn't help it . . . there were all these Unitarian Ministers, Friend Service Committee [members] . . . I felt a strong spiritual identity throughout the experience."[33]

Unlike the members of the New England CNVA, the fifteen or so hardcore members of the Boston CNVA directed their attention exclusively toward the Vietnam War. Although they were pacifists and were deeply concerned about the proliferation of nuclear weapons, the worsening situation in Vietnam, they felt, deserved all of their attention. They set up their first office in Roxbury but because of inadequate plumbing and wiring, later moved to an old barn in Brookline, complete with "milk-crate-modern furniture" and mimeograph machines for producing leaflets. They were extremely well informed regarding the Geneva Accords and could, in conversation or leaflet form, detail the history of American involvement in Vietnam since the 1940s. One of their regular activities involved going to the movie theater where *Doctor Zhivago* played and passing out leaflets that stressed the peace theme in the film and how it applied to Vietnam. They also planned their own peace marches in which they inevitably ran into the usual intolerant bystanders. On a Boston-to-Provincetown march, they were regularly jeered and occasionally beaten up. Phillips recalled, "going through Plymouth . . . very naive . . . walking through the center of town and finding the whole center of town mobbed with people ready to do all kinds of things to mess us up . . . one lady in particular squirting us with a water pistol full of mustard—because we were yellow."[34]

On March 25, 1966, the group turned its attention to the Boston Army Base, a massive building on Boston Harbor, as its contribution to the Second International Days of Protest. They distributed leaflets and sat in the road to block buses of draftees and anyone else from entering or exiting the base. In general they hoped to be able to "gum up the works." It did not last long. At the army base, which is located in South Boston near the waterfront, hundreds of longshoremen and other onlookers spat on the demonstrators, yelled obscenities, and called them all "cowards." One burly longshoremen approached the group and offered them a gallon of gasoline, "so you can burn yourself," a reference to Norman Morrison, a Quaker who had set himself on fire outside the Pentagon several months before. This prompted David Benson to take out his draft card to burn it. As he attempted to light it, a longshoreman knocked the matches from his hands. The police quickly stepped in and arrested the demonstrators—eleven of them—and hauled them off to the police wagon. As two officers dragged Benson away from the gates of the army base, he ripped up the card and tossed the pieces to the ground. Several hecklers yelled sarcastically to the police: "Be careful. Don't hurt them." As Suzanne Williams remembers it, they were arraigned for "sauntering and loitering in such a way as to engender a breach of the peace and likely to endanger passersby." They were released on their own recognizance and ordered to appear for trial at the South Boston Courthouse on March 31, thus setting in motion the events that would lead to their beatings.[35]

Benson did not destroy his draft card casually. The Boston CNVA had quickly recognized the draft as an ideal target for the kind of confrontational direct action about which they had been learning in Voluntown. It required more than the usual commitment to standard civil disobedience; participants had to be prepared to face the penalties of the draft card destruction law and, for those who had deferments, to face the inevitable change of draft status to 1-A (draftable) by their local boards. They also had to face the hostility of those whose sons and brothers were being conscripted.

The Boston resisters' emphasis on the draft coincided with a sharp increase in the number of men being called for induction. By the end of 1965, between 35,000 and 45,000 men were being drafted every month nationwide; monthly calls in 1962 and 1963 had averaged between 6,300 and 9,400 men. Americans had grown comfortable with the peacetime draft but the sudden intrusion of the Selective Service System on their lives brought the war home and made the draft a subject of heightened scrutiny.[36]

AMERICA AND CONSCRIPTION, 1789–1965

Not until after World War II did the American people tolerate a peacetime draft. During the Revolution, the War of 1812, the Mexican War, and the Spanish-American War, the armed forces of the United States relied on volunteers—as they do today. The behavior of British troops stationed in the thirteen American colonies in the 1760s and early 1770s convinced most Americans of that era, and for generations after, that standing peacetime armies encroached on the liberties of the citizenry and, at their worst, could be used as forces of repression. Moreover, to Americans who embraced classical republican notions of service to one's community, conscription seemed unduly coercive. Throughout most of the nineteenth century, Americans expected that all free citizens would spring to the defense of the nation during periods of crisis.[37]

The earliest uses of conscription in America were therefore carried out with caution. President Lincoln introduced the first draft in 1863—and bloody riots resulted—but he terminated it soon after Lee's surrender at Appomattox. Woodrow Wilson, too, initiated conscription in 1917, upon American entry into the war in Europe but ended it once victory was achieved. The draft that Franklin Delano Roosevelt signed into law in 1940 (long before the Japanese attack on Pearl Harbor) created the first of its kind in peacetime and ultimately resulted in ten million inductions by the end of the Second World War. Having helped to win the war, the draft ended on March 31, 1947. But policy makers openly contemplated renewing the draft law even without an attendant national emergency, for soon after the old law expired, the armed services began to lose 15,000 men from the armed services each month due to attrition amid growing tensions with the Soviet Union (which were exacerbated by the Communist coup in Czechoslovakia). On June 24, 1948, Congress passed the Selective Service Act.[38]

The establishment of a peacetime draft did not occur without criticism. In 1947, the War Resisters League sponsored the first public draft card burning and turn-in in New York City. More than 400 people participated, including social critic and essayist Dwight MacDonald, who spoke against conscription under any circumstances: "When the State . . . tells me that I must 'defend' it against foreign enemies—that is, must be prepared to kill people who have done me no injury in defense of a social system which has done me considerable injury—then I say that I cannot go along. In such a serious matter as going to war, each individual must decide for himself; and this means civil disobedience to the State power that presumes to decide for one."[39] In addition, ongoing segregation within the military led A. Philip Randolph, the black labor leader and civil rights activist, to tell the Senate Armed Services Committee in 1947 that he would "personally pledge . . . to openly counsel, aid and abet youth . . . in an organized refusal to register and be drafted" should a peacetime draft be enacted. A month after passage of the new draft law, President Truman issued Executive Order 9981, which ended segregation in the military.[40]

The administration of the Selective Service remained essentially the same as during the war, but Congress did make some key changes in the new law. First, they reduced the draftee's term to twenty-one months (in World War II, draftees served for the duration of the war) and placed a two-year limit on the life of the draft; after that, Congress would have to re-evaluate the need to continue it. (Eventually, the draft came up for review every four years through the fifties and sixties and Congress extended it every time.) As Congress reviewed a possible extension of the act in 1950, North Korean armies streamed across the thirty-eighth parallel into South Korea, prompting the United States, under the auspices of the United Nations, to take action against North Korea. Congress quickly extended the draft law, and the Selective Service sprang into action, drafting 220,000 men by the end of 1950. Such events seemed to confirm the need for—and the practical advantage of—an ongoing Selective Service Act.[41]

As the Korean conflict wound down and manpower needs declined, some members of Congress worried about the structure of the draft. They feared that the Armed Forces Qualification Test, an intelligence test, resulted in the rejection of too many draftees and that, consequently, the nation was sending too many of its brightest and healthiest off to fight while its weakest and least intelligent stayed home to procreate. L. Mendel Rivers, a congressman from South Carolina, suggested lowering the standards of the qualification exam because, he said, "Korea has taught us one thing if it has taught us anything. You don't need a Ph.D. degree to fight those Chinks." At approximately the same time, the Selective Service implemented a system to distribute draft deferments to America's best and brightest. Starting in 1951, draft boards began granting deferments to college students who placed in the top half of their class or who scored well on a national aptitude test. Soon, more than 75 percent of the nation's college students were effectively put out of harm's way.[42] During the rest of the decade and well into the 1960s, very few Americans were drafted and no draftees were killed in combat; thus, Americans seemed willing to tolerate not only a peacetime draft but the concomitant inequities assured by a complex system of deferments.[43]

Attitudes toward the draft did not change substantially until the American escalation in Vietnam. Up to that point, the Selective Service enjoyed considerable approval among policy makers. In 1962, President John F. Kennedy praised the state directors of the Selective Service, saying that "the pressures upon them are tremendous, yet I cannot think of any branch of our government in the last two decades where there have been so few complaints about inequity." Furthermore, in 1963 the Pentagon acknowledged the importance of the draft, noting that one-third of all enlisted men and 41 percent of its officers would not have entered the service if not for the draft as a motivator.[44]

Much of the popularity of the agency could be traced to its director, General Lewis B. Hershey, who after supervising the draft during World War II, served as director of Selective Service from 1948 to 1970. Hershey personified his agency in a way unequaled by anyone, save J. Edgar Hoover. Politicians loved him for the folksy Will Rogers style he brought to his testimony before congressional committees. In 1966, syndicated columnist Mary McGrory described him as "everybody's grandfather" and noted that "if the system is inhuman, its director at least is not."[45]

Hershey liked to promote the agency's flexibility and the fact that rather than being run as a massive government bureaucracy out of Washington, the Selective Service was decentralized, administered by over 4,000 local boards made up of "little groups of neighbors." This actually made it into a much larger bureaucracy, and the "neighbors" on local boards were hardly representative of mainstream America. As Lawrence Baskir and William Strauss pointed out after the Vietnam War, Hershey shaped the agency in his own image, "converting what was originally a civilian agency into a paramilitary organization, 90 percent of whose top-ranking officials and state directors were officers in the armed forces. In turn, they appointed local board members with perspectives like their own."[46]

From the end of the Korean War until 1965, under Hershey's direction, these draft boards oversaw a deferment system based on a theory called "manpower channeling." Under the new system, the Selective Service extended its mission beyond merely delivering men to the armed forces; through the use of attractive deferments and the threat of induction, it "channeled" men into fields of study and occupations deemed to be in the nation's interest. Thus, in the mid-1960s if a potential draftee had the grades and planned to study physics (scientists were important in the arms and space races), he could expect a deferment for four years of undergraduate work, additional deferments for graduate study, and a final occupational deferment if he were successful in securing the right kind of job. Such a system could easily ensure the safety of a man from age eighteen to twenty-six and beyond. Of course, it was completely unfair, but Hershey argued that the protection of "vital activities and scarce skills" were keys to national security. Those who were ineligible for such deferments, because they were poor or not as smart or worked in their fathers' businesses, more likely viewed the system as Bellow's character Joseph viewed American society. As he put it, "Personal choice does not count for much these days."[47]

Despite the inequities, by July 1965 the deferment system had long been accepted by the public as an integral part of the draft. But as President Johnson increased the number of troops in South Vietnam to more than 185,000 by the end of the year, more manpower became necessary, and it could come from only two places: the reserves or the draft. The president and his advisers believed that activating the reserve armed forces would be more disruptive to the homefront than increasing draft calls, so the Selective Service quickly swung into action. As Hershey's biographer notes, however, after twelve years of relative dormancy, "deferments had been translated into exemptions" in the minds of many draft-age men. "To now revive the draft in order to fight a limited war in Southeast Asia might prove troublesome." Indeed. Whereas monthly draft calls had been kept to fewer than 9,000 men before the war's escalation, the jump to between 25,000 and 40,000 men called (the Selective Service drafted 300,000 men a year in 1966, 1967, and 1968) snapped Americans back to reality—and the nation's system of conscription soon came under scrutiny for the first time in many years.[48]

Early protests against the war included the occasional draft card burning which resulted in the August 1965 passage of legislation (sponsored in the House by Mendel Rivers and in the Senate by Strom Thurmond) prohibiting the destruction of draft cards. In addition, General Hershey began using reclassification as punishment for antiwar protesters. After more than thirty people, many of them students at the University of Michigan, staged a sit-in at a Local Board 85 in Ann Arbor in October, Hershey revoked the deferments of thirteen male students and made them eligible for the draft. This invited considerable criticism from newspaper editorial boards across the country, but Hershey argued that "reclassification is quicker at stopping sit-ins than some indictment that takes effect six months later." When a reporter from the Michigan campus paper interviewed him about this decision, he responded, "I'm one of those old-fashioned fathers who never let pity interfere with a spanking." Some months later, Mendel Rivers told Hershey, "God bless you, you did right."[49]

In a matter of months public interest in the draft had heightened considerably. Between September 1965 and January 1966, 170,000 men had been drafted and another 180,000 enlisted after being classified 1-A. Men seeking deferments quickly became fathers or enrolled in college. By January, two million men had secured college deferments, effectively becoming the first draft dodgers. That spring, in less than five months, 11,000 copies of the eighth edition of *The Handbook for Conscientious Objectors*, published by the Central Committee for Conscientious Objectors and "designed to serve the committed objector, not to challenge the draft system," were sold and the book went into a second printing. At the same time, Hershey, in an attempt to tap into the student population, resurrected the long unused Selective Service Qualification Test in order to target the least successful students. In 1963, when the test had last been offered, only 2,145 men sat for it. In 1966, however, 767,935 men—all anxious to secure deferments—took the exam.[50]

"I FOUGHT THE LAW, AND THE LAW WON," MARCH 1966 TO MARCH 1967

Into this atmosphere of increased attention to the draft stepped the Boston Committee for Non-Violent Action. On March 26, 1966, the day after the arrests of the men at the Boston Army Base for "sauntering and loitering," many CNVA members participated in a march from the Cambridge Common to the Arlington Street Church. In coordination with the Second International Days of Protest, local organizers decided to hold the rally in the church in hopes that they would be able to avoid the kind of hostility that had ended the October demonstration on the Common. The location made no difference. In contrast to New York, where 50,000 turned out for a peaceful march, fewer than 2,000 marched in Boston, and those who did were jeered and pelted with eggs over much of the route. A group of counterprotesters marched ahead of them chanting derogatory epithets and calling the parade the "long yellow line." When the demonstrators arrived at the church, a group of 1,500 hostile onlookers awaited them. As the marchers entered the building, dozens of eggs and several beer cans rained down on them. Many of the eggs splattered on the doors of the church, staining them a slimy yellow. On the steps of the church, MIT professor Noam Chomsky asked a police officer, "Don't you think you ought to stop this?" The officer just smiled. When an egg connected with his uniform, he rapidly changed his demeanor. "Then they cleared everybody away in about three seconds," Chomsky recalled.[51]

For two straight days, the members of the Boston CNVA had faced considerable enmity as they protested against the war. Still, several of them decided that on the day of their "trial" for the sit-in at the army base, they would use the South Boston courthouse steps as a "natural stage" for a draft card burning. Part of their training in civil disobedience taught them to seek to make every event into an opportunity for protest, to get the message out. They wrote press releases, took them to the State House press room, and distributed them to as many print, radio, and television reporters as they could, never realizing that this activity could result in the beating that they received. Years later, John Phillips said, "For some reason, I think we were oblivious to the possibilities there. This was something we never expected to happen."[52]

After the attack, the victims went to the courtroom to be sentenced each to a $20 fine for their roles in the army base sit-in. In keeping with standard nonviolent tactics, they refused to pay the fines. They believed that rather than giving money to the system that they were fighting, it made more sense to have that system incur some expenses to support them for twenty days in jail. The judge told John Phillips that, given his broken nose and two black eyes, he had already paid a sufficient penalty, but Phillips insisted on going to jail, too. There the group quickly learned, however, that the Massachusetts correctional system did not spend much money to house and feed them. Their cells at the Charles Street Jail were overrun with cockroaches, and they were served disgusting meals. Suzanne Williams recalled trying to eat "women's fist sized" meatballs that were impossible to penetrate with the large spoons with which they were expected to eat. "It was some kind of double boiled gristle or something," she recalled. "We all called them hand grenades."[53]

On the day that they were released from jail (an uncle had paid bail to get Phillips out the first night, but the others stayed), a crowd of reporters, about ten police officers, and five FBI agents waited outside. To their satisfaction, Gary Graham Hicks, one of the eleven from CNVA, and one of the few black men in the movement, burned his draft card. Hicks had been involved in the civil rights movement, primarily in Boston, since 1963 and had attended a 1965 meeting at which Carver Neblett of the Student Nonviolent Coordinating Committee (SNCC) had reported that the organization was looking for the first available opportunity to come out against the war. The draft, in particular, looked promising as a target of protest because it selected a disproportionate number of minorities to serve when, as Hicks later recalled, "we couldn't even guarantee a free election in Mississippi." Hicks also based his decision to burn the draft card on his jailhouse reading of Albert Camus's *The Plague*, which taught him that "you're either on the side of the plague, or you're on the side of its victims." As he carried out his protest, two FBI agents stood directly behind him, peering over his shoulder; one relayed information that he read off the draft card to the other who wrote it down in a notebook. After Hicks dropped the burning remains to the ground, the first agent snuffed out the flame and collected the pieces. Even though Hicks, as did his four friends before him, had openly broken the law—and said so to the media as they did it—the FBI agents diligently collected evidence at the scene as if it were a clandestine deed, evidence that within a year put Gary Hicks in prison.[54]

The government wasted no time in taking legal and possibly illegal action against the Boston CNVA men who had burned their draft cards.

On April 15, 1966, two weeks after the draft card burnings on the South Boston Courthouse steps, a grand jury in U.S. District Court in Boston indicted David O'Brien, John Phillips, David Benson, and David Reed each for violating the federal law prohibiting the destruction of one's draft card (Hicks's indictment came down later). At almost the same time, each man heard from his draft board. By April 22, two of the men—Phillips and O'Brien—had been reclassified to 1-A. By mid-May, two of them—Phillips and Reed—had been called for their pre-induction physicals (which they ignored), and by mid-June both had been called for induction (which they also ignored). On August 18, Phillips and Reed were indicted for failure to comply with the Selective Service laws directing them to appear for their physicals and to submit to induction. These were the early days of draft resistance, and a determined federal government brought its full force to bear on those who challenged its authority.

When each of the CNVA cases came to trial, the defendants and the government argued their cases from two completely different perspectives. The prosecution, led by Assistant U.S. Attorney John Wall, a former paratrooper who served in Korea, stuck to proving that the defendants did "knowingly and willfully" burn their draft cards or refuse induction. These facts were easily proven since the defendants had generally perpetrated the acts in public or announced their intentions in letters to their draft boards. In contrast, the defendants, all of whom served as their own counsel, used some of the evidence introduced by the prosecution against them—their letters to their local boards—not to dispute the government's presentation of the facts but to make an argument to the jury based on the moral value of their acts as compared to the immorality of the "war machine" and, sometimes specifically, American efforts in Vietnam.

David O'Brien faced the government first. In his trial of June 1, 1966, he did not object to any of the evidence presented by Wall and, after hearing the testimony of FBI agent Thomas McInerney, thanked the man for saving his life (in fact, O'Brien did not believe that McInerney had saved his life; he rather resented the way McInerney had treated him that day during the janitor's closet interrogation. But he made this gesture out of concern that the CNVA be seen as civil and thoughtful, not anti-FBI or anti-American). In his cross-examination of the state's assistant director of Selective Service, Col. Paul Feeney, O'Brien read aloud the letter that he had sent to Local Board 18 in March. He had informed the board that he severed his ties to the Selective Service because it was the "only moral course" he could follow. "I could never serve in the armed forces in any capacity for I consider the existence of the war machine the furthest step taken toward the demise of mankind, not only physically but morally." He told the board that he would not accept a civilian position as an alternative because "this would amount to my being placed in a special category, and I am not special. This would be saying that there is a right to draft others in the killing machine."

During his one-day trial, O'Brien's arguments rested more on his pacifist beliefs than on his particular opposition to the Vietnam War. He acknowledged that he could have applied for conscientious objector (CO) status— which would have kept him from being drafted into a combat role but probably would have resulted in his having to fulfill noncombat responsibilities for two years—but such exemptions were generally given only to Quakers or to those who could demonstrate a religious basis for their pacifism. O'Brien could not. Moreover, he felt that even to accept CO status would be tantamount to acceptance of and participation in an institution designed to kill others. "I could not go along with the system," he said in his final statement to the jury. "I had to refuse to cooperate with what I considered to be evil."[55]

John Phillips had presented similar arguments in a letter that he wrote to President Johnson (a copy of which he sent to his draft board, and thus made its way into his trial as evidence). But he went beyond O'Brien's expressions of pacifism to address more Thoreau-like questions of the place of the individual in a civil society. He stated that he, too, objected conscientiously to all wars. "To participate in the war effort," Phillips wrote, "whether in combat or as a noncombatant, would be a betrayal of my moral beliefs." He did not seek CO status through his draft board, he said, because "I am really a conscientious *affirmer*, for I wholeheartedly affirm the values of life and conscientiously pursue the good of all men." But, equally important, Phillips said, he found the Selective Service System intolerable because it sought "to coerce a man to do the bidding of his state, under threat of punishment should he refuse." In a truly free society, he argued, "individuals will act from a genuine desire to attain a better life for their fellows, not from an acceptance of standards imposed by the government." Without room for individual conscience, men, as Thoreau said, "serve the State . . . not as men mainly, but as machines." Phillips and the others would not accept that. He concluded with a pledge to continue his efforts to convince his fellow citizens that "war is senseless and immoral" and that in Vietnam, "as in all wars[,] men are being made their brothers' murderers for the selfish interests of political leaders." He said he knew the president would "recognize the urgent need for such a task" and would encourage him in his "mission for peace."[56]

In the letters that they wrote to their draft boards and in statements made at their trials, David Reed and Gary Hicks—as if to prove Thoreau's point that by means of men's respect for the law, "even the well-disposed are daily made the agents of injustice"—expanded on the critiques of O'Brien and Phillips to directly question the morality of American policies on Vietnam. In early 1966, Reed wrote to his local board and reminded it that he faithfully registered for the draft in 1964 but that since then he had "seen the government of the United States rain bombs upon the people of Vietnam" and "American soldiers burn the homes of Vietnamese peasants with cigarette lighters, with flame-throwers, and with napalm bombs." He also referred to the American invasion of the Dominican Republic and government threats to "wage total war—nuclear war—against the people of the Soviet Union and China." All of these actions, Reed charged, "are crimes under the Constitution of the United States; they are crimes under the Charter of the United Nations, and under international law; and, most importantly, they are crimes against humanity." As a result, he wrote, "I refuse to participate in these crimes, and I declare my intention to do all that I can, as one citizen, to stop my government from behaving in this manner." Reed told the local board that he would henceforth refuse to participate with the Selective Service System. "I think it is the duty of every American to say 'NO' to the government," he wrote, "and face jail rather than fight in a brutal war of aggression against the people of Vietnam." When his board called him for induction in May, Reed responded: "I refuse to serve in the armed forces because . . . my loyalty to humanity lies above my loyalty to any government."[57]

Hicks, who had fled to Montreal after being indicted—only to turn himself in two months later—also used his January 1967 trial to highlight the hypocrisy of the government in expecting its citizens to obey the law while it "openly violate[d] international law, the Geneva convention and the Nuremberg decisions and the Charter of the United Nations" in prosecuting its war in Vietnam. "This country has committed and is committing genocide in Vietnam," he argued. Furthermore, in a way that the other card burners did not, he emphasized his perspective as an African American. "The United States," Hicks told the judge during sentencing, "can't even send Federal Marshals to protect people who try to vote in Alabama," but marshals shuttled him back and forth to court every day. Moreover, he said, "this is the only country in the world that says that I should deal nonviolently with the Ku Klux Klan. This same country will actually pay me to go out and commit genocide against someone whom I don't even know." Hicks concluded by telling the court that "carrying a draft card in this country is equal to a black man carrying a draft card in South Africa or of a Jew being forced to wear a Star of David on an armband in Nazi Germany." The law prohibiting the burning of draft cards, he said, was made to "suppress legitimate political expressions of legitimate American dissenters to foreign policy." When Americans start enacting and tolerating such laws, he finished, "then we no longer live in a democracy and we may as well stop pretending that we do."[58]

In the fall of 1966 and early 1967, when Reed and Hicks were tried, such charges were gaining currency at home (albeit among a limited number of people) and especially abroad. During much of 1966, Bertrand Russell, the aging British philosopher and mathematician, almost single-handedly organized an International War Crimes Tribunal to hear evidence of possible American war crimes in Vietnam. After Prime Minister Harold Wilson and President Charles DeGaulle refused to hold sessions of the tribunal in either Britain or France, it finally got down to business in Stockholm in May 1967. There, consistent with the charges levied by Americans like David Reed and Gary Hicks, international researchers presented evidence that American planes had bombed civilian targets in both North and South Vietnam, including, for example, a leprosarium in Quinh Lap, which was bombed thirteen times over nine days in June 1965. Such acts led the tribunal to find the United States guilty of war crimes. Consequently, a growing number of draft resisters invoked the Nuremberg principles as support for their decisions to defy orders to commit immoral acts.[59]

The American media and the Johnson administration, despite being invited to defend itself before the tribunal, largely ignored the proceedings. Secretary of State Dean Rusk, referring to Russell, told reporters that he had no intention of "playing games with a 94-year-old Briton." Jean-Paul Sartre, executive president of the tribunal, had trouble understanding this comment, coming as it did from "a mediocre American official." The American press seemed even less interested, calling the tribunal an "anti-American propaganda ploy" and claiming that its members were "not interested in peace." At this early date, one historian has noted, the American media could be depended upon to view the tribunal as "a political circus orchestrated by left-wing nuts."[60] The evidence presented to the tribunal would be confirmed by Vietnam veterans at the Winter Soldier hearings in 1971, but such stories had no effect on American war policy.

Similarly, the early appeals to morality by draft card burners had no impact on the way their cases were handled by the judicial system. By early 1967, all five of the Boston CNVA draft resisters were serving prison sentences of anywhere from two to five years, except for David O'Brien, who, after two months in prison, secured bail while his case went through the appeals process. The judges who heard the cases allowed the defendants to make their cases in closing statements but would not tolerate their trying to put American war policy on trial. Consequently, all such cases were easily processed. At the end of 1966, the government had secured 450 draft-related convictions, a substantial increase over the 262 convictions of 1965 and the 227 of 1964.[61]

Charles DeBenedetti has noted that "the draft issue provided the link between political action and personal commitment and life-style that radical pacifists had been seeking."[62] CNVA members sought to challenge the nation's war policies on the issue of morality as one way of calling attention to Americans' growing callousness and attraction to violence. David O'Brien got to the heart of the matter in his statement at sentencing when he described draft card burning as symbolic of his "choice to work for the betterment of our society in a very radical way, radical in that all our motivations, all our actions, all our beliefs must be reexamined and those that are incompatible with the well-being of the individual and those that deny love must be changed." The horrors of war are so great, he said, it mystified him that "so many people, even those who have fought in wars, seem unable to feel any compassion for those who are affected." He concluded: "The cry we have heard in the past to bomb Hanoi with its thousands of innocents has been acted upon, and now the same people cheer over the cries and screams of their victims. I cannot understand how the warriors fail to see in this the rape of their own sensitivity."[63] Such pleas did little to affect policy makers in Washington, Selective Service officials, the courts, or the public at large. Soon the Boston CNVA ceased to exist, since the men who comprised much of its core found themselves in federal prison.[64]

The Boston CNVA draft resisters set important precedents for future resisters. In addition to raising questions about individuality and free will in a republic at war, they framed their dissent as an issue of citizenship, an impatient brand of citizenship that justified confronting one's government when circumstances warranted it. Furthermore, the rapid, effective response of the federal government to the draft resistance threat set an example of prosecutorial zeal that led later draft resistance leaders to believe that they could rely on the Department of Justice to attempt to prosecute thousands of draft resisters at once, thus clogging the courts and straining the Selective Service System.

On October 16, 1967, John Phillips, then over twelve months into his sentence, watched the nightly news in the prisoners' lounge at the federal pen in Petersburg, Virginia, and, to his amazement, saw hundreds of men turning in (and some burning) their draft cards in an elaborate ceremony at the Arlington Street Church in Boston. "I remembered," he later recalled, "our little band of bold pioneers" and the beatings they received for doing essentially the same thing as these men, who now were backed by thousands of supporters. Much had changed in eighteen months, but in that intervening period, many opponents of the war must have remembered the experience of the Boston CNVA, for public draft resistance disappeared between April 1966 and October 1967 in Boston. Although some resurrected the idea in other parts of the country in the spring of 1967, Boston's leading protesters turned to other means of undermining the Selective Service System and the war effort before October 16.

2 THE DRAFT AS A POLITICAL ISSUE AND A MOVEMENT TARGET

Sarge, I'm only 18, I got a ruptured spleen, and I always carry a purse / I got eyes like a bat, my feet are flat, and my asthma's getting worse / Yes, think of my career, my sweetheart dear, my poor old invalid aunt / besides, I ain't no fool, I'm going to school, and I'm working in a defense plant.
—Phil Ochs, "Draft Dodger Rag," 1965

For more than a year after the attacks on the CNVA draft card burners, protests targeting the draft faded from public view. The impatience exhibited by early draft resisters receded as the courts consistently ruled against the burners and sent them off to prison quickly and quietly. Protest against the war continued but sporadically and still on a relatively small scale. On the morning of April 15, 1967, however, draft resistance resurfaced in dramatic fashion. As 100,000 to 400,000 people (estimates varied) gathered in New York for a march that organizers called the Spring Mobilization to End the War in Vietnam (more than 60,000 also marched in San Francisco), about 170 men, most from Cornell University, and a former Green Beret burned their draft cards together in Central Park's Sheep's Meadow. Newspapers across the country splashed their images across their front pages. The following day, Martin Luther King Jr., the main speaker at the New York march, told panelists on television's *Face the Nation* news program that although he didn't condone the draft card burning in the park, he did support resistance. "In the true spirit of non-violence," he said, "I have only advocated doing what we do to resist it openly, cheerfully, and with a desire to reconcile rather than to estrange and really appeal to the conscience of the nation on what I consider a very unjust and immoral involvement" in Vietnam.[1]

On the same day of the marches in New York and San Francisco, a full-page "We Won't Go" statement appeared in the *Harvard Crimson*:

> We, the undersigned, as American men of draft age, may be asked by our government to participate in the war in Vietnam. We have examined the history and the nature of this war, and have reached the conclusion that our participation in it would be contrary to the dictates of our consciences.
>
> We therefore declare our determination to refuse military service while the United States is fighting in Vietnam. Our intention in signing this statement is to unite with other draft-age men who share our convictions, in order to turn our personal moral rejection of this war into effective political opposition to it.

That eighty-six men signed this statement on a day when one hundred seventy others burned their cards in New York made it significant. Draft noncompliance reemerged as one of the primary strategies of antiwar protest, but this time on a larger scale. Gone were the days of fighting the draft individually or even in small groups. This new brand of defiance recognized the power of numbers.

Nevertheless, even with its emphasis on converting moral outrage into "political opposition," the Harvard We Won't Go statement did not commit the signers to action or even a clearly defined strategy of resistance. "Our policy is open," admitted one spokesman for the group (tentatively calling itself the Harvard Draft Resistance Group). "Draft resistance could include applying for draft deferments as conscientious objectors, emigrating to Canada or accepting prison sentences rather than undergoing induction." He estimated that between 500 and 700 men had signed similar statements nationwide and—as if to demonstrate the absence of risk—mentioned that he knew of no resulting prosecutions.[2] In a strategy that was altogether different than the CNVA practice of open confrontation with the government, the "We Won't Go" signers deliberately chose to be vague because, as one of them later noted, they were still debating their plans; they discussed numerous strategies but did not want to commit to anything beyond the statement.[3]

The Boston CNVA exposed not only the inherent risks of open draft law defiance but, perhaps more important, that it was ineffective. One key figure in the draft resistance movement that developed a year later recalled that the actions of Phillips, O'Brien, Reed, Benson, and Hicks, seemed "politically very dumb." Although one had to respect their pacifist, non-violent stand, he said, the "stupidly provocative" incident in South Boston did not win many converts among the larger citizenry.[4] Consequently, the "We Won't Go" statement promised no such violations of the law nor did the mere signing of it constitute a crime.

This more cautious—perhaps ambivalent—approach of courting confrontation without actually going face to face with the government did, however, represent the beginning of a shift back toward more radical defiance of the government's will regarding conscription. In fact, despite the absence of draft resistance through most of 1966 and the winter of 1967, the impulse to challenge the draft never completely died. Indeed, the draft remained a constant concern for the American people and, consequently, continued to loom as an obvious target for the growing antiwar movement. As the Selective Service escalated draft calls, more and more Americans began to question the fairness of a conscription system that appeared to play favorites; local draft boards, it seemed, valued some draft-age citizens more than others. Increasingly, as the military inducted disproportionate numbers of working-class, poor, and minority men (while upper- and middle-class men hid behind deferments), more and more anti-war activists saw an opportunity to expose the nation's system of conscription as both unfair and un-American. Making the draft the focus of their protest, it followed, could form the foundation for a massive grass-roots movement against the war.

The Harvard "We Won't Go" statement and dozens of others like it derived from this rationale. And if the "We Won't Go" statements did not outline a clear program of protest, the organizations they spawned did. In particular, the formation of the Boston Draft Resistance Group (BDRG) is critical to understanding the growth of the movement. Instead of aiming for dramatic confrontations that were sure to garner media (and government) attention, the BDRG adopted a more low-key approach that focused on building grass-roots support through campus and community organizing.

THE DRAFT AS A POLITICAL ISSUE

In the autumn of 1966, as John Phillips and David Benson adjusted to their prison cells and as David Reed and Gary Hicks prepared for similar arrangements, an article in the *Harvard Crimson* reported that the war in Vietnam had "had virtually no effect on the graduate plans of Harvard seniors." The university's Office of Graduate and Career Plans, the article noted, had determined that 74 percent of graduating seniors from the Class of 1966 had gone on to graduate school while only 7 percent went into the military. These figures virtually matched those of the Class of 1965. At the same time, however, the editors predicted that the 1966–67 school year would be the "Year of the Draft." Events would prove them right.[5]

In fact, for some conscription-age men, 1966 had already become the "year of the draft" as Selective Service calls climbed dramatically. But students at universities such as Harvard did not have to worry, for they were protected by deferments issued by their local draft boards. As long as they scored well on the Selective Service mental aptitude test or attained rankings in the upper half of their classes, deferments were practically guaranteed. Such deferments raised serious questions about the fairness of the draft; working-class men who lacked the financial resources to attend college full time, for example, were more likely to be drafted than middle-class, full-time students. Meanwhile, a host of deferments continued to protect some men while others were left exposed (see Table 1).

At Harvard in the fall of 1966, few students questioned the legitimacy of the 2-S (student) deferment. When the Harvard Undergraduate Council sponsored a referendum to gauge student opinion on the draft and, in particular, on the requirement that the university provide class rankings to the Selective Service, only 43 percent of the student body turned out to vote. Those who did cast ballots overwhelmingly opposed the computing of students' ranks for the Selective Service. More telling is that 65 percent indicated that they believed they deserved draft deferments "solely because they were students" while 70 percent expressed their aversion to proposals for a more equitable lottery system to replace the existing one. Insofar as they were willing to see changes made, 84 percent favored some kind of alternative service system in which one could fulfill one's duty to the country by accepting a nonmilitary appointment in lieu of being sent to boot camp and possibly Vietnam. Clearly, these results reflected a strong instinct on the part of the students to keep themselves from being drafted.[6]

This is not to say that Harvard students were apathetic regarding the Vietnam War. Since 1965 the campus had seen a fairly steady stream of speakers, leafleters, and other activists (many from New Left organizations such as the May 2nd Movement and Students for a Democratic Society) coordinating teach-ins and campaigning against the war. These events occurred sporadically, though, and the numbers of students involved remained relatively low.

TABLE I. Selective Service Classifications

Class	Definition
1-A	Registrant available for military service
1-A-O	Conscientious objector registrant available for noncombatant military service
1-C	Member of the Armed Forces of the United States, the Coast and Geodetic Survey, or the Public Health Service
1-D	Qualified member of reserve component, or student taking military training, including ROTC and accepted aviation cadet application
1-O	Conscientious objector available for civilian work contributing to the maintenance of the national health, safety, or interest
1-S	Student deferred by law until graduation from high school or attainment of age 20, or until end of his academic year at a college or university
1-W	Conscientious objector performing civilian work contributing to the maintenance of the national health, safety, or interest, or who has completed such work
1-Y	Registrant qualified for military service only in time of war or national emergency
2-A	Occupational deferment (other than agricultural and student)
2-C	Agricultural deferment
2-S	Student deferment
3-A	Extreme hardship deferment, or registrant with a child or children
4-A	Registrant with sufficient prior active service or who is a sole surviving son
4-B	Official deferred by law
4-C	Alien not currently liable for military service
4-D	Minister of religion or divinity student
4-F	Registrant not qualified for any military service
5-A	Registrant over the age of liability for military service

Source: U.S. National Advisory Commission on Selective Service, *In Pursuit of Equity: Who Serves When Not All Serve?* (Washington, D.C.: GPO, 1967)

There were some exceptions. In early November 1966, several hundred antiwar students, largely led by SDS, managed to corner Secretary of Defense Robert McNamara on the hood of a car. McNamara had come to campus to lunch with a group of undergraduates as part of the Kennedy Institute's Honorary Associates program. In anticipation of his appearance, SDS had tried to arrange a debate on the war between the secretary and Robert Scheer, managing editor of *Ramparts* magazine. McNamara refused and, as a result, roused SDS to action. Using walkie-talkies to communicate, the students monitored the exits of Quincy House waiting for

McNamara's departure. A decoy car failed to fool them, and they quickly surrounded McNamara's vehicle as the driver tried to leave Mill Street. They began rocking it. As demonstrators sat down in front of and behind the car, the driver slammed the car into gear and started driving forward into the students. Thinking better of it, he stopped before anyone got hurt. Finally, an obviously annoyed McNamara edged out of the car. Hal Benenson, a junior and cochair of SDS, persuaded the secretary to stand on the hood of a convertible parked at the curb. McNamara, impeccably dressed, hair neatly greased back in his trademark style, scrambled onto the front of the car and shouted into the SDS microphone: "I spent four of the happiest years of my life at Berkeley's campus doing some of the same things you're doing here. But there was an important difference. I was tougher and more courteous." This brought catcalls of "fascist!" and "murderer!" to which McNamara responded, "And I was tougher then and I'm tougher now!"

He then asked Benenson to organize a nonviolent meeting that he promised to attend but hastened to add that he had another meeting in five minutes on the other side of the Charles River. The crowd was in no mood for a later meeting. Finally, he relented: "O.K. fellas, I'll answer one or two of your questions." Michael Ansara, the chair of SDS, called for two questions from the crowd. Someone immediately asked why the administration kept insisting that the war resulted from aggression by North Vietnam in 1957. "The war didn't begin in '57," McNamara answered. "It started in '54–55 when a million North Vietnamese flooded into South Vietnam." Another student then yelled, "Yeah, and they were all Catholics."[7] "A report from the International Control Commission states that it was aggression," the secretary replied. "I didn't write it. All you have to do is read it. You haven't read it and if you have, you obviously didn't understand it." "We've seen it," someone shouted. Now McNamara was irritated: "Why don't you guys get up here since you already seem to have all the answers?" It soon turned into a shouting match. Someone asked, "How many South Vietnamese civilians have we killed and why doesn't the State Department disclose the figures?" When McNamara responded with a weak "We don't know," another person in the crowd yelled, "Why don't you know? Don't you care?" The jeering reached such a level that McNamara could not have been heard even if he had answered. To his relief, ten Harvard and Cambridge police officers pushed their way toward him, helped him from the car, and ushered him into McKinlock Hall, where he escaped the throng through an underground tunnel.[8] Harvard officials condemned the students for their behavior, but the event electrified the campus—if only briefly.

Within a couple of weeks, life returned to normal at Harvard. Even the dramatic confrontation with one of the architects of the American war effort did not galvanize students to sustained protest. Indeed, Harvard's was symptomatic of all antiwar efforts in the Boston area up to that point. Certain groups and individuals held demonstrations and organized occasional marches, teach-ins, and rallies, but taken together these events constituted little more than spasms that were easily ignored by those running the war. They failed to create a cumulative effect that even approached comparison with the civil rights movement or other precedent-setting political activism. Antiwar activists continued to seek ways to unify their efforts and attract greater numbers of citizens to their cause.

By the end of 1966, the number of draftees being called for induction numbered more than four times that of 1964 levels. As a result, the draft (and the war) touched the homes of a far greater number of families than it had since the end of the Korean War. But as the *Harvard Crimson* made clear, it did not affect everyone equally. That fact alone convinced many Americans that the complex system of deferments that had evolved over a decade of relative peace warranted closer examination.

Rumblings about the Selective Service had started as early as 1964 when Barry Goldwater, the Republican nominee for president, had called for the end of the draft. In response, President Johnson announced that he would launch a comprehensive study of the Selective Service. Historian George Q. Flynn notes that Johnson recognized that the "draft issue was politically sensitive because of the class bias of the deferment system." One labor official wrote to the president in 1964, "When [United Automobile Workers Union president] Walter Reuther realizes his people are doing the dying while the auto executives' sons keep getting school deferments, there could be hell to pay." Johnson won in a landslide in 1964, but the results of the study were not released. Not until April 1965 did Robert McNamara receive the Department of Defense (DOD) report Johnson ordered. McNamara concluded that continuing the draft was imperative and that, since the study showed that 40 percent of all enlistees joined because of fear of the draft, any notion of an all-volunteer force (as some were suggesting) should be dismissed. McNamara made his recommendations to Johnson, but the DOD report remained unpublished until July 1966, when increased criticism of the draft in the wake of sharply increased calls for manpower forced its release. McNamara himself grew uneasy with the inequities of the existing system of conscription and in one speech even floated the idea of two years of "national service" as a solution.[9]

One of the most obvious cases of Selective Service unfairness involved Hollywood actor George Hamilton. Hamilton lived a fairly public social life—most notably as a frequent date of President Johnson's older daughter, Lynda Bird—and news of his deferred status caused controversy. On June 23, 1966, Congressman Alvin O'Konski, a Republican from Wisconsin and a member of the House Armed Services Committee, told his fellow committee members that although all of the 100 men drafted from his congressional district over the previous six months came from families with annual incomes under $5,000, George Hamilton, "a young Hollywood actor with a $200,000 home, a $30,000 Rolls Royce, and a $100,000 income," continued to receive a hardship deferment to support his mother, a woman, the congressman noted, who had been married four times. "The system is undemocratic and un-American," O'Konski concluded. "It nauseates me. How can I defend it to my people?" Although O'Konski carefully avoided accusing the White House of arranging preferential treatment for the first daughter's boyfriend, Hamilton's deferment made the president look bad. Muhammad Ali's lawyer, Hayden Covington, told the champ, "George Hamilton gets out [of the draft] because he's going with the president's daughter, but you're different. They want to make an example out of you."[10]

To placate critics of the draft, Johnson issued Executive Order 11289, creating the National Advisory Commission on Selective Service under the chairmanship of Burke Marshall, the former head of the Justice Department's civil rights division. Johnson instructed the commission to review draft "fairness" (especially student deferments), classification methods, the appeals system, and the impact of the draft on society, among other things, and to submit its report to him early in 1967 so that he and Congress might be fully informed when they took up the renewal of the Selective Service Act in the spring.[11]

More than any of America's previous armed conflicts, the Vietnam War relied mostly on the working class to fight it. Historian Christian Appy estimates that enlisted ranks in Vietnam were "comprised of about 25 percent poor, 55 percent working class, and 20 percent middle class, with a statistically negligible number of wealthy."[12] In fact, he shows that the inequities of the sss were not limited to its structure of deferments but also arose from policies designed to induct the less intelligent. Appy explains that in the early 1960s, half of the men called by local boards failed one or both of their physical or mental exams; most failed the Armed Forces Qualification Test. Of those who failed this test, almost half came from families with six or more children and an annual income of less than

$4,000. Daniel Patrick Moynihan, the assistant secretary of labor for policy planning, viewed this as "de facto job discrimination" against "the least mobile, least educated young men." Intent on putting such men to work in careers that would teach them skills that could be useful outside the service, he called for reform that would facilitate such training through military service. But, according to Appy, as draft calls increased dramatically in 1965, the military, "with no intention of engaging in any social uplift . . . simply accepted more and more men with terribly low scores on the mental examination."[13]

Shortly thereafter, in 1966, Robert McNamara created Project 100,000, a program that addressed Moynihan's concerns by admitting 100,000 men who failed the exam into the military every year. "The poor of America," McNamara said, "have not had the opportunity to earn their fair share of this nation's abundance, but they can be given an opportunity to serve in their country's defense and they can be given an opportunity to return to a civilian life with skills and aptitudes which for them and their families will reverse the downward spiral of decay." Appy reports that officials in the Johnson administration fashioned this program as part of the War on Poverty and the Great Society initiatives more than as an extension of manpower mobilization. Of course, to reap the promised rewards one would have to first survive the Vietnam War. Ultimately, "the promised training was never carried out" and half of the 400,000 men who joined the military through Project 100,000 went to Vietnam. Worse, they had a death rate twice as high as that of American forces as a whole and 40 percent of them were black—compared to 10 percent for the military overall.[14]

The Marshall Commission went to work in the summer and fall of 1966, then, just as Project 100,000 unfolded, sending even greater numbers of poor and poorly educated men off to fight in the place of better educated, middle- and upper-class men. From the start, commission members were aware of the inequities—at least those resulting from deferments—and the public's view of them because they received over 500 unsolicited letters from the public, the majority of which urged the abolition of all deferments. As a result, George Flynn notes, by their second or third meeting, Marshall and others had successfully shifted the focus from a critique of the existing system toward a new plan for national service.[15]

WE WON'T GO

Although the strategy of confronting the Selective Service directly had lost some of its appeal among the war's opponents, the heightened level of attention focused on the draft served to hold it aloft as an ever-present, tempting target. By late 1966, a certain momentum developed that brought even the recalcitrant SDS to move toward draft resistance. Following two local meetings in New Haven, a national discussion of noncompliance took place in late August at the AFSC building in Des Moines, Iowa. There, about fifty participants from various student organizations discussed plans for community antidraft unions that would counsel and organize men around the issue of the draft. In addition, they resurrected the idea of a We Won't Go pledge—first used by the May 2nd Movement in the spring of 1964—and made plans for a national "We Won't Go" conference in the fall.[16] As Michael Ferber and Staughton Lynd later described it, the December 4 We Won't Go conference in Chicago "brought together representatives of every significant strain of antidraft activity—at a moment when that activity was on the verge of assuming mass proportions." Over 500 representatives from across the country left the meetings planning to start dozens of local We Won't Go projects.[17]

Most significant, the Students for a Democratic Society were at last poised to join the battle. SDS originated at a conference of sixty-two college students in Port Huron, Michigan, in 1962. That conference produced a manifesto, the Port Huron Statement, that became the most enduring intellectual contribution of the New Left. Authored primarily by Tom Hayden, a twenty-two-year-old former editor of the University of Michigan's student newspaper, the statement chastised American society for failing to live up to its potential. In particular, it expressed the students' horror at the treatment of African Americans in the segregated South and their anxiety over the threat of a nuclear holocaust (their fears were almost realized several months later when the United States and the Soviet Union nearly went to war over missiles in Cuba). Most important, the manifesto indicted modern conceptions of man as "a thing to be manipulated . . . inherently incapable of directing his own affairs." It called for the establishment of "a democracy of individual participation" in which "the individual shares in those social decisions determining the quality and direction of his life." This "participatory democracy" would allow individuals to escape the alienation and conformity of modern society and encourage independence and creative fulfillment of all citizens. For thousands of college students in the 1960s, these ideas struck a chord.[18]

Still, in spite of the Selective Service's power over the direction of so many young American lives, SDS had a long history of ambivalence regarding draft resistance. Kirkpatrick Sale writes that, by fall 1966, when some members of SDS were thinking of coming out against the 2-S deferment or refusing induction, "even many of those willing to take such personal risks—and there were a number in SDS—tended to acknowledge that this was more an expression of middle-class guilt, or a 'politics of masochism,' than an effective way to build up a mass antidraft organization." When the SDS National Council met in Berkeley in December, however, "everyone wanted to talk about the draft." In part, this shift in attitudes could be attributed not only to the participation of some of its prominent members in both the Des Moines meeting and the We Won't Go conference but also to a growing recognition that the timing made sense given the government's need to review and probably renew the Selective Service Act within six months. Just before the National Council met, John Spritzler of Dartmouth SDS, sensing the mood, wrote an essay in *New Left Notes*, SDS's national newspaper, proposing a mass draft card burning by 10,000 men.[19]

After more than a year of doubt regarding the political efficacy of protesting the draft, and after nineteen hours of debate over two days, the National Council adopted a militant antidraft resolution that described the war as "immoral, illegal, and genocidal" and reaffirmed its opposition to "conscription in any form" as well as any attempt to "legitimize the Selective Service System by reforms" (a clear reference to the Marshall Commission). More important, SDS pledged to organize "unions of draft resisters," members of which would be "united by the common principle that under no circumstances [would] they allow themselves to be drafted." In addition, they promised direct-action demonstrations at draft boards and recruiting stations, as well as reaching out to draft-age men in high schools, universities, and communities all over the country. With this statement, SDS took a bold step, moving, as one of its leaders said, "from protest to resistance." In protesting against the war, SDS would no longer be content with the spasmodic occurrence of marches and sit-ins; they had now made a commitment to action. Soon, members began wearing buttons expressing one word: "Resist." The Berkeley statement effectively set the course for antidraft activity across the country for the next six to eight months.[20]

Certainly, its impact became obvious in Boston and especially at Harvard. Although many students seemed to take what one future draft resistance leader called the "morally opaque" view of the draft as an inconvenience early in the 1966–67 school year, by the end of the fall semester, discussions took a more sober turn.[21] The influence of some members of the faculty proved significant in this regard. On December 6, just two days after the national We Won't Go conference opened in Chicago, sixteen members of the departments of government and philosophy offered a resolution that characterized the 2-S deferment as "unjust" and stated that "it strikes us as implausible to suppose that it is in the national interests that students, regardless of their fields, should be deferred while the disadvantaged are compelled to enter military service." Not all faculty agreed, and even if they did, most of them thought such views should be expressed individually rather than collectively; they tabled the resolution by a 141–88 margin. Still, the debate served to elevate the draft as the most prominent issue on campus.[22]

The majority of the faculty seemed unwilling to tackle the draft, but the students soon began to dedicate more attention to the issue. After another failed attempt by some professors to bring their resolution to a vote early in the spring semester, the editors of the *Harvard Crimson*, though notoriously timid on such issues, published an editorial in support of a lottery system. It anticipated the release of the Marshall Commission report and laid out the arguments for and against the 2-S deferment: "The best defense of the student deferment is that it is economical," the editors wrote. They challenged the proposition that without the student deferment, the United States would suffer the "decimation of a generation of college students" as Great Britain did during the First World War. "America," they wrote, "has simply too great a wealth of human resources to justify a procedure based on the premise that a loss of some portion of its students would be catastrophic." The paper acknowledged that there are times when a nation "must ignore moral principles" and put self-preservation first. "Now is not such a time," the editors concluded. "Because of its clear social inequity, the 2-S deferment should be discarded."[23] It turned out that the Marshall Commission agreed.

DRAFT REFORM?

Within a week of the *Crimson* editorial, two competing commission reviews put the draft on the front pages again. The first report was the product of a congressionally ordered review of the sss led by retired army general Mark Clark. Essentially, it argued that the existing Selective Service Act and its attendant policies and procedures were basically fair and, therefore, the law should be renewed. Like General Lewis Hershey, the director of Selective Service, the Clark Commission advocated continued use of local draft boards and keeping the undergraduate deferment and opposed any kind of lottery. The only significant change Clark recommended was the calling of the youngest men—rather than the oldest—in the pool first. In addition, it urged that draft card burners and other draft violators be "severely and expeditiously punished" and pushed for the application of tighter standards on conscientious objectors.[24] Under these proposals, the system would change little.

The Marshall Commission report, *In Pursuit of Equity: Who Serves When Not All Serve?*, released the next day advocated more sweeping reforms, including the elimination of the 2-S. It reported that it had "sought to find the means of securing the manpower needed for our national security in a manner as consistent as possible with human dignity, individual liberty, fairness to all citizens, and the other principles and traditions of a democratic and free society." Its major recommendations included inducting men at age nineteen, selecting them "through a system of impartial random selection among those equally vulnerable," and eliminating occupational and student deferments. On this last point, they noted that "student deferments have become the occasion of serious inequity. . . . Even though educational opportunity is increasingly widespread, the opportunity to go to college still reflects a degree of social and economic advantage not yet shared by all."[25] The commission thus validated one of the fundamental critiques leveled by the draft's opponents.

Equally important, the commission recommended the elimination of local draft boards and the centralization of power in regional offices that would use a computerized system; in this way the capricious nature of local board decision making could be replaced by a more uniform process. The commission bolstered its recommendation with a telling analysis of draft board composition: most local board members were middle-aged and elderly (71 percent were fifty or older; 22 percent were seventy or older), had military backgrounds (66.3 percent), and were overwhelmingly white (96.8 percent). These "little groups of neighbors" were not representative of the people most Americans encountered in their own neighborhoods.[26] Another study of over 16,000 draft board members, published in 1966, confirmed such statistics, noting that more than 70 percent were middle- and upper-class professionals (managers, proprietors, public officials, white-collar workers) over fifty years old while only 25 percent were blue-collar or agricultural workers.[27]

Two days later, on March 6, 1967, Lyndon Johnson asked Congress to renew the Selective Service Act. In his address, he pushed many of the Marshall Commission's proposals. He acknowledged the inequity of the deferment system: "Deferred for undergraduate work, deferred further to pursue graduate study, and then deferred even beyond that for fatherhood or occupational reasons," he said, "some young men have managed to pile deferment on deferment until they passed the normal cut-off point for induction." He urged the elimination of graduate deferments except in the fields of medicine and dentistry and the ministry. On the termination of undergraduate deferments, however, the president balked. He cited the split vote of the commission and asked for congressional and public debate on the subject. In addition, Johnson called for the induction of the youngest men first, urged centralization of the sss administration into regional boards, and ordered the implementation of a lottery system to be in place by January 1, 1969.[28] Between March and June, the fate of the draft lay with Congress and the American people.

THE BOSTON DRAFT RESISTANCE GROUP

The contrasting perspectives of Congress and the incipient draft resistance movement regarding the new proposals could not have been more opposed. By March and April, Ferber and Lynd note, "We Won't Go statements and antidraft unions proliferated from coast to coast, some of them instigated by sds, some arising independently."[29] Promises of draft reform meant little to the protesters. In fact, the growing number of students supporting draft resistance had grown so suspicious of the administration and the Selective Service that nothing short of the abolition of the draft and American withdrawal from Vietnam would have satisfied them.

Much of this cynicism was well-founded. Shortly after sds made its commitment to draft resistance, Peter Henig discovered a Selective Service document that stunned even the most hard-line opponents of the draft and the war. Called the "channeling memo" and published in the January 1967 issue of *New Left Notes*, the piece became one of the draft resistance movement's best recruiting tools. The Selective Service included the memo in training kits, and activists correctly assumed that it came from the desk of General Hershey; as they read it, most imagined the wizened, half-blind old man—a sinister Gepetto of sorts—sitting at his desk typing out the ominously matter-of-fact phrases: "Delivery of manpower for induction, the process of providing a few thousand men with transportation to a reception center, is not much of an administrative or financial challenge. It is in dealing with the other millions of registrants that the System is heavily occupied, developing more effective human beings in the national interest." The memo went on to describe the pressure, "the threat of loss of deferment," reinforced through periodic reports to the local draft board, felt by every registrant. "He is impelled to pursue his skill rather than embark upon some less important enterprise," it stated, "and is encouraged to apply his skill in an essential activity in the national interest." Finally, as if boasting of America's ability to program some of its citizens' futures under the illusion of democracy, the memo concluded: "The psychology of granting wide choice under pressure to take action is the American or indirect way of achieving what is done by direction in foreign countries where choice is not permitted." To the surprise of even the most jaded, the document offered evidence that the Selective Service System was not only inducting men into the military but engaging in the kind of social engineering practiced by America's totalitarian enemies.[30]

Furthermore, the channeling memo implied that the men who could not afford to go to college but worked as, say, an electrician's apprentice or a cab driver were much more likely to be drafted. Likewise, those who did manage to go to college but graduated only to pursue careers in music or the arts, for example, could expect their local boards to regard their career choices as something short of being "in the national interest." These were stunning revelations. Certainly, the channeling memo highlighted the kind of manipulation of lives that sps criticized in the Port Huron Statement. Any innocence retained by the nascent draft resistance movement surely now was lost. "At last, 'the American way' laid bare," wrote Kirkpatrick Sale.[31] The old movement slogan (with roots in existential and Beat criticism of modern society), "Human Being: Do Not Fold, Spindle, or Mutilate," seemed particularly germane once again.

In the face of such deceit, draft resistance attracted more and more men who were willing to organize against the sss and to do so in bold fashion. Despite the initially unclear mission of the Harvard We Won't Go group, a sense of solidarity quickly developed. Within ten days, at a meeting on April 25, a number of the We Won't Go signers organized themselves into the Boston Draft Resistance Group (BDRG) and brought their objectives into focus a little more sharply. Using the statement as their primary recruiting tool, the men (no women yet worked with the group) "set out to mobilize the Harvard campus" by going door to door, inviting students to meetings where they could discuss the draft and the war. Sixty people turned out for the first meeting a few days later.[32]

The tactic of canvassing the campus for more men made sense at the time. Just days before, Martin Luther King Jr. and famed pediatrician Benjamin Spock had come to Cambridge to launch Vietnam Summer by visiting a few homes to talk to families about the war as television cameras captured it all on film. The organizers of Vietnam Summer aimed to fuse politically inactive middle-class Americans into a powerful antiwar lobby by sending thousands of volunteers into thousands of communities across the country to talk about Vietnam. The idea had been conceived by Gar Alperovitz, a fellow at the Kennedy School's Institute of Politics at Harvard. He modeled it on Freedom Summer, the 1964 civil rights project that injected over 1,000 college students and civil rights activists into Mississippi to work in Freedom Schools and to register blacks to vote. Organizers chose Cambridge as the national headquarters for Vietnam Summer and staffed it with 11 people and 100 recruiters. Eventually, over 4,000 volunteers took to the streets of 770 of their own communities as part of the nationwide project. It is virtually impossible to gauge the impact of Vietnam Summer, though most scholars have concluded that it did not prove as successful as its movement forebear. According to Charles DeBenedetti, the far-flung engagement of the project made it difficult to manage: volunteers "worked sporadically. Staff members were not consistent. Ideological animosities were all too predictable" in a project more or less supported by the American Friends Service Committee, the Committee for a Sane Nuclear Policy (SANE), the SNCC, the Southern Christian Leadership Conference, and some factions of SDS.[33]

Even with its shortcomings, the national office of Vietnam Summer exerted heavy influence on the Boston Draft Resistance Group. A booklet called "Vietnam Summer: Project Profiles" described antiwar projects allied with Vietnam Summer, including the BDRG. The still small draft resistance organization's own depiction of itself demonstrated the impact of Vietnam Summer: "The Boston Group's program is built on the view that constructing a radical constituency through draft resistance is the tactic most likely to mobilize opposition to the war where it will be felt. Draft-age men and their parents, especially parents in the middle class, meet the war most closely through the draft system; draft resistance hits them at their present concerns." The emphasis on constructing a movement from the middle class while reaching out to the working class directly echoed the Vietnam Summer approach, but the BDRG soon found its own identity.

In just a matter of months, the Boston Draft Resistance Group transformed itself into one of the most important antiwar organizations in the city, largely due to the efforts of three organizers: Bill Hunt, Tim Wright, and Harold Hector. All three were older than typical draft protesters. Hunt and Wright were Ph.D. candidates in the Harvard history department, and both were married. Wright was an army veteran, and Hunt had children. Hector, twenty-six and African American, came from Roxbury, a working-class community in Boston and brought a much needed blue-collar background to the organization. Hunt essentially recruited the other two. As Wright later noted, Hunt was a "spellbinding storyteller and charisma-filled visionary in style" who "seduced" Wright into taking a leading role in the BDRG. Hector agreed. Once he talked with Hunt, he became committed to fighting the draft and the war makers.[34]

But the commitment of the three ran deep for other reasons. Bill Hunt, for instance, possessed a fairly long record of social activism before he took up draft resistance. He had participated in the civil rights movement, marching with Martin Luther King Jr. and the SNCC in Selma, Alabama, in 1965 and had been concerned about Vietnam since before John F. Kennedy's assassination. When he arrived at Harvard, he joined the May 2nd Movement because it was the only group doing anything to protest the war; they had issued the first We Won't Go statement in 1964 and at Harvard regularly manned tables distributing leaflets about the war. (Eventually Hunt tired of M2M's Maoist/Leninist rhetoric and joined SDS as it grew more radical.) Draft resistance for Hunt became a logical extension of his other activist interests.[35]

Tim Wright, on the other hand, had not been much of a social activist before he went to Harvard. He viewed his time in the army as "the most politically educational experience" of his life "because it was a situation in which [the army] put people of radically different social class and ethnic background into an identical environment." The result was what he called a "kind of barracks socialism" in which class origins were not important. Before going into the service, he had been a very "provincial suburban kid," but the "latently radicalizing experience" of serving in the army changed all that. He figured that by the time Vietnam heated up, he would have been "urging most middle-class people I knew to go *into* the army to learn about their own provinciality." Under the circumstances, however, the escalating war in Vietnam made it inappropriate to urge *anyone* into the army, he thought, and so he found himself working with the BDRG to keep men out. According to Bill Hunt, Wright had "the liveliest and clearest mind" of any of his contemporaries in the Harvard graduate program; his sharp intellect and army experience made him a natural leader in the BDRG.[36]

Harold Hector, one of the few blacks to participate in the draft resistance movement in Boston, did not have either the activist or the military background of Hunt and Wright but was ripe for protest in 1967. Hector sought to join the navy in 1959 but was rejected because he was overweight. He watched civil rights workers on television as they were beaten and attacked by dogs and saw news reports on the disappearances and deaths of others. He and his friends knew that they could not be nonviolent if they went south. "We go south, we [will] kick ass," they thought. But they never did. However, soon after the good natured and exuberant Hector met Bill Hunt and Tim Wright through four Radcliffe students who lived in Roxbury and found that his views of America as an oppressive society dovetailed with Hunt's and Wright's convictions regarding the war, he joined them as a leader of the BDRG.[37]

At first, the Boston Draft Resistance Group—made up of about thirty signers of the We Won't Go statement—operated out of the basement of Harvard's Memorial Hall, but over the summer of 1967, with $1,000 in seed money from Vietnam Summer, the BDRG opened an office on River Street in Cambridge that they staffed initially for three hours every day. In the early days, the group's work focused primarily on legal research regarding the draft and on organizing through canvassing. They targeted other Boston-area college campuses and soon had over 400 signatures on the We Won't Go pledge. That summer, one worker noted, the BDRG was a "talking machine." They talked to draft-age men wherever they could find them, distributed leaflets, and visited army bases.[38]

For the most part, the talking aimed to engage and provoke others to do something—*anything*—to protest the war. An early leaflet challenged draft-age men to make choices:

WE WON'T GO—WILL YOU?
Right Now
   Americans are killing in Vietnam—and are being killed
   What will you do about it?
   Will you kill?
   Will you be killed?
What can you do about it?
   —silence is inexcusable
Are you going to fight, kill, and die for an unjust war?
   Can you let others die?
   We Won't
     We Won't Go
   We refuse to be silent
We, the Boston Draft Resistance Group, have signed a statement declaring our rejection of the war, and a refusal to serve in the armed forces while the Vietnam War continues. So strong a stand is necessary now. A

faculty supporting statement is now in circulation. *We hope to turn our individual rejection of the war into effective group opposition to it.* What is your stand? Are current means of dissent effective for you in your position as a draft age man? Come discuss your views: We invite you to discuss the issues that led us to sign this statement.

Readers were invited to stop by the BDRG office to speak with one of the organizers or to come to one of the regularly planned meetings designed to provide information on the war and the draft.[39]

In May and June 1967, students at Harvard paid attention to appeals made by groups like the BDRG, especially as debates over the future of the draft took place in Washington. When members of Congress finally voted to extend the draft in late June, the new bill they came up with did little to change the existing system. In spite of the president's message to them and the recommendations of the Marshall Commission, they rejected a lottery system and dictated that the president could not institute such a change without congressional approval. They did include language indicating that graduate deferments (except for medical and dental school students) would be eliminated sometime in 1968 but set no timetable. Meanwhile, undergraduate deferments remained intact.[40] The most significant change involved the ending of marriage and fatherhood deferments for men married after 1965. Still, all of the fundamental inequalities about which there had been so much concern when Johnson appointed the Marshall Commission remained. Yet his aides urged the president to sign the bill. "Congress went a long way towards meeting the recommendations in your message," domestic adviser Joseph Califano told the president. He calculated that by limiting graduate deferments and eliminating marriage deferments, "some 200,000 additional men will be made eligible for the draft in 1968."[41]

Although the system remained basically the same, the possibility of change continued to make students anxious. That they might not be exempt from the draft when they entered graduate school prompted many men to seek out the BDRG. The group often received mixed responses, however, from those who might join. As one BDRGer wrote, "almost immediately we realized the need to make a clear distinction between draft evasion and draft resistance" in order to avoid misrepresenting themselves "as affluent draft dodgers whose political dissent was a function of class privilege."[42] They decided, therefore, to issue a statement opposing *all* conscription while the war continued, but this had little tangible effect. They still had not developed a plan of *action*.

By midsummer, the BDRG moved to address this shortcoming. First, the organization decided to "minimize" the act of signing the We Won't Go statement "as an end in itself" and instead sought to make signing one's name "a symbol of commitment to work actively against the war through other activities of the Group." This decision reflected a desire on the part of organizers to treat draft resistance "as a unique issue around which to organize people who opposed the war for widely divergent reasons." As one member wrote, the BDRG strived "to reach those who were anti-war out of self-interest as well as those who had firm moral and political conviction." No kind of moral litmus test would be applied to potential activists because, ultimately, the group aimed "to help ordinary young guys move from fear and alienation to active radical commitment." The draft, then, because it touched every young man in some way, offered the perfect opportunity to organize protest against the war, and "the social and political structure which makes such wars possible." In addition, part of that goal involved reaching working-class Bostonians, again with the idea that once galvanized, they would learn how to "flex their own political muscle."[43]

As the organization experimented with new tactics, eventually a strategy of meddling with the draft evolved. "We are unabashedly using every means possible to inhibit, retard, and be dishonest with the Selective Service System," said Ray Mungo, the outgoing editor of the *BU News*, a signer of the We Won't Go pledge, and an early BDRG activist. "Our position has been philosophically anarchistic. That is, we make no moral judgements about why a kid wants out. If he wants out, we get him out the best way we can." He made it clear that the group did not specialize in helping men obtain conscientious objector status (those who wanted it were referred to the American Friends Service Committee), and that instead "loopholes" were the BDRG's specialty. "It is perfectly legal," he explained "to refuse to sign the security oath at the pre-induction physical, and you don't even have to give a reason for refusing. The army generally doesn't want anything to do with non-signers and classifies them I-Y."[44] Mungo could speak with some authority on this last point for, by then, the BDRG knew the army well—and the army was getting to know the BDRG.

THE EARLY MORNING SHOW AND THE HORROR SHOW

Two of the most ingenious programs developed by the Boston Draft Resistance Group came to be known as the Early Morning Show and the Horror Show. Almost every day in suburban Boston, a draft board would send a group of men to the Boston Army Base either for induction or for pre-induction physicals (usually done a few weeks before the call for induction). The Early Morning Show got its name from the BDRG staff and volunteers who rose very early in the morning to drive out to draft boards and speak with potential draftees before the bus arrived for the trip downtown. The name for the Horror Show came from a related program in which BDRG members would pose as potential draftees and, upon entry into the induction or physical examination proceedings, create a disruption by making political speeches, questioning army officials about the war in Vietnam, or something similar (often Horror Shows took place when a BDRGer had himself been called for a physical).

Early Morning Shows began when members of the BDRG recognized that potential draftees felt most vulnerable and anxious during the time period between the pre-induction physical and the induction itself. "This gives us a crucial opportunity to reach them before it is too late," they wrote. "Therefore BDRG has set up a program to hit each local board when they send in their quota." Dozens of local boards operated in the greater Boston area, making an Early Morning Show possible on almost any weekday. Consequently, through some "forever secret" ploy, the BDRG obtained a schedule noting when each draft board planned to send its men. Five or six staff and volunteers would arrive before the board opened, careful to park far away (after the first few episodes, the police in some towns began taking down license plate numbers). Generally, some pre-inductees would be waiting there already. A few of the BDRGers would approach the young men, while the others stayed behind. They learned not to appear at a local board all at once for several reasons. First, they did not want to overwhelm the men they hoped to counsel. Equally important, however, they wanted to avoid making the impression that they were an organized group; as long as the draft board clerks and bus drivers thought that the BDRGers were simply friends of the pre-inductees, the prospect of their ejection from the premises remained remote.

Once there, the BDRG men and women tried to engage the potential draftees in conversations about the war and specifically about the draft. Sometimes, if space and time allowed, one of them would make a speech. Either way, one BDRG newsletter reported, "many of these guys want to talk; a good percentage of them are already consciously against the war, and a lot more are badly confused. We tell them about deferments, exemptions, and their right to refuse the Security Questionnaire. We also hand out Draft Fact Cards with our address and phone and even make appointments for them to come in for counseling." By the fall, a full complement of draft counselors staffed the BDRG office and they were supported in their work by researchers who continuously looked for "loopholes" in the Selective Service regulations. They also maintained lists of sympathetic doctors and psychiatrists who would be willing to see clients who could be candidates for physical or mental deferments.

After conversing with men at the draft board, the counselors would try to board the bus for the ride into Boston. When they were successful, they had more time to talk to the pre-inductees. Getting on the bus could be difficult. Sometimes, the bus driver worked for a charter company and held no particular loyalty to the Selective Service; getting on these buses required little ingenuity. But frequently it required some kind of clever maneuver like those listed in a special memorandum for Early Morning Show participants: "1. Board the bus when the driver is not nearby. Often if you get on, several of the pre-inductees will follow. 2. If clerk instructs everyone to show a bus token for return trip to bus driver, show a token. 3. If checking names at the bus door, get to the end of the line and try to see the list to see whose name has not been checked, and say, while pointing: 'that's my name.' 4. Sometimes you can get on using your own old papers. Tell the clerk that you're going for induction and want to ride down to induction center on the bus (because you just moved there)." Upon arrival at the army base, BDRGers would inconspicuously leave the base and catch a regular city bus back to town. Later that afternoon, if they had collected the names of any of the pre-inductees, they would call them to see how things went and to again offer assistance.[45]

The Early Morning Show became an essential element in BDRG operations and in the group's identity. By early February 1968, a pool of more than 100 volunteers helped to pull off Early Morning Shows at more than twenty draft boards each month.[46] The program continued for over two years, until the breakup of the organization in the summer of 1969.

The proportion of men approached under such circumstances who then came to the BDRG for counseling, however, was quite small. As Tim Wright later reflected, "Mostly we were not successful. Probably half of the kids who showed up [for the bus] were openly hostile. Another third were kind of passive and maybe two or three or four in each group were openly sympathetic . . . those were the people we would try to work with." But mainly, as one BDRG staffer wrote, "the basic rationale for the 'early morning show' is to broaden the anti-war movement. Unless you get a man's name and phone number we can't see if he knows other men who need counseling or whether he or his friends will help us with anti-draft and anti-war work in his area." Thus, even the activists who participated in the Early Morning Shows had limited expectations for actually helping the men they met there to escape the draft; the education and politicization of young men mattered most.[47]

BDRGers sought to educate and politicize in the Horror Shows, too, but they also aimed to have a little fun at the army's expense. Whenever the Selective Service called a male BDRG member for his own pre-induction physical and whenever BDRGers could pose as potential draftees, they did everything possible to "demystify the nature of power as it affects the guys who are being forced to fight." They did this by talking to the other draftees about the war and the draft during the proceedings and by constantly challenging the authority of the army officials running the physicals. These men gained access to the base easily. Tim Wright, the veteran, in an early newsletter wrote, "As [far as] the military-industrial complex goes, the Boston Army base is a pretty bush-league operation, considering its crucial role in the lives and deaths of the young men of Boston." He noted that public buses leaving South Station at ten-minute intervals carried passengers ranging from army personnel, to inductees, to BDRG members to the interior of the base. "The security (!?) guards are civilian," he continued, "with what seems to be a median age of 86, who can often be bullied and/or cajoled. So far we have allowed ourselves to be sluggishly evicted, although not without making a vivid impact on incoming draftees and passers-by. Our purpose is, in the classical formula, to instruct, to inspire, and to delight." This kind of witty description conveyed an accurate sense of the spirit BDRG members brought to their work. Early descriptions of Horror Shows include frequent use of adjectives like "entertaining" and "provocative." Tales of BDRG exploits made antiwar work seem fun and bred confidence in activists who might otherwise hesitate to take part in such bold confrontations.[48]

Horror Shows did not occur with the same frequency as Early Morning Shows. They were much more difficult to organize and to sustain. Usually, it required a few men because once one began a political speech during the physical, he would be hauled off; others were needed to carry on after the first one or two were taken out of the room. Most of the time leaflets had been distributed to all of the men in advance. As one BDRGer noted, the leaflets conveyed three key ideas. First, those worried about the draft and the war were not alone: "More and more guys are coming to feel this war isn't worth one American life, and the draft resistance movement can stop it." Second, legal alternatives to the draft, including a range of deferments and exemptions, did, in fact, exist. And third, the BDRG supported "the boys in Vietnam." In contrast to stereotypes of antiwar protesters being anti-soldier, the BDRG made it clear that America needed its young GIS and veterans home from Vietnam "to build a decent society right here." The army confiscated such documents at first, but the BDRG soon learned that the army could not legally take the leaflets and began each subsequent leaflet with the declaration, "This is yours to keep! The Army may not take it away from you!"[49]

Those who participated in Horror Shows, then, did attempt to engage pre-inductees in serious discussions about the war and the draft—but only on a limited basis. For the most part, they tried to disrupt the army's proceedings and to do on-the-spot educating by making speeches and arguing with army officials. By one account, the BDRG nearly took over a physical one day, "adroitly turning a menacing harangue by an army officer into a debate on the war, and calling for a straw vote on it." Forty-eight out of fifty voted against the war.[50] Occasionally, a scuffle would break out. One time, in 1968, Sergeant Brown, the man in charge of inductions and pre-induction physicals, lost his tie to a BDRG man in such an altercation. Later the tie graced the wall of a coffee house started in Cambridge by the BDRG; they named the establishment "Sgt. Brown's Memorial Necktie."

As a political tactic, Horror Shows never became as effective as the Early Morning Shows, though they became legendary throughout the movement and were copied in other parts of the country. Quite often, a kind of moratorium on Horror Shows would have to be instituted because the army grew better prepared for them. After a couple of months of successful Early Morning Shows and several Horror Shows in the summer of 1967, the raids on the induction center were suspended because "the Army got very hip very quickly, and our last two or three visits ended in almost instantaneous eviction." Curiously, the participants were never arrested for such stunts (some speculated that the army did not want to make martyrs out of them in court cases).[51]

As the fall of 1967 approached, the BDRG began its first real self-evaluation. At the August 8 Steering Committee meeting, members discussed group ideology and asked the "burning" question: "Does the BDRG gain more effectiveness by (a) encouraging the idea that it is committed to a hard-core, direct-action, somewhat alienated brand of radicalism, or by (b) underplaying the alienation and seeking a surface alliance with more 'acceptable' anti-war groups, such as Vietnam Summer, the AFSC, etc.?" Their answer, it turned out, fell somewhere in between. The BDRG continued to conduct its "direct-action" programs (the Early Morning Shows and the Horror Shows) but also decided to become much more involved in community-oriented draft counseling.[52]

DRAFT COUNSELING

While the Boston Draft Resistance Group had always been influenced in part by the work of the Students for a Democratic Society, it became more so in the fall of 1967. At that time Nick Egleson, Vernon Grizzard, and John Maher joined BDRG and turned it more toward counseling and the Early Morning Shows. Egleson and Grizzard both were national SDS officers, and Maher had been heavily involved with Vietnam Summer.[53] Their training in these organizations had stressed community organizing, and they brought this perspective to the young and still malleable BDRG. It also resulted in continued emphasis on the politicization and radicalization of everyone with whom they came into contact. Implicitly, they offered each "client" a deal: in exchange for draft counseling the BDRG expected a personal commitment against the war.

The BDRG recognized an opportunity in draft counseling because the primary provider of draft counseling in the area, the American Friends Service Committee, focused on preparing conscientious objection appeals. "The AFSC counseling course is no longer adequate for our purposes," wrote one BDRGer, "because it is non-political, not aimed specifically at the War in Vietnam and, in consequence, somewhat out of date." Consequently, the BDRG established its own counselor training course with the help of a couple of AFSC counselors and the information that the first small group of BDRG counselors had gathered through research over the summer.[54] The new office on Columbia Street in Cambridge was open six days a week, staffed with dozens of volunteer counselors tending to long lines of men seeking information on the draft.

Unlike the AFSC or the individual resisters from the Committee for Non-Violent Action, BDRG counselors advised men to take advantage of the system any way they could. If a counselee felt that he could not in good conscience comply with the Selective Service System at all, outright resistance became an option; but few such discussions took place. Counselors more often sought to find something in the young man's life that made him eligible for a deferment. Popular artists like Phil Ochs had described nearly every available escape from conscription in songs like "Draft Dodger Rag," but many men remained unaware of their options. Counselors, then, would lay them out as Ochs had. They looked for men who were still too young ("Sarge, I'm only 18"); who had physical ailments ("I got a ruptured spleen . . . I got eyes like a bat, my feet are flat, and my asthma's getting worse"); who were homosexual ("I always carry a purse"); who could get a hardship deferment ("think of my . . . sweetheart dear, my poor old invalid aunt"); who were enrolled in college or graduate school full time ("I'm going to school"); or who were qualified for work in the national interest ("and I'm working in a defense plant"). Therefore, rather than counseling men to refuse to cooperate with the draft, the BDRG told them to *over-cooperate* by applying for a deferment allowed by the system. In addition, local board decisions could be appealed, sometimes repeatedly, with the goal that eventually a bureaucratic error would occur; if that happened, the process could be dragged out for years and chances of such individuals being inducted became very small.

The BDRG was not satisfied with simply helping individuals stay out of the service, however. From the start, BDRG counselors maintained a broader agenda. One directive issued in September 1967 cautioned counselors to "be always conscious of the total situation—every deferment that you get for someone else, for yourself, just means that another ghetto cat who can't get deferments, gets drafted." It then reinforced the BDRG's aim of moving as many counselees as possible toward more radical action: "Try to awaken the guy you are counseling to how the SS System works, etc. Touch, expand his consciousness. . . . We must hit these guys so they don't just take their deferments and forget about the draft. We must look for ways to politicize them, to get them indignant about the draft." Here, again, the channeling memo proved useful in helping counselees understand that they were, in some ways, being programmed.[55]

As part of this philosophy, counselors took great care in providing information about the draft. "You don't tell a guy what to do, you don't make decisions for him," remarked one counselor. "Lay out the decisions open to him, but he should make the decisions. Force him to think about what he's going to do and what his choice means . . . the only way you'll get him to work against the war is if he's convinced it's the right thing to do." Ultimately, counselors hoped that they would not only provide useful information that would help their clients to escape the draft but also convince them of the importance of continued action against the war and move them "toward a more radical perspective." Although it didn't happen as often as the BDRG would have liked, some counselees went on to organize in their own neighborhoods, become counselors themselves, or even volunteer for Early Morning Shows.[56]

Counselees were not always receptive to the political "rap" that they received when they came for draft information, however. Most just wanted service without having to make a commitment on their part. Some counselors had little patience for such individuals.[57] The records that the BDRG kept for each man it counseled no longer survive, but in 1973, Charles Fisher, a sociologist at Brandeis University and himself a former BDRG counselor, used more than 5,000 counselee forms to draw some conclusions about these individuals. According to Fisher, despite the efforts of the BDRG to reach into the working-class community, 60 percent of the men that they counseled were college students and, therefore, mostly middle class. Overall, however, in spite of the high percentage of students, 50 percent were classified 1-A (draftable) and 35 percent were 2-S (student deferment). Another sociologist and former BDRG counselor, Barrie Thorne, estimated that most of the BDRG's clientele were "middle-class students who came for technical advice on how to avoid the draft." Moreover, she wrote, "at least two-thirds and perhaps even 80 or 90 percent were white, middle class college students."[58]

Thorne noted that draft counselors preferred to work with working-class and minority clients because of the obvious imbalance in who was drafted. These counselees were few in number, however. As a result, the most favored clients were "registrants who were similar to the counselors—white, middle-class, college-educated, *and* concerned about the war and the draft as political issues." Conversely, Thorne reported, the clients whom counselors most disliked were "typified by an upper-class, pampered, college senior, politically apathetic and trying to evade the draft for reasons of self-interest." Such men already benefited from the inequities in the system; thus "if these clients weren't radicalized through the draft counseling process, BDRG counselors were hard-pressed to offer a political justification for giving them service."[59] Harold Hector, a BDRG founder and a master counselor, hated it "when a Harvard guy would come in and want to get out, wanting to get out to spend more time at Harvard. [That] used to piss me off. I'd say, 'Hey man, there are a lot of guys who don't have that student deferment, you know, who are really in trouble with going [to Vietnam], who need this counseling.' "[60]

If it seemed a client would not be able to take advantage of one of the legal loopholes, he was left with three choices: accept induction, refuse induction and go to prison, or leave the country. In examining thousands of client records, Charles Fisher found that 40 percent of the men counseled by BDRG tried to fail their physicals; 30 percent applied for conscientious objector status; and only 3 to 4 percent considered induction refusal or leaving the country. (The choices made by the remaining 26 percent are unclear. Many, no doubt, attempted to fail the mental examinations, acted crazy, or claimed to be homosexual—all of which could get a potential draftee disqualified).[61] Ultimately, however, as one BDRG counselor noted, the course of action taken by an individual client on his own draft case did not matter as much as his *outlook*, "whether or not he was strongly opposed to the Vietnam War and could be mobilized for radical political activity."[62]

Measuring the success of moving young men to such levels of activism proved difficult. No one knew what most counselees did after they left the BDRG office. Certainly, only a few started their own neighborhood antidraft programs and most were not heard from again. Consequently, a sense that the counseling and Early Morning Shows were too tame developed among some BDRGers. On the one hand, organizers could claim that, even in that first summer of operation, they had "been able to expose the draft as merely the more conspicuous symptom of a broader pattern of corporate manipulation." "In doing so," the group asserted, "we help[ed] transform alienation and fear into conscious political radicalism." On the other hand, to a large extent the BDRG continued to play by rules set by the Selective Service and did so almost inconspicuously. Very few of their actions received significant press coverage (as the draft card burnings of 1966 had), and any sense that they were making progress was difficult to gauge. Furthermore, challenging the draft on moral and ethical grounds, the strategy pushed by the CNVA the year before, was undermined by the BDRG's willingness to work the system to its advantage. As the war raged on, some men began to resurrect the idea of total noncompliance as another complementary response. Michael Ferber and Staughton Lynd have noted that "a means had yet to be found that would tie together in one political process the hundreds of signers of We Won't Go statements and the bold tactics of the draft card burners." A new strategy was needed, one that would openly confront the government on a massive scale. As summer slipped into fall, momentum began to build for what would become the driving force of Boston's antiwar movement.[63]

3 OCTOBER 16
A RESOLUTE
SHOW OF MORAL
FORCE

> If any man would come after me, let him deny himself, and take up his cross, and follow me. For whosoever would save his life shall lose it; and whosoever shall lose his life for my sake shall find it. For what shall a man be profited, if he shall gain the whole world, and forfeit his soul? Or what shall a man give in exchange for his soul?
> —Matthew 16:24–26[1]

As the Boston Draft Resistance Group refined their draft-counseling and draft-meddling tactics, plans for an ambitious national confrontation with the Selective Service originated in California and began to move east. On April 15, 1967, the same day that the "We Won't Go" advertisement ran in the *Harvard Crimson*, former Stanford University student body president David Harris announced the formation of an organization called the Resistance to a capacity crowd assembled for the national mobilization in San Francisco's Kezar Stadium. From the stage, Harris, who had returned his draft card to his local board the previous August and pledged total noncompliance with the Selective Service, told the crowd that the war in Vietnam was "a logical extension of the way America has chosen to live." He called on the draft-age men in the crowd to join him on October 16, when men in cities across the country would sever their ties to the Selective Service by returning their draft cards to the government. "As young people facing that war," he said, "as people who are confronted with the choice of being in that war or not, we have an obligation to speak to this country, and that statement has to be made this way:

that this war will not be made in our
with our hands, that we will not carr
people, and that the prisons of the
people who will not honor the order;
to receive his own induction notice at
the induction center in his hometowr
cal. But, as he told the crowd, he pla
prison sentence instead.

David Harris and several friends
mune in Palo Alto arrived at their per;
many months of discussion in 1966. C
experienced activist who had worked
nating Committee in Mississippi, rem
compliance beginning in the spring o_ _, _ _ . . . . commented on the army as one of the best tools for educating the poor and
minorities. "It became obvious," Sweeney noted, "that it was pointless to
say you 'won't go' if you weren't being asked to."[3] But he also knew it would
be pointless to refuse induction if only a few people did it. "I was sure I was
going to do it but I was sure I wasn't going to do it by myself," he said,
"because I believed that to have an impact, to have some kind of political
effect, it had to be a number of people doing it together." Although the
timing did not seem right in 1966, David Harris went ahead and returned
his card anyway.

Early in March 1967, Harris and Sweeney met Lennie Heller and Steve
Hamilton from Berkeley. Heller and Hamilton had independently arrived
at the same idea for a draft resistance movement. In fact, they carried
leaflets that they had produced that bore the name of their budding organization: the Resistance. The name had important historical antecedents.
First, it most obviously referred to resistance to Nazi occupation in Europe
during the Second World War. The reference to fascism was deliberate:
Heller and Hamilton feared that the Vietnam War might lead to the dawn
of an American style of fascism designed in part to crush dissent. Bettina
Aptheker, another Berkeley activist, later recalled that "when you said the
word *resistance* [in 1967], it was with a capital R, and you meant the
resistance to fascism in Europe. . . . People had a sense of very great
repression in this country . . . like fascism was creeping in on us from a lot of
different directions." General Hershey's channeling memo and the obvious
inequities in the draft only fueled this perception. Second, in the early

...d the term "Young Resistance" to describe their
...s colonial war in Algeria. This group included sev-
...ho refused induction into the French army. The Amer-
... clearly the parallels between the French students' out-
...lgerian war and their own anger over Vietnam.[4]

...ornia, the Resistance distributed its first leaflet in early April,
...the Mobilization, and in it they articulated the basis for recruiting
...e members: "The war in Vietnam is criminal and we must act together,
...t great individual risk, to stop it. . . . To cooperate with conscription is to
perpetuate its existence, without which the government could not wage
war. We have chosen to openly defy the draft and confront the government
and its war directly."[5] With such rhetoric the Resistance raised the standards for antiwar protest. To keep a student deferment while protesting the
war, to flee to Canada, to seek conscientious objector status, to intentionally try to fail a physical, or even to counsel a potential draftee to do
any of these things was "to effectively abet the war." As another early leaflet argued, "the American military system depends upon students, those
opposed to war, and those with anti-Vietnam war politics wrangling for the
respective deferments. Those opposed to the war are dealt with quietly,
individually and on the government's terms."[6]

The draft, they suggested, used deferments as built-in safety valves to
disarm dissenters. A genuinely universal draft, as writer Michael Walzer
noted, "would almost certainly be a major restraint upon peacetime war-
making, if only because it would mean that the sons of politically articulate
and effective classes would die in greater numbers, though for no more
significant purposes." Or, as Staughton Lynd pointed out in April 1967, if
there were not student deferments, "a little arithmetic makes clear the
immense and sobering fact that . . . 100,000 men would refuse to go and
the war would end." Thus, by refusing to be pigeonholed into one of those
safety valves, the members of the Resistance sought confrontation, the
kind of confrontation the government would find uncomfortable.[7]

Resistance organizers, then, not only argued for draft resistance as a
matter of conscience but as a strategic breakthrough, too. The prospect of
thousands of middle-class men being marched off to prison for failure to
carry their draft cards would bring terrible publicity to the government and
enrage countless other Americans. They anticipated a ripple effect: with
each resister, more and more people (family, friends—and then their family and friends, etc.) would learn of his plight as he went through each

stage of resistance; by the time the government sent him to prison, dozens of people would have turned against the war. Furthermore, organizers believed that ten to twenty thousand draft resisters would be a sufficient number to swamp the relatively small federal court and penitentiary systems. Draft resistance, therefore, combined an act of moral witness with a new practical approach to ending the war. And it appealed to many people who opposed the war and felt guilty about their privileged place in the Selective Service System.

Over the next year, draft resistance became the driving force of Boston's antiwar movement. On October 16, Resistance leaders collected more cards in Boston than in any other city in the country, save San Francisco. The men and women who organized Boston's October 16 draft card turn-in—most of whom were Vietnam Summer and BDRG veterans—had been protesting the war in Vietnam for more than a year, but in the summer and fall of 1967, they grew impatient. In spite of their letters to Congress and their participation in teach-ins, marches, and other demonstrations, the war ground on unabated. The time had come, they decided, for more radical action. By returning their draft cards to the government, those who chose to become draft resisters raised the stakes for themselves as opponents of the war and placed the administration in the uneasy position of having to consider the prosecution of almost 1,000 young men nationwide.

Within the broader New Left, draft resistance generated considerable controversy. Consequently, the ideological debates between proponents of draft resistance and their critics in SDS and other organizations merit attention here. Like a child striking out on her own for the first time, the Resistance owed much of its view of the world to its ideological parents in the New Left; at the same time, however, an interesting amalgam of anarchist, existentialist, and especially religious thought distinguished the New England Resistance, in particular, from other New Left organizations. Most significant, despite SDS accusations of "bourgeois moralism," Resistance faith in building a mass movement of mostly middle-class students (as opposed to leading the poor and working-class to revolution) complicated what it meant to be a New Leftist. Resistance organizers sought only to end the war—not foment revolution—and supposed that if thousands of articulate, educated, middle-class young men confronted their government through a series of somber draft card turn-ins, and began filling the courts and prisons, they could apply enormous public pressure on the Johnson administration to withdraw from Vietnam. If they had any doubts about this approach, they were erased by the success of October 16.

SEEDS OF RESISTANCE

The rise of the Resistance took place as the public's views of the war started to turn against the Johnson administration. A Gallup Poll taken in the middle of the summer showed for the first time the majority of Americans (52 percent) disapproving of "the way President Johnson is handling the situation in Vietnam."[8] For years the White House and Pentagon had been able to claim that despite protests, the majority of Americans supported their actions in Southeast Asia. But those days had passed, and the timing for large-scale draft resistance could not have been better.

In Boston, however, the Resistance did not at first find a receptive audience. Lennie Heller, to whom the task of organizing draft resistance efforts east of California had been assigned, arrived there in the late spring, shortly after the publication of the Harvard "We Won't Go" statement and the formation of the Boston Draft Resistance Group. The men and women behind those efforts had little time between Early Morning Shows and Horror Shows to consider further dramatic action. Moreover, it was not at all clear that they would not be rounded up and arrested for their current activities, so to contemplate upping the ante at such an early stage seemed unwise. In the late spring and early summer, few individuals besides Robert Talmanson seemed interested in turning in draft cards. Talmanson had burned his draft card in Boston's Post Office Square in April 1966 to demonstrate his solidarity with the CNVA men and women who were attacked in South Boston; in June 1967, the government convicted him for failing to report for induction and sentenced him to three years in prison. Although he responded enthusiastically to Heller's plan for a national draft card turn-in, by the end of the summer, despite setting up shop in the BDRG's office, he had compiled only a short list of names of Boston men who were interested in October 16.[9]

In September the situation changed dramatically. The concentration of colleges and universities in Boston were full of potential activists, and it took only a few students to spark a movement. In previous months, several graduate students, all experienced organizers, gravitated independently toward resistance. Bill Dowling, a Harvard Ph.D. student in English first seized on the idea to transform Talmanson's small Resistance operation into a formidable political force. Dowling had grown up in New Hampshire and graduated from Dartmouth College, where he had excelled as a student and served as editor of the college's humor periodical, the *Jack-O-Lantern*. In his senior year, despite being awarded one of only a handful of senior fellowships, Dowling nearly got himself expelled for an incident at a campus appearance by General Hershey. Dowling and a few other students had turned out to picket Hershey's appearance and later went inside to hear the Selective Service director's speech. In the hall, a student who supported the war effort began taunting Dowling and one of his friends. Dowling cold-cocked the other student. He escaped expulsion in part because of his scholarly record and in part because the college did not want to draw wider attention to the politics of the war.[10]

Similarly, Alex Jack, a seminarian at the Boston University School of Theology, had been active with the BDRG and Vietnam Summer. Before that, as an undergraduate at Oberlin College, he had twice gone to Mississippi (where he narrowly escaped violence at the hands of segregationists) and spent a week in Selma, Alabama, doing civil rights work. He also had been editor of the school newspaper, a job that led to three months of reporting early in 1967 from South Vietnam, where he wrote two to three articles a week for twenty-five to thirty school and small-town newspapers. He met the American ambassador, Henry Cabot Lodge, there and flew with American forces on combat missions. But he also became close to a number of Buddhists and interviewed the Zen master Thich Tri Quang, who profoundly influenced his own life because Quang was so "completely calm and clear" about the war. Equally important, Jack also managed to visit hidden hospital wards where he saw children who had been burned in American napalm attacks and were kept away from the mainstream press. Such experiences affected him deeply.[11]

Over the summer, Alex Jack's father, Homer Jack (then social action director of the Unitarian Universalist Association and former head of SANE) introduced Alex to Michael Ferber, a Harvard graduate student in English and a classmate of Dowling's. Like Jack, Ferber grew up in the Unitarian Church. As a high school student in Buffalo, New York, he had peppered his representatives in Congress with letters protesting nuclear testing and participated in a march across the Peace Bridge to Canada on Hiroshima Day in 1959. Later, as a student at Swarthmore College, Ferber got involved in civil rights work in nearby Chester, Pennsylvania. His first arrest came when he participated in protests at city hall calling for better funding of schools in black neighborhoods. After graduating summa cum laude with a degree in Greek, he went on to Harvard in 1966. During his first semester, Ferber participated in the blocking of Robert McNamara's car and other antiwar activity. In 1967, he took part in Vietnam Summer, worked a little with the BDRG, and moved toward resistance.[12]

Sometime in late August, during a demonstration at the Boston Army Base, Ferber, who had become interested in the idea of a draft card turn-in through Bill Dowling, introduced Dowling to Alex Jack. Dowling and Ferber had discussed noncompliance several times over the summer, though Dowling, like Alex Jack, was more committed to the idea. Ferber took a more gradual path to resistance. Earlier in the year, feeling guilty about his student deferment, he wrote to his draft board saying that he should be categorized as a conscientious objector. "I was about as close to a pacifist as I could be without having really been put to the test," he later remarked. But since the Selective Service did not recognize Unitarianism as a denomination with the kind of pacifist tradition of, say, the Quakers or the Mennonites, they rejected his claim and reclassified him 1-A. By the end of the summer, he remembered, "I got more and more kind of sick of it and felt guilty for even trying to be a CO. On the one hand I wanted to get the claim so I could have it as a fall-back position, but on the other hand, I began to feel bad for even trying to get it. I was quite torn." So when Alex Jack and Bill Dowling started organizing draft resistance, Ferber grew more interested.[13]

Soon the three attracted others to help organize for October 16. Alex Jack recruited Nan Stone, a young Methodist minister then also attending the School of Theology at Boston University, to help organize as well. Although she could not be drafted, Stone, who grew up in a conservative farm family in Iowa, had a long history of social activism and had been outspoken in her opposition to the war. Over the next two years, despite her "continual struggle" with the male organizers for equal participation in strategic decisions, Stone became the backbone of the day-to-day operations of the New England Resistance. In addition, three former schoolmates from Bill Dowling's undergraduate days at Dartmouth, Neil Robertson, Steve Pailet, and Ric Bogel, joined the budding movement. Bogel had gone on to graduate school in the English department at Yale and thus became one of the point men in New Haven (hence the name New England Resistance). Robertson, who had dropped out of Dartmouth, came to Boston to study jazz drumming under the legendary Alan Dawson, and Pailet, Robertson's best friend and a superb musician, soon followed.[14] Bill Hunt of the BDRG also joined the effort. Within weeks this small group of activists, almost all of whom were twenty-two to twenty-four years old and enrolled in graduate school, planned the largest—and most dramatic—antiwar demonstration Boston had ever seen.

INTELLECTUAL ROOTS AND DEBATES ON THE LEFT

The New England Resistance, and indeed the national Resistance effort, differed from other New Left, student, and antiwar organizations in its unusually complex intellectual grounding. Although the Resistance owed much to the early ideals of the New Left, the draft resistance movement in Boston, in particular, derived its theoretical underpinnings from a blend of existentialism, anarchism, nonviolence, and especially religion.[15] In some ways, this mix of influences made the movement appealing to certain people, but it also led to very public disagreements with other influential New Left and antiwar organizations.

Existentialism most obviously influenced Resistance organizers on the West Coast who seemed to adopt the trappings of modern-day existential cowboys. They wore their hair long, rode motorcycles, and read Kierkegaard, Sartre, and Nietzsche. As Bill Hunt recalled, "there was a real kind of Western, gun-slinger, macho style" to the Bay Area resisters.[16] They were very glamorous. The New England Resistance lacked that flair but still showed similar influences. Literature promoting October 16 often included one quote or another from Albert Camus. For example, a campus newspaper ad for October 16 used a Camus quote as an epigraph: "Whether these men will arise or not I do not know. It is probable that most of them are even now thinking things over, and that is good. But one thing is sure: their efforts will be effective only to the degree they have the courage to give up, for the present, some of their dreams, so as to grasp more firmly the essential point on which our very lives depend. Once there, it will perhaps turn out to be necessary, before they are done, to raise their voices."[17] In addition, as Michael Ferber later noted, existentialism inspired in many resisters a sense of the "unexpectedness and absurdity of life, the contingency of life, and the importance of living life with passion." These were sometimes vague concepts for resisters, but they inspired some individuals in the educated leadership ring of the Resistance to plunge into certain causes without worrying about the probability of success. "It sort of discouraged waiting until you got a whole correct theory," Ferber concluded.[18]

Most important, however, draft resistance philosophy in Boston distinguished itself as a merger of religious and political beliefs; the group reflected its own geographical ties in being, as one member said, much more "Unitarian and transcendentalist" in its philosophical grounding.[19] The influence of the two organizers from the BU School of Theology (Jack and Stone) and the lifelong Unitarian (Ferber) set the group apart from the more typical New Left strain of Resistance chapters popping up all over the country. Alex Jack, in particular, pushed the organization in this direction. In his efforts to reach out to clergy and laity in the weeks leading up to October 16, he produced his own newsletter, which, on behalf of the Resistance, first articulated a strategy not simply of undermining the draft but of building a community of religious people who would continue to work to reshape America into a more compassionate society. In his call to clergy and laity, he described the Resistance as a "first step in building a mass movement that can aspire to win the respect of young people and their active support." They planned to organize "first 3,000, then 10,000, then 30,000, then 100,000" young men to resist. "We will make the government either end the war, or fill the jails," he said, but prison would not be the ultimate objective. "Prison," he declared "is the price we may have to pay for effective resistance." More important, "we must be willing to live (however restrictedly in jail for a few years) for our supreme convictions. . . . Both in jail and afterwards, we will create a community of men to transform the society into a fully human one. We choose to stay and struggle for the America we believe in." He concluded by quoting the Jewish theologian Martin Buber, who, when asked why protests against social injustice so often failed, responded, "They are only addressed to other people and do not involve any personal commitment." Through draft resistance, Alex Jack argued, clergy and laity could demonstrate their personal commitment, end American involvement in Vietnam, and, simultaneously, begin to transform America itself.[20]

Jack's focus on personal commitment resulted not only from his own religious upbringing but also from his experience in Vietnam earlier in the year. He returned from Vietnam believing that the "thousands of burned villages and Vietnamese deaths" caused by American forces constituted "no less a crime against humanity than Nazi genocide of the Jews." He likened the napalm and phosphorus burning of Vietnamese civilians to the use of German death camp ovens in World War II. Jack told of seeing Vietnamese hamlets "encircled, their inhabitants massacred, and the remains bulldozed over by US Marines," equating it to the 1942 Nazi destruction of Lidice, Czechoslovakia, where German forces killed the town's entire male population, shipped women and children to concentration camps, and burned the town to the ground. Michael Ferber later described Alex Jack as "modest and quiet in his behavior, almost inscrutable in his oriental calm." That kind of personality, combined with his experience in Vietnam, made him that much more persuasive when he appealed to fellow seminarians by saying, "We must now act, as well as speak."[21]

The religious foundation of the New England Resistance also fostered a continued commitment to Gandhian teachings of nonviolence among the organization's founders. Although by 1967 many participants in the civil rights movement had begun to move toward the more radical Black Power perspective and away from nonviolence, the Resistance remained confident in the potential for nonviolent protest to end a violent war. The organizers' strong belief in this strategy evolved in part from their own experiences as activists in the civil rights movement and their reverence for Martin Luther King and his commitment to nonviolence; at least a few of them had attended the 1963 March on Washington and heard King's "I Have a Dream" speech. In addition, Alex Jack's father, Homer Jack, knew King quite well and had himself published a widely read edition of Gandhi's writings.[22] So, although they recognized that they might be attacked—physically attacked—for resisting the draft, there was never any question that the movement had to remain nonviolent.

In addition to the existential and religious influences, the organization reflected a unique blend of political ideologies. For example, some organizers possessed an uncommon affinity for anarchist theorists of the late nineteenth and early twentieth centuries. They preferred the arguments of Mikhail Bakunin, for example, over those of Karl Marx and were well aware of the critiques of the Russian Revolution made by Peter Kropotkin, Rosa Luxemburg, and the American anarchist Emma Goldman. The anarchist spirit also served to introduce some levity into the serious work of confronting the government. Dan Tilton, a twenty-eight-year-old Coast Guard veteran and constant presence in the New England Resistance office after October 16, successfully encouraged a number of his Resistance colleagues to form a chapter of the anarchosyndicalist organization the Industrial Workers of the World (IWW). Although the government all but crushed the IWW in the early 1920s, the Resistance felt a historical connection. Organizers liked the Wobblies' "willingness to do anything to make their point," Tilton later reflected. "It was a fun link to the past."[23]

Resistance founders also were influenced by the original Port Huron–era SDS anarchist spirit. SDS's call for participatory democracy—that is, for all citizens to participate in making decisions that affect their lives—illuminated a distrust of centralized government that dovetailed with anarchist principles. Indeed, what made the New Left *new* was, in part, its recognition that the Soviet model was a betrayal of Marxist ideals. In general, then, the New England Resistance rejected any kind of concentrated power and, instead, hoped to build a broad-based draft resistance movement, one that operated from the grass roots and did not turn on the whims of a small core of leaders. Organizational decisions were made at meetings not by majority vote but by consensus, thus making the meetings notoriously long but also more purely democratic.

Finally, like other New Left organizations, the New England Resistance showed the influence of Frankfurt School social theorist Herbert Marcuse, who until 1965, had taught at nearby Brandeis University. Marcuse's writings, especially *One-Dimensional Man*, *Essay on Liberation*, and *Negations*, urged his readers to "negate" the totally administered world, to overcome the ideological waves of the establishment, and to assert their individuality in the face of the technologized status quo. Most important for the student generation of the 1960s, Marcuse saw in the civil rights movement and the Berkeley Free Speech Movement of 1964 reasons to believe that young people (as opposed to, say, the proletariat) might be the ones to lead the revolution against one-dimensional society in America. As Marcuse scholar Douglas Kellner has noted, *One-Dimensional Man* showed that the problems confronting radicals in the 1960s "were not simply the Vietnam War, racism or inequality, but the system itself."[24] Resistance founders recognized this and saw the Selective Service, with its channeling strategy, as one of the most hideous examples of the one-dimensional "system" at work. They did not need Marcuse to confer legitimacy on their planned confrontation with the government—after all, students across the country had been leading social movements throughout the decade—but his ideas were important to shaping the way they viewed their society, their government, and the Vietnam War.[25]

Although the Resistance shared these ideological influences with other New Left and antiwar groups, not everyone in those larger movements agreed on the efficacy of draft resistance. Within national and local antiwar organizations the Resistance endured considerable criticism in the early days. The Boston Draft Resistance Group, for instance, remained aloof until just days before the planned action. Even though the words "draft resistance" made up half of the organization's name, the BDRG's attitude toward complete noncompliance with the Selective Service made it clear that "resistance" meant different things to different people. In their first newsletter of the summer, the BDRG described noncompliance as an act of "foolish bravado" and although they admitted that draft resistance represented "a serious intensification of anti-war activity" they feared that it presented just as many "new pitfalls" as opportunities.[26]

An August BDRG newsletter betrayed sarcasm in expressing its doubts about the value of resistance. "The Resistance," they wrote, "has so far announced its presence in Boston only by the somewhat cryptic 'October 16' button worn by a few BDRG members. (Too cryptic, maybe: Resistance people have been finding out that the button is mostly a good way to meet passers-by with birthdays in mid-October.)" They went on to point out that in some cities, the Resistance had become the "major focus of anti-draft activity" but that in Boston it remained "only an unofficial project of the BDRG." Such a portrayal implied a kind of turf war between the two groups, yet the rest of the newsletter's description of the Resistance made it clear that the real source of contempt arose from a disagreement over tactics: "The October 16 protestor will have to withstand, right up to the last moment, the argument that he is set on an act of useless martyrdom. The task of locating and enlisting those people committed to radical protest at great personal risk is the major job that lies before the Resistance in the weeks ahead. But beyond this, there is the problem of creating a unity of purpose and belief which is the only final answer to cynicism and doubt."[27] The BDRG, therefore, grudgingly continued to accept student deferments and steadfastly kept its focus on trying to organize the working class and the inner cities through community outreach. Unlike the Resistance, BDRG members professed no interest in mobilizing the middle class either in the suburbs or on Boston-area campuses.

The Boston Draft Resistance Group's adherence to community organizing mirrored that of Students for a Democratic Society, who were then also busy debating the pros and cons of draft resistance in their weekly national newspaper, *New Left Notes*. In late June, Mark Kleiman wrote, "The prospect of putting 200 to 500 of our people in jail for such a long time in such a reckless fashion concerns me. I have no desire to expend either the organizational or human resources required in such an action. We are not the Wobblies—we cannot fill the jails." The following month, the issue of resistance came up at the national SDS convention. Discussion resulted in a new resolution that stated that "a draft resistance program must move beyond individual protest to collective action." That said, the resolution reaffirmed SDS's call for "the formation of draft-resistance unions" and argued that Resistance-like tactics "such as civil disobedience and disruption of the Selective Service System are among those advocated" but only "when they complement the overall strategy of resistance to the draft and to other forms of oppression." Just what SDS meant by an "overall strategy of resistance" was not clear, however. And although the resolution clearly stated that "SDS does not urge going to jail as a means of resisting the draft," it persisted in its ambiguity by expressing support for "all those whose actions result in imprisonment."[28]

In the weeks leading up to October 16, though, criticism from SDS grew more strident. Steve Hamilton, one of the original Berkeley founders of the Resistance, broke ranks and wrote a blistering column in *New Left Notes* in which he condemned what he saw as middle-class elitism at work in the Resistance: "I don't think moral witness on our part can have any concrete effect on those who cannot afford to make a moral witness. . . . No revolution is built on bad consciences but on the organizations of those who are exploited. Middle-class tears and money mean very little." Instead, he called on those who had "the perspective of being political organizers" to "get off the campus and do draft resistance work . . . in communities, on high school and junior college campuses." As Hamilton saw it, the goal of the Resistance had shifted from political organization to "public effect" and the "primary mistake" of such an approach lay in "building a movement that hoped to stir one more wave of middle-class liberal sentiment against the war and American militarism" in lieu of organizing "those who can make revolutionary change—black, poor white and working-class people."[29]

Locally, SDS leaders agreed with both Kleiman and Hamilton on targeting the working class. As Steve Shalom of MIT SDS put it, "Whether we get out [of the draft] with . . . bizarre behavior [at a pre-induction physical] or whether we get out by a student deferment or whether we get out by going to jail, a Cambridge working-class kid—that slot is still made available for him." So, for SDS, the goal became "how can we best bring the war to an end so that Cambridge kids are not going to have to go? And a lot of us thought that probably the best way was not to be in jail, but to be out organizing . . . it wasn't an easy decision, because we realized . . . the moral conflict of interest that not going to jail was also very personally pleasing." But the overriding concerns involved organizing not the middle class but the working class, and staying out of jail to do so.[30]

Hamilton's and Shalom's argument against widespread draft resistance by middle-class college students reflected an Old Left kind of faith in the working class that remained strong in SDS. Just a few years earlier, from 1963 to 1965, the organization had focused much of its attention on an economic research and action program intended to galvanize the poor and working class in northern cities to tap their potential political power, much like the civil rights movement had done in the South. In the fall of 1967, although many SDS members, faced with persistent inequality between the races and the ongoing escalation of war in Vietnam, began to swerve away from a more moderate Left liberalism toward Marxism-Leninism, that emphasis on mobilizing the masses in their neighborhoods toward some kind of leftist revolution remained prominent.

The key difference between SDS and the Resistance, then, arose from an issue of ultimate objectives. Whereas Steve Hamilton and others in SDS urged continued appeals to the poor and working class as a way to create "revolutionary change," the Resistance sought more specifically to end the American war. Although Resistance founders in Boston and elsewhere held out some hope of attracting working-class men to their movement, making the mobilization of large numbers of poor and working-class men to revolution the main objective of an antiwar movement seemed an unnecessary distraction away from their primary goal of stopping the war. While the Resistance sought to instigate an uprising against the Selective Service, it harbored no illusions about beginning a revolution against the government.

The New England Resistance organizers, therefore, found the arguments of SDS and the BDRG unpersuasive. The notion of keeping oneself out of jail to continue one's antiwar work sounded, as Bill Hunt (one of the few BDRG-NER crossovers) put it, "a little bit like you're saving yourself for the junior prom." The question came down to an individual's view of politics, history, morality, and how important he thought he might be, as an individual, to the movement. Hunt later recalled: "Who the fuck *are* we, frankly? . . . I mean, if you really see yourself building a conspiratorial network that's eventually going to overthrow the world, [that is one thing] (and this is what Lenin would, of course, have done . . . Lenin was quite unscrupulous about protecting his own butt, because he figured he was *Lenin*)." But if individuals did not see themselves that way and "did not really support that notion of social change," then the resisters' "power to go to jail was probably the best weapon that we had in a sense that it was going to be embarrassing [for the government] to do that. We were educated, we were articulate, we could make good speeches in the courtroom. . . . We might be *nuts*, but we were clearly not self-interested here—that could come across."[31] Thus, proponents of draft resistance recognized that, for the most part, they came from positions of relative privilege that were tied to their middle-class upbringings. In acknowledging their class status, they hoped to preempt charges of elitism and, in turn, use it to their advantage in garnering big headlines. As they told the media, "We will not be bought off with draft deferments and exemptions that keep most of us who are white, middle-class, and educated free and alive, while blacks, poor people, and working-class people who could not afford an education are sent to the war and die."[32]

Ironically, the Johnson administration's decision to maintain student deferments gave Resistance leaders reason to be confident. According to James Reston of the *New York Times*, the administration chose to continue the 2-S deferment because it estimated that without it, one out of every four male undergraduates might refuse induction. Knowing that the White House feared such a development and had taken positive action to try to prevent it, the Resistance sought to make it happen anyway. Citations from Reston's article appeared in the New England Resistance's first newsletter along with a widely quoted piece written by Tom Wicker in May 1967 in reaction to heavyweight boxing champion Muhammad Ali's induction refusal. Wicker wondered what would happen if "enough citizens simply refuse to obey the positive commands of government and of the national majority . . . if only, say, 100,000 young men flatly refused to serve in the armed forces." The result, he theorized, would be that the government's "real power to pursue the Vietnamese war or any other policy would be crippled, if not destroyed. It would then be faced not with dissent but with civil disobedience on a scale amounting to revolt."[33]

Crippling the government's ability to prosecute the war became the primary objective of the New England Resistance and other Resistance chapters around the country. No one expected to get 100,000 men to pledge refusal on October 16, and even if they thought they could, Resistance organizers were not so naive as to believe that the military could not go on without those 100,000 men. Too many acquiescent conscripts prevented that. Still, the scale of dissent was important. Thousands of middle-class college students breaking the Selective Service laws would cause an uproar not only in Washington but in suburbs across the country. The administration would have to react. And when it did, the resisters believed, the resulting confrontation would shatter public support for the war, once and for all. America would have to get out of Vietnam.

PLANNING OCTOBER 16

At first, the New England Resistance went to work trying to mobilize campuses across the region for October 16. The numerous colleges and universities in Boston alone occupied most of the organizers' time, but they also sought to reach out to the state universities in Rhode Island, Connecticut, Vermont, New Hampshire, and Maine. They sent speakers to Brown, Dartmouth, Middlebury, Amherst, Williams, Yale, and the Rhode Island

School of Design. At most of those schools, they relied on SDS chapters for assistance, but given the ambivalence of the national SDS, such efforts were rarely enough. The second and final newsletter put out before October 16 boasted that the NER planned to distribute 50,000 leaflets "in a serious effort to hit everyone in the New England area who holds the II-S deferment."[34]

Resistance organizers divided up assignments and spoke with each other daily. Bill Dowling ironed out most of the details for October 16, getting permits for the demonstration planned for Boston Common, arranging speakers, and doing outreach to other antiwar groups. Michael Ferber promoted October 16 on college campuses, thus doing most of the public speaking for the group. Alex Jack and Nan Stone focused on the religious community, reaching out to clergy, seminarians, and laypeople for support. In this last respect, especially, the Boston plan for October 16 developed much differently from other cities.[35]

In late September, Alex Jack suggested that the Boston draft card turn-in take place in a church. The others loved the idea immediately, for as Michael Ferber later wrote, "what better way to underscore the moral gravity of the act we were embarking on than to hold it in a place of worship? It was a little like a confirmation or a baptism: a rite of passage into manhood, from slavery and 'channeling' to the promised land of peace and freedom." The difficult task, they thought, would be in finding a church that would allow such a controversial ceremony to take place in its sanctuary. As usual, though, Alex Jack had a plan.[36]

Jack and Ferber arranged a meeting with the Reverend Jack Mendelsohn of the Arlington Street Church, a Unitarian Universalist church adjacent to Boston's Public Gardens. At the time, Jack and his parents were parishioners there, and the minister was an old family friend. Mendelsohn had been preaching against American involvement in Vietnam for a long time and could be counted upon to be sympathetic. Even so, he hesitated when first asked to hold the draft card turn-in in his church. His reluctance stemmed not from any misgivings about the nature of the ceremony but from his appraisal that everyone in Boston would *expect* such a ceremony at Arlington Street. "It was assumed that things of that nature would occasionally be held there," he later remarked. Therefore, he suggested that the organizers approach some of the more establishment churches in town. Newspaper and television images of hundreds of draft resisters assembling in Copley Square and marching into Trinity Church, Henry Hobson Richardson's great architectural masterpiece and a monument to Boston's rich intellectual and cultural legacy, would have stunned the city. To be welcomed in such a place would imply that even the most powerful families in Boston so firmly opposed the war that they were willing to approve a plan of radical civil disobedience. In the end, however, it did not happen. Those establishment churches rebuffed Resistance organizers, who returned to Arlington Street.[37]

The history of the Arlington Street Church made it an ideal site for a draft card turn-in. The church itself, the first public building built on the newly filled Back Bay, was constructed in 1861. Three congregations from other churches had combined to create the one that Rev. Mendelsohn led in the 1960s. The first parish, started by Scots-Irish immigrants who had moved to Boston from Londonderry, New Hampshire, in 1729, named itself the Church of the Presbyterian Strangers. Eventually, it relocated to Federal Street, where, in 1803, the parish recruited a young minister named William Ellery Channing. Channing transformed the church by applying its ministry to social justice causes and a more liberal theology. In 1825, he founded the American Unitarian Association at the Federal Street Church, and he himself later became an articulate champion of the abolitionist movement. According to Daniel Walker Howe, the leading historian of Unitarianism, Channing "called upon New England to provide the American body politic with its conscience and rationality." In ensuing decades, the Arlington Street Church played an integral role in the development of Unitarianism, and in the twentieth century it eventually merged with two other churches: the First Unitarian Church and the Church of the Disciples. During the Vietnam era, draft resisters and parishioners alike found reassurance in the history of the Church of the Disciples as well. Under minister James Freeman Clark, the church issued the following resolution, signed by Clark and 130 others, in opposition to the Mexican War:

> We the undersigned members of the Church of the Disciples, or religiously connected therewith, wish by a solemn declaration to free ourselves, as far as possible, from the responsibility of the war of invasion now waged by the United States against Mexico.
>
> We take this step because we believe this war to be unjust + inhuman, + to be carried on from the lust of territory and for the extension of slavery, because the attitude of silence in which this country stands before the nations with regard to this war is one of approval + because thus our influence and character individually + collectively, as Americans and Christians goes to strengthen a scheme of oppression and blood.

We therefore, as far as by this public act we can, absolve ourselves before God + the Christian world of all participation in or approval of this deed of violence, + we protest in the name of humanity + religion against the existence + continuance of this war, as dishonorable to our name + race, as the forfeiture of our mission as a people + as one of the great crimes of modern history.

During the 1960s, the original copy of that resolution hung, framed, on the wall of the entry foyer of the Arlington Street Church's offices at 355 Boylston Street. One needed little imagination to apply that 1846 resolution to 1967, and many church members looked to it for inspiration during the difficult days of draft resistance.[38]

Despite a legacy of commitment to social activism in the nineteenth century, the Arlington Street Church grew fairly conservative in the twentieth century through the late 1950s. It had itself become an establishment church. During the thirties, forties, and fifties, many of the church's Brahmin members who had moved to some of the affluent suburbs outside Boston still came in on Sundays to hear "one of their own," the Reverend Dana McLean Greeley, preach. But when Jack Mendelsohn came to Arlington Street, that changed. Mendelsohn entered the Unitarian ministry because it was turning its attention toward social issues and he wanted to work in an institution that would apply itself to "trying to find better approaches to solving human problems." He quickly set to work transforming Arlington Street into a vibrant urban church, one that reached out to the city's diverse population.[39]

Most important for the Resistance organizers, Jack Mendelsohn and the Arlington Street Church already possessed a record of commitment to antiwar activity. The march that ended with counterprotesters hurling eggs at antiwar activists on the steps of the church in the spring of 1966 had firmly established Arlington Street as a home for such activity. Alex Jack and Michael Ferber were not too surprised, then, when Rev. Mendelsohn agreed to host the draft resistance service and volunteered to participate. "The notion of the 'bully pulpit,' which we apply generally to the President of the United States," the minister said years later, "equally applies to a downtown religious institution. It's a great place for great thoughts and people who express great thoughts—or at least who express unconventional thoughts."[40] Certainly the notion of returning Selective Service documents in an elaborate church ceremony did seem unconventional.

The plan for October 16 now included a rally on the Common to be followed by a march to the church, where the draft card turn-in would take place. Organizers recruited from among the usual suspects of the antiwar movement to speak on the Common: Boston University professor Howard Zinn, MIT professor Noam Chomsky, former SDS national president Nick Egleson, and former *BU News* editor Ray Mungo. In contrast, the service outlined for the church leaned, appropriately, toward the religious community: Alex Jack and Michael Ferber planned to speak in addition to Yale chaplain William Sloane Coffin Jr., Father Robert Cunnane of the Boston Committee of Religious Concern for Peace, and George Hunston Williams, Hollis Professor of Divinity at Harvard Divinity School.

The inclusion of several older sympathizers in the plans for October 16 runs counter to the popular belief that participants in the student movements of the sixties trusted no one over thirty. In fact, the Resistance, both locally and nationally, benefited from the invaluable support of a deeply committed group of older men and women who were not subject to the draft but wanted to register their disgust regarding the war in Vietnam by supporting draft resisters. The most obvious example of this commitment resulted in the "Call to Resist Illegitimate Authority," a statement published in the *New York Review of Books* and the *New Republic* in early October and signed by 320 people. Much like the student "We Won't Go" statements of the previous spring, dozens of such petitions circulated among intellectuals and prominent antiwar activists in 1966 and 1967. They expressed the intention of the signatories to counsel and assist young men in resisting the draft and were therefore presented to the public (and the government) as complicity statements, sufficient evidence for indictment under Section 12 of the Selective Service Act.

The Call to Resist became the most successful and widely known of these complicity statements, eventually attracting over 2,000 signatures over the next year. The statement itself turned out to be rather lengthy, but its underlying theme underscored the "moral outrage" felt by a growing number of citizens regarding the war in Vietnam. Its authors, Marcus Raskin and Arthur Waskow, both from the Institute for Policy Studies, a Washington think tank, and Robert Zevin, professor of economics at Columbia University, argued that the war was unconstitutional and violated the United Nations Charter and the Geneva Accords of 1954. They cited examples of American war crimes: "The destruction of rice, crops, and livestock; the burning and bulldozing of entire villages consisting exclusively of civilian structures; the interning of civilian non-combatants in concentration camps; the summary execution of civilians in captured villages who could not produce satisfactory evidence of their loyalties . . .; the slaughter of peasants who dared to stand up in their fields and shake their fists at American helicopters." These deeds, they argued, were exactly like those determined to be crimes against humanity by the Allies following World War II. As a result, they argued, "every free man has a legal right and a moral duty to exert every effort to end this war, to avoid collusion with it, and to encourage others to do the same." They acknowledged the "excruciating choices" facing young men in the military or threatened by the draft and praised the courage of those resisting the "illegitimate authority" of those institutions. The authors pledged to support those who resisted the war by raising money, organizing draft unions, and supplying legal defense and bail. And in the most eloquent passage of the statement, they justified their actions: "We feel we cannot shrink from fulfilling our responsibilities to the youth whom many of us teach, to the country whose freedom we cherish, and to the ancient traditions of religion and philosophy which we strive to preserve for this generation. We call upon all men of good will to join us in this confrontation with immoral authority. . . . Now is the time to resist." Despite the length and what poet Allen Ginsberg called the statement's "humorless prose," the list of signatures attached to it gathered over the summer included names that most Americans and, in particular, readers of the *New York Review* and *New Republic* recognized, such as Ginsberg, artist Alexander Calder, columnists Nat Hentoff and Jack Newfield, clergymen Philip Berrigan and William Sloane Coffin Jr., famed pediatrician Benjamin Spock, and academics Noam Chomsky, Paul Goodman, Herbert Marcuse, Hilary Putnam, and Howard Zinn.[41]

During the summer, as organizers of the Call to Resist realized that enthusiasm for their statement overlapped with growing interest in the national draft card turn-in planned for October 16, they sought a way to bring the two together. Specifically, Mitch Goodman, a writer and teacher, conjured up the idea of delivering the cards collected across the country on October 16 to the Justice Department on October 20, the day before the massive march on the Pentagon. On October 2, several of the educators, clergy, and literary figures who signed the call gathered for a press conference in New York. They discussed the statement and Goodman's plans for returning the draft cards to the Justice Department. Rev. Coffin promised that resisters would be granted sanctuary in churches and synagogues across the country, and the group issued a statement that again combined its members' sense of history with their moral outrage: "We hope that by using traditional American tactics of nonviolent civil disobedience against conscription and militarism, we will spur further antidraft activity and help to build the tidal wave of revulsion that will lead to the withdrawal of our Army from Vietnam and an end to the unconstitutional intrusion of the Pentagon into policymaking." On the same day, a Louis Harris poll indicated that only 31 percent of Americans supported President Johnson's handling of the war and that continued support for the war dropped from 72 percent in July to just 58 percent.[42]

In Boston, the kind of backing evident in the Call to Resist had been present for some time. The ubiquitous professors Zinn and Chomsky could be heard at almost all antiwar demonstrations, and an organization started by Harvard philosophy professor Hilary Putnam, the Boston Area Faculty Group on Public Issues (BAFGOPI), laid the groundwork for continued interaction between the two generations of activists. Since 1965, the BAFGOPI had been running antiwar ads in the *New York Times* and working with students to organize teach-ins and other protests. By the time the New England Resistance began to organize for October 16, a well-established antiwar infrastructure—the kind needed for large-scale activism—made planning easier.[43]

OBEDIENCE TO A HIGHER ALLEGIANCE

October 16 dawned clear and bright. Organizers carried chairs and sound equipment from the basement of the Arlington Street Church to the dewy, green rise of Flagstaff Hill, the only remaining hill on the Common. Flagstaff Hill and the parade grounds on its western slope (approaching Charles Street) have played host to innumerable public events in Boston's history, and in some ways, it was the ideal choice for the location of a rally aimed at encouraging resistance to conscription. The city once stored its gunpowder supply on top of the hill, and the Marquis de Lafayette, hero of the Revolution, ceremonially fired a cannon from the hill during a visit in 1824. Most significant for the Resistance, army officers used Flagstaff Hill as their recruiting station during the Civil War—the war to preserve the Union. Although the organizers who now set up chairs and a speaker system on that hallowed ground did so in preparation for an event that those Union officers might have found puzzling, the hill's patriotic heritage dovetailed seamlessly with their own sense of the Resistance's adherence to—and desire to preserve—the best of American traditions.[44]

By 10:00 A.M., small groups of young people began approaching Flagstaff Hill from all directions. When speeches began at 11:00, over 5,000 people stood or sat on the now-dry grass, listening. Buses filled with students from Dartmouth, Yale, Brown, the University of Rhode Island, the University of Massachusetts, and nearly every Boston-area college circled the Common looking for parking spots. Uniformed officers stood by with police dogs to cope with any potential violence. On the hill, in the middle of a group of seated young people, a middle-aged woman, blonde, wearing sunglasses, held a sign that read "LBJ KILLED MY SON." Dozens of people held signs. Some of the slogans included, "Suppose They Gave a War and Nobody Came?"; "The Resistance: Don't Dodge the Draft, Oppose It"; "Wars Will End When Men Refuse to Fight"; "The Resistance Shall Not End"; "UMB [UMass-Boston] Veterans Against the War"; "They Are Our Brothers Whom We Kill"; "No Draft—Don't Enlist—Refuse to Kill." Counterdemonstrators came armed with placards, too. One said "Tough Enough to Criticize, Too Weak to Defend—USMC," another, "Draft the Draft Dodgers—Yes LBJ." Two others, held by self-described Polish Freedom Fighter Josef Mlot-Mroz, said "Lets Fight Communism, Red Dupes, Vietniks, Peaceniks, and Clergy" and "Fight Communism and Zionist Stooges, Peaceniks, Vietniks, and Anarchists." When Mlot-Mroz tried to disrupt the speeches, Bill Dowling attempted to force him out of the area; although the struggle did not escalate, police eventually took Mlot-Mroz into "protective custody."[45]

Homer Jack chaired the rally and introduced the speakers, each of whom took turns at the microphone in the shadow of the Soldiers' Monument. Everyone who addressed the crowd emphasized morality, conscience, and the responsibilities of citizens. Rev. Harold Fray of the Eliot Church in Newton and chair of the Committee of Religious Concern for Peace stood first before the vast crowd in his clerical robe. "What does it profit a nation," he asked, "to impose its military might upon peoples of the world, while in so doing it loses its soul?" He called it a dark period in the nation's history but added, "The light will shine again when the moral conscience of America will not submit to national policies that violate honor, decency, human compassion and those qualities of life which alone make a nation strong." Fray praised the "great courage" of the men who would resist the draft on this day but told them that, henceforth, they would have to "bear the penalty of adverse public opinion and the long arm of government suppression." Better to endure those penalties, he concluded, "than to allow your consciences to atrophy because you were afraid to give expression to them." Ray Mungo, the director of Liberation News Service, spoke next, taking up the issue of draft resistance. He told the crowd that the prospect of going to jail should not be feared; indeed, he saw prison as "an honorable alternative to serving in Vietnam."[46]

When Nick Egleson took the microphone next, he was not as sanguine about the prospects of a protest rooted in "individual conduct." Egleson possessed extensive Movement credentials. He had been national president of SDS, and in the fall of 1967 he assumed a leadership position in the Boston Draft Resistance Group. The thrust of what he said to the crowd sounded much like the SDS line—only more persuasive. First, he lamented the antiwar movement's lack of a "base of power" and what he saw as the resulting shift toward "moral acts" of protest. Specifically, he warned of the temptation to "measure actions in the movement by a code of individual conduct," to establish certain moral acts as minimum standards for appropriate dissent. He argued that "such an individual code easily becomes the primary or only standard for political conduct" and pointed to the nation's "individualist ethic," the "religious frame of reference," that so many protesters had adopted and the "absence of widespread political experience" as factors that pushed the movement toward an individual code and closed off the possibility of other political standards.

Ultimately, Egleson acknowledged that that standard of individual conduct might be useful in organizing people on campuses—those not immediately threatened by the draft—but noted that "all the while the men of Charlestown and South Boston and Riverside, of Roxbury and Dorchester and of the working-class parts of cities all over the country are threatened by the draft and are more gently coerced by the security of enlistment." To address this issue he urged a prescription more consistent with the missions of the BDRG and SDS: "Our solution," he said, "must be to begin to organize those most threatened by the US armed forces. How many people gave out information about the October 16 rally in Boston in poor and working-class neighborhoods? Who put up posters speaking the language of those communities? Who tried to counter, thereby, the image the press promotes of us as hippies, cowards, and peace finks?" The BDRG, of course, had already been working in this direction for several months through the Early Morning Shows and their counseling efforts, so the Resistance saw no need to duplicate BDRG's work.[47]

Egleson's speech startled some in the assembled crowd. Suddenly, they had to come to terms with one of the day's main speakers choosing not to provide the kind of ringing endorsement of draft resistance offered by the others. In fact, Egleson implied that draft resistance might amount to the kind of "useless martyrdom" that the BDRG had warned of in its recent newsletter. Although he did not address one of the Resistance's central hopes—that widespread resistance might actually create the base of power for which he longed (through the imprisonment of thousands of resisters and the resulting outrage of their parents)—his arguments gave some potential resisters reason to pause and reassess their plans for the day. David Clennon, a third-year graduate student at the Yale School of Drama, for instance, recalled that Egleson's speech prompted him to completely rethink his reason for being there. "When I heard Nick Egleson make his speech, I really began to have some serious doubts about what I was doing. Here was a guy who . . . had a lot of political savvy, much more than I had, [and he disagreed with the draft resistance strategy]." Clennon, who "came at [the movement] mostly from a kind of politically naive point of view [and] a very strong moral point of view" found himself "easily confused and easily swayed" by Egleson's arguments.[48]

Just in time for Clennon and others, though, Boston University government professor and World War II veteran Howard Zinn strode to the microphone. Zinn, like Noam Chomsky, was by then a well-known critic of the war. He frequently participated in antiwar teach-ins on area campuses, and his recently published book, *Vietnam: The Logic of Withdrawal*, attracted a wide readership. Zinn did not respond directly to Egleson's critique of draft resistance as creating an uncomfortable standard of individual conduct by which all antiwar activity might be judged, however. Instead, the older man raised issues of a government's responsibilities to its citizens and the citizen's loyalty to his government. "Ever since governments were first formed and tyranny, the natural companion of government, began," he observed, "people have felt the need to gather in the forest or the mountains or in underground cellars, or, as here, under an open sky, to declare the rights of conscience against the inhumanity of government." The tyranny of the present administration had already killed 13,000 Americans, he said, and he criticized those men in positions of power for appointing themselves "guardians of every spot on the earth against Communism." Zinn derided policy makers for trying to save people everywhere from Communism, "whether the people want to be saved or not, and even if they have to kill them all to save them," and assailed President Johnson for breaking his pledge to those who supported him in the 1964 election on a peace platform. A government guilty of such betrayals and abuse of power, Zinn reasoned, no longer deserved the allegiance of its citizens. "I don't believe we owe loyalty to a government that lies to us," he said. "I do believe we owe loyalty to our fellow Americans who are in danger of being killed by the incompetence of this government."

Rather than emphasize the individual principled acts of defiance decried by Nick Egleson, Zinn argued for holding the government to a reasonable moral standard. He said he felt ashamed, "deeply ashamed," to call himself an American when he read, "and in the most conservative newspapers," that the U.S. Air Force had "bombed again and again the residential areas of North Vietnamese cities, that it has bombed, again and again—too often to be an accident—villages that are devoid of military significance, that it has bombed a hospital for lepers in North Vietnam 13 times." He repeated, "I am ashamed, and I want to disassociate myself from these acts. That is not my idea of what America should stand for." In the end, although individual morality surely intertwined with responsibilities of citizenship, for Zinn the latter provided the most compelling reason for draft resistance. "We owe it to our conscience, to the people of this country, to the principles of American democracy," he concluded, "to declare our independence of this war, to resist it in every way we can, until it comes to an end, until there is peace in Vietnam."[49]

As the last speaker at the demonstration, Zinn called on those who planned to turn in their draft cards to assemble in one area of the hill from which they would be directed to take their places in the column of marchers that would walk to the Arlington Street Church. David Clennon, his doubts assuaged, joined the line. Zinn "spoke so eloquently about the horrors of the war," he remembered, "that I was convinced all over again that turning in my draft card was the right thing to do." He felt so committed, he began to weep. "I was crying with relief I think . . . that I was about to do the right thing as dangerous and controversial as it seemed to be. . . . I was just overcome emotionally but I really felt solid then in my decision about what I was doing."[50]

Most participants marched purposefully, quietly. Others were more expressive and playful. Marshals organized the marchers into distinct groups. The clergy led, followed by Veterans for Peace, then the resisters. This order gave the march a well-planned look of respectability. Moreover, the resisters themselves did not look like "hippies, cowards, and peace finks." The hair on some men touched their ears and collars, but most hairstyles were fairly clean cut. A few beards could be seen, but the vast majority of men had bare faces. Many wore coats and ties, perhaps because they were going to church, or because they wanted to somehow demonstrate the gravity of the act they were about to undertake. The second Resistance newsletter had instructed its readers to "smile as you march, but think defiance." They marched across the Common to Tremont Street, down Tremont to Boylston Street, and down Boylston to the church at the southwest corner of the Public Gardens. According to one report, a woman crossing Tremont Street saw the marchers and, obviously disgusted, turned to a police officer and said: "Why don't you send them all back to Cambridge?" "Oh, they're from all over," he answered. As the marchers approached their destination, the carillon in the tower of the church played "We Shall Overcome."[51]

The church filled quickly, leaving nearly 3,000 other participants outside waiting to hear the service over loudspeakers. The actor Peter Ustinov, in town for a performance, mingled with the crowd. (When reporters asked him if he was with the Resistance, he responded: "No, because I am British. But if I were an American I would be part of the group.") Like some of the oldest churches in New England, the pews at Arlington Street are separated into boxes that the church's earliest parishioners (or "proprietors") could purchase. About 1,000 people squeezed into these boxes and the balconies above and sat on the lumpy cushions filled with horsehair. Reporters took notes, flashbulbs flashed, and an NBC News photographer standing in the balcony with correspondent Sander van Ocur trained his camera on the sanctuary below. The atmosphere was hushed, respectful—and *electric*.[52]

The printed programs called it "A Service of Conscience and Acceptance," and all of the speakers emphasized moral and religious justifications for civil disobedience. After Jack Mendelsohn gave the invocation, the congregation sang "Once to Every Man and Nation":

Once to every man and nation
Comes the moment to decide
In the strife of truth with falsehood,
For the good or evil side;
Some great cause, God's new Messiah,
Off'ring each the bloom or blight,
And the choice goes by forever
'Twixt that darkness and that light.

A responsive reading ("The Young Dead Soldiers") followed, and, after that, Alex Jack read a Vietnamese prayer.

The real power of the service, however, derived from the four addresses—or sermons—given. Like the speeches on the Common, the statements given in the church are worth considering in detail because of their incomplete coverage in the press. Two graduate students spoke first. Jim Harney, a Catholic studying for the priesthood at St. John's Seminary in nearby Brighton, told the congregation that he had spent the last few weeks reading about German "men of faith" who stood up to the Third Reich and paid for it with their lives. "Their witness," he said, "has affected my life enormously." He quoted Father Alfred Delp, a German priest who did not survive the concentration camps: "The most pious prayer can become a blasphemy if he who offers it tolerates or helps to further conditions which are fatal to mankind, which render him unacceptable to God, or weaken his spiritual, moral or religious sense." Harney then cited the German peasant Franz Jagerstatter, who also died "in a solitary protest": "For what purpose did God endow all men with reason, and free will, if, in spite of this, we are obliged to render blind obedience, or if, as so many also say, the individual is not qualified to judge whether this war started by Germany is just or unjust? What purpose is served by the ability to distinguish between good and evil?"

Angered by his country's actions in Vietnam and burdened by a conscience that would not allow him to study quietly for the priesthood while his ministerial deferment protected him from the draft, the twenty-seven-year-old seminarian found inspiration in the example set by these little-known German heroes. "For me," he explained, "these words from the past have great meaning: my faith is put on the line, and above all, my life is directed to the cross-roads of the living. . . . Now I must take a stand on behalf of the living. Conscience must prevail." Harney argued that "man's transcendent dignity brings him not only inalienable rights but also an awesome responsibility" and that, consequently, he could not stand by "while the very survival of the Vietnamese people is in jeopardy." Indeed, to make his stand with Franz Jagerstatter and Father Delp, "who opted for life rather than death," Harney added his voice to the 2,500 ministers, priests, and rabbis who urged Johnson to, "in the Name of God," stop the war. "And further than this," he concluded, "on this October the 16th, I resist."[53] A year later, Harney went on to greater notoriety as a member, with Bob Cunnane, of the Milwaukee 14, a group of Catholic pacifists who, following the examples of Daniel and Philip Berrigan, raided a Milwaukee draft board and destroyed thousands of files. As a seminarian about to break the law on October 16, however, he risked being barred from the priesthood, for which he had been preparing himself for so long.

Michael Ferber followed Harney to the pulpit. He felt comfortable in such situations. He had delivered sermons at his home church in Buffalo, and as one of the main speakers for the New England Resistance (for whom he gave talks or "raps" almost daily), his "low-key Harvard style" seemed ideally suited for this moment. In what Howard Zinn later called an "extraordinary, passionate, personal statement,"[54] the twenty-three-year-old graduate student began: "We are gathered in this church today in order to do something very simple: to say No. We have come from many different places and backgrounds and we have many different ideas about ourselves and the world, but we have come here to show that we are united to do one thing: to say No. Each of our acts of returning our draft cards is our personal No; when we put them in a single container or set fire to them from a single candle we express the simple basis of our unity."

Still, Ferber warned, they would not be able to form a real community "if a negative is all we share." Albert Camus, he noted, said that "the rebel, who says No, is also one who says Yes, and that when he draws a line beyond which he will refuse to cooperate, he is affirming the values on the other side of that line. For us who come here today, what is it that we affirm, what is it to which we can say Yes?" Before they answered that question, Ferber told the congregation, they must acknowledge the differences that existed within the inchoate Resistance community. For one, many of those assembled might feel a sense of hypocrisy for participating in the religious trappings of the day's ceremonies because they themselves were not churchgoers. In response, he told of the "great tradition within the church and synagogue which has always struggled against the conservative worldly forces that have always been in control." In modern times, he said, that radical tradition "has tried to recall us to the best ways of living our lives: the way of love and compassion, the way of justice and respect, the way of facing other people as human beings and not as abstract representatives of something alien and evil." That religious tradition, he said, "is something to which we can say Yes."

Ferber then warned the assembly not to "confuse the ceremony and symbolism" of the service with the "reality" that they were only a few hundred people "with very little power." He told them that American policy would not change overnight, that, indeed, the "world will be in pretty much the same mess it is in today" and that because they, as a community, would have to "dig in for the long haul," October 16 represented not the end, but the beginning. To change the country, he said, would mean "struggles and anguish day in and day out for years . . . it will mean people dedicating their lives and possibly losing them for a cause we can only partly define and whose outcome we can only guess at."

As he moved toward his conclusion, in the most important part of the sermon, Ferber engaged the critique of "moral acts" as protest made by his old friend and former roommate at Swarthmore, Nick Egleson. To Egleson's charge that resistance grew from moralistic and personal, rather than political, motivation, Ferber again cited Camus, who, he said, "believed that politics is an extension of morality, that the truly moral man is engaged in politics as a natural outcome of his beliefs." The issue is not the difference "between the moral man and the political man," he said, but the difference "between the man whose moral thinking leads him to political action and the man whose moral thinking leads him no farther than to his own 'sinlessness.' It is the difference between the man who is willing to go dirty himself in the outside world and the man who wishes to stay 'clean' and 'pure.'"

Ferber, therefore, acknowledged the potential damage that moral actions could have on the antiwar movement. This kind of "sinlessness" and "purity," he said, is "arrogant pride" and "we must say No to it." "The martyr who offers himself meekly as a lamb to the altar is a fool," he warned. "We cannot honor him . . . unless he has helped the rest of us." The morally pure act of draft resistance would be useful in ending the war only if it produced a tangible political effect beyond cleansing the souls of those who carried it out. Ferber concluded:

> Let us make sure we are ready to work hard and long with each other in the months to come, working to make it difficult and politically dangerous for the government to prosecute us, working to help anyone and everyone find ways to avoid the draft, to help disrupt the workings of the draft and the armed forces until the war is over. Let us make sure we can form a community. Let us make sure we can let others depend on us. If we can say Yes to these things, and to the religious tradition that stands with us today, and to the fact that today marks not the End but a Beginning, and to the long hard dirty job ahead of us—if we can say Yes to all this, then let us come forward together and say No to the United States Government. Then let our Yes be the loudest No our government ever heard.[55]

Michael Ferber's emphasis of community formation as the key to supporting the moral purpose of the Resistance and moving it into the political arena highlighted an issue about which organizers truly worried. Up until the end of the ceremony, planners thought that everyone who resisted might well be rounded up and arrested on the spot. When that did not happen, they committed themselves to maintain the solidarity felt in the church among the now-scattered brethren of the Resistance. It would not be easy. They soon learned that the government would not go after them as a community, but individually. Building a community under such circumstances could be difficult. But in the church on that day, the sense of fellowship engendered by Ferber's speech and the simple feeling of being surrounded by others who were equally passionate about ending the war inflated their hopes.

For the keynote address of the service, Alex Jack had recruited Rev. Coffin, a veteran of the Second World War, a former CIA operative, and now a chaplain at Yale University and a tireless antiwar protester. He also had a playful sense of humor. When he arrived that morning and encountered Jack Mendelsohn, he told him that he wished the service were taking place in a Presbyterian church but said, "I have to hand it to you Unitarians: you really know how to combine a thin theology with a thick ethic."[56]

For nearly two years, Coffin had been one of the leading lights of Clergy and Laymen Concerned About Vietnam (CALCAV) and gained considerable notoriety as one of its most articulate spokesmen.[57] That quality was in evidence on October 16. He began by quoting Socrates and St. Peter, both of whom chose to follow their consciences before obeying others. Their words, Coffin said, "tell us that because there is a higher and hopefully future order of things, men at times will feel constrained to disobey the law out of a sense of obedience to a higher allegiance." To hundreds of history's most revered heroes, he said, "not to serve the state has appeared the best way to love one's neighbor," and he cited Milton, Bunyon, Gandhi, Nehru, as examples. Coffin then answered the charges of critics who argued that civil disobedience is the first step on the road to anarchy. The "heroes" he listed did not try to "destroy the legal order," Coffin said. In fact, "by accepting the legal punishment, they actually upheld it." Furthermore, like those assembled before him, these men broke the law as "a last, not as a first resort" and once they did, "they were determined to bend their every effort to the end that the law reflect and not reject their best understanding of justice and mercy."

The central force driving the incipient Resistance, Coffin argued, was the issue of conscience: "Let us be blunt. To us the war in Vietnam is a crime. And if we are correct, if the war is a crime, then is it criminal to refuse to have anything to do with it? Is it we who are demoralizing our boys in Vietnam, or the Administration which is asking them to do immoral things?" He then called on churches and synagogues to provide sanctuary for draft resisters. He quoted from the twenty-third Psalm ("Thou spread-est a table before me in the presence of mine enemies") and explained that the passage referred to "an ancient desert law which provided that if a man hunted by his enemies sought refuge with another man who offered him hospitality, then the enemies of the man had to remain outside the rim of the campfire light for two nights and the day intervening." In the Middle Ages, Coffin explained, this practice expanded until every church in Europe was considered a sanctuary even for common criminals. Coffin acknowledged that if the American government decided that "the arm of the law was long enough to reach inside a church," the church would be unable to prevent an arrest. "What else can a church do?" he asked. "Are we to raise conscientious men and then not stand by them in their hour of conscience?" He concluded by noting that the resisters assembled that day were taking action within two weeks of the 450th anniversary of the Reformation. He urged them on in their new reformation, their reformation of conscience: "You stand now as Luther stood in his time. May you be inspired to speak, and we to hear, the words he once spoke in conscience and in all simplicity: 'Here I stand, I can do no other. God help me.'"[58]

The Reverend George H. Williams, also recruited by Alex Jack, his nephew, spoke last and gave the call for draft cards, the "Call to Acceptance." The appearance of this very distinguished looking man, a Harvard professor and one of the nation's leading scholars in religious history, shocked many of the faculty and students at Harvard. Few of them would have expected him to align himself so publicly—and so forcefully—with the leading edge of the antiwar movement. Alex Jack remembers that "the general feeling about my uncle was that he was trapped in the twelfth century . . . people would assume he was conservative." Williams himself stated on October 16 that he was one of the more "conservative" members of the clergy to participate. On this day, though, he displayed a moral outrage that belied that image.[59]

Williams began by explaining that during a just war he would view the exemption of clergy and conscientious objectors favorably, as an act representative of "a high degree of moral sensibility" on the part of the society in question. But he did not believe the war in Vietnam to be a just war. Therefore, he agreed to stand with the resisters in their protest. He told the congregation that, like "countless others," he had sought to register his opposition to the war in Vietnam through all the "appropriate channels of democratic, academic, and religious activity." When that failed, however, Williams concluded that the administration would "only take notice of a resolute show of moral force." He said, "I am driven to show my solidarity with fellow seminarians in an act of civil disobedience out of moral indignation at the miscarriage of American ideals of international behavior. What we are doing in Vietnam is not appropriate for a great society with a long religious heritage."

Perhaps more important, Williams made a case for draft resisters as acting within firmly established democratic and religious traditions: "We interpret the action of these seminarians as moral courage, and we trust that the democratic society of which we are a part will look upon this solemn action of moral dissociation as redemptive for our society, that the Church herself in all lands and in times to come will count these young men as true servants of the peaceable kingdom." To understand the act of resistance in this way, Williams said, did not detract from the heroism of "our fighting men in Vietnam," and he also recognized that "an orderly nation has the right to make grave demands upon its citizens in time of conflict or emergency." But citizens also have the right "to determine what constitutes licit demand" upon their lives—"in other words," he argued, "what constitutes a just war."[60]

As he neared the end of his address, perhaps anticipating that in addition to the collection of draft cards, some men might burn their cards, he argued against such an act. "I deplore the burning of draft cards," he said. "The more solemn and responsible act is to withdraw from the social covenant on this specific issue of conscience against a barbaric, unnecessary war being waged between pitifully unmatched opponents in quite disparate stages of national and social evolution. The manner of dissociation from this unjust war should be solemn and not impetuous, anguished but not disorderly, respectful but resolute."[61] He then asked the resisters to come forward, and he stepped down from the pulpit to the edge of the chancel, where the Reverends Mendelsohn and Coffin, Father Cunnane, and Harvard philosopher Hilary Putnam (who had been recruited to accept cards from the nonreligious resisters) joined him. Each held an offering plate for the collection of draft cards.

All eyes (and cameras) turned toward the forward pews. Flashes popped as the first man rose, jiggled the stubborn latch on the old door at the end of the pew, and stepped out into the aisle. As he walked forward, several other men stood and began moving toward the aisle and their moment of truth. Although the promotional leaflets predicted that 500 men would turn in their draft cards and join the Resistance in Boston, organizers had commitments from only about 20 to 25 men. They were hopeful for maybe

50. It soon became apparent that many, many more would resist on this day. The first trickle of men quickly became a steady stream that continued to swell for over twenty minutes. They came not just from the pews reserved for resisters but from all corners of the church. At one point, someone pushed open the massive church doors to let resisters in from outside. At least one woman, the Reverend Nan Stone, joined the long line as it moved slowly, quietly. When she reached the altar, she burned Steve Pailet's card in the flame of a candle held by one of William Ellery Channing's own candlesticks. As they turned over or burned their cards, some of the men smiled. Others wept softly. No one spoke above a whisper. The loudest sounds came from the TV cameras whirring away in the balcony. It seemed like the procession would never end. There were brief exchanges of encouragement between the resisters and their older accomplices holding the plates. When a student he recognized from the law school at Yale handed him his card, though, Coffin tried to give it back. "Don't be a fool," he said. "With this on your record you would destroy a law career." The resister replied, calmly, "I don't care. I know I'm not going to become a lawyer." He then broke the law.[62]

When the last man placed his card on top of the pile sprouting from one of the collection plates, elated Resistance organizers hugged one another. "The most irreligious of us," Bill Dowling later said, "perhaps, are ready now to believe in miracles." After the service ended, they counted 214 cards turned in with another 67 burned at Channing's flame. NBC News correspondent Sander van Ocur, tears in his eyes, descended from the balcony to speak to his friend Bill Coffin. "What a country this would be," he said, "if something like this were now to take place in every church."[63]

Indeed, it had been a surprisingly moving day for many of those in attendance and a gratifying culmination to many long hours of planning by New England Resistance organizers. As the strategy of noncompliance came under attack by other antiwar and New Left groups in preceding weeks, few of them could have predicted the success of October 16. The call for draft resistance resulted in the mobilization of the largest antiwar rally the city had yet seen and a much greater number of returned draft cards than anyone anticipated. More important, the day signaled the successful transformation of the CNVA pacifists' individual defiant acts into a large-scale, mass protest that organizers believed would have lasting political effect. And, as Sander van Ocur's reaction indicated, the moral clarity of the participants came through in a serious, respectful, and thought-

ful confrontation with the government. In the days and weeks that followed, the media and the public often missed that point, but leaders of this
new driving force in the antiwar movement were heartened by the extensive coverage they did receive. Draft resistance, it seemed, could not now
be ignored.

CONFRONTATIONS AND MISCONCEPTIONS

FILTERED RESISTANCE
DRAFT RESISTERS' IMAGE AND REALITY

4

Naturally, the common people don't want war; neither in Russia, nor in England, nor for that matter Germany. That is understood. But after all, it is the leaders of the country who determine the policy, and it is always a simple matter to drag the people along, whether it is a democracy, or a fascist dictatorship, or a parliament, or a communist dictatorship. Voice or no voice, the people can always be brought to do the bidding of the leaders. That is easy. All you have to do is tell them they are being attacked, and denounce the pacifists for lack of patriotism and exposing the country to danger. It works the same in every country.

—Herman Goering, testifying at Nuremberg[1]

In post–Vietnam War memory, the image of draft resisters has been shaped most successfully by their detractors. Cartoonish images of long-haired hippies burning draft cards and of cowards fleeing to Canada persist to this day. This condition is undoubtedly the chief explanation for resisters' virtual absence in the national narrative of the war and protests against it. The origins of such images date to the coverage of the actual events themselves when the media played an important role in interpreting, or misinterpreting, dissent. Despite the best efforts of Resistance planners, the national press, including the Boston newspapers, almost always ignored their message and portrayed resisters in a condescending and negative light.[2]

For example, almost as soon as the service at Arlington Street ended, New England Resistance writers and speakers attempted to shape public

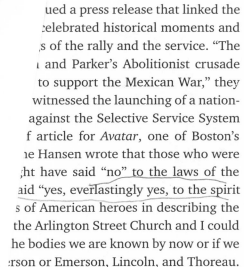

ued a press release that linked the
:elebrated historical moments and
,s of the rally and the service. "The
ı and Parker's Abolitionist crusade
to support the Mexican War," they
witnessed the launching of a nation-
against the Selective Service System
f article for *Avatar*, one of Boston's
ıe Hansen wrote that those who were
;ht have said "no" to the laws of the
aid "yes, everlastingly yes, to the spirit
s of American heroes in describing the
the Arlington Street Church and I could
he bodies we are known by now or if we
were Paine and Franklin aıı᾿ ᾿rson or Emerson, Lincoln, and Thoreau.
We were all of them, all of them on our way to becoming more of them, for
the knowledge that was theirs is yet for us to learn, but we are learning, the
pure vision that was theirs we must yet see, but we are seeing, and the
strength to manifest that vision that was theirs, must be ours also—and yet
we do not have it, but we will." Likewise, for Bill Hunt, the graduate
student in history, one of the most appealing sides to the Resistance was its
association with "an indigenous, patriotic, American tradition of protest
and dissent."[3]

In the end, few news outlets bought this line. The Resistance took some
pleasure in seeing NBC Nightly News anchor John Chancellor turn to the
camera after viewing the Sander van Ocur report from Boston and say, "If
men like this are beginning to say things like this, I guess we had all better
start paying attention." But such comments from the media came few and
far between.[4]

The Boston press, for instance, took a completely different approach,
emphasizing the *burning*—not turning in—of draft cards. The headline
on the front page of the *Boston Globe*'s October 16 evening edition said,
"Youths Burn Draft Cards on Boston Church Altar." The next morning,
surrounded by no less than three photographs of flaming draft cards, the
Globe headline read: "67 Burn Draft Cards in Boston." The sub-headline, in
much smaller type, said, "214 Turn in Cards, 5000 at Rally." The *Boston
Herald Traveler* and the *Boston Record American* also ran images of cards being burned and similar headlines. The *Record American* echoed the *Globe*,

saying "67 Burn Draft Cards at Hub Peace Rally," while the *Herald*'s headline read: "291 [*sic*] Youths Burn, Turn in Draft Cards."

In addition, reporters from each newspaper emphasized the speeches of Howard Zinn, William Sloane Coffin Jr., and, to a lesser degree, George Williams. The articles did not even mention Jim Harney, Michael Ferber, or Nick Egleson. Each newspaper instead provided details on the physical appearance of the resisters. The *Herald Traveler* said they looked more "mod" than "typical American" and "scholarly rather than athletic" and that some were even "neatly attired in suit and tie or in casual college wear," but the *Record American* (which boasted the "largest daily circulation in New England") focused its readers' attention on a few "shaggy-haired, bewhiskered youths" that they had photographed burning draft cards at the altar. Several of the men in the photograph *were* "shaggy-haired" and "bewhiskered," though no more so than Peter Ustinov, whom the paper did not describe in the same way. In the accompanying story's lead sentence, *Record American* reporters Tom Berube and Al Horne characterized the church service as a "macabre ceremony."[5]

Only the *Herald Traveler* addressed the motivations of the resisters but did so superficially. Reporter Earl Marchand quoted several resisters saying things like "the war is wrong" and "it's an immoral and illegal war," but he offered no follow up on how the resisters had arrived at those conclusions or why they believed draft resistance would be an effective way to protest the war.[6]

In an October 17 editorial, the liberal *Boston Globe* expressed its doubt that the Resistance had accomplished anything for its cause. The editors acknowledged the inequities of the draft system but argued that a better way to challenge it would be to "obey the law and seek to change it." Like a condescending father talking to his wayward son, they cited Gandhi in warning that a campaign of civil disobedience would succeed only "if a large majority of the people support it." They concluded that "the Resistance will result only in making martyrs out of some students who have great courage but little judgement." Meanwhile, the *Record American*, the paper favored by Boston's working class, argued that the demonstrators "once again inevitably will be helping to prolong the war instead of shortening it." American forces, they said, were "clearly winning in Vietnam," but the enemy, encouraged by the antiwar movement in the United States, still had reason to keep fighting.[7]

On the whole, New England Resistance organizers were elated with the _verage that October 16 received and were essentially _its generally negative tone. Media attention, *any* media atten-_y believed, served their purposes. But in the weeks following Octo-_ 16, it became clear that the press proved more successful than the Resistance at shaping public opinion. And public opinion was often unfavorable. Without the benefit of scientific polling data, it is impossible to say just how the public's view of draft resisters broke down statistically, but evidence from letters to the editor and other newspaper sources indicates that a significant segment of the population either misunderstood or disagreed with draft resisters. Those who participated in the Arlington Street service were widely regarded as hippies, cowards, or communists and were accused of being disloyal and unpatriotic.

Consequently, it is worth comparing these images of draft resisters with actual demographic data on the resisters themselves. Such an analysis demonstrates that the media's tendency to focus on the more unusual aspects of a story contributed to the development of a false image of the typical draft resister. In fact, very few of Boston's draft resisters were hippies or communists, and they were not cowards either; a coward would be more likely to try to save himself by *dodging* the draft than to openly resist it and risk a five-year prison sentence. The men who turned in their cards, many of whom were seminarians and theology students (and many more who were not religious), did so because they believed they had a moral and civic duty to commit civil disobedience. They did not commit draft resistance thoughtlessly. Most came to their decision after months, if not years, of protesting the war through legal channels and, more significant, after lengthy periods of soul searching. The majority of these resisters viewed the war and the draft with a moral clarity that derived in part from earlier civil rights and antiwar work. The civil rights activists, especially, felt comfortable confronting the government.

Perhaps most important, the overwhelming majority of draft resisters came from ordinary, middle-class homes. Their parents were not communists but professionals who lived in the suburbs. Consequently, at the time of the turn-in, most of them held deferments that protected them from the draft; by protesting in this way they risked losing those deferments (as most did) and subjected themselves to immediate prosecution. They chose resistance in part because they believed the country could not tolerate its government locking up the sons of the middle class, particularly if their actions were rooted in a conscientious adherence to values that their parents had taught them were consistent with the best American traditions.

INFLAMMATORY IMAGES

Some readers of the Boston papers were so outraged by what they saw and read in their daily paper regarding the October 16 events that they immediately wrote to the editors condemning the protesters. Every single critical letter that the *Boston Globe* printed (six letters attacking the resisters were published compared to two supporting them), consistent with their own reporting of the original story, emphasized the *burning* of draft cards. Central to their themes were issues of patriotism, loyalty, and duty to country. Letters published in the other two papers were similar. The *Record American* printed only three letters, all attacking the antiwar demonstrators, two of which specifically condemned draft card burning. "All those who participated in the demonstrations," one writer said, "should go to Russia and see how they would like living under Communism." Likewise, the *Herald Traveler* printed seven letters, all negative, six of which focused on card burnings. "Must the meaning of unity, loyalty, and love of country," one Unitarian woman wrote, "go out the window with the burning of draft cards on a church altar?" Another woman, exasperated, asked the *Herald Traveler* to run weekly articles about the "nice young people of our wonderful country." She had grown tired, she said, of all the stories about "hippies and draft card burners."[8]

Paul Christopher of Wakefield (a suburb north of Boston), reacted so angrily to photographs of draft cards being burned that he decided to organize a rally to demonstrate support for the war. The Boston papers carried numerous stories on the nineteen-year-old Christopher in the days leading up to the event. Like the letter writers, Christopher emphasized responding to the unpatriotic draft card burners. His promotional leaflet for the rally read: "Outward rebukes of our nation's policies with relation to the draft and Vietnam cannot go unchallenged. To be silent when confronted with draft card burning, sit-ins, and other demonstrations only consoles those hippies and others who are bent upon desecration of our great country." Senator Saltonstall and even the White House called to praise Christopher. Entertainer Wayne Newton offered to sing at the rally. Ultimately, after just two weeks of planning, Christopher hosted a demonstration that brought 25,000 to 50,000 people (estimates varied) to the Wakefield Common, where, across the street from a memorial to the "Spanish American War, Philippine Insurrection, and China Rebel Expedition," attendees waved flags, recited the Pledge of Allegiance, and listened to the bells in the Congregational Church across the green play the "Battle Hymn of the Republic."

The role of the Boston draft resistance ceremony as a catalyst for this rally should not be overstated (the large Wakefield crowd may have turned out for the rally in any case). But the rally's speakers made repeated reference to the Arlington Street event. Joseph Scerra, national commander of the Veterans of Foreign Wars, proclaimed: "All of our young people are not burning up their draft cards. All of our young people are not tearing up the flag. All of our youth are not supporting North Vietnam and carrying Viet Cong flags." As young men in the crowd waved signs that said "We Will Carry Our Draft Card Proudly" and "Draft the Anti-Demonstrators," Scerra told the crowd, "It's too bad we can't give pictures of what's happening here today to every individual in the country who asks for a pause in the bombing." A photographer captured one man in the crowd kissing his draft card as his sweetheart smiled her approval. Massachusetts governor John A. Volpe also spoke briefly. In an obvious reference to draft resisters, he said that some Americans were "forgetting their duty and responsibility to their country" and accused them of being unpatriotic. "Patriotism," he said, "may be old fashioned today to some, but it should never be out of fashion." Nearby, an effigy of Ho Chi Minh—holding a gun marked "USSR"—hung from a maple tree with an arrow through its chest and a knife stuck in the back of its head.[9]

In contrast to their coverage of the Resistance events, Boston newspapers openly supported the Wakefield rally. *Boston Record American* columnist John Sullivan revealed that the rally moved him to tears. The Wakefield demonstration, he wrote, "told a nation and a world that we are united and that we are proud and that we are Americans. And we are—you and I—and, by golly, a Wakefield kid proved it." The *Boston Herald* quoted several high schoolers in the crowd who, like Paul Christopher, were disgusted with the draft card burnings of October 16. They told reporters that they thought resisters were "mostly hippies," "cowards [who] should be drafted" or "banished if they don't want to fight for their country." The *Boston Globe* had sent reporter Alan Lupo to Wakefield to profile the young man behind the rally. Lupo wrote glowingly of Christopher, describing him as "good-looking" and possessing "maturity uncommon for his age." He also noted that Christopher hoped to join the Special Forces. Despite portraying themselves as the heirs of a patriotic American legacy, members of the New England Resistance could not get the kind of fawning media coverage afforded Paul Christopher.[10]

In the decades since the end of the Vietnam War, defenders of American policy have long viewed the media as a "major factor in the United States' failure in Vietnam." According to Clarence Wyatt, one side of this popular perception argues that the press fulfilled the role of a "savior" that "pulled aside the veil of official deception" and led the American people to demand an end to the war. On the other hand, others have seen the media as the "villain" that, "inspired by political and ideological biases," intentionally misrepresented the nature and progress of the war, "thus leading the American people to turn their backs on a 'noble cause.'" If such charges are valid, it follows that the press should have been at least mildly sympathetic to the antiwar movement, and especially to a group of educated, articulate young men who saw themselves as heirs of Thoreau. But as the articles and letters published in the Boston papers demonstrate, the press did little to help draft resisters win a more favorable public view. This was entirely consistent with media treatment of the antiwar movement nationwide. In *Covering Dissent*, historian Melvin Small has shown that "time and time again," the nation's newspapers, magazines, and television networks concentrated on the most "colorful" behavior (which sometimes meant emphasizing violence or some other displays of fringe radicalism) and "ignored political arguments the protesters' leadership presented."[11] Readers of the Boston papers learned little about the motivations of the resisters or even that most were giving up the security of deferments to risk prosecution for their beliefs. Mostly, they saw flaming draft cards.

Just why draft cards were burned at all on October 16 is a point worth exploring. In the weeks leading up to the service, and even during the proceedings that day, Resistance organizers emphasized the returning—rather than burning—of draft cards. Most of the men who decided to participate in the day's events recognized that by turning in their cards—with the understanding that they would be delivered to the Department of Justice—the government would know the identity of the resisters and could take measures to punish them. Burning a draft card essentially destroyed the evidence of one's protest and greatly minimized personal risk. David Clennon later reflected: "I was persuaded that turning them in was the better way to go because it was a way of saying this is who I am, this is where I can be found, and if you are serious about enforcing the laws that you have passed, then come and get me. And so that's what I did."[12]

At the same time, however, the Resistance planners made allowances for cards to be burned at the altar. They knew that some men, because they were required to carry two cards (a registration certificate and a classification certificate) at all times, would want to turn in one card and burn the other. In addition, they did not feel that they could deny those who saw the burning of their cards at the altar as a kind of sacramental act the opportunity to follow through on that view. Moreover, no one knew how the police and the FBI were going to react to the ceremony. It seemed quite possible that everyone who burned or turned in a draft card could be arrested immediately following the service. Simple failure to carry one's draft card could lead to arrest, in which case it did not matter if the evidence had been destroyed. Finally, for Nan Stone, the only woman to participate in the ceremony, burning a draft card was the only act of protest available.[13]

Perhaps the most persuasive case for burning—but the one that received the least mainstream exposure—came from seminarians and theology students who favored the tactic as "symbolic identification with Buddhist monks and American immolators like [Quaker pacifist Norman] Morrison." Alex Jack, in particular, offered a vigorous defense of card burning on these grounds. "Draft card burning," he wrote in an early position paper, "is designed to challenge and change people's perspectives." Since most American war resisters did not express their protest by setting themselves on fire, destroying one's draft card in this way demonstrated "symbolic understanding and support" for those who did. In addition, burnings were useful in dramatizing American war crimes: "The crime at issue in America is the burning of people, not a piece of paper. Those who enflame the Vietnamese countryside with napalm and white phosphorus and burn down villages and entire forests, not those who put the match to the ticket that stands for their compliance and service of this inhuman system—they are the real non-cooperators." Jack invoked the historical precedents of abolitionist William Lloyd Garrison's burning of the American Constitution and the burning of passbooks in South Africa to support his argument that torching symbols of "oppression and inhumanity" have long been judged as acceptable forms of protest. He saw no reason to "abandon the historical significance of fire" just because the Ku Klux Klan burned crosses and the Nazis burned books.[14]

Of course, not everyone agreed. In addition to George Williams, neither Jack Mendelsohn nor William Sloane Coffin approved of draft card burnings. Coffin was quite distressed when the burning of cards began because he believed it to be "needlessly hostile." He later recalled that, as he stood there accepting cards, he could see Sander van Ocur "pushing his cameraman to zero in on these cards that are in the flame. [I thought], 'Aw, shoot, we lost it.'" The following week, when many regular members of the Arlington Street Church expressed their unhappiness over the burning of draft cards in their church, Jack Mendelsohn, who had final authority to allow it in the first place, addressed the matter in his sermon. "It may come as surprising news to some that I react very negatively to the burning of draft cards," he said. "It is too flamboyant for my taste, too theatrical, too self-indulgent." He went on to tell his congregation, however, that although he did not encourage the burnings, he had not forbade them either. He decided that because the leaders of the Resistance possessed such a great degree of "integrity and moral depth," he agreed to go along with whatever plan of action they chose. And since they felt compelled by the moral outrage of a minority who wanted to burn their cards and "made orderly, respectful provision for it," Mendelsohn permitted it. In fact, the handout distributed to resisters when they arrived at the church included a "Suggested Procedure" section that said: "Hand your draft card to the clergy member of your choice, or, burn it in the altar candle. Make it smooth." That the card burnings were orderly and respectful did not, however, make it into the press accounts.[15]

CHILDREN OF THE AMERICAN DREAM

For draft resistance organizers, the overwhelming success of October 16 greatly overshadowed the inflammatory headlines. They had pulled off the largest antiwar rally in the city's history, the number of draft cards collected far exceeding their expectations, and they were thrilled that a real sense of solidarity seemed to have developed over the course of the day. They had, it seemed, built the foundation for a powerful movement that would not only challenge their government to rethink its policies in Southeast Asia but likewise dare their fellow citizens to consider the moral implications of tacit acceptance of the war.

When authorities failed to take any resisters into custody immediately following the service at Arlington Street, Resistance organizers went back to their office in Cambridge and began sorting through the collected draft cards. They created a "Master File" that included key information on each resister (since the cards themselves were destined for the Justice Department by the end of the week, most participants filled out a brief form for this purpose). Using these cards, organizers produced a mailing list so that everyone could stay in touch and begin building the kind of community that Michael Ferber described in his sermon. Fortunately, a sizable portion of the Master File has survived thanks to Alex Jack, who held on to it for thirty years. These records have been very helpful in constructing a kind of group biography of rank-and-file draft resisters.

It is important to note that, in standard movement fashion, the chore of typing up index cards with pertinent information for each resister fell mostly to the one woman then working in the office, Nan Stone. In 1967, even organizations dedicated to principles of fairness and equality continued to exhibit sexist tendencies (see Chapter 6). In Boston, a considerable debate had developed over Stone's participation in the October 16 service, and in the week that followed, male organizers argued over Stone's status again, disagreeing over whether an index card with her name on it should be kept in the Master File of resisters. Stone could not be drafted, but as a Resistance organizer she had been complicit in "aiding and abetting" the violation of Selective Service laws. Furthermore, she had clearly broken the law when she burned Steve Pailet's draft card at the altar. In the end, it took the appearance of FBI agents—who were then investigating all of the October 16 resisters and showing interest in Nan Stone at the same time—for Stone's index card to find a place in the Master File.[16]

The Master File that Stone created shows that most of the men who resisted on October 16 were white college- and graduate-school-age men—educated at some of the more prestigious schools in New England—who were willing to give up the security of the draft deferments assigned by their draft boards. The average (and median) age of the men who turned in their cards in New England that fall was twenty-two. Students made up 76 percent of the resisters who took part, with the largest contingents coming from Harvard, Boston University, and Yale. The Selective Service classifications assigned to these students varied, however (see Table A.1). Forty-nine percent were classified either 2-S (the standard student deferment) or 4-D (the deferment for ministers and divinity students). Most telling, though, is that only 17.5 percent of resisters were classified 1-A, available for military service. Therefore, at least 82 percent of the men who resisted in Boston risked their deferments by breaking the law, an important detail never reported to the public by the media.[17]

What the draft cards that were collected could not say, however, was that the resisters who returned them were children of the American dream. This is apparent from a 1997 survey administered to former resisters and resistance activists. For the most part, they grew up in comfortable homes, raised by parents who were better educated than previous generations and who worked at professional careers. Nearly 50 percent of resisters' fathers graduated from college, with a total of 37 percent going on to graduate school; 22 percent held professional (M.D., J.D., etc.) or doctoral degrees (see Table A.2). Forty percent of resisters' mothers were college graduates, with 15 percent possessing advanced degrees. These educational achievements meant that most resisters' fathers (70 percent) held professional jobs as physicians, attorneys, accountants, engineers, academics, scientists, and ministers, etc., or ran their own businesses as real estate and insurance brokers or were other kinds of small business proprietors (see Table A.3). More than half of their mothers were homemakers, but another nearly 30 percent held professional positions (most as teachers, librarians, and nurses). Nearly 80 percent of resisters in Boston identified themselves as coming from middle-class (44 percent), upper-middle-class (33 percent), or upper-class (2 percent) families (see Table A.4). The fact that they came from families that were quite ordinary, they believed, was their greatest strength. They grew up in the years following the Second World War as children of a burgeoning middle class and lived in middle-class neighborhoods all across America. They were the boys next door.

In addition, the men who resisted the draft in Boston do not seem to have been bred for this kind of activism any more than other middle-class children. Although most resisters identified their parents (84 percent of fathers and 91 percent of mothers) with one or another religious denomination (see Table A.5), none was a member of the historically pacifist (and antiwar) sects such as the Quakers or Mennonites. Four of the resisters themselves were Quakers but had not been raised so. In fact, 40 percent of the resisters surveyed came from homes in which one or both of their parents were veterans of the armed forces, many of whom had seen combat duty during World War II (see Table A.6). Most significant, however, is that few resisters' parents ever took part in any kind of social activism or protest themselves. Only 25 percent of Boston's resisters grew up with a parent who had a history of activism, including only 15 percent with a union member for a parent.[18]

If, as Polish Freedom Fighter Josef Mlot-Mroz believed, the draft resisters had been "duped" by "Reds," it is clear that it did not happen under their parents' roofs. While many draft resisters saw themselves as members of the New Left, they were not "red diaper babies," that is, children of Old Left communists. Indeed, the majority of resisters' parents were Democrats and the rest Republicans (see Table A.7). Of 121 resisters surveyed, only five identified both of their parents as either socialist, communist, or anarchist (see Table A.8). In 80 percent of resisters' homes, both parents belonged to the same political party;[19] the vast majority (62 percent) were Democrats. Thus, by challenging the draft and Lyndon Johnson's foreign policy, most resisters confronted an administration voted into office by their own parents. Even among the resisters, 46 percent called themselves Democrats; less than 2 percent were Republicans (Table A.7). That said, it is true that a significant minority of resisters (39 percent) thought of themselves as either socialists, communists, or anarchists. Yet it is apparent that this did not mean that these New Leftists were hell-bent on revolution. Actually, only about 20 percent of them felt comfortable with radical labels like "revolutionary" or "politico." Rather, more than two-thirds of Boston's draft resisters saw themselves as "activists." Most felt very American and, like Michael Ferber, "fully engaged in a big struggle with my country . . . having what Coffin always called 'a lover's quarrel with my country.'" This distancing from their parents' political ideology no doubt originated in some of their prior social activism, not in a love of the Soviet Union.[20]

For the overwhelming majority of the Boston draft resisters, the decision to join the Resistance followed their earlier participation in protest movements. Three-quarters of them had a history of prior activism, including working with campus or community peace and civil rights organizations. More than half of the resisters in Boston (50.4 percent) had been involved in either campus or community civil rights work. Likewise, 53 percent worked in either campus or community peace efforts before coming to the Resistance. A smaller number of these men (15.7 percent) worked on Vietnam Summer in the months before October 16. In addition, even though SDS officially doubted the value of draft resistance, 30 percent of the resisters in Boston were present or former members of that organization. Such experiences helped to demystify civil disobedience and imprisonment for many. Michael Ferber, who had spent a night in jail for civil rights protest, noted that by the time he helped launch the New England Resistance, he no longer cared that he had an arrest record. "Some of the finest people in America," he said, "are now getting arrested for one thing or another."[21]

These figures notwithstanding, the statistics still peg nearly one-quarter of Boston's resisters as men who were participating in a protest movement for the first time. And although more than half of the men who turned in or burned their cards knew friends in the movement, 45 percent did it on their own and knew no one else among the hundreds who resisted with them. These individuals were so highly motivated by their outrage regarding the war that they were willing to take the risky step of defying the draft to make their protest. And they did it all by themselves.[22]

For weeks, Resistance leaders tried to make plain the degree of potential peril that participation in the October 16 service might bring. Leaflets included warnings to resisters that turning in their cards could result in arrest and that if they were found guilty of breaking Selective Service laws they could receive a five-year prison sentence and a $10,000 fine. They hoped that no one would turn in or burn his card without having thought it through completely, in advance, in the cool light of reason and *not* in the emotional atmosphere of the ceremony itself. For the most part, resisters heeded their advice. More than half of Boston's resisters (54 percent) planned in advance to turn in or burn their draft cards. An additional one-third said they had been considering resistance carefully in the weeks before they did it but did not decide to turn in their cards until the day of the event. Only 13.4 percent spontaneously turned in or burned their cards in the heat of the moment.

In some ways, organizers were unrealistic in expecting that no one would resist on the spur of the moment. The skilled oratory of the speakers assembled at each turn-in, coupled with the church setting (as on October 16), made these services a little like low-key revival meetings. Some could not help having, as Alex Jack described it, "a conversion experience." For example, Bill Bischoff, a Harvard graduate student in history and a veteran, recalls that the array of passionate, reputable speakers assembled on October 16 made him think of the demonstration as a kind of test of his commitment to protesting the war. "Well," he thought to himself, "I don't know how I can stay out of this when I feel as strongly [about the war] as I do." Similarly, Harold Hector, a leader in the Boston Draft Resistance Group and one who did *not* advocate risking jail through open confrontation with the Selective Service, turned in his card on the same day. He did it because it was "one of the most moving days" of his life, so moving that he thought he "would have done anything that day." "I could not *not* turn it in," he said. "I couldn't walk out of there with my card in my pocket. . . . You knew there were FBI agents up in the balcony; I felt like I wanted to wave it under their nose—that's how I felt that day. . . . There were moments when you just couldn't hold back."[23]

The vast majority of resisters, though, came to their decisions after long periods of careful consideration. Just as William Sloane Coffin, George Williams, and Michael Ferber had criticized and protested the war through other more moderate means in previous years before moving toward a more direct confrontation with the government, many of the resisters now felt that the time for civil disobedience had arrived. As Coffin noted, for each person, a time arrives when, "having done everything legal, you really have to decide . . . you've done what you could, so you can now tuck your conscience into bed, and sort of move on. Or you can say, 'alright, we've exhausted the legal possibilities' . . . so, you have to look into possibilities of civil disobedience, which challenge the injustice of the law." And, he said, civil disobedience is also a way of "being more dramatic about calling attention to the horrors of whatever you're opposing."[24] Draft resisters had marched. They had written letters and attended teach-ins. They had protested more than most of the war's opponents, but they were not prepared to tuck their consciences into bed. Instead, they chose to act in the strongest way they knew, short of violence, to protest the inequities of the draft and what they believed to be the illegality and immorality of the war in Vietnam. And in making the emotional, life-altering decision to resist their government's authority, resisters justified and rationalized their acts using moral and political arguments.

Most resisters recognized the potential political impact of widespread draft resistance. They aimed to make the government face the prospect of jailing thousands of middle-class sons in order to continue on the same course in Vietnam. They gambled with their own freedom, believing that enough men would join them and that the costs of the war would become too high for the government to continue the war. The greatest cost, one resister argued, would be "the criminalization of large numbers of elite college students—future 'leaders.'" Eventually, they believed, "upright, respectable, middle-class citizens," the kind who were potentially influential, would not stand for their children going to prison.[25]

More important, draft resisters—both leaders and the rank and file— recognized their place within society, within the system of conscription, as symptomatic of an existential dilemma that needed to be addressed. Instead of being asked to serve in the military alongside their less fortunate fellow citizens, many of them were being protected through an unfair draft apparatus. As working-class and minority men died each day in rice paddies and jungles on the other side of the world, they breathed in the aroma of the drying leaves then blanketing the grounds of their picturesque New England campuses. They felt guilty. Most deferment holders could live with that guilt.[26] But those who would resist the draft could not ignore it or the reality that their own senses of good and evil, morality and immorality, spawned that guilt. Many of them, therefore, committed themselves to the risky business of openly defying their elected government out of a sense of personal integrity and a deep sense of morality. For Michael Zigmond, a twenty-six-year-old postdoctoral fellow at MIT, the decision to resist resulted from "at least equal parts trying to be more effective and just trying to get the weight off." Zigmond, who attended the October 16 service but did not return his card until the following month, felt a "need to respond somehow and also to basically come out of the closet from being this protected . . . kind of person." He felt like his draft card "was getting very heavy . . . it was really heavy," and the opportunity to resist relieved the moral strain of keeping it. Similarly, David Clennon felt like he had to "do something personally to help to end the war."[27]

Many resisters reported similar experiences of agonizing over their decision to resist and then being overwhelmed with emotions at the moment of resistance. For Larry Etscovitz, a twenty-one-year-old junior at Boston University, two years of anguish over the Vietnam War culminated on October 16, 1967. Since entering BU with a deferment in 1965, he, as well as many of his friends, had grown more and more involved, emotionally and intellectually, with the war. The war "was just getting worse and worse," he said. "After a while, it was the only thing any of us talked about." On October 16 he went to the Common because he had heard that a huge antiwar rally was scheduled and that BU professor Howard Zinn would be speaking. Despite Resistance publicity, he did not know about the scheduled draft card turn-in. When Zinn finished his speech and told the resisters where to line up, Etscovitz, not fully aware of what this meant, simply thought, "Yes, I'm a resister. OK, I'm going to line up over there." He marched with the group to the church and took a seat in one of the forward pews. "Even then," he said, "I had no idea or knowledge or intention of taking my draft card out; I felt I just needed to be there and be a part of this event." When the call was made, Etscovitz turned in his draft card. He was scared but resolute. "Everything was leading up to this moment and . . . this is the moment when I was going to let my voice be counted. Up until that moment, whether I was at a demonstration or not, was not a matter of record. I wanted it to be a matter of record, that I was there. . . . That was my protest." When he caught a ride back to BU with some friends, one of them, a woman, told him: "Today, you are a man."[28]

Like Etscovitz, many draft resisters later viewed the moment of their turn-in as a kind of rite of passage into manhood. In resisting the draft publicly, they overcame tremendous anxieties and fears of openly defying the will of their government. They were, after all, middle-class children, raised in an era of confidence and taught to revere the promise of the American dream. But suddenly that dream seemed tainted by a war they found repulsive. James Oestereich, a seminarian at Andover-Newton Theological Seminary, recalled debating the merits of draft resistance with one of his professors while taking a Green Line trolley car from Newton Centre on the way to the service at Arlington Street. Oestereich emphasized to his mentor that by turning in his card he would be making a statement, and that was what mattered. "I mean I was definitely taking a step to criticize my government." Despite his firm belief that he planned to do the right thing that afternoon, he could feel the knots in his stomach tighten as they got closer to downtown. The prospect of challenging the authority of one's government chilled him. "It's *hard*," he later said. "You know, we know how to pay our taxes . . . but we don't know how to oppose our government in a way that's responsible and that will be listened to. None of us knew that." When he walked up the aisle toward Rev. Coffin, draft card in hand, a wave of mixed emotions swelled within him. He felt strongly that through this act he was saying, "Whatever this movement is, I'm in . . . I'm not going to read about it, I'm not going to be this isolated sort of graduate student on the hill; I'm in." At the same time, he was overcome with the gravity of the act. "When I dropped that card in the tray . . . I really just had a very emotional reaction to it. I was very moved at what we were doing. It hit me just that, my God, this is important. I don't think it was fear or anything, I was just very emotional about it. I had a lot of tears in my eyes."[29]

Others simply felt fear. On October 16, no one knew what would happen to the men who chose to resist the draft. "We knew that the faster the movement grew, the better off we'd all be," explained Bill Hunt. "But if you found yourself out there, you know, just a handful of us out there alone, that was going to be a lonely experience." Very few draft resisters knew what it would be like to experience the full force of the government's law-enforcement powers. Some of them had been arrested at other peace and civil rights demonstrations, but those resulted in minimal fines at worst. Those choosing resistance knew that the penalties for not cooperating with the Selective Service would be severe. "So it wasn't a lark," recalled Hunt. "It wasn't something people did as a gag." Years later, Rev. Coffin echoed Hunt as he reflected on the resisters he encountered. "I was very moved by the seriousness with which they were organized, the seriousness with which they took their actions," he said. "This wasn't something they decided to do when they were high on dope or something like that," nor was it carried out by "the far Left or the flakiest at all." Indeed, he recalled, the participants "were very conscientious. And there were some very fine students in the group," but what was most "courageous" about them, he asserted, was "that they had an out—staying in college—and they refused to take the out. And that was really fine."[30]

Critics of the sixties generation and the antiwar movement in particular have been successful in using stereotypes of radical movement minorities to portray the whole movement, but it would have been difficult for an observer of the October 16 rally on Boston Common and the service at Arlington Street Church to confuse the assembled protesters with the hippies, Yippies, and Weathermen (the radical SDS splinter group) that dominate those portrayals.[31] True, a significant number of resisters (50 percent) thought of themselves as members of the "counterculture"—undoubtedly because they grew their hair longer than their fathers', listened to Bob Dylan, and smoked an occasional joint—but far fewer called themselves "hippies" (16.5 percent). Similarly, although the majority of resisters claimed membership in the New Left (66 percent), only one in five felt like "revolutionaries." But as historian David Farber has argued, the myths that portray antiwar protesters as either stoned hippies or dupes of an international communist conspiracy—both "officially promoted by guardians of the standing order"—die hard in America. In Boston, draft resisters did not fit either stereotype. Indeed, they defied David Horowitz's and Peter Collier's much publicized stereotypical claim that sixties activists "assaulted and mauled" the American system, destroying "that collection of values that provide guidelines for societies as well as individuals." They do not fit into historian Stephen Ambrose's portrayal of the antiwar movement as having chosen "to print a license to riot, to scandalize, to do drugs and group sex, to talk and dress dirty, to call for revolution and burn flags, to condemn parents and indeed anyone over 30 years of age, in an excess of free will and childish misjudgement seldom matched and never exceeded."[32]

The men (and woman) who chose to resist the draft rather than submit to it or "dodge" it do not, in the final analysis, seem to conform to the traditional perceptions about Vietnam-era antiwar protesters. They came from stable homes, had parents who were professionals and who had inculcated their children with mainstream, not radical, political ideas. They were themselves well-educated and often in the process of pursuing graduate degrees. As a result, most were protected from the draft and, like millions of beneficiaries of an unfair Selective Service System, could have ignored both the war and the draft. Before 1967, many resisters participated in other types of social protest, including the civil rights movement. Just as civil rights leaders sought nonviolent moral confrontation with state and federal authorities, draft resisters hoped to use similar tactics in confronting what they saw as a war machine out of control in Southeast

Asia. Also like civil rights leaders, members of the New England Resistance, because of the efforts of certain organizers, contributed a unique blend of religious and political rationales for their work. In the days and weeks that followed October 16, resisters would be faced with the reaction of the federal government and with the task of sustaining a movement that burst onto the Boston antiwar movement like a supernova but that might easily be snuffed out in the face of official pressure.

5 UNEASY WAITING
DRAFT RESISTERS AND THE JOHNSON ADMINISTRATION

> What really prevents the great majority from refusing to take
> part in military service is merely fear of the punishments which
> are inflicted by the governments for such refusals. This fear,
> however, is only a result of the government deceit, and has no
> other basis than hypnotism.
> —Leo Tolstoy, "Carthago Delenda Est," 1899

On October 20, 1967, four days after Boston's most stunning antiwar demonstration to date, Michael Ferber delivered the draft cards collected at the Arlington Street Church (along with the charred remains of those burned) to the U.S. Department of Justice in Washington. This weekend capped a week-long national protest against the draft that began on October 16 and that was marked most notably by violent clashes between protesters and police outside the Oakland, California, induction center. Ferber was one of 500 draft resistance activists from across the country who gathered early on the twentieth at the Church of the Reformation at 212 East Capitol Street in anticipation of the march to justice. Like Ferber, other resisters brought draft cards with them from ceremonies held on October 16. Many older advisers joined them, including William Sloane Coffin Jr., Benjamin Spock, Mitch Goodman, Robert Lowell, and Dwight MacDonald. After marching the mile and a half to their destination, they arrived to find three rows of policemen, outfitted in helmets and other riot gear, guarding the building's massive bronze doors. Across the street a crowd of reporters and photographers jostled one another for the best viewing positions.

Once again, Coffin filled the role of featured speaker. On the steps of the gleaming white building, he spoke into a bullhorn, telling the crowd and the mass of reporters that he and other older supporters intended to "aid and abet" draft resisters in every way possible. "To stand up in this fashion against the law and our fellow Americans is a difficult and even fearful thing," he said, echoing some of the themes in his Arlington Street sermon. "But in the face of what to us is insane and inhumane, we can fall neither silent nor servile." He stressed that the resisters and their supporters, many of whom were veterans, felt the "highest sympathy" for the men fighting in Vietnam and their families at home, but he asked those who backed the war out of loyalty to their "sons or lovers or husbands" in Vietnam to understand that "sacrifice in and of itself confers no sanctity." "There can be no cleansing water," he said, "if military victory spells moral defeat."[1]

Mitch Goodman then issued the call for draft cards. Young men from the crowd walked up the stairs of the Justice Department building, stated their names, announced the city or college that they represented, and told how many cards they carried on behalf of their fellow resisters. Each then turned to the tall man holding a plaid Fabrikoid briefcase open before them. Dr. Spock, wearing his trademark three-piece suit, smiled as the men took turns dropping the returned Selective Service documents into the satchel that he held in his hands. Norman Mailer, the novelist who later won a Pulitzer Prize for *Armies of the Night*, his book chronicling the events of this weekend in Washington, stood in awe of the number of draft cards put in the bag and especially of the young men doing it:

> As these numbers [of draft cards collected] were announced, the crowd . . . gave murmurs of pleasure, an academic distance from the cry they had given as children to the acrobats of the circus, but not entirely unrelated, for there was something of the flying trapeze in these maneuvers now; by handing in draft cards, these young men were committing their future either to prison, emigration, frustration, or at best, years where everything must be unknown, and that spoke of a readiness to take moral leaps which the acrobat must know when he flies off into space— one has to have faith in one's ability to react with grace en route, one has, ultimately, it may be supposed, to believe in some kind of grace.[2]

For the Resistance representatives and their supporters, the time to confront their government, their moment of truth, had arrived. Although every resister had taken the personal step toward outright resistance on the sixteenth, their identities remained unknown to those in power—until now. When the line of resisters finished, Spock's briefcase held 994 draft cards from across the country. To complete what Alex Jack later called the "largest collective act of civil disobedience in modern American history," the cards needed only to be delivered to U.S. Attorney General Ramsey Clark.[3]

A small group of resisters and supporters, including Spock, Coffin, Marcus Raskin and Arthur Waskow, authors of the "Call to Resist Illegitimate Authority," and Bay Area resister Dickie Harris, entered the Justice Department building. There they hoped to be greeted by the attorney general himself. An escort led the group down a long hall to a conference room, where, instead of finding Ramsey Clark, they met Assistant Deputy Attorney General John McDonough and John Van de Kamp, the deputy director of the Executive Office of U.S. Attorneys. Clark sent McDonough in his stead because he believed that receiving "evidence of potentially criminal conduct" would be irresponsible and "not the role of the attorney general." McDonough, on leave from his teaching post at Stanford Law School, had joined the Department of Justice only six weeks before. Although he greeted the group cordially, he disagreed with their tactics. Specifically, McDonough thought that the "solicitation" of young men to resist the draft "was not appropriate behavior," and, more generally, he saw civil disobedience as a precursor to "anarchy."[4]

After offering coffee to the men, McDonough told them that he represented the attorney general in this meeting and that Clark had instructed him to report back to him on the substance of the discussion. He then recorded the name and address of each visitor. He sat through brief statements made by each protester and conspicuously ignored Marc Raskin when he asked if the Justice Department planned to investigate alleged war crimes in Vietnam. Years later, McDonough acknowledged that he did not "undertake to discuss with them . . . the merits of the points which they raised"; he simply wanted to make an accurate report to Clark. After being subjected to an intense "rap" by the flamboyant Harris, McDonough pulled a piece of paper from his pocket and read a brief statement warning the group that they might be breaking the law. Then, he began an unusual verbal tango with Coffin. He turned to the Yale chaplain and asked, "Am I being tendered something?"

"Tendered something?" Coffin responded.

"Yes, tendered something."

Coffin suddenly understood. "Yes, Mr. McDonough," he said, "you are herewith being tenderly tendered these draft cards and supporting statements," and he held out the briefcase for the assistant deputy attorney general. Perhaps McDonough thought that after he read the draft law the group would take their briefcase and go home. When they did not, he refused to accept the bag. Indeed, according to Coffin, he nearly recoiled. Coffin tried again, but McDonough kept his hands in his lap. Coffin later recalled that when he finally put the briefcase down on the table in front of McDonough, the assistant deputy attorney general "stared [at it] as though it contained hot coals."[5]

Such accounts of McDonough's response are probably exaggerated, for although Ramsey Clark later speculated that McDonough was uncomfortable participating in this meeting, the Stanford legal scholar knew what he was doing. As John Van de Kamp understood, McDonough refused to accept the cards because he "did not want to give countenance to the turn-in of draft cards." To have accepted the cards only would have encouraged more protesters to seek meeting with the attorney general for similar purposes.[6]

Nevertheless, on this day, the activists were nonplused. Even after Arthur Waskow exploded, demanding that McDonough fulfill his duties as a law enforcement officer (and collect the evidence of a probable crime), McDonough did nothing. Disgusted, the group left the building to tell the crowd what had happened. As they walked down the hall to the door, two FBI agents burst into the conference room and scooped up the briefcase. The following week, FBI agents began their investigations of draft resisters by swarming down on college campuses across the country, including Harvard, Yale, and Boston University. The government, it appeared, had taken an interest in the resisters' protest.[7]

The Johnson administration had been aware of opposition to the war for some time; it had seen the marches and demonstrations. Some cabinet members (Robert McNamara, for instance) had been targeted personally by these protests. But the episode at the Justice Department marked a new phase of antiwar protest and a new challenge to the administration. For the first time, the antiwar movement brought its protest to the seat of power and confronted the administration directly. Just as resisters raised the personal stakes for opponents of the war, their mass civil disobedience likewise upped the ante for the administration. Now, the White House could no longer ignore the antiwar movement. The president's men would have to act. The Resistance counted on it.

Draft resisters soon learned, however, that the government's response would not be as quick and decisive as they imagined. Just as John McDonough surprised the Resistance emissaries with his reaction to them at the Justice Department, the administration did not follow the course most resisters believed—and hoped—it would follow. Most expected to be arrested, perhaps swiftly, once the government received their draft cards, the evidence of their crimes. But their showdown with the administration did not work out that way.

The two months following October 16 produced sharp disagreements between key Johnson administration officials that contributed to an ambivalent, sometimes conflicted, government response. This uneven and inconsistent reaction, to the extent that it was perceptible to outsiders, caught the Resistance off-guard; as the FBI investigated resisters and local draft boards moved to punish some of them, the Resistance scrambled to respond—while still anticipating arrests or indictments. In the weeks after October 16, resisters and the administration engaged in a kind of uneasy dance, like two prizefighters sizing each other up in the first round; as each side tried to evaluate the other, both showed signs of uncertainty regarding their next moves. The confrontation the resisters sought simmered a while before reaching full boil.

ALL THE PRESIDENT'S MEN

News of the meeting at the Justice Department infuriated the president of the United States. At 7:30 that evening, Lyndon Johnson pulled Joseph Califano, his top assistant for domestic affairs, into the Oval Office. Next to the president's desk, a teletype machine pumped out wire reports from news organizations. Obviously agitated, Johnson tore off the United Press International report from the tape spitting out of the machine. He read the news to Califano that nearly 1,000 draft cards had been left at the Justice Department. "I want a memo to the Attorney General tonight," he told Califano. "I want the FBI investigating." Soon after, Attorney General Ramsey Clark received a terse memo from the president:

> With reference to reports that several individuals turned in their draft cards to an official of the Department of Justice this afternoon. I would like you to inform me promptly, as well as periodically, thereafter, concerning:
>
> —The progress of investigations by the Federal Bureau of Investigation of any violations of law involved.
>
> —Steps you are taking to prosecute lawbreakers in accordance with established procedures.
>
> It is important that violations of law be dealt with firmly, promptly, and fairly.
>
> LBJ

On separate copies of the same memo sent to J. Edgar Hoover and Lewis Hershey, the president wrote, "I want you to be personally responsible for keeping me informed on this." Johnson did not know that, a few hours earlier, at 4:30 P.M., John McDonough and John Van de Kamp had already yielded the briefcase full of draft cards to FBI agents. The following day, a teletype went out to all FBI field office special agents in charge instructing that individual cases be opened up on each person who turned in his card. "Indices are to be searched, respective Selective Service files reviewed, and registrants interviewed," the memo said. The government had joined the battle.[8]

Meanwhile, Johnson and his administration focused on a more pressing matter: the march on the Pentagon scheduled for October 21. The National Mobilization to End the War in Vietnam (Mobe), had organized the protest under the direction of David Dellinger. In addition, Dellinger had recruited Jerry Rubin to be program director. Hoping to fuse antiwar activism with countercultural flair, Rubin publicized the march by announcing plans to levitate the Pentagon, flip it over, and empty it of all its bad spirits. The administration feared much worse. Some of Johnson's advisers believed that the event coordinators planned to encourage rock- and egg-throwing at the windows of the Pentagon, and possibly breaching the massive building's security through basement windows. Defense Secretary Robert McNamara suggested on October 3 that the president might consider being somewhere other than Washington on the day of the march, but Johnson responded, "They are not going to run me out of town!"[9]

The president did feel sufficiently concerned, however, to ask Ramsey Clark for daily updates on plans for the demonstration. Clark assigned the responsibility of planning for the event to his deputy, Warren Christopher. By 8:00 P.M. every night for the next two weeks, reports from the Justice Department appeared on Johnson's desk. He read not only of the administration's preparations for the march, but also of details of the protesters' plans, including who would speak at various locations and details on the Mobe's leaders and their ties to other organizations. Although the president spent most of the day of the march in the Rose Garden, fashioning for reporters an image of a chief executive with a full schedule of meetings (and with only a slight interest in the demonstrations), Joe Califano fed Johnson frequent updates on the progress of the protests throughout the day and night.[10]

The president learned that perhaps as many as 100,000 people congregated in front of the Lincoln Memorial that day to hear speeches condemning his policies in Vietnam. The gathering constituted the most significant antiwar demonstration in the nation's capital to date. Although the rally and the march that followed had only indirect ties to the draft resistance movement, the speakers' rhetoric that day reflected the influence of October 16. David Dellinger told the crowd, "This is the beginning of a new stage in the American peace movement, in which the cutting edge becomes active resistance."[11]

But if organizers intended to send a message of "active resistance," it got lost in the media's attention on the clash between marchers and the federal troops assigned to protect the Pentagon. As approximately 35,000 marchers approached the Pentagon from the Arlington Memorial Bridge following the earlier rally, they could see that U.S. marshals and army regulars surrounded the building. It marked the first time since the 1932 Bonus Army March that the federal government called out the armed forces to protect itself against its own citizens. Almost everyone in the crowd assembled in the Pentagon's north parking lot, a space for which march organizers had secured a permit. Several small groups of militants, however, charged the troops and attempted to enter the Pentagon (a few succeeded and were beaten and arrested for their efforts). When these flare-ups settled down, the afternoon actually took on a "festival atmosphere" as musicians played for the crowd and speakers conducted what amounted to an impromptu teach-in. That night, however, events turned ugly.

After midnight, when only a few hundred demonstrators remained on the plaza in front of the Pentagon—most sitting and sleeping directly in front of the troops—the officials in charge of security ordered the marshals and soldiers to form a wedge and begin driving the protesters away from the building. As one official later reported to the attorney general, in some cases the marshals "used more force than was warranted."[12] The troops used batons and their rifle butts to club the protesters. A number of women suffered the most severe beatings—apparently as part of a strategy to provoke male protesters into attacking the troops. The demonstration fizzled the next day, and at the end of the weekend, the Justice Department counted 683 arrests, 51 jail terms (of up to 35 days), and $8,000 in fines.[13]

Most significant for the draft resisters who had taken their fateful step of defiance the previous week, the media coverage of the march completely obscured the previous day's events at the Justice Department. The 100,000 participants at the Lincoln Memorial made the gathering of 500 people who turned out for the demonstration at the Justice Department on Friday seem puny. Moreover, as historian Charles DeBenedetti has observed,

Rubin's provocative rhetoric and the violent clashes between a small number of protesters and the soldiers and marshals guarding the Pentagon "reinforced the image of the antiwar movement as a radical fringe and pushed it further to the political margin." By Monday, October 23, the papers and television newscasts were reporting only on the wild events of the previous forty-eight hours; Friday afternoon's draft card turn-in had been forgotten.[14]

In Boston the following week, however, resisters soon learned that, despite the attention focused on the Pentagon demonstrations, the Federal Bureau of Investigation did not overlook the receipt of their cards in Washington. Beginning on October 24, FBI agents from the Boston field office visited dozens of resisters at their homes and on campus. They also appeared at the homes of resisters' parents. Generally, agents pressed resisters to respond to three questions: 1) Did you turn in your draft card purposefully and knowingly? 2) Were you coerced in any way? And 3) Why did you do it? Parents were asked if they knew of their sons' activities and if they were aware of the possible consequences. Most resisters and their families had always been law-abiding citizens and had no experience with being questioned by federal authorities. Since few had ever even seen an FBI agent before, opening their doors to find two FBI agents displaying their credentials could be a little unnerving.[15]

The New England Resistance, knowing that many resisters might be easily intimidated when confronted alone by FBI agents, scrambled to respond. Several pages of a hastily produced newsletter dated October 25, the day after the first FBI visits, addressed the issue. Organizers warned all resisters that the federal agents were visiting people singly, "with a heavy emphasis on parents." With such "harassment," they argued, the FBI tried to "intimidate or frighten" resisters, "split families," and scare off others who might consider becoming resisters. They noted that the FBI arrested no one on its first day, and, in their first efforts at maintaining solidarity, organizers urged rank-and-file resisters to stay committed to the cause and to one another: "THE SINGLE MOST IMPORTANT WEAPON WE HAVE IS OUR COMMITMENT AND UNITY AS A GROUP. WE MUST LET THEM KNOW THAT HARASSMENT OR ARREST OF ONE OF US WILL MEAN A RESPONSE BY ALL OF US. WE ARE FREE MEN NOW AND WILL NOT BE INTIMIDATED. WE WILL STAND UP FOR OUR LEGAL RIGHTS AND MORAL CONVICTIONS. WE HAVE TOLD THE ADMINISTRATION AND SELECTIVE SERVICE SYSTEM WHERE IT [SIC] CAN GO, AND THE FBI AND JUSTICE DEPARTMENT CAN FOLLOW THEM . . . NOT WE, BUT THE GOVERNMENT WILL BE FORCED TO BACK DOWN." The newsletter also included a lengthy section on how to handle an FBI visit. First, it reminded resisters that they did not have to speak with the agents or let them into their homes (unless they were equipped with a search warrant), and resisters should submit to interviews only with an attorney present. Second, the newsletter provided tips on how to handle an FBI search, recommending that a resister allow agents in his home only after getting a lawyer or minister on the phone so that he could describe everything the agents did. They also recommended keeping the agents together to "make sure nothing is planted or taken." The newsletter did not, however, indicate how compliant one could expect the FBI agents to be with such demands. Finally, Resistance organizers counseled their brethren never to be on the defensive. "The FBI is generally a bunch of political hacks," they wrote, "who threaten loudly but back down when their bluff is called." Interviews by FBI agents constituted standard operating procedure for the Justice Department, the newsletter said, noting that civil rights workers in the South had been subjected to the same kind of treatment.[16] Most important, they concluded, no one had yet been arrested.

NER MEETS FBI

That the FBI arrested no one in that first fortnight following October 16 surprised the New England Resistance; they had expected "rapid and massive prosecutions" of the first resisters. Not only did resisters remain free and uncharged of crimes, but the FBI did not even interview some of them. The slow pace and inconsistency of government response bewildered Resistance organizers. In fact, when representatives of Resistance groups from across the country met to discuss strategy following the scene at the Justice Department on October 20, they made few plans. Other than agreeing on responsibilities for maintaining a communications network through newsletters and setting December 4 as the target date for the next national action (though Michael Ferber indicated that Boston would probably do something earlier), the resisters made no significant decisions about how to move forward over the following weeks and months. They waited for a government crackdown they believed to be imminent.[17]

Only in rare instances did resisters feel the force of the government's wrath in the first two months following the turning in of their draft cards. In Boston, authorities singled out one resister, Chris Venn, and even that took six weeks. Venn had grown up in the Back Bay neighborhood of Boston and in the fall of 1967 had taken a semester off from the University of Colorado. On October 16, he worked as part of a painting crew on the

Mystic River Bridge. At work the next day, when the draft card turn-in came up in conversation, Venn found himself defending the resisters in a heated argument with the rest of the crew. Eventually, one of his coworkers asked Venn why he, if he felt so strongly, did not turn in his own card. So he did. Venn tracked down Michael Ferber at his Phillips Street apartment on Beacon Hill and gave him his draft card in time for it to be conveyed to Washington with the rest. He immediately began working in the New England Resistance office in his spare time. A few weeks later, FBI agents interviewed him with his parents in their four-story house on Gloucester Street in the Back Bay. The meeting was civil. In fact, Venn today remembers the agents being surprised that someone who lived in one of the nicest neighborhoods in the city might have broken the law. Venn continued to work with the Resistance after the interview.

Chris Venn's personal history, however, made him more vulnerable than other resisters to an accelerated reaction to his draft card turn-in. Venn had been arrested earlier that year for drug possession as he reentered the United States on his way back to Colorado following a vacation in Mexico. The judge in El Paso saw that Venn did not have a prior record and gave him a suspended sentence but required him to see a federal probation officer on a regular basis. On Friday, December 1, 1967, when Venn made his monthly visit to the federal building in Boston's Post Office Square, U.S. marshals arrested him and locked him up. Venn's draft resistance had prompted it. They immediately began preparing him for extradition to Texas, but Venn's lawyer interceded and demanded a hearing to review whether or not probation had been violated. In a hearing held the following Tuesday, Venn was found guilty of violating his probation. His lawyer filed an appeal to have his case transferred from Texas to Boston, but when it was denied, the state of Texas extradited him. After a couple of weeks in jail in Boston, two marshals put him in a car with some other prisoners and started off down the Massachusetts Turnpike toward Texas. Venn's parents appeared in the El Paso courtroom with him, and again the judge let him go. Venn returned to Boston and resumed his work with the Resistance. He continued to fulfill his probation obligations and never heard from the FBI again.

Chris Venn's arrest and cross-country odyssey demonstrated that federal authorities would at least exploit opportunities to punish draft resisters when other factors made it possible. Resistance organizers seized on Venn's story to warn fellow resisters about law-enforcement officials. That the marshals tried to ship Venn to Texas without a probation hearing, in particular, alarmed them. It demonstrated that the authorities were willing to "completely disregard a person's rights in favor of their 'law enforcing' instincts," a notion that most resisters found frightening. "We must always be on the defensive," the newsletter read, "in the event that any of us are arrested."[18]

When it became clear that the authorities did not have plans to move swiftly and decisively against most other draft resisters, however, a flaw in Resistance planning revealed itself: its leaders did not know how best to sustain the movement. As Michael Ferber and Staughton Lynd later wrote, "Beyond the single tactic of draft card turn-ins, [the Resistance] had no political program, no plan of day-to-day work (comparable to, say, voter registration in the South) which could help individuals and groups keep themselves together." According to Neil Robertson, one of the original organizers and a full-time paid staffer by late October, after being "catapulted into notoriety" by the remarkable success of October 16, Resistance leaders "were totally confused about what to do next." They believed they had created an organization, "or the beginnings of one," Robertson later recalled, "but that was always a misunderstanding." Just because 281 men had "in one way or another divested themselves of their draft cards" did *not* mean they had an organization of that many men. In Robertson's view, the Resistance possessed "more of an appearance of solidity in the newspapers than it did in reality."[19]

Indeed, mobilizing the first rank-and-file resisters to sustained levels of protest proved to be very difficult. Just keeping track of all the resisters and other supporters could be a challenge; in the first post–October 16 newsletter, organizers listed more than thirty men who had turned in or burned their draft cards that day for whom addresses remained unknown. When the third newsletter after October 16 went out, Resistance organizers pleaded with rank-and-file resisters to maintain a higher degree of activism. They were beginning to conclude that the "majority" of resisters treated the Resistance as little more than "another extracurricular activity." In particular, they were alarmed that when they called some resisters to ask them to join a squad of men willing to demonstrate at any time, some responded, "I can't be bothered," or "I don't want to be awakened at weird hours," or "I have papers and exams." The organizers retorted in the newsletter, "*All* of us have papers and exams, or something that takes up our time . . . nevertheless, we have lots of work to do and everyone should be doing *something*." Neil Robertson later concluded that by turning in their draft cards, by committing "that defiant act," most men had taken "an incredible step . . . that was a really pivotal event in their lives," or a "watershed event," and that alone made many men feel like they had done their part—and risked enough—to end the war. "For a lot of guys it summarized many, many different things, a good deal of which were not articulated or" of which these men were not "even fully conscious." The attempt to build community among "such a disparate group of people," each of whom had moved toward Resistance for individual reasons, Robertson believed, may have been "doomed to failure."[20]

In some respects, an individual's decision to participate in draft resistance activism beyond turning in his own card depended on his temperament. As Robertson suggested, some rank-and-file resisters wanted to resist quietly, alone. They turned in their cards like everyone else and chose to simply wait for an official response. Bob Bruen, an undergraduate at Northeastern University later remarked that resisting "was something I was going to do and take a stand at that point, but I wasn't going to go around getting people all excited, giving speeches, and participating in all the other stuff. I thought a lot of that was a waste of time." Others chose to work on draft resistance in their own communities. For example, many of the resisters who were seminarians offered draft counseling in the parishes where they conducted youth ministries rather than in the Resistance office. In addition, some resisters were intimidated by the Resistance ringleaders. Howard Marston Jr., a resister from the North Shore town of Rockport remembered that when he visited the Resistance office in Cambridge, "they all made me very nervous" because they were "just so gung-ho." To some eighteen- or nineteen-year-old resisters, an encounter with a Harvard graduate student who worked twelve hours a day almost every day on draft resistance activity could be a little overwhelming.[21]

In several ways, however, Resistance organizers did make efforts to reach out to their brother resisters. Every Monday night, they held potluck dinners in the basement of the Arlington Street Church. They invited all resisters and supporters, and, although the conversation almost always revolved around the war and protest against it, the event remained a social occasion where anyone might feel at home. As one resister later put it, "Mike Ferber, Bill Hunt, and the Community feeling in the resistance were probably more convincing than the war as reasons to hand in your draft card." On October 31, the New England Resistance hosted a masquerade party to raise money for future draft resistance events. It was also one of the ways leaders were trying to bring rank-and-file resisters together in one place. A few weeks later, they arranged some football games between the New England Resistance and the Boston Draft Resistance Group, or the

"Peace Creeps" and the "Commie Dupes," as they called themselves. Anyone could play for the Resistance, and when the team won, the players joked that "rumors have it that BDRG men were weighted down by the mass of their draft cards." The New England Resistance also adopted the Greek letter omega, Ω, as a symbol of their "determination to resist the draft and the war machine until the last." Omega is the symbol for the ohm, the unit of electrical resistance in physics, and, as Michael Ferber later wrote, it suggested many useful metaphors: "friction in the machine, attrition in the supply lines, turbulence in the conduits to Vietnam." Moreover, the omega is also the last letter—or the end—of the Greek alphabet and therefore stood for the end of the draft and the end of the war. It made an ideal symbol for the Resistance, and eventually Resistance chapters nationwide adopted it. Dozens of white buttons with a large black omega printed on each were distributed to resisters as another way of making everyone feel like they were part of a much larger, growing community. Rather than "leave for Canada," NER leaders wrote when they introduced the omega, "we choose to stay in America . . . and build an effective political movement to inaugurate the greater society that we believe in."[22]

Even with some sense of solidarity and community, individuals on their own are often vulnerable, and law-enforcement officials were skilled at bringing pressure to bear on people one at a time. Resisters never reported being interviewed by only one FBI agent; they always worked in twos. Resisters who did not turn them away immediately could expect the standard questions about why they made their decision to resist and whether they had been coerced. Frequently, however, the conversations extended to discussions of the draft system and even the war. Often the agents disagreed with a resister about his duties as a citizen; tensions would rise, and the feds usually left saying something like, "You'll be hearing from us."[23]

Still, although encounters with the FBI were remarkably similar from resister to resister, there were a few notable exceptions. Faculty and administrators at Yale Divinity School were so outraged at the disruption agents caused tracking down resisters that they posted a note where the agents would see it: "Dear FBI, 'Let your foot be seldom in your neighbor's house, lest he become weary of you and despise you.'" One resister who met with two agents in Boston wore a button that said "J. Edgar Hoover Sleeps with a Night Light." The most celebrated meeting took place in the offices of the Boston University *News* between two agents and Alex Jack. Jack had been expecting a visit, and he and his colleagues in the office were well prepared when the agents arrived. Jack welcomed the agents and invited them to sit down. Before they could pose the first question, he turned the tables on them. As he sat down and put his feet up on the desk, he said, "Thank you for coming. I just have a few questions." Then he handed each of them a three-page document called "FBI for the Resistance: Questionnaire." It included a waiver of Fifth Amendment rights not unlike the one agents often used with resisters, a questionnaire, and a pledge sheet that would, when completed, make the agents members of the Resistance. The questionnaire asked questions like "Do you believe the war in Vietnam is illegal, immoral, unjust, and not in the interests of America's national security?" and "Do you feel it is the patriotic and legal duty of the Bureau to investigate President Johnson, Secretary [of State] Rusk, Secretary [of Defense] McNamara, the Joint Chiefs of Staff, the CIA, and General Hershey for war crimes, crimes against humanity, treason . . . on the basis of the US Constitution, the UN Charter, the 1954 Geneva Agreements, and the Nuremberg Statutes?" After a few moments, the agents realized that Alex Jack was giving them a taste of their own medicine. They terminated the interview and left "in a huff." A group of Resistance "agents" followed them and teased them all the way to their car by looking them up and down, scribbling in note pads, and saying "Ah, yes" and "very interesting" until they drove off.[24]

News of this confrontation spread quickly within the antiwar community in Boston. Wayne Hansen, a resister, reported the incident in the *Avatar*, one of the city's leading underground newspapers. The piece also included Hansen's description of two FBI agents who had come to *Avatar*'s offices and then left after failing to find the resister they sought for questioning. Hansen departed the office a few minutes after the agents. Outside, he found the two agents jiggling a coat hanger through the window of their car; they had locked themselves out. He asked the G-men if they would mind him photographing the scene, but when the agents begged him not to, he relented. Stories like this made great copy in movement newspapers. Another group of students at UMass-Boston followed Alex Jack's example. Soon after two agents sat down with a resister in an empty room, a group of the young man's supporters jammed into the room with several cameras and photographed the agents in midsentence. The pictures later appeared on leaflets and in the student paper.[25]

Although such instances of counterharassment of federal agents soon entered Resistance lore because of their bravado and apparent playfulness, the perpetrators of these pranks took their actions seriously. At least some of those resisters felt, as Alex Jack later reflected, that since "the government was immoral and illegitimate," noncooperation made sense. "Now we were kind of moving into that vacuum where you're creating your own government," Jack continued, "almost like a provisional authority in which you begin to assume in the name of humanity, or the Nuremberg statutes, or whatever, some kind of civil authority and put these people on record that their actions are being monitored." The agents, and even Resistance supporters, might have viewed such episodes as pranks, but from the perspective of those who pulled them, they were "an exercise of legitimate counterauthority," Jack said.[26]

Some Resistance activists, particularly those involved in day-to-day operations, eventually found humor in their relations with the FBI. Nan Stone recalls that, at first, meetings with the FBI could be fairly intimidating. FBI agents benefited from a widely held image (bolstered by *The FBI*, the successful television show featuring Efrem Zimbalist Jr.) that portrayed them as elite members of the law-enforcement community. After a while, however, that luster began to fade and Resistance activists grew more bold. "It got to be a game for us," recalled Stone. They learned to pick FBI agents out of a crowd—each agent usually standing incongruously in trench coat, fedora, and sunglasses among scores of young people—and pose for them as the G-men photographed demonstrators. Similarly, Bill Hunt recalls trying to hand out leaflets to FBI agents at a demonstration; when an agent asked him what he did for a living, Hunt, a graduate student in history at Harvard, told him he was that university's head of the anthropophagy (i.e., cannibalism) department. In addition, resisters sometimes found FBI investigative methods and tactics to be amusing, such as the time Harold Hector found three agents, dressed as homeless men sleeping (or pretending to be asleep) in the hallway of his Cambridge apartment building. Although they were "dressed like bums," they were clean shaven and still wore white socks and shiny wingtip shoes. After Hector yelled at them to get out of his hallway, he looked out the front window of his place and watched them all pile into a cream-colored car and speed away. "It was so crazy," he said, "It was even funny at the time."[27]

Whether or not FBI agents were inept, such examples point to the lengths to which they would go to investigate their targets. A reporter from the *Harvard Crimson* and a Resistance sympathizer once saw FBI agents standing outside the Arlington Street Church on a Monday night when the New England Resistance held a potluck supper. As resisters and supporters entered the church, agents would, the reporter claimed, "aim umbrellas at you and take your picture, click." Similarly, Nan Stone learned years later, when she first found photographs in her FBI file (which she acquired through the Freedom of Information Act), that agents had tailed her to a friend's wedding on Cape Cod, an event completely unrelated to draft resistance, and took pictures of her enjoying the celebration with friends. Stone and others also reported finding wiretap devices in their home phones, and everyone in the New England Resistance believed that the office phones were bugged. Given the president's personal interest in the investigation of draft resistance, the use of such tactics on the part of the FBI seems plausible.[28]

These encounters with the FBI notwithstanding, the kind of information the FBI relayed back to Washington and the White House (though resisters could never hope to know the substance of it) is what should have concerned the Resistance most. Resisters would have been interested to know that, from the start, the president seemed a little perplexed about the nature of the protest directed at his administration. At an October 23 meeting with Secretary of State Dean Rusk, Secretary of Defense Robert McNamara, and chairman of the Joint Chiefs of Staff, General Earle Wheeler, Johnson said, "I am concerned as to how we handle the draft card burners who are *handing in* their draft cards at various federal centers." The Resistance practice of allowing the burning of draft cards at ceremonies where cards were collected no doubt contributed to the president's confusion. The FBI capitalized on it. First, the bureau challenged the Resistance's claim that 994 draft cards had been returned to the Justice Department on October 20. According to a memo sent to the president from Ramsey Clark, an FBI inventory of the briefcase found 185 registration certificates and 172 notices of classifications, "which due to duplication appears to represent approximately 300 individuals." In addition, they found 14 facsimile registration cards, photostat sheets with reproductions of 155 registration certificates and notices of classification, an envelope containing the ashes of 67 draft cards, and numerous letters, statements, and discharge orders expressing antiwar and antidraft views. According to these figures 593 people, at most, turned in their cards on that day. By the time President Johnson met with Democratic congressional leaders on October 31, he felt comfortable using a figure of only 256 people and claiming that, according to the FBI, those individuals were "crazy people" with a history of being institutionalized. Furthermore, he said, informants in the Communist Party reported that "the communists decided to do all they could to encourage demonstrations against the draft." The president told his audience that he did not want to sound like a "McCarthyite," but he believed the country was in "a little more danger than we think and someone has to uncover this information."[29]

The reference to Senator Joseph McCarthy is telling because, by 1967, aides to the president frequently saw him exhibit a kind of paranoia regarding communist manipulation of congressional opponents of the war as well as the antiwar movement itself. Speech writer Richard Goodwin later wrote that as early as 1965, "Johnson began to hint privately . . . that he was the target of a gigantic communist conspiracy in which his domestic adversaries were only the players—not conscious participants, perhaps, but unwitting dupes." As far as the president was concerned, this collusion included not only antiwar activists but doves in Congress, too. He used both the Federal Bureau of Investigation and, beginning in 1967, the Central Intelligence Agency to gather information on his critics and especially to seek to find communist ties to these people. Operation Chaos, the illegal domestic spying program run by the CIA to gather information on the antiwar movement, relied on burglaries, interception of activists' mail, and wiretapping in investigating their targets. According to Eric Goldman, historian and special assistant to the president, Johnson claimed to have information from the FBI and CIA proving that the Soviets were manipulating certain antiwar senators. These senators, the president suggested, attended luncheons and social functions at the Soviet embassy; and children of their staffs dated Russians. "The Russians think up things for the [antiwar] senators to say," Johnson argued. "I often know before they do what their speeches are going to say."[30]

In the fall of 1967, the president's belief that communists controlled the opposition to his Vietnam policies became a frequent theme of his meetings that addressed antiwar opinion and activism. Reports fed to Johnson by J. Edgar Hoover convinced the president that the individuals planning the march on the Pentagon were communists; he then leaked this information to the press in hopes of reducing the number of mainstream antiwar sympathizers coming to Washington. In a meeting with congressional leaders a few days after the march, he read a "secret report" that allegedly proved that the demonstration's planners were Hanoi's puppets. The report dealt primarily with a conference that had taken place in Bratislava, Czechoslovakia, a few months earlier, during which some of the activists, the report charged, had made contacts with the National Liberation Front and the North Vietnamese government. House Minority Leader Gerald Ford (R-Michigan) found the president's charges so compelling that, from the floor of the House, he remarked that the march had been "cranked up by Hanoi." Several days later, the president told Ramsey Clark, "I'm not going to let 200,000 of these people ruin everything for the 200 million Americans." Johnson wanted investigated any antiwar activists who left the country: "where they go, why they are going, and if they're going to Hanoi, how are we going to keep them from getting back into this country." By mid-November when CIA director Richard Helms presented a report concluding that "no significant evidence" existed to "prove Communist control or direction of the U.S. peace movement or its leaders," Johnson and several of his aides refused to believe it. They simply could not understand, as Joe Califano said, how "a cause that is so clearly right for the country . . . would be so widely attacked if there were not some [foreign] force behind it." Despite the evidence to the contrary, the president continued to press the FBI and CIA to investigate the antiwar movement for its ties to the communist world.[31]

The job of uncovering information on draft resistance belonged primarily to the FBI, but the accuracy of their intelligence remains suspect. Given the demographics of the resisters from Boston, the assertion that most of the people who had returned their draft cards were former mental patients is silly. Perhaps only J. Edgar Hoover knew why the FBI characterized the protesters this way. The question of how many actual draft cards were turned in, however, is another issue. Unfortunately, neither side (the resisters nor the government) can today support its own figures; the evidence is gone.[32] Michael Ferber acknowledges that, although he brought actual draft cards from Boston, the briefcase left at the Department of Justice did contain photocopies of hundreds of other draft cards. These copies, he believes, came from many different parts of the country where resisters had turned in the originals to their local draft boards, FBI offices, and U.S. Attorneys; in order for the cards to be counted in the nationwide tally in Washington, these groups sent copies of the ones they had collected and had already returned to the Justice Department. From the administration's perspective, the facsimiles of draft cards did not constitute sufficient evidence to warrant further investigation or prosecution of the men who turned them in. Stating the "true" number of cards left with John McDonough also helped to make the Resistance seem less significant as a force in the antiwar movement. If the FBI had its figures right, 256 returned draft cards would not have been very significant to the White House. Nevertheless, the president wanted something done about it.

THE SELECTIVE SERVICE RESPONDS

On the evening of October 20, when his concern over communist control of the antiwar movement seemed to be at an all-time high, the president continued to stew over the draft card turn-in at the Justice Department. According to Joe Califano, he seemed genuinely bewildered about why anyone would want to burn a draft card and also wondered who the "dumb sonofabitch" was who "would let somebody leave a bunch of draft cards in front of the Justice Department and then let them just walk away." In fact, the day's events only reinforced the president's concern about the attorney general's commitment to prosecuting draft violators. Consequently, Johnson went after the resisters by another route. That night, in addition to instructing his attorney general to keep him informed about draft resisters, the president called the director of Selective Service, to see if anything else could be done. Even before he had received the FBI's analysis of the evidence left at the Justice Department, Johnson gave Hershey "an earful" about the need to punish draft protesters. According to George Q. Flynn, a historian of the draft and Hershey's biographer, the old soldier responded by telling the president about the provision in the draft law that discussed the drafting of any registrant who becomes delinquent. In Hershey's view, turning in or burning a draft card, both illegal forms of protest, seemed obvious cases of delinquency. "Johnson immediately approved the idea and instructed Hershey to send out the orders." This directive ultimately led to an embarrassing spat between Ramsey Clark and Hershey and a more serious crisis over how to handle dissenters who targeted the draft.[33]

Following the orders of his commander in chief, Hershey moved to quash draft resistance the only way he could. Just four days after Coffin and the others left the bag of draft cards at the Justice Department, the Selective Service chief issued Local Board Memorandum No. 85, which effectively established procedures for the drafting of resisters. It said, in part:

Whenever a local board receives an abandoned or mutilated registration certificate or current notice of classification which had been issued to one of its own registrants, the following action is recommended:

(A) Declare the registrant to be delinquent for failure to have the card in his possession.

(B) Reclassify the registrant into a class available for service as a delinquent.

(C) At the expiration of the time for taking an appeal, if no appeal has been taken and the delinquency has not been removed, order the registrant to report for induction.

On October 26, Hershey followed this memo with a letter to all members of the Selective Service System explaining the rationale for the new policy. Before laying out his argument, he emphasized that the military obligation for young men was universal and that deferments were given *only* "when they serve the national interest." Any action that "violates the Military Selective Service Act or the regulations, or the related processes," he wrote, "cannot be in the national interest." Therefore, he continued, "it follows that those who violate them should be denied deferment in the national interest." Local boards who receive information regarding an illegal protest by a registrant, Hershey said, should reopen the classification of the registrant and "classify him anew." He also asked local board officials to consider sending some cases to the nearest U.S. Attorney, but as Flynn notes, the board members had years of experience and they "knew the director preferred a draft action to a prison term."[34]

When news of the Hershey directives surfaced in early November, a firestorm of protest erupted. Scores of letters poured into the White House. Big-city newspapers across the country, including the *Boston Globe* and the *Boston Record American*, criticized Hershey. The *Globe*'s editors wondered whether Hershey had "outlasted his usefulness" in attempting to use the U.S. armed forces as a "penal colony." The director's "meat axe approach" to draft resistance demeaned the draft act, they said. Even veterans groups felt disgraced by Hershey's action. Eugene D. Byrd, chair of the American Veterans Committee sent a telegram to the White House urging "the removal of General Hershey as Director of Selective Service System as essential to the national interest." Most of the protest focused on the vague wording of Hershey's letter. If, as Hershey declared, "any action" that violated Selective Service "processes" could be considered illegal and not in the nation's interest, critics envisioned thousands of youths being reclassified simply because they participated in a sit-in at a local board. They remembered the 1965 reclassification of student protesters at Ann Arbor, Michigan, and did not want to see it repeated.[35]

Since Hershey's instructions to local boards originated with his conversation with the president, the general expected Johnson to back up his letters. Hershey, too, remembered the outrage over the reclassification of the Ann Arbor protesters, so he sought to solidify his position by authoring an executive order on the subject, which he submitted to the White House for Johnson's signature and, thus, his endorsement. The executive order would have changed the regulations so that the definition of delinquency would include "positive actions" against the draft in addition to the standard provisions requiring a failure to register or appear for induction. Anyone disrupting the operation of a draft board, even through picketing or sitting in, would be subject to prosecution. As the first draft of the executive order circulated around the White House, many aides urged restraint.[36]

Some members of Congress also severely criticized Hershey. Senators Edward Kennedy, Philip Hart, Mark Hatfield, Jacob Javits, and others co-sponsored a bill to outlaw the drafting of protesters. In the House, John Moss, a Democrat from California, led the charge against the director. In a series of letters to Hershey, Moss, then chair of the Foreign Operations and Government Information Subcommittee of the Committee on Government Operations, called repeatedly for Hershey's resignation. "Your October 26 'recommendations' to local Selective Service Boards concerning reclassification procedures," Moss wrote in the first missive, "can only serve to underscore once again your callous disregard and contempt for the law, the Constitution, and the rights of Americans. . . . I cannot comprehend how a person in your position could exhibit so blatantly [sic] a total lack of understanding of fundamental democratic principles." Hershey's responses, often "unintelligible and wholly confused," according to Moss, only made matters worse and prompted Moss to continue pressing for the general's resignation.[37]

Several aides to the president joined the chorus of protest regarding Hershey's directive and the proposed executive order. Although most of them felt the same contempt for the draft resisters as their boss, these advisers unanimously cautioned the president (through Joe Califano) that signing Hershey's executive order would be extremely ill-advised. Special counsel Larry Temple, deputy special counsel Larry Levinson, and White House aide Matt Nimetz each wrote to Califano urging the president to rein in Hershey and not to issue the executive order. All three emphasized that criminal courts—not draft boards—were the proper forums for imposing penalties on law breakers and that a prison sentence—not service in the armed forces—was the most appropriate punishment. "The obvious argument," wrote Temple, "is that if induction is to be used as a type of punishment here then what are the hundreds of thousands of young men who serve willingly being punished for?" Califano agreed. In a memo to Johnson, he wrote: "I believe it is important for you to stay out of this controversy" and recommended against the executive order. He advised the president in this way not because he thought Hershey had stepped out of line. In fact, Califano speculated that Hershey might actually have had the authority to reclassify draft resisters, and if he did, he wrote to the president, "then he should continue to proceed on that basis . . . and keep you out of it." Hershey, Califano urged, should be left to "carry the can" alone.[38]

Most important, however, the president's own attorney general, Ramsey Clark, disagreed with Hershey's new policy and proposed executive order. That Clark and Hershey shared a long personal history complicated matters. Hershey had known Ramsey Clark and his father, former Supreme Court justice Tom Clark, for years. When the elder Clark had been an assistant attorney general during the Second World War, he had prosecuted some of the earliest draft violation cases; he had also protested punitive reclassification of registrants at that time. By 1967, Hershey made a habit of telling people that he had known the current attorney general since young Ramsey's high school years. To Clark, Hershey was "a little nutty but basically sweet." On the other hand, the director's new policies obviously had not been authorized by Congress and Clark believed that there were "grave doubts" about their constitutionality. Even if induction could be used as punishment, he wrote, "registrants are certainly entitled to procedural due process in the proceedings for determination of whether they have violated the law and should be punished."[39]

Ramsey Clark's views on the prosecution of draft resisters originated in an understanding much deeper than the law, however. In 1944, Clark joined the marines at the age of seventeen (though he was ineligible to go overseas), but many of his friends chose to be conscientious objectors to the war. "In many ways, the most sensitive and thoughtful and good (if there is such a thing) people among my classmates were those who resisted," he reflected in 1998. "And some of them were permanently hurt by the social ostracization" that resulted among their peers. That ostracization made a lasting impression on the future attorney general. Clark felt that the nation had "needlessly damaged many of [its] best young people" and that it should always seek to eschew doing so again. Inflicting such pain on people of conscience is not, he said, "a decent thing for a society to . . . expose people to." In addition, Clark had seen enough draft-law prosecutions to conclude that those who lacked money or status, "the poorer and defenseless," were the ones who went to jail: "And to see lonely youngsters (because it's finally lonely when it happens to you; you're by yourself even if all your buddies get indicted, too, you're by yourself) face this alone, face this without resources more times than not, face it without maturity or experience or background, is cruel and not productive of the best law because the law wouldn't be thoroughly considered; each case would just be processed through." Clark therefore felt a duty to "avoid injuring innocent people." Resisters, he believed, were not innocent in the sense that they had not broken any laws but innocent in that they were "not engaged in an act of moral turpitude"; they were "acting on conscience and they were probably right," he said. About Vietnam-era resisters, he later remarked: "These are the gentlest we have. And these are the ones that we should want to protect the most, perhaps. They tend to have more initiative—it's a hell of a lot easier to go than not to go." Consequently, he instructed all U.S. Attorneys that they were not to prosecute any cases in which a registrant had, because of draft resistance activism, seen his call for induction accelerated thanks to Hershey's directive.[40]

The attorney general's action—or inaction—displeased Johnson. Clark claims that the president leaned on him only lightly, yet Joe Califano's records recall a November 18 meeting between the president, Hershey, and Clark in which Johnson started off by demanding to know why the Justice Department had prosecuted only 1,300 of 7,300 men who had been arrested for failing to report for induction. Clark, who today is certain that Hershey had been "pumping" the president with statistics on draft violators who were not being prosecuted, responded that many of these no-shows were unintentional and, therefore, should not have been arrested in the first place. When Clark concluded by saying that he was doing all he could under current law, the president blustered, "If you need more laws, submit your suggestions at once!" Shortly after the meeting, Johnson sent another memorandum to Clark detailing every criminal statute on sabotage, espionage, and interference with the government. He directed Clark to pass the information along to all U.S. Attorneys with instructions to prosecute anyone who participated in illegal acts covered by these laws. "If you need further legislation in this connection," Johnson again commanded, "please submit your suggestions at once." Indeed, when Congressman Mendel Rivers heard about Clark's concerns regarding punitive reclassifications, he said, "If there exists the slightest doubt in the attorney general's mind that General Hershey's action is not fully supported by the law, he need only say so and I am certain the Congress will correct any deficiency."[41]

Despite the president's intense interest in the Justice Department's pursuit of draft resisters and his role in encouraging Hershey to go after protesters, Johnson ultimately grew tentative on the issue of reclassifying resisters. He offered no public sign of support to Hershey, and the general's proposed executive order never made it out of the White House. And when Johnson received advance warning of an unflattering *New York Times* article on Hershey in early December, he brought Hershey together with Ramsey Clark again to issue a joint announcement on the subject, which he hoped would lay to rest any more concerns regarding the director's memoranda on punitive reclassification. Before the White House released the statement, Johnson himself read it and, according to Joe Califano, approved "every word of it."[42]

Both Clark and Hershey compromised on the content of the communiqué. Hershey consented to leave lawful protesters alone. There would be no more Ann Arbors, a point repeatedly emphasized in most press reports. But Clark gave up even more. Despite his own experiences as a young man and his philosophical beliefs regarding the prosecution of those acting on conscience, the attorney general went along with Hershey's existing policy of reclassifying the men who turned in their draft cards and pledged the Justice Department's cooperation in prosecuting those who refused an accelerated induction resulting from reclassification:

> A registrant who violates any duty affecting his own status (for example, giving false information, failing to appear for an examination, or failing to have a draft card) may be declared a "delinquent" registrant by his local draft board. . . . When a person is declared to be a delinquent registrant by his local board, he may be reclassified and becomes subject to the highest priority for induction if otherwise qualified. If he fails to step forward for induction, he is subject to prosecution by the Department of Justice.

The Justice Department, meanwhile, would not prosecute a draft resister simply for his failing to possess his draft card. In addition, the department planned to form a special unit in the Criminal Division in Washington to oversee the prosecution of draft-law violators. U.S. attorneys general across the country could expect to work closely with this new unit in bringing cases against draft resisters in their cities.[43]

Most Justice Department lawyers regarded the joint statement as a victory for the attorney general: it stopped Hershey from targeting demonstrators and made no commitment to prosecute men who returned their draft cards. Years later, however, as Ramsey Clark reflected upon his acquiescence to Hershey's reclassification and induction policy, he acknowledged the difficult situation he had been in during that period. Even though he saw draft card turn-ins as an issue of free speech and an expression of conscience, he felt obligated to uphold the Selective Service laws. Clark believed that if one accepted the idea of a conscription system like the Selective Service (which he did because he thought it was "more compatible with civilian authority and government, and less likely to lead to militarism"), then the Selective Service rules had to be upheld. "As much as I opposed the war," he said, "the law has to have integrity. It has to do what it says even if what it says is wrong. I thought, therefore, that I had to act to protect the Selective Service System."[44]

At the same time, however, Ramsey Clark sought to minimize the impact of the joint policy on individual resisters. He asked John Van de Kamp to head up the Criminal Division's new special unit on draft resistance, and rather than have him focus on individual draft-law violators, Clark instructed him to look into the existence of a possible conspiracy aimed at inducing young men to resist the draft. Clark was much more concerned with the notion that older advisers may have been soliciting draft-age men to resist the draft than with pursuing individual resisters. Until the Justice Department could make a determination on the conspiracy, therefore, Clark directed all U.S. Attorneys to suspend prosecution of men who had refused induction when the call to report was based on a punitive reclassification. This order effectively nullified one part of his agreement with General Hershey, who wanted to see resisters reclassified and indicted.[45]

In the end, in spite of Clark's concessions, the joint statement did little to allay the controversy caused by General Hershey's October instructions to local boards. To the president's dismay, Hershey violated an agreement negotiated by Joe Califano that neither Clark nor Hershey would discuss the issue with the press. Within days, the Selective Service director told Neil Sheehan of the *New York Times* that the recent clarification did not invalidate his October letter. Furthermore, he acknowledged a fundamental difference of opinion between himself and the attorney general regarding the definition of delinquency. "When a fellow goes into a draft board and pours ink on his own file, then there's no disagreement," Hershey told Sheehan, "he's affecting his own status. But when he goes in and pours ink on his brother's file—there's the disagreement." In the latter case, Hershey would declare the perpetrator delinquent and accelerate his induction process. Clark, on the other hand, would not assert delinquency but would have him prosecuted for criminal conduct. Sheehan's piece caused further outrage among the war's critics and the public, and it left Hershey backpedaling.[46]

Suddenly, the already beleaguered president was caught in the middle of the "embarrassing public spectacle" of Clark and Hershey's feud. Califano appealed to Johnson for some kind of decision, complaining that Hershey "keeps citing you [Johnson] to Ramsey and me as authority for his earlier memorandum." Still, the president tried to stay out of the way. Only when the presidents of eight Ivy League colleges and universities signed a letter of protest did Johnson instruct Califano to write to them with the pledge that he would not advocate using the draft as "an instrument to repress and punish unpopular views." This, too, did little to settle the issue. As Colonel Paul Feeney, the Massachusetts director of Selective Service noted, the joint statement reinforced existing policy. Illegal forms of protest, he said, included nonpossession or mutilation of draft cards; therefore, anyone turning in or burning a draft card could expect to be reclassified and called for induction. Only the courts would be able to settle the issue once and for all, and it seemed that in 1968 they would get their chance as dozens of draft resisters challenged punitive reclassification across the country that fall.[47]

On the whole, the country's four thousand local draft boards did not handle draft resister cases according to any universal standards. Unfortunately, the Selective Service System destroyed all of its local board records in the late 1970s when the agency went into "deep standby" status, making it impossible to learn how individual draft boards interpreted directives from General Hershey. But the anecdotal evidence that survives shows that some boards clearly took a hard-line approach and immediately reclassified resisters per Hershey's instructions. By December 1, 1967, draft boards had declared approximately twenty-five of the men who had turned in their draft cards at the Arlington Street Church delinquent and changed their classifications to 1-A. Eventually, almost two-thirds of Boston's draft resisters received reclassification notices from their draft boards.[48]

When the New England Resistance learned that the government might reclassify rather than indict resisters immediately for failure to carry their draft cards, the organization urged resisters to notify the Resistance office promptly if they thought their local boards might take that course. They then directed resisters to a group of lawyers who would plan an "aggressive legal injunction as soon as possible," before the resisters received induction notices. As the new year approached, more and more men needed the legal assistance offered by a growing number of antiwar lawyers. Of course, draft resisters simply could have let the Selective Service reclassify them and call them for induction and in turn, they could have refused induction and awaited prosecution (as some, indeed, did; see Chapter 7). The sense of strength they derived from the October 16 service, however, emboldened them to seek confrontation with the government not just in the courts but anywhere they could find it. Legal injunctions against local boards, for example, fit neatly into the broader strategy of putting their bodies "upon the gears of the machine."[49]

At the same time, some draft boards did not follow General Hershey's instructions with the same degree of enthusiasm as others did. Many apparently tried to give resisters a second chance and, consequently, tested some resisters' commitment to their cause. Both David Clennon, the Yale Drama School graduate student, and Bob Bruen, the Northeastern University undergraduate, were offered new draft cards with their student deferments intact. In Bruen's case, his local board, located in Malden, Massachusetts, wrote to him to tell him that he should apply for a new draft card if he had lost or misplaced his originals. Three weeks later, when Bruen did not reply, they simply sent him a new card with his original deferment. Clennon's draft board in Waukegan, Illinois, did the same thing (though without the preliminary letter). The Resistance had warned its members that their draft boards might try to tempt them, "bribe" them, "with a luxurious deferment or exemption." If that happened, Resistance leaders advised, the rank and file was to "treat it [the deferment] just like . . . the last one." Soon after receiving a new card from his draft board, Clennon turned it in at a ceremony in New Haven similar to the one at Arlington Street. A small number of resisters chose not to be so aggressive. Out of 121 resisters surveyed for this study, nineteen (15.7 percent) either asked their draft board for a new draft card or accepted the unsolicited one sent to them. Bob Bruen, for instance, simply did nothing after his draft board sent him a new card. He did not carry it with him, but neither did he send it back. Bruen figured that someone on his local board knew his father, a career military man, and decided to give him another chance; perhaps his father had intervened on his behalf. To this day, Bruen is not sure why his draft board did not go after him. In any case, he decided not to return the new card. "I just took it as it was pointless to push it," he said later, "because if they chose to pretend that I didn't do anything wrong, they weren't that interested." Draft boards did not have to worry about resisters who, for whatever reason, did not rise to the challenge and resist all over again. Naturally, this greatly simplified the situation for both the resister and his local board.[50]

Some resisters heard little or nothing from their local boards. Given the intensity of debate regarding official response to resisters in Washington, that some men would be altogether ignored seemed odd. After all, the strategy of turning in one's draft card appealed to many men because they believed it made it easier for the government to track them down. Thirty years later, the reasons behind draft board inconsistencies are no more obvious, but the example of Boston's resistance community offers some clues. In Boston, 27 out of 105 men (25.7 percent) who turned in their draft cards (this does not include those who burned their draft cards) were not contacted at all by their draft boards following their act of defiance. The majority of this group were much older than the average resister. In fact, 12 of the 18 resisters over the age of twenty-six—two-thirds—were left alone by their draft boards. In these cases, it seems, local boards decided to go after the men more likely to be drafted once they were stripped of their deferments. In other instances, some draft boards appear to have steered clear of resistance movement leaders. Alex Jack's draft board, for instance, never contacted him after October 16 even though he was classified 1-A when he returned his card. Bill Hunt, on the other hand, received a letter from his Akron, Ohio, draft board demanding to know why it suddenly found itself in possession of his draft card. It instructed him to explain himself either in Akron or at the nearest draft board. Rather than return to Ohio, Hunt visited the Cambridge draft board with a film crew led by Norm Fruchter of Newsreel, the underground film collective. He made a speech about the war to several bewildered draft board secretaries. He never heard from his draft board (or a U.S. Attorney) again. That Hunt held a fatherhood deferment (3-A) at the time may have contributed to his draft board's reluctance to punish him, but it could be that the Akron draft board, like Alex Jack's, wanted nothing to do with a crusading draft resister. Drafting him would only make a martyr of him and give him a forum for more antiwar speeches.[51]

Perhaps the most striking instance of the government ignoring a draft resister (purposefully or not) occurred in the case of former *BU News* editor Ray Mungo. During Mungo's tenure at the school paper, the *News* had become a leading critic of the Johnson administration's policies in Vietnam. Mungo's name and image became well known throughout the city. After turning in his draft card on October 16, Mungo's Lawrence, Massachusetts, draft board called him for induction (he was 1-A at the time of the turn-in). Mungo responded by doing just about everything he could to draw the government's ire. About 600 people turned out at the gates of the Boston Army Base on the morning of Mungo's scheduled pre-induction physical and watched him stand on the hood of a car, tear up his induction papers and cast them into the frigid coastal wind. He never set foot on the base itself and thus did not appear for his physical. Despite this flagrant violation of the law, neither the Selective Service nor the Justice Department moved to punish him. He received additional orders for physicals and induction, and the FBI interviewed him several times, but nothing ever came of it. Today, Mungo is certain that his notoriety in Boston protected him from prosecution. "It was an open and shut case," he said. "I expected to be prosecuted . . . but they never prosecuted me . . . I can only conclude that they didn't want to give me the right to make a martyr out of myself"[52]

In the first weeks and months following October 16, draft resisters were left with few clues about how the administration would react to their protest. And so, for many resisters, the wait—the uncertain, awkward dance with the government—continued. The experience of earlier draft resisters like the men from the Committee for Non-Violent Action, who were indicted within a month of their protest, led the new resisters to believe that their dissent would be handled with dispatch by law enforcement authorities. Yet, despite FBI interviews, no arrests or indictments followed October 16. Even the proposed response of the Selective Service—the reclassification of resisters—clearly did not have the full support of everyone in Washington. But as resisters awaited their fate, other consequences of their actions began to unfold. Family members, friends, employers, and others alternately expressed anger, support, and concern. Resistance organizers, meanwhile, had to plan to settle in for a long fight with the government rather than a quick knockout. They needed more financial and moral support. Most important, they needed to maintain the momentum generated on October 16.

6 GETTING BY WITH A LITTLE HELP FROM THEIR FRIENDS

> You all know me and are aware that I am unable to remain silent. At times to be silent is to lie. For silence can be interpreted as acquiescence.
>
> —Miguel de Unamuno, Salamanca, Spain, 1936

On the eve of the October 16 draft card turn-in at the Arlington Street Church, David Clennon wrote a letter to his parents from his New Haven apartment. He drank heavily that night as he wrestled with the prospect of returning his draft card. He found himself, he later said, without "anybody that I could really confide in." That night, he dropped the letter to his folks and another to his Waukegan, Illinois, draft board into a street-corner mailbox. Clennon awoke the next morning with a mean hangover, but he drove to Boston with some friends and, inspired by Howard Zinn's speech, turned in his draft card.[1]

A few days after the Arlington Street ceremony, Virginia and Cecil Clennon received their son's letter. They were not pleased. David's sixteen-year-old sister, Jean, immediately noticed the tension. Ordinarily, whenever her brother wrote home from Yale, her parents left the letters out for Jean to read. This time, however, they broke with routine, and when Jean inquired about the letter she knew had arrived, her mother withheld it. "Your brother's done something bad," she explained in a tone that Jean understood to mean that there would be no further discussion. The girl walked away puzzled, wondering just what kind of crime her brother had committed.[2]

Virginia Clennon, in particular, always maintained her family's privacy assiduously, and although no one knows the extent to which she and her husband discussed David's situation between themselves, with others she limited mention of it to brief one-sentence pronouncements. Jean, for example, last heard her mother refer to it that first night after the letter came. She said simply, "Your father is going out to see Dave," and they never talked about it again, even after her father returned from Connecticut. Likewise, Virginia brought up David's situation only rarely to her sister, Joan, and never mentioned it to her older daughter, Kathy, both of whom also lived in Waukegan.[3]

Meanwhile, the tension between David and his parents sharpened. Cecil Clennon boarded a plane bound for New Haven within days of receiving the letter. He hoped, as David later recalled, to "talk some sense" into his son. But the younger Clennon anticipated the visit and arranged for a meeting between his father and Yale chaplain William Sloane Coffin Jr. David figured that since his parents were "good Catholics," talking to a man of the cloth (even though Coffin is Presbyterian) might help his father to better understand his position. The meeting did not go well. Although the discussion remained respectful, Cecil Clennon disagreed emphatically with Coffin's views of the war. He expressed his concern for his son's well-being and left without being comforted or persuaded by the pastor. Before he returned to Illinois, Clennon urged his son to seek a job teaching in the inner city; David's draft board would give him a deferment, he reasoned, and he would send money to David to support him. The son refused, and a kind of cold war began between them.[4]

The FBI soon made the crisis in the Clennon family even worse. Within weeks of the draft card turn-in, two agents from the Chicago field office knocked on the door of the Clennons' house in Waukegan. They were not home, so the agents went next door and spoke to their neighbors, inquiring about David. Naturally, word slowly began to spread that Cecil and Virginia Clennon's son was in trouble with the FBI. It is unlikely that the FBI had any legitimate reason to ask anyone about David Clennon or his whereabouts. His case, no doubt, had been referred to them by his local board after it received his letter and/or draft card; the FBI had all the information it needed to find him. These visits were aimed more at pressuring his parents into getting their son to reconsider his actions. And a visit to the neighbors added a twist: the possibility that their peers might learn of their son's illegal activities.[5]

The threat of such humiliation could be a powerful motivator. Except for David, the Clennons never told anyone else about the FBI visit, not even their daughters or other relatives. Virginia Clennon, her sister said, "wanted everything to be right, to look right, to seem right. . . . [She] didn't want any crises in her life." Both her son's defiance and the potential embarrassment of a public trial caused her considerable anxiety. "I sensed from her," David reflected years later, "that it would be a profound humiliation just to have a son on trial for *anything*, never mind a matter of principle. . . . She feared that there would be a tinge of the unpatriotic about it." David's sister Kathy confirmed that her parents "were extremely concerned with 'what would people think.'" And so, when another Waukegan youth, Bill Drew, went on trial for "crimes" in connection with his own antiwar activism but was supported by his parents, Virginia Clennon remarked to her sister that "of course the Drews are a house united whereas we are a house divided."[6]

It would be a mistake, however, to view the Clennons' reaction to their son's draft resistance as rooted solely in a fear of public embarrassment, for the source of their response grew out of the complicated dynamics of familial relationships. According to David Clennon, his father was a dedicated family man. A veteran of World War II (he served in a clerical position in North Africa), Cecil Clennon worked as an accountant and later a data processing supervisor for the Johns Manville Corporation from 1946 until he retired. He worked nine to five every day, rarely more, and always put his family first. He was very active in the Boy Scouts, serving as scoutmaster of the Mount Vernon, New York, troop to which David belonged. Under his father's guidance, David became an Eagle Scout at thirteen, and he also won the *Ad Altare Dei* award for outstanding Catholic scout. Clennon's mother was a homemaker and local Democratic Party activist. Both of his parents were lifelong Democrats and encouraged their children to get involved in mainstream politics; in 1960, they urged David and his sister Kathy to campaign door-to-door in support of John F. Kennedy. In 1964 they supported Lyndon Johnson.[7]

The Clennons were an active, liberal, middle-class family, and in 1967, with the exception of David, they still believed in their president. Lyndon Johnson possessed more information than the general public knew, they thought, and must have good reason for pursuing the current course in Vietnam. Consequently, they very much disapproved of their son's protest—especially his method of protest—against the war. In addition, as members of the World War II generation, the Clennons harbored a strong sense of duty to their country. Not only did Cecil Clennon serve in the war, but both of Virginia's brothers fought in it, too, including one who was killed. Although David's sister Kathy believes today that her mother would have been devastated if David had been drafted, her Aunt Joan (Virginia's

series of indignities ultimately resulting in estrangement between a son and his parents. By the time Chris Venn resisted and prompted his extradition to Texas, his parents were resigned to accepting that he had—at twenty years old—stepped out from under their influence. No arguments resulted, but Venn's parents, although they went to El Paso, offered him no support for his stand on the war or the draft. The philosophical gulf that existed between some resisters and their parents frequently meant that the issue went undiscussed. In rare cases, though, the initial disaffection created by draft resistance could be bridged. Neil Robertson's father, for example, at first saw his son's draft card turn-in as the culmination of troubles that began with his withdrawal from Dartmouth College. Robertson's parents chose to break off contact, and they essentially "disowned" him. When Robertson informed his fellow resisters of his deteriorating relationship with his parents, one of them suggested that he send them a copy of Howard Zinn's book, *Vietnam: The Logic of Withdrawal* and the Selective Service memo on channeling. Two weeks later, his parents wrote a letter of apology and told him that they supported his resistance. In an amazing transformation, Robertson's mother soon got involved with antiwar and women's liberation activism; his father went to the Democratic National Convention in Chicago in August 1968 as a delegate for Eugene McCarthy and was arrested after leaving the convention to march with comedian and presidential candidate Dick Gregory. Neil Robertson posted bail for his father.[12]

There is not much evidence to suggest that many parents did completely disown their sons because of draft resistance. The New England Resistance Master File noted that the parents of one resister from Northeastern University should not be contacted because, as the card read, they "don't want anything to do with him." Such cases seem rare, however. What appears to have occurred more frequently is that resisters who knew their parents well enough to realize that resistance would not meet with their approval simply chose not to discuss it with them. As one resister wrote, "While I never informed my parents of my 'activities,' if I had I'm sure their reaction would have fallen into the 'strongly disapproved' category." There did not seem to be much of a reason for a resister to talk about his resistance activity with parents who he knew would not understand or would not approve; they experienced enough stress just waiting for the FBI to visit. Debates with mom and dad over draft resistance would not improve the situation. Keeping parents in the dark actually made matters easier for those resisters who expected disapproval. Resisters such as David Clennon who were not sure how their parents would respond, only to experience disapproval, suffered the most. "I thought they might well disapprove," Clennon reflected in 1998. "I hoped they would understand. I hoped that they would see my actions as a reflection of values that I learned from them."[13]

Some parents could understand their sons' outrage over the war but disagreed with their method of protest. Total noncooperation seemed too extreme. Virginia Clennon thought David's willful surrender of his deferment was foolhardy. Similarly, Homer Jack, the father of New England Resistance founder Alex Jack, would have preferred that his son seek conscientious objector status while still protesting against the war. The parents of Michael Zigmond, a postdoctoral fellow at MIT, believed the strategy of draft resistance was futile. Michael and his comrades would never get enough men to resist the draft to actually slow or stop the war, they asserted. But Zigmond himself argued that if he wanted to continue speaking out against the war, doing so would be much easier if he refused to cooperate with the Selective Service than if he submitted to their rules.[14]

Most of all, parents of resisters just worried. They worried about their sons' safety and about their futures. When they learned of a son's decision to resist, the prospect of a prison sentence loomed most prominently in their minds. Most middle-class parents could not bear to think of one of their children in a place as alien to their placid suburban lifestyles as a federal penitentiary. On one level, then, they quickly grew concerned with the physical protection of their law-breaking sons. This describes the parents of Ray Mungo and David Clennon. And this concern for safety was not limited to parents who disapproved of draft resistance. Indeed, several respondents indicated that although they supported them, their folks could not help but be nervous and anxious about the course of action chosen by their boys. One resister said that both of his parents were "fearful of the effects of a jail term on me," and another noted that his parents did not want him to go to jail any more than they wanted him to go to Vietnam. Like any parents who have given so much of themselves to raise a child until he is eighteen or nineteen years old only to see him drafted into the army, the parents of resisters feared losing their sons—only in the case of resisters' parents, not on a battlefield but in a prison. They also feared how American society might treat them years later, long after the war ended.

Resistance simply did not fit the vision of life that parents planned for their children. Harold Hector's family thought his draft resistance activity as both a resister and a draft counselor might keep him from ever getting a decent job. Women who worked in draft resistance organizations especially heard this line of thinking from their parents. The father of Connie Field, a full-time worker in the New England Resistance office after October 16, kept telling her that if she kept this kind of behavior up, she would never get a good position working for the government. Likewise, the parents of Bliss Matteson, an office manager for the Boston Draft Resistance Group, feared that she was losing out in the "career chase." Matteson's summary of the effect of her draft resistance work on her relationship with her parents seems to fit the experience of most participants: draft resistance, she said, "didn't really wreck our relationship, but I think it was very hard for them."[15]

At the same time, of course, that 27 percent or so of parents who supported their resister sons included the rare few who appeared fearless. Howard Marston of Rockport, Massachusetts, took the position that until his son, Howard "Chick" Jr., reached the age of twenty-one, he and Chick's mother were responsible for him. Therefore, the elder Marston forbade his son to submit to the draft. Marston later recalled that he had his parents' "full support and then some." At times he felt that his parents—especially his father—"really pushed" him into resistance. By the time the younger Marston refused induction (see Chapter 7), his father had become a virtual fixture on Boston TV newscasts and in the papers. Reporters found the flamboyant Marston Sr. to be articulate and controversial, so they covered his son's draft case closely.[16]

On the whole, very few parents took their support of their sons' resistance as far as Howard Marston. And most disapproved of draft resistance and were simply bewildered by their sons' actions. Resisters who hoped for support from home, then, often had to turn elsewhere. David Clennon found some comfort in regular telephone discussions with his Aunt Joan, but many resisters found that just as their parents disapproved, so too did others from whom they might ordinarily expect support. Sometimes resisters overestimated the amount of sympathy that they could hope for from others. Draft resistance, it turned out, could get pretty lonely.

UNEXPECTED CONSEQUENCES

Resisters may have been able to predict a possible clash with their parents following their protest, but they did not anticipate the fallout that resulted in their places of employment, their schools, or among people from whom they thought they could expect understanding. In one of its first post–October 16 newsletters, the New England Resistance called on its readers to help assemble a job file for resisters "in the event they are fired."

In just a short time, a few resisters had lost their jobs because of their expression of dissent, and the Resistance hoped that sympathetic employers and friends would be able to provide temporary or permanent work for those who lost their jobs.[17]

The Reverend J. Michael Jupin, newly installed as an associate rector at an Episcopal church in Winchester, Massachusetts (a suburb just north of Boston), learned the hard way about the combustible effect of one man's decision to part with his draft card. News of Jupin turning in his registration certificate to Rev. Coffin at the Arlington Street Church on October 16 stunned his parishioners at the Parish of the Epiphany. Neither the twenty-five-year-old Jupin nor the church's rector, the Reverend Jack Bishop, had any idea that they were about to set off a firestorm of protest when they announced Jupin's resistance in the weekly parish newsletter, *Three Crowns of the Epiphany*. Indeed, Bishop (who wrote the newsletter) sandwiched the rather matter-of-fact announcement of Jupin's stand between other routine parish notes. He indicated that Jupin returned his draft card and that the associate rector would report on his draft protest (and his experience in the march on the Pentagon) in a sermon on November 26. Here, however, Bishop misjudged his flock. Most parishioners, it turned out, could not wait over a month to hear from Jupin—or from Bishop. Not a few assumed that Jupin's resistance and Bishop's support of it had been planned ahead of time, and they felt insulted that the parish had not first been consulted. They demanded explanations almost as soon as the newsletters landed in their mailboxes.[18]

Both Mike Jupin and Jack Bishop arrived at Epiphany with a history of social activism. In the year or so that they had worked there, they sought to raise the parish's level of concern for contemporary issues of social justice and, in particular, civil rights. Bishop came to Winchester in the autumn of 1966 straight from a sabbatical leave at the Episcopal Theological School in Cambridge, where he worked under Harvey Cox. (A theologian and sociologist, Cox stressed making religious faith relevant in an increasingly secular American society. His first book, *The Secular City* (1965), became a best-seller.) Prior to his year in Cambridge, Jack Bishop had been active in the civil rights movement. He marched from Selma to Montgomery with Martin Luther King Jr. and later did civil rights work in Boston. Early in 1967, Bishop went to Washington to join the first mobilization organized against the war by Clergy and Laity Concerned About Vietnam (CALCAV). Similarly, Mike Jupin had answered the Southern Christian Leadership Conference's call for college students to protest segregation in St. Augustine, Florida, in April 1964, the month before King himself brought national attention to that city's racist ordinances. In addition, Jupin had been protesting American involvement in Vietnam since November 1965, when he participated in the SANE-sponsored march on Washington. He arrived at the Parish of the Epiphany soon after Jack Bishop; then in his last year at the Episcopal Theological School, he started as a student minister and became so well-liked by the congregation that the church hired him as assistant minister when he graduated from seminary in June 1967. Given their personal histories, Mike Jupin's decision to resist the draft and Jack Bishop's readiness to support him did not seem unusual, at least not to the two of them.[19]

The parishioners, led by their wardens (elected representatives of the congregation), however, found these developments shocking. The two wardens, one a successful businessman and the other a retired rear admiral and veteran of World War II, asked Rev. Bishop for a special meeting on October 21. Almost immediately, the former navy man defined this crisis as the worst the parish had known in its eighty-five-year history. The two asked Bishop how they could "get rid of Mike." When a stunned Jack Bishop replied, "you get rid of the rector," the meeting ended at an impasse.[20]

Bishop later said that he should have seen this kind of reaction coming. He viewed Winchester, a wealthy town, as a "very conservative suburb" that attracted highly educated working professionals from the city. The parish itself, made up of 1,200 members, flourished economically. In one of his first meetings with the wardens the year before, one of the two suggested that Bishop bring the American flag forward while the congregation sang "God Bless America" at the start of every service. He refused. He later regarded the parish's suggestion as representative of its patriotism and a clear harbinger of the request for a meeting following the announcement of Michael Jupin's draft card turn-in. But Bishop did not notice it at the time. And in the meantime, he had been pleased with the way the church had responded to some initial social-action work, especially with respect to civil rights. He had no idea what he and his assistant were walking into in the fall of 1967.[21]

On October 22, 1967, the day after the wardens sought Mike Jupin's removal, Jack Bishop spoke of the controversy from the pulpit. He noted that certain members of the parish had expressed deep concern over the draft card turn-in and that he wanted everyone to know that he supported Jupin in his protest. This announcement did nothing to minimize the unrest. Over the next week, Bishop felt obliged to devote almost all of his time to "countless meetings, appointments, telephone calls" to let parishioners air their complaints. One man, a respected Winchester physician and influential parish member, came to see Bishop in those early days. As the rector later recalled the story, the doctor told him, "Jack, I want you to know that I've been a member of this parish for twenty years and I've been close to the clergy all along, and my family has been raised here, and my kids have grown up here, and it means everything to us. And I have to say you're the worst thing that's happened [to this church]." On Thursday, October 26, the vestry (a committee of members elected to administer the temporal affairs in the parish) convened a special meeting to discuss the clergy's participation in antiwar activities. Although two members of the vestry had already resigned in protest, no fireworks erupted at this meeting. Instead, the group recommended that Bishop and Jupin address the issue squarely the following Sunday and that the entire parish be notified that this would be the focus of the services that day.[22]

On October 29, the parish finally heard from the assistant minister himself. In an address that lasted about fifteen minutes, Jupin detailed all of the factors that brought him to his decision to choose draft resistance. First, he discussed the "immoral" nature of the American war in Vietnam. He cited statistics comparing the number of civilians killed to the number of soldiers killed at "somewhere between five and ten to one." More bombs had already been dropped by American planes on North and South Vietnam, he asserted, than on Germany during all of the Second World War. He described the relocation of nearly one million South Vietnamese civilians and the American forces' use of napalm and antipersonnel bombs on civilians. But he also explained to the parish that he did not make his decision to resist solely on the immorality of the American war effort. He argued that fighting the war to stop the spread of communism, a commonly held rationale for supporting the war effort, did not jibe with American policy toward other communist nations. After all, the United States traded with the Soviet Union and other Eastern bloc nations, he said. He did not accept the notion that Americans were fighting in Vietnam to contain China, noting that historically, China and Vietnam were at least distrustful of one another and frequently enemies. He had come to the conclusion, he said, that "the administration's arguments for our presence in Vietnam are totally inadequate."[23]

In fact, Mike Jupin had been opposed to the war since 1965, when American escalation of the war began in earnest. He wrote protest letters to his Indiana congressman and Senators Vance Hartke and Birch Bayh. They assured him of their concern and their efforts to "do something about it," but two years later, he told his parish, "nothing has happened but greater escalation." Since coming to Massachusetts, he had spoken with Senators Edward M. Kennedy, Edward Brooke, and his congressman, but they had done nothing serious to end the war. Since none of the traditional legal channels of protest seemed to be working, Jupin said, he and his friends began to contemplate nonviolent civil disobedience. He chose to violate Selective Service laws, he said, "because with others I firmly believe that what this administration is doing is evil and that as a follower of Jesus Christ and as a member of his Church I have no choice but to oppose evil. In this act I accepted the consequences of breaking the law of the land because I felt I must respond to a higher law of opposing evil which to me and many is a clear and present danger in this country." Jupin also noted that even before committing themselves to draft resistance, he and his friends had been called "unpatriotic, cowardly, vicious, rebellious, un-American, and even treasonous." He asked the congregation, "Where did democracy and freedom and individualism end in this country and unthinking blind obedience to even that which may be evil begin?"[24]

Finally, the young minister acknowledged that he had misread the members of the Parish of the Epiphany. "I thought that my position was understood by most and that my action would be understood," he said. "In this I have erred and I am sorry." He also wanted them to know that he felt the greatest sympathy for those with loved ones in Vietnam. "I want them home and unhurt," he said. "I do not want to see all these American boys killed for what appears to me to be an absurd war." He closed by reminding his listeners that he had nothing personally to gain from draft resistance. He was not trying to "dodge" the draft; as a minister he could not be drafted. Instead, he asserted, "I do this as an act of conscience out of love for this nation and the desire that it truly search its heart, and know and do the will of God." Several weeks later, reflecting on the crisis with some detachment, Jack Bishop said that "October 29 surpassed any day I have known in its power and dignity."[25]

Jupin's sermon affected parishioners in various ways. Following the 9:00 A.M. service, all members of the church were invited to the normally scheduled adult education class where they were given the opportunity to write down their personal reactions to the morning's service. More than 100 parishioners wrote comments—most of which have survived to this day—and others sent letters over the subsequent week. A review of these comments reveals that a majority (56 percent) of the parish supported

Jupin's protest (see Table A.10). One woman noted that "this may be the shot in the arm the parish needs!" Others were moved by Jupin's sermon. "We feel that Mr. Jupin has conducted himself with dignity and humility, and we have great respect for his commitment," wrote one couple. "His statement in church today was impressive in its clarity, intelligence, and concern for both the larger issues and the problem of his relationship with this particular parish."[26]

Still, a significant number of parishioners disapproved of Jupin's actions, some strongly. Nearly 20 percent were so upset that they called for some kind of disciplinary action, including firing Jupin. Several themes emerged from these responses, but three stood out: First, many parishioners simply could not tolerate an assistant minister who broke the law for any reason; second, some were concerned about the influence Jupin would have on the younger members of the parish; and third, many believed Jupin's own youth, immaturity, and naïveté (not his conscience) were responsible for his actions. Some critics incorporated all of these themes into their notes. "Responsible citizens," wrote one, "do not perform acts of treason and take the law into their own hands by either destroying or turning in their draft cards. . . . I do not care to have my children taught disrespect for their country and its laws." Another woman was most concerned with the impact the event would have on her children. "I must accept Mr. Jupin's action as an individual willing to accept whatever penalty the government wishes to impose," she wrote, but since Jupin also taught and advised young people, he could not "behave solely as an individual." As a mother of three children, she wondered, "Do I tell them that in critical situations they should let their consciences be their guides, regardless of the law? Would it not be better—morally and ethically—to use their most conscientious efforts, within the law, to combat difficult situations?" Others were certain that Jupin did not know what he was doing. Some of them called the young minister "naive" or "gullible" or described his resistance as "an uncounseled act of youth." One parishioner saw Red behind this apparent ignorance: "When well-intentioned but not very well-posted individuals . . . go out and preach and practice Civil Disobedience, and worse breaking the Law; they are dupes and instruments of [an] Anti-Christ by the name of Communism."[27]

Finally, the last large group of parishioners (about 17 percent) disapproved of Jupin's views and his methods but did *not* think he should be punished for what amounted to an act of conscience. Like their fellow members who were more upset, this group also feared the example that draft resistance set for the younger members of the church and questioned using illegal methods to make a political point. But overall, their criticisms were muted by their faith in freedom of expression and their admiration for anyone who stood up for his beliefs. At times, these parishioners showed an ambivalence that even they seemed to recognize and sometimes found frustrating. For instance, one man wrote that he, too, opposed the war and saw the loss of American lives as "horrendous and futile" but that he remained unsure about how to effect a change in policy. "How to withdraw from Vietnam at this point is an enigma to me!" he said. Civil disobedience, he knew, was not the answer. "Thus, Mr. Jupin, I agree with your opinion but not your method. But at least you have the courage of your conviction—which is more than most of us!"[28]

Despite the support Jupin received in the parish and the grudging respect paid to him even by some of those who disapproved of his behavior, Jupin's sermon on the 29th did not quell the upheaval in the parish. In the middle of a service on November 1, All Saints Day, several parishioners walked out in protest; three others refused to take Communion from the hands of a draft resister. Meanwhile, several people suggested that Jupin was a Communist and a marijuana dealer. Jack Bishop, for his part, continued to meet with angry members of the church, including one of the wardens who hoped Jupin might consider getting a haircut as a gesture of goodwill. At the same time, the story began to creep into the local weekly newspaper, the *Winchester Star* in the form of readers' letters. Over several weeks in November, letter writers accused Jupin (though usually without naming him specifically) of being "Un-American," "disrespectful," and "fostering anarchy." Defenders responded with their own missives equating Jupin and his fellow draft resisters with participants in the Boston Tea Party, abolitionists, and Christ himself. One man said they were guilty only of "the highest form of responsible patriotism."[29]

Ultimately, Jack Bishop sought outside assistance to help placate the discontented in his parish. On November 26, the Sunday of Thanksgiving weekend, the Right Reverend Anson Phelps Stokes, bishop of the Episcopal Diocese of Boston, addressed the Winchester congregation. The two services at which he preached were packed, but the timing was not ideal; three days earlier Winchester learned that it had lost its second son in Vietnam. Marine corporal Francis J. Muraco, known to friends as "Butch" and already a Purple Heart winner, died when he stepped on a land mine while he was on patrol duty in the province of Quang Tri. He was twenty-one years old and a "short timer"—due to come home in six weeks.

Jack Bishop worried about the juxtaposition of this war hero's funeral at St. Mary's, the Catholic church in town, with his own church's recruitment of Bishop Stokes to attend to its draft resistance crisis.[30]

When Bishop Stokes came to Winchester and spoke at both services that Sunday, he said all the right things for people on both sides of the issue. Looking resplendent in his full bishop's regalia, Stokes ascended to the pulpit and at first spoke generally about the church's long-standing concern with war, war's victims, and those who fight against war. Historically, he noted, Christians frequently sought conscientious objector status or noncombatant options. He told the parish that he, personally, thought the turning in or burning of draft cards was "unnecessary and unwise." Nevertheless, Stokes continued, "if done prayerfully, after consultation and with a willingness to bear whatever criticism or penalty must be born," draft resistance could be "one expression of a desire to face the evil of war and to bear witness against it." After all, he said, "a man who gives up his card to the government is not doing a popular thing and he is certainly not avoiding any penalty."

Though apparently supportive of Michael Jupin's general stand of resistance, the bishop gave clear signals that he understood how uncomfortable this kind of law-breaking made some members of the parish. In certain cases, he counseled, thoughtful people use such measures to press their point. "Obviously, we must seek to avoid unlawful steps," he said, "except as a very last resort, as law and order are necessary for freedom." Stokes invoked the illegal methods of abolitionists—maintaining an underground railroad, for example—in the movement to end slavery. In difficult times there would always be a few people whose "strong convictions" would lead them to take "unusual measures" to underscore their positions of protest even though it might rankle their families, friends, and acquaintances. He continued,

> The Reverend Mr. Jupin in his action at least reminds us of the complexity and importance of some of the issues. He let us hear clearly what many are saying secretly. He is concerned on a conscientious basis with a great contemporary issue. If we do not approve the form his protest takes, at least we can learn from his action the depth of concern of many people. I am sure that he is willing to recognize that on these issues no man can have easy or altogether satisfactory answers. I am sure that he is willing to bear the legal costs he may have to bear. He has not been furtive. He can help make us think, and I believe we can trust the pro-

cesses of thought and discussion. . . . Let us in the name of Christ be big enough to understand and appreciate those whose concerns lead them to such actions as he has taken.

Stokes concluded by seeking some common ground on which the entire parish could stand. If parishioners disagreed over Jupin's actions, Stokes hoped that out of the disagreement might at least come "a new unity here, not of opinion, but of concern." The church community, he suggested, could at least agree that the war in Vietnam was an issue that warranted the attention of the church, its members, and its clergy. "If together you turn your back on [Jupin] now," Stokes warned, "it will indicate that you cannot tolerate all concern."[31]

The bishop's visit to the Parish of the Epiphany had an almost immediate calming effect. Following the service, one parishioner approached Mike Jupin. "I understand better now," he said as he shook the assistant rector's hand. "I couldn't have done this before." About ten days later, after another meeting of the vestry, the two wardens issued a letter to all members that they hoped would bring the matter to a close. They enclosed copies of the bishop's statement and a position paper on civil disobedience produced by the National House of Bishops in 1964. That document, written in response to the civil rights movement, made it clear that the Episcopal Church recognized the right of anyone to break laws "for reasons of informed conscience," as long as the person violated the law nonviolently, accepted the legal penalty, and exercised restraint in "using this privilege of conscience." The wardens also included a paragraph in their letter noting that the clergy (Jack Bishop and Mike Jupin) had apologized for the unexpected "unrest they have caused" and assured parishioners that neither of them would take any similar future action without first consulting with the wardens and the bishop. The vestry concluded that Jupin could continue in his role as assistant minister and "as a leader of our youth."[32]

The wardens and the remaining members of the vestry hoped that the letter would begin a period of reconciliation, and, indeed, in the weeks following the bishop's visit, the clergy at the Parish of the Epiphany sought to establish a ministry that would foster greater communication, understanding and, as the bishop had urged, unity of concern. The church, after all, had weathered the loss of several families, some of whom were long-time members, and other parishioners' pledges of financial contributions; at the end of the year, approximately $12,000 in pledges (out of about $82,000 total) had been withheld by angry parishioners. In addition, sore feelings lingered among members on both sides of the issue. Even the rector's two older sons, ages ten and twelve, were teased and ridiculed by other children who heard about the controversy. The vestry and the clergy now sought to heal those divisions.[33]

At the same time, however, the thrust of the wardens' letter insinuated that, by apologizing, the two ministers had admitted to making a mistake, to accidentally stirring up trouble; the vestry appeared unwilling (at least in the letter) to consider the larger implications of Michael Jupin's draft card turn-in as an act of protest and instead portrayed it as merely an error of judgment. This point weighed on Bishop as he and Mike Jupin moved forward with adult education classes designed to discuss ways to bridge the new divisions in the parish. In mid-December, as he reflected on the crisis for the first time in an address to a group of fellow ministers, Bishop told his colleagues that the swirl of controversy had been so intense that for most of the parish, it may have obscured the most important issue: the church's role in matters of war and peace. The frequent references to Mike Jupin's youth and naïveté in the parishioners' written responses supported this assertion. Despite Bishop Stokes's hope that the church would unite in its concern regarding the war in Vietnam, the reconciliation within the parish, it seemed, would take place at the expense of confronting difficult societal dilemmas. "In all of it," Jack Bishop later remarked, most parishioners "didn't face the real issue." Instead, they focused on returning the church to its former noncontroversial state by pointing to aspects of Bishop's and Jupin's ministries that they *could* support. Several months later, in May 1968, the Parish of the Epiphany sent a busload of volunteers to Washington to take part in the Poor People's Campaign, an undertaking that may not have happened before Jack Bishop and Mike Jupin began to turn the parish's attention toward contemporary issues, but it never returned to the issue of Vietnam.[34]

To Mike Jupin's relief, the *Boston Globe*, at least, seemed to soften its position on draft resistance in light of the Winchester controversy. The day after Bishop Stokes spoke at Epiphany, the *Globe* ran an editorial that cited Jupin's situation as a basis for defending civil disobedience. In part, the paper issued a clarification that defined civil disobedience not as a "dissociation from society" but as "an act of profound commitment to it." Some Americans, like Michael Jupin, saw the war in Vietnam, it said, "as so contrary to national ideals and personal beliefs as to warrant civil disobedience." This was a point resisters had been trying to make from the start but had failed to receive much consideration from the press. "While not agreeing with them, we should not condemn them," the editorial concluded. "They are brave and honorable men." This characterization of draft resisters demonstrated an important shift in thinking at the newspaper; only five weeks before, the editors had characterized the resisters of October 16 as "misguided" and possessing "little judgement."[35]

Michael Jupin now believes that if he had still been in seminary in October 1967, no outcry would have resulted from his draft resistance. But his position in Winchester made his protest much more difficult. "I really hadn't understood the move that I made, that I lived in a completely different community that would respond in a completely different way," he reflected. "Fools rush in," he chuckled.[36]

A NETWORK OF SUPPORT

The New England Resistance and other advocates of draft-centered protest recognized that individual draft resisters might be left feeling, like Michael Jupin, isolated and alienated in the weeks and months following their initial acts of defiance. Organizers knew that they could not realistically expect that an individual resister's depth of commitment might not wither under the weight of FBI visits, letters from draft boards, and the palpable concern of (if not alienation from) family and friends. Thus, as it became evident that the federal government did not plan the kinds of mass arrests or indictments that might act as a crucible from which Resistance solidarity would continue to grow spontaneously, members of the Resistance and other groups began to devote some of their energies to holding the movement together. This happened deliberately within groups like the New England Resistance but often, as in the case of some of the older supporters, it occurred organically as different people gravitated to draft resistance in the belief that it was the most effective way to protest the war.

Just like draft resisters themselves, those who were rallied to activism by the zeitgeist of draft resistance were children of the American dream. They came to the cause with varied backgrounds and different expectations, but, in general, most supporters of draft resistance came from middle-class homes, were well-educated, and had a history of social movement activism. Frequently, they were older than the resisters themselves. The 1997 survey of draft resistance activists from Boston revealed an average age of twenty-five and a median age of twenty-three among the sixty-eight respondents who could be classified not as resisters but as supporters. Nearly

50 percent were students; the second largest group, which constituted approximately 15 percent of supporters, were academics (see Table A.11). In addition, as many as half of all supporters may have been women.[37]

Those who stood behind resisters in their confrontation with the government came from the same kinds of homes and neighborhoods as the resisters did. Their parents were mostly professionals and proprietors (see Table A.12). Eighty-one percent of supporters' fathers, for instance, held professional jobs or ran their own businesses. And although 40 percent of their mothers were homemakers, another 42 percent of them held professional positions or were entrepreneurs. Moreover, when supporters were asked about their class backgrounds, nearly 85 percent identified themselves as coming from middle-class, upper-middle-class, or upper-class families (47, 36, and 2 percent, respectively) (see Table A.13). Like resisters, then, other draft resistance activists came from the same social strata as those in power, as those responsible for American policies in Vietnam. In some cases, such as that of novelist James Carroll, whose father ran the Defense Intelligence Agency, draft resistance supporters were actually the children of the war makers.[38]

Resistance supporters from Boston came from varied backgrounds, most of which offered no hint that they would become activists. Although most supporters' parents identified themselves with a religious denomination (82 percent of fathers and 87 percent of mothers), only one parent, a Quaker, came from any of the historically pacifist sects (see Table A.14). Indeed, in addition to the 43 percent of supporters who came from homes in which at least one parent was a veteran of the armed services (similar to the 40 percent for resisters), 25 percent of the men who supported draft resistance in some way were themselves veterans (see Table A.15). Unlike the parents of resisters, however, more parents of supporters had histories of social activism and protest of their own (38 percent compared to 23 percent for parents of resisters), including 19 percent who had a parent active in a union.[39]

In their less-than-radical political leanings, however, supporters' parents were more like resisters' parents. Although many of the activists viewed themselves as part of the New Left (69 percent) (see Table A.16), their parents were overwhelmingly mainstream in their politics. In 75 percent of supporters' homes, both parents belonged to the same political party; 57 percent of these couples were Democrats (see Table A.17). Among the supporters themselves, although 49 percent identified themselves as either socialist, communist, or anarchist, 51 percent also were Democrats (see

Table A.18). Again, by protesting the draft in this way, many resistance supporters confronted an administration that either they or their parents (or both) had put in office. Even among the supporters who thought of themselves as New Leftists, nearly 43 percent were Democrats, too.[40] Their protest against the draft, then, had less to do with political affiliation or ideology than it did with outrage over the war.

The activism of draft resistance supporters also seems to have stemmed in part from earlier participation in protest movements. Compared to the draft resisters, supporters came to draft resistance equipped with more impressive protest résumés. Out of 68 supporters surveyed only 7 had no prior activist experience—which means that nearly 90 percent of all supporters came to draft resistance with a previous history of activism (see Table A.19). Almost 21 percent had participated in Vietnam Summer, 34 percent were members of Students for a Democratic Society, 56 percent had been active with various peace organizations, and 62 percent came from a background in the civil rights movement. This level of experience fueled the rapid growth of a community of supporters for draft resisters in late 1967 and early 1968. As the New England Resistance gained more prominence through its demonstrations and draft card turn-ins, more and more men faced the pressures brought by the FBI, their draft boards, and often their parents. In Boston, groups of young supporters flocked to organizations like the Boston Draft Resistance Group or other draft counseling organizations, while older supporters joined organizations like Resist. All of these groups were critical to the ongoing efforts of draft resisters.

BDRG AND THE RESISTANCE

In the fall of 1967 and winter of 1968, resisters could rely on a budding draft resistance community formed first and foremost by the alliance of the New England Resistance and the Boston Draft Resistance Group. By October and November, BDRG had firmly established itself as a leading antiwar and antidraft organization in Boston. It continued to mount Early Morning Shows and Horror Shows and its draft counseling efforts grew dramatically. Dozens of young men sought the group's services at its office on Columbia Avenue in Cambridge every day. More significant, the BDRG's initial reluctance to support draft card turn-ins gave way to a more general sense of collaboration.

In addition to sponsoring touch-football games, social events, and Monday night dinners, both the NER and the BDRG encouraged their members to turn out for each others' demonstrations and public events. An early Resistance newsletter noted that it was "working closely" with the BDRG and that the two groups shared "considerable overlap in membership." The newsletter urged draft resisters to plan to do regular work for the BDRG when they were not occupied with a specific NER project. "Unless we are to do nothing but pull off spectacular demonstrations once a month, we must all be ready to do serious, steady, unspectacular work."[41]

This kind of bipolar characterization of each group's mission ("spectacular" and "unspectacular") betrayed a certain snobbery on the part of the Resistance, but the BDRG activists directed a similar strain of condescension at the NER. "Tensions continue to exist," one BDRG newsletter noted, "between those who see draft resistance as essentially an act of moral witness and those who see it as an organizing program with broad implications for radical change." For several reasons, however, the two groups put their differences aside in the months following October 16. First, as BDRG counselor Charles Fisher later commented, the "BDRG grudgingly admitted that the Resistance did attract attention and convert people." That attention resulted in financial assistance not only to the Resistance but also to the BDRG, whose fund-raisers, Fisher said, were "acutely aware of how much BDRG's affluence" owed to donations solicited from Resistance contributors. Furthermore, BDRG activists suggested that while Resistance chapters clashed with their draft counseling counterparts in other parts of the country, in Boston a gradual "convergence of attitudes" had occurred, in which both groups realized that their approaches were complementary. "It would seem that demonstrations can be an important adjunct to anti-draft organizing," a BDRG newsletter noted, "particularly by creating a sense of a city-wide movement." Indeed, through the fall, the BDRG's counseling caseload doubled, a development they attributed to its participation in Resistance rallies and draft card turn-ins. By February, some BDRG members were starting to worry that the organization might be getting too "hung up on mass actions to the detriment of its ongoing organizing programs." In the early months of draft resistance, however, the sense of solidarity and camaraderie that resulted from collective action warranted the combined efforts of these organizations. Not a day went by, it seemed, when one could not find work to do for either the BDRG or the Resistance.[42]

"GIRLS SAY 'YES' TO GUYS WHO SAY 'NO'"

Although the draft did not threaten women directly, a significant number of them sought work in Boston's draft resistance movement, and it attracted them for the same reasons it attracted draft-age men: it seemed like the most direct way to challenge the government's war policies.

The kind of work that women could find in draft resistance organizations, however, was frequently limited even within support roles. In 1967, women who chose to target the draft as their primary focus in protesting against the war in Vietnam generally had two options open to them. They could work with the local Resistance organization or work with draft counseling groups like BDRG. (In time, a small number of women joined groups of the so-called Ultra-Resistance in raiding draft boards to either steal or destroy draft files). The male-centered experience of the draft and draft resistance often marginalized women within these organizations. That this occurred within the civil rights movement and elsewhere in the New Left has been well-documented. Indeed, historian Sara Evans's interpretation of the origins of women's liberation in the civil rights movement and the New Left, which she first spelled out in her enormously influential 1979 book, *Personal Politics*, is one of those rare scholarly arguments that has persisted virtually unchallenged for two decades. Evans has argued that women who gained valuable organizing experience and insights into the meaning of equality within the civil rights movement and the New Left nevertheless faced constant unequal treatment within those movements, thus necessitating their own movement.[43] But in the Boston draft resistance movement, depending on their backgrounds, their expectations and aspirations, and the organizations in which they worked, women's experiences of marginalization—and their responses to it—varied in significant ways. Despite obvious inequities, draft resistance provided a nurturing environment in which some women could do the kind of antiwar work they wanted to do, and with room to grow; for others, it offered only limitations, frustration, and conflict—and thus served as a catalyst for the women's liberation movement. While some women described the draft resistance movement as the "point of ultimate indignity" for women in the New Left, others experienced it as an extension of the civil rights movement's "beloved community."[44]

The dramatic public events staged by the New England Resistance attracted support from women, though they often found themselves channeled into the most mundane work. On October 16, the first draft card turn-in yielded 214 cards, with another 67 burned in the flame of a church candle. Although the mass of reporters in attendance did not report it, Nan Stone, the young Methodist minister then enrolled in Boston University's

School of Theology, burned one of those cards; she was the only woman to participate in the ceremony. In fact, Stone had fought hard with the event's other organizers for the right to do so. In anticipation of mass arrests at the church, the planners decided that several people—including Nan Stone—would not participate, thus guaranteeing that someone would be available to arrange bail and find legal assistance for the others. But Stone, perhaps more than the others, felt a powerful need to somehow put herself at the same level of risk as the men, not only to demonstrate her passionate stand against the war but also to prove herself an equal within this young organization. As she later recalled, "Most of the guys sort of dismissed that. . . . They looked at me as not having the risk that they had, 'cause I didn't have a draft card, wouldn't be drafted." Steve Pailet, one of the few sympathetic men, pushed for her participation and gave her his own card to burn.[45]

This episode is representative of the kind of treatment women could expect in those resistance organizations that made draft noncompliance their primary tactic. As Sara Evans has found in other New Left and civil rights organizations, women were most often limited to doing the "shitwork": typing, stuffing envelopes, and making coffee. The men who founded the Resistance, after all, conceived it as a kind of brotherhood of resisters. Like a college fraternity that admits women only as "little sisters," the New England Resistance welcomed "resister sisters" only in clearly defined support functions.[46]

Still, some women like Stone were able to attain positions of influence in the New England Resistance, though it was a "continual struggle." First, they had to put up with frequent sexist allusions to women that appeared in NER literature. One leaflet intended for resisters, for instance, noted that organizers were planning a "huge, incredibly noisy, chick-laden" party for the night following the April 3, 1968, draft card turn-in. Another leaflet targeting GIs invited them to another gathering that would offer "beer and chicks and things." These kinds of statements were consistent with the prevailing understanding of women's place in draft resistance as articulated by some of the leading women in the movement. Folksinger Joan Baez, the wife of Palo Alto resister David Harris, perpetuated this mode of thinking when she coined the expression "Girls Say 'Yes' to Guys Who Say 'No'" as a way of attracting more men to draft resistance. The downside of that campaign—which included images of beautiful young women on posters emblazoned with the Baez quote—was in the alienation it created among women who took their draft resistance work seriously, only to be viewed as sex objects.[47]

At the same time, a kind of romantic mystique attached to the resisters existed, and it made them and their cause appealing to some women. Historian and Boston draft resistance activist Ellen DuBois recalls a particular "giddiness" as late as 1968 among her female peers at Wellesley College in anticipation of a campus rally to which Michael Ferber, a nationally known draft resister and one of Dr. Benjamin Spock's codefendants, and several other resisters came to speak.[48] For DuBois, coming from a women's college, the "presence of lots of men was a thorough attraction, not a discouragement." And their mystique was naturally rooted in rebellion. "I kind of imagined motorcycles," DuBois remembers, "that they all had motorcycles." In fact, compared to the Resistance men in California, many of whom did have motorcycles, the men in Boston seemed tame. But the act of resistance, of defiance, nevertheless fueled this romanticism.

In several instances, romanticism led to romance, and some of the women who worked in the New England Resistance office became involved in relationships with men in the leadership. This sometimes resulted in feelings of distrust and competition among some of the women, particularly between women involved with men in the organization and women who were not. For example, the men would often forget to tell Nan Stone about a meeting to which some of their girlfriends (who also worked in the office) would go. Stone resented one woman in particular, she said, "because she had this boyfriend that gave her . . . an in, somebody who would listen to her. She was paid attention to because of who she was fucking." Sue Katz, another prominent woman in the New England Resistance, on the other hand, saw such relationships as useful in attaining positions of responsibility in the organization. Until she started sleeping with one of the Resistance leaders, she says today, "I know I was sort of like nobody, just a 'chick.'" Her relationship made her "somebody" and provided entrée into "those . . . all-night meetings, solving the problems of the world."[49]

Clearly, the draft resisters' struggle to overcome the popular image of them as "cowards," "sissies," and "faggots" did much to shape the gender dynamics of the draft resistance movement. In Boston, as draft resistance came to dominate all antiwar efforts in the city, organizers not only emphasized the risk attached to open defiance of draft laws but also fostered a kind of machismo that did much to frame the experience of both men and women in the movement. Surrounding themselves with women and objectifying them served to reinforce their own virility and masculinity. This at first seems consistent with Doug Rossinow's findings elsewhere in the New Left that "sexuality and danger mingled closely in the existential search for a fuller life and a just society," but in the more apocalyptic ethos of late 1967 to late 1969, stopping the war took precedence over the search for a fuller life.[50]

At the same time, the kind of male swagger that developed in the movement may have sustained the courage of some draft resisters, but it also alienated others, particularly gay men. Peter Schenck, a BU sophomore from Springfield, Massachusetts, turned in his draft card largely because the idea of a community of draft resisters emerging from this act of defiance appealed to him. "I certainly felt like I was giving up a lot of elements of community," he later said. "This was a decision that was going to make my life a lot more difficult with a lot of other people in my life. And I hoped that something was going to replace that." For a gay man, however, the Resistance's promise of community was never fulfilled. After the FBI called to interview him, Schenck went to the New England Resistance office to seek advice and was alarmed to encounter a group of draft resisters "just kind of hanging out" in the Resistance office "telling fag jokes." Those present casually tossed about words like "faggot" and "cocksucker" as Schenck stood there wondering what to make of this new "community." He left the office and never returned. It is difficult to know just how common this experience might have been, but it is clear that no openly gay men (or women) actively participated in Boston's draft resistance movement; those gay men and women who did take part, including Ray Mungo, the editor of the *BU News*, kept their sexual orientation hidden.

Meanwhile, regardless of the intimate relationships between the men and women in the Resistance, a fairly pronounced sexual division of labor did exist. Dana Densmore, who worked in both the New England Resistance and the Boston Draft Resistance Group, has recently described the weekly dinner meetings of the Resistance as "exercises in self-laceration" for the women members. "It went without saying that we cooked and cleaned up while the men bonded, strategized, and postured." Indeed, women were expected to take on the traditionally female tasks of cooking, cleaning, and secretarial work: bookkeeping, typing, filing, stuffing envelopes. While women such as Nan Stone, Connie Field, and Rosemary Poole tended to the books, kept track of hundreds of resisters, bought office supplies, and made up leaflets on the mimeograph machine, the men held strategy sessions, met with reporters, and gave informal "raps" at some of the numerous college or church venues in greater Boston.[51] Although women like Nan Stone did become (and all of the men now acknowledge this) an essential member of the New England Resistance leadership, Stone notes, "I was never invited in to the inner circles, I had to push my way in."[52]

In the BDRG, circumstances for women differed somewhat from those of the New England Resistance. Although women did most of the clerical work in the Cambridge office, participation in the group was not as starkly gender coded in the same way that it was in the Resistance.[53] At least half of the draft counselors were women, and many of them also took part in Early Morning Shows. Unlike draft card turn-ins and induction refusals, such activities were open to both men and women. Ellen DuBois, who worked for the BDRG while an undergraduate at Wellesley College, recalls that although draft counseling was not at all sexualized, the Early Morning Shows, which were usually carried out with more men than women, did take advantage of female participants' femininity. "We wouldn't call it flirting, but we would earnestly try to convince [the inductees] to resist the draft," she recalled. "I'm not sure how conscious we were that we were playing on the fact that we were women and they were men, but somebody must have been conscious of it."[54]

BDRG women, however, disagreed then (as they do today) about the extent to which they participated in leading the organization. Generally, those who held one of the few paid staff positions claim to have experienced very little male chauvinism. Both Sasha Harmon and Bliss Matteson, successive office managers for BDRG, agree that they never "felt any particular discrimination or any particular shutdown" in weekly steering committee meetings or in the office itself. They acknowledge, however, that if they had not assumed clearly defined roles as part of the office staff, they might have felt "at more of a disadvantage."[55]

Other women in the BDRG recall the situation differently. Ellen DuBois believes that although women such as Harmon and Matteson were influential, a fundamental inequality kept them and other women from "advancing beyond a certain point." Women in the BDRG had greater responsibility than women in the Resistance, "but there was something wrong at the top." A kind of glass ceiling existed, and as DuBois remembers it, the women who had reached it would eventually "sort of mysteriously disappear." Dana Densmore, Abby Rockefeller, and Roxanne Dunbar pushed this view further, charging that an "astonishing male hierarchy," most apparent in steering committee meetings, dominated the BDRG. According to Densmore, just as it occurred in New England Resistance meetings, "if a woman spoke up" in a BDRG steering committee meeting, "there would be a dead silence for a few seconds, and then they would pointedly pick up exactly where they were before her comment." Eventually, such experiences led Densmore, Rockefeller, and Dunbar to leave the draft resistance movement in 1968 and form Cell 16, one of the first radical feminist groups in the country.[56]

Steering committee meetings at the BDRG, like those at the New England Resistance, were notoriously long since decisions were reached by consensus rather than by majority rule. As a result, those who excelled in debate and carried themselves with confidence (the "highly aggressively verbal easterners . . . New Yorkers," according to one woman) often dominated these sessions. Although there were some exceptions, far fewer women felt comfortable with this kind of confrontational dynamic than men. One male BDRG founder remarked that he had always been proud of the organization's emphasis on this informal style of decision making until years later when he recognized that it had resulted in a kind of "tyranny of informality" that yielded to a "charisma-based" form of leadership. Since few women in those days were socialized to master the "mass-haranguing style" needed to make a point in meetings, men dominated decision making. Sue Katz later raised the issue of masculinity when she described the debates that occurred in similar meetings in the Resistance as a "dick sport for wimpy radicals." Instead of an athletic competition, the men in the Resistance jousted with one another by seeing, she said, "who could conceptualize a longer sentence that would obfuscate more ideas than the next person." Ideological discussion provided a forum to assert "who was the big cock on the block. . . . [It] was as much a competitive sport as anything else. It was just *their* competitive sport," Katz recalled. "Women were not picked for the teams until last."[57]

Ultimately, the evidence seems to suggest that a clear-cut case of male insecurity (resulting from draft resisters' collective refusal to go to war) led to the development of a group culture in which sexism and male chauvinism were accepted expressions of one's manhood. This culture, consistent with the Evans thesis, marginalized many of the women in the movement and eventually led them to create their own movement. Indeed, women from the New England Resistance and the Boston Draft Resistance Group felt sufficiently alienated to come together in the city's first consciousness-raising groups (which later became part of the larger socialist-feminist organization Bread and Roses) and to form Cell 16, which began teaching women Tae Kwon Do to defend themselves against their male oppressors.

But the gender dynamics in the draft resistance movement were more complicated than these conclusions imply. Men did not simply dominate the movement, and women did not simply wait to begin fighting sexism in the movement only after they left it. To infer as much suggests that women experienced the draft resistance movement primarily as victims. In fact, many women found draft resistance work fulfilling in spite of male dominance, and many also challenged that dominance within resistance organizations long before and even after discovering women's liberation. Women certainly experienced sexism and frustration, but the extent to which they were limited or not depended on the individual and often could be tied to individual expectations and aspirations.

Like some of the women at BDRG, female Resistance activists today disagree on the degree to which the men kept them in subordinate roles. In particular, with the exception of Sue Katz, the women who were involved in relationships with Resistance men are less likely to recall male chauvinism as a defining characteristic of their experience. Even though their very presence in the Resistance inner circle derived largely from their attachment to male leaders, and could be seen, consequently, as more pointedly sexist, the consensus among these women seems to be, as one said, that "you weren't treated any differently than you were anywhere else in the Movement." The male chauvinism present in the draft resistance movement, they suggest, was simply an extension of the male chauvinism that permeated American society. Another female Resistance activist is certain that women in the Resistance participated actively in the leadership of the organization: women "certainly spoke out at meetings whenever they wanted; there was no attempt to silence women. And I certainly didn't feel that I wasn't a part of the organization nor that I couldn't speak up if I wanted to speak up." Indeed, she said, "power is in the hands of those who seize the power."[58]

By the time the New England Resistance had run its course in late 1969, the two women who recall most acutely the oppression of the men in the organization, Sue Katz and Nan Stone, had largely succeeded in their personal struggles to overcome male dominance, in "seizing power." Both Katz and Stone eventually took on public speaking assignments, directed their own programs, and wrote articles for the organization. Moreover, according to Katz, the men in the group made her their head of security. All of these responsibilities had formerly been reserved solely for men.[59]

The contrasting accounts of women's experiences in the draft resistance movement can be explained in part by a combination of their prior activist experience, their motives in joining the antiwar movement, and, extending from those two factors, their levels of expectation regarding their roles. The slightly older women—or those in at least their mid-twenties—who came to draft resistance as graduate students, for example, arrived with years of experience in the civil rights movement or elsewhere in the New Left where they felt that they had been marginalized to a far greater degree than in their draft resistance work.

Some of these women possessed a sense of comparative perspective that others did not. Unlike Nan Stone and Sue Katz, for whom draft resistance work constituted their first sustained activism of any kind, Rosemary Poole came to the Resistance after working with the Congress of Racial Equality (CORE) in California in the early 1960s and Students for a Democratic Society (SDS) at Harvard in the mid-1960s. Poole had faced sexism in both places but saw relative improvement in the New England Resistance. Even though Poole acted as Resistance bookkeeper and did the kind of clerical work often expected of women, she asserts that "there was freedom" in the Resistance. "There was openness. There was the same old shit, but it was malleable. . . . It was really a place where things could grow. And of course we did grow and there were lots of arguments and fights and feelings . . . but it was a great situation, in my opinion, for women to move out of that kind of position." When draft resistance faded by 1970, Poole got more involved with women's liberation, but not as a direct reaction to her draft resistance experience. For her, the New England Resistance surpassed her expectations. "It was *family* . . . it was just like 'God, these people really do stuff together, and have fun together, and they care about the things I care about, and they go off and do them together.' It was wonderful. It was absolutely wonderful." Penney Kurland Lagos of the Resistance agreed: "I did whatever needed to be done; I was just so happy to be doing something [to end the war]."[60]

Similarly, Janine Fay, who was instrumental in establishing the BDRG's coffeehouse for GIs, Sgt. Brown's Memorial Necktie (named for the army sergeant in charge of inductions at the Boston Army Base who had lost his tie in a scuffle with protesters) never felt thwarted in the group. She came to the organization after working on civil rights in Chester, Pennsylvania, for several years while she was an undergraduate at Swarthmore College. Fay later recalled that she joined the BDRG because she "just couldn't bear the news about what was going on in Vietnam and I wanted to do something." She also simply sought a place in the antiwar movement that at the same time would be enjoyable. "I tried to find a place where I could do something that I kind of liked," she later said. "Given the context that I wanted to participate, and give part of my life over to ending the war, to doing what I could, I made it also so I could kind of enjoy myself as much as possible." As Heather Booth, Evi Goldfield, and Sue Munaker wrote in 1968, coffeehouse work constituted one way in which women could do antiwar work without being in an "auxiliary" position. According to Fay, in her work for the BDRG and the coffeehouse, she enjoyed considerable autonomy. "There wasn't something that I was yearning for that someone was stopping me from doing," she said. Years later, she could see how other women with higher aspirations to *lead* the BDRG might have felt stifled and then left the organization, but that does not accurately describe her experience.[61]

Likewise, Ellen DuBois notes that although she saw the glass ceiling that kept women from advancing beyond a certain point in the organization, she regarded the BDRG as also providing the kind of "beloved community" environment associated with the early civil rights movement, "a place where men and women came together in loving union with hopes of transcendent goals."[62] In part, DuBois experienced this sense of community even as she felt that her "leadership capacities," which were already developing at Wellesley, were "at least overlooked" at BDRG; and although she did not assert herself as strongly in the BDRG as she did at Wellesley, she recalls, "I never felt that I wasn't allowed to do or say anything." DuBois and other women "didn't quite get it" that draft resistance was "supposed to be a men's movement." They tried to extend it "to be a fully integrated movement" from the start, and the men in the organization did not actively restrain them. "The amazing thing is that I *didn't* hit any walls," she recalled. "I sort of noticed . . . that there was something odd about the women [in BDRG], but only because they *were* in the leadership."[63]

In addition, the "beloved community" quality of BDRG also contrasted sharply with the sexually predatory nature of SDS and the Weathermen and the macho "strutting" of the New England Resistance. As a twenty-one-year-old woman, DuBois notes, her work in the BDRG coincided with her "sexually coming of age" and in that organization she found a safe place to "get introduced to a full-fledged heterosexual culture in the context of the movement," which, she said, "was pretty nice." Women's primary motivation for participating in the draft resistance movement may not have been to pursue relationships, but the generally respectful and safe quality of those relationships contributed to a gender dynamic often overlooked in the descriptions of the subjugation of women in the New Left (which tend to emphasize the more exploitative experience of women in SDS and the Weathermen).[64]

To the extent that men did limit the roles of women in the Resistance and BDRG, some women have suggested that they did so only as much as women allowed it; as soon as they challenged the arbitrary limits set by the men, the women claim, they were given room to grow. "I dearly loved some of [the men], and none of them restricted me in a way that I felt I didn't participate in," recalls Rosemary Poole. "[If] I was willing to put up with it, then I got it; if I wasn't willing to put up with it, then I didn't get it—'it' being abuse." When Poole was clear about her limits, "they were respected" by the Resistance men. "God knows there was a lot of sexism that went on right and left, but I didn't feel like I couldn't do something about it," she recalled. Women "could make an emotional space that was really good for the people involved in [the Resistance]."[65]

Perhaps the most frequently cited example of men marginalizing women in draft resistance and throughout the New Left focuses on the dominance of men in meetings. Like Dana Densmore, Roxanne Dunbar recalled women being routinely ignored in Resistance and BDRG meetings. Dunbar, a graduate student in history at UCLA who came to Boston in part to begin dissertation research, later remembered: "I'd be rattling off all this stuff, historical stuff and everything, and see these eyes glaze over—these men—in meetings where I'd make a suggestion . . . and I realized that it wasn't just me." Women did not speak as often as men, "and when they did, sometimes they'd be politely listened to and then [the men would] go on as if that woman hadn't even spoken . . . and that really burned me, because I was used to people listening to me."[66]

Not all women felt excluded in organization meetings. For example, Rosemary Poole asserts that she was willing to tolerate a few men's dominance of Resistance meetings in a way that Sue Katz, Nan Stone, and Roxanne Dunbar were not. She admits that she grew accustomed to just listening at meetings and could generally count on someone finally saying what she thought anyway. Likewise, Penney Kurland today recalls that she did not like to see the men dominating but that she also did not necessarily want a leadership role for herself. Kurland remembers only that the women in the Resistance struggled with men who "were really nice people, good intentioned, but [who] couldn't help dominating whatever situation they were in." Poole agrees that "those guys just talked their heads off—they took up too much space" but recalls that the women were not totally passive. When the women established their limits, they were respected. Eventually, Poole recalls, "[we would] get up our spunk and come in and blast them all. . . . We taught each other how to shut up a little bit so that those of us who had a harder time speaking in a group like that could speak." Bliss Matteson experienced an analogous situation in the BDRG. "If you're used to functioning in groups, if you're used to being listened to," she later reflected, "then you just didn't let them *not* listen to you." In addition, a statistical analysis of BDRG steering committee meeting minutes done by Charles Fisher, a Brandeis University sociologist and BDRG activists, circa 1970, indicated that the ratio of women who spoke to men who did was three to four, though, as Fisher noted, the women were "less likely to contribute to strategic or political discussions."[67]

Restricted participation in meetings also did not extend to women such as Bernardine Dohrn of SDS, who used her physical appearance and revealing attire to advance her own leadership aspirations. Both men and women in Boston's draft resistance movement remember Dohrn as much for her provocative sexuality as for her political savvy. Rosemary Poole recalls that when Dohrn once attended a Resistance meeting in Boston in 1968 wearing one of her trademark miniskirts and then sat with her legs spread apart, "all of the guys were just flipping out." According to Tim Wright, a BDRG founder, though, Dohrn was one of a few women who could be "respected intellectually and politically" even if they "dressed like sex objects." When Dohrn came to town, Wright recalled later, "not only was she bewitchingly attractive—so we all wanted to fuck her—but . . . part of her charisma was her mind, which was razor sharp: she was a lawyer [and] she was really smart."[68] Dohrn was an exception, however; most women did not participate equally with men in draft resistance meetings, either because they were less inclined to do so or because they were largely ignored when they did.

From its inception the draft resistance movement attracted many women and could not have sustained itself without their efforts. How those women experienced the movement varied significantly and shaped their subsequent activism in important ways. In the wake of the first draft card turn-ins, however, their steady presence among the various movement supporters helped minimize the alienation so many resisters felt from other quarters.

"A CHILD HAS SPAWNED PARENTS"

Draft resistance organizers found out soon after October 16 that they could count on encouragement from individuals and groups other than the BDRG. Although an early New England Resistance newsletter boasted that for the "first time in history . . . a child has spawned parents," in fact many of the organizations that allied themselves with draft resistance groups had been protesting the war for a long time. Members of the Committee for Non-Violent Action and the American Friends Service Committee, for example, showed up at all NER demonstrations and draft card turn-ins. When Bill Hunt of the BDRG and the Resistance later reflected on this, he remarked that in those first months after October 16, resisters came to realize that they could always count on the Quakers and other pacifists to be there. Although many resisters may not have been strict pacifists (e.g., believers in the just-war theory), their demonstrated opposition to the Vietnam War was sufficient to merit assistance from the AFSC and the CNVA. On the other hand, although liberal Democrats might have shared the Resistance's analysis of the war, Hunt said, most of them felt that nothing justified damaging the party; thus they could not be expected to publicly back draft resistance.[69]

On the surface, though, the notion of a child spawning parents seemed more accurate with respect to Resist, the organization formed out of the "Call to Resist Illegitimate Authority." Certainly, most of the older advisers of Resist, like those of the AFSC and CNVA, were longtime dissenters to American involvement in Vietnam; yet they acknowledged that the impetus to make draft resistance their main focus came in response to the actions of their younger counterparts. "We are certainly in an embarrassing position to be looking to the young to make our will effective," Paul Goodman wrote in the *New York Review of Books* earlier in the year. "I am ashamed to be so powerless."[70]

In fact, intellectuals were not powerless to protest the war effectively; indeed, some had been trying to marshal support from their colleagues for a long time. Noam Chomsky, in particular, churned out numerous articles imploring his fellow academics to act. In the fall 1966 issue of the *Harvard Educational Review*, he wrote: "One can only be appalled at the willingness of American intellectuals, who, after all, have access to the facts, to tolerate or even approve of the deceitfulness and hypocrisy [of the administration]." His most influential essay, "The Responsibility of Intellectuals," which appeared in the *New York Review* in February 1967, moved scores of academics to act in ensuing months. "It is the responsibility of intellectuals to speak the truth and to expose lies," he wrote. Regarding Vietnam, Chomsky implied, intellectuals had been content through the 1950s and 1960s to quietly accept the decisions of foreign policy and national security "experts" in successive administrations. In light of this inaction, Chomsky alerted his colleagues, "no body of theory or significant body of relevant information, beyond the comprehension of the layman . . . makes policy immune from criticism." He expected them to speak out against what he viewed as an obviously "savage American assault on a largely helpless rural population in Vietnam."[71]

Although Chomsky issued this charge to the academic community in February, the actual catalyst for the intellectual community's activism—anticipation of the national draft card turn-in on October 16—did not arrive until the end of the summer. At that time the Call to Resist began to gather momentum; scores of adoptive "parents" lined up to support the resisters. As Sandy Vogelgesang has written, Chomsky's strategy aimed both to stop the war and to "resolve the larger dilemma of powerlessness which underlay the Vietnam experience." He hoped that the addition of older adults to the resistance movement would raise the economic and political stakes for the government and would make it "impossible for the government to ignore the protesters." He then counted on what he called "the unpredictable effects of a really large-scale repression" of the resisters and their supporters to raise "questions about the range of meaningful political action." The popular outrage generated by this repression would, it followed, cripple the administration's capacity to wage war in Southeast Asia.[72]

Not all intellectuals agreed with Chomsky, however. As Vogelgesang had pointed out, prominent figures like Michael Harrington, Theodore Draper, and Michael Walzer thought intellectuals should stick to speaking and writing against the war rather than resorting to civil disobedience—even if it was nonviolent. Harrington, for instance, warned that trying to reach Americans through "middle-class tantrums" of draft resistance risked turning the antiwar movement into a "morally self-satisfied but ultimately impotent cult." Walzer commented that no one could be "morally justified in acting (however heroically) in ways that defeat his own stated purpose."[73]

Despite such criticism, a significant group of older advisers, mostly academics, moved ahead with a program to support draft resisters. Following the October 2, 1967, press conference announcing the "Call to Resist Illegitimate Authority," Columbia University economist Robert Zevin hosted a large group of the participants at the Columbia Faculty Club, where they laid out plans for a new organization called Resist. As the first donations came in to support the Call to Resist, Zevin hired Herschel Kaminsky to open an office in New York. Meanwhile, in Washington on the eve of the Pentagon march, Resist held the first steering committee meeting, at which the members administered grants to antiwar and draft resistance organizations. In their first newsletter (printed in early November), Resist organizers outlined their intention to mount two fund-raising programs, one for general support and another to save money for a defense fund that they expected would be necessary once the government started indicting draft resisters. At this early stage, Resist members primarily wanted to continue to apply pressure on the administration. "We cannot emphasize too strongly the need to stay together," they wrote. "On occasion when we have mobilized strength, we have made them back off or overreact, as in Hershey's recent pronouncements [in the October 26 memo], and thereby jeopardize their legal power." The advisers of Resist, like Resistance organizers, expected the government to try to intimidate them; they were challenged with successfully maintaining their momentum in the face of that intimidation.[74]

As members of Resist received their own visits from FBI agents and as some of the younger professors among them saw their own draft status changed (punitively), Resist responded with very public support for draft resisters. Chomsky, again writing in the *New York Review*, declared, "It is difficult for me to see how anyone can refuse to engage himself, in some way, in the plight of these young men." He suggested that older adults might help resisters through legal and financial aid, participation in demonstrations, learning to counsel potential draftees, and signing complicity statements. In addition, Resist sent over 100 letters to poets, writers, and other academics and activists, asking that they "add appearances for Resist to their scheduled speaking engagements" or that they offer to speak at Resist-sponsored events. From New York Resist and New York Resistance came a suggestion—modeled after the original Cornell graduated turn-in plan—that "students opposed to the war . . . be asked to sign a conditional pledge stating the minimum number of students (along a scale, from 1,000 to 50,000) they would join in refusing the draft." The conditional pledge would allow each student to set a benchmark for himself as the point at which he would commit to possibly going to jail. "Those who need the reassurance of great numbers can set a high quota for participating," the planners said. "Those, who for whatever reason are ready to incur greater risk, can set a low quota." The project never got off the ground, but it demonstrated the close relations between Resist and local Resistance organizations.[75]

By the middle of December, Resist leaders grew unhappy with the inefficient operations of the New York office. They decided to move the office to Cambridge, Massachusetts, where Louis Kampf, a professor of American studies at MIT, believed the organization could easily find activists to run it.

Kampf's confidence stemmed from his experience with a local organization called the Educational Cooperative, which had attempted to set up a community school in Cambridge in 1966. Within the Educational Cooperative a young faculty group, made up of at least ten people, had formed. This group, Kampf figured, was "ready-made" to handle running the new Resist office. Paul Lauter, another expert in American studies and an experienced political organizer from his work with the American Friends Service Committee and SDS, became national director for the organization, and Kampf took on the role of associate national director. In January, Lauter, Florence Howe, and Kampf set up the new Resist office across from the post office in Central Square in Cambridge. Not long after, a postal employee informed them that an FBI agent regularly staked out the Resist office from the attic of the post office building. Kampf recalled Resist staffers and volunteers waving to the agent and mugging for his camera as they entered and exited the office.[76]

Most important for draft resisters, Resist raised and distributed money to local draft resistance groups nationwide. Bob Zevin conceived the idea of a monthly pledge system that sustained levels of funding from the start, and when the indictments of the Boston Five came down in January 1968 (see Chapter 7), the money poured in. Regular steering committee meetings were held, most often in New York, to make grant decisions. At first, most of the groups that applied for funding were well known to the Resist leadership, but in an effort to spread the wealth more evenly, the steering committee divided the country into geographical zones and assigned each zone to one or two of the younger faculty volunteers. These regional representatives or "area people," as they were known, took responsibility for finding and communicating with local organizations that might need funding. Whenever possible, members of the steering committee and the regional representatives accepted lecture invitations and found other reasons to travel as a way of scouting other parts of the country for potential grantees.[77]

As an organization, Resist was so concerned with avoiding disproportionate funding of local organizations (which they already knew so well) that the steering committee assigned two regional representatives just to Boston and its environs. Hilde Hein and Saul Slapikoff, both of whom were on the faculty of Tufts University at the time, were charged with operating their own kind of mini-Resist just for Boston. As Hein recalls, they did all the outreach that other area people did but also were responsible for doing their own fund-raising distinct from the national effort. "We did all the equivalents of bake sales," she recalled. She and Slapikoff organized art shows, concerts, and poetry readings to raise money for local groups. The money went back to Resist, where funding decisions for Boston-area organizations still were made by the steering committee. Of course, the New England Resistance and the BDRG did their own fund-raising, too, but Resist could always be counted upon for the largest regular donations (or grants) to such organizations. These monies funded the salaries of the few paid office workers, helped pay the rent and other bills, and covered production costs for Resistance and BDRG newsletters and other literature. Resisters were grateful for the moral support provided by older advisers, but it was the financial benevolence of Resist and other individual patrons that kept the draft resistance movement afloat; without it, the Resistance might have crumbled soon after October 16.[78]

Although Resist consistently buttressed the draft resistance movement for the next eighteen months following October 16, like their younger counterparts, the older organizers experienced their own divisions and strained internal relations. Not long after the organization began distributing grants, the majority of the steering committee advocated expanding Resist's objectives to include the funding of other groups working for social change. While some members, notably Paul Goodman, thought the grants should be limited to draft resistance organizations, the others thought that draft resistance was meaningless outside of a broader context of the antiwar movement and other movements for peace and justice. Some of the younger draft resistance leaders themselves agreed with Goodman. At one point, about a dozen draft resistance leaders from different parts of the country crashed a steering committee meeting being held at Paul Lauter's mother's house in New York. They demanded that Resist fund only draft resistance organizations. Noam Chomsky answered for the group by suggesting that the Boston draft resistance representatives present return to Cambridge and sift through Resist records to see if they could honestly disagree with any of the funding decisions. The steering committee never heard such complaints again.[79]

Resist's hierarchical organizational structure also created some tension, most notably around gender issues. Men dominated the steering committee, and although it included Florence Howe and Grace Paley, Hilde Hein was the only female regional representative in the organization. The staff, in contrast, consisted almost entirely of women who were, as Hein says, "just errand runners." The men in the group were guilty of the same sexism as their younger draft resistance counterparts. Hilde Hein recalls that neither Florence Howe nor Grace Paley felt intimidated at steering committee meetings, but she did. "I certainly know that if we went around the room expressing opinions and I said something, nobody paid any attention. And if somebody two seats down repeated exactly what I had said—and was male—it would be heard." The male "stars" of the organization—Chomsky, Lauter, Goodman, and others—dictated the course of discussions. In addition, though she did not think much of it at first, it later rankled her that male members of the steering committee asked her husband, George Hein, a chemistry professor at Boston University, to do some public speaking on behalf of Resist, instead of asking Hilde. "It suddenly dawned on me that this was a little odd," Hein remarked, particularly since she did so much more work for Resist than her husband.[80]

In spite of these difficulties, Resist's support of draft resistance, both financial and moral, helped to sustain the movement from the very start. As resisters faced counterprotesters, intimidating FBI agents, hostile draft boards, and often-skeptical parents, the community of supporters that sprung up among their peers and especially among this group of older academics and advisers assuaged their doubts about their work that naturally crept in when resisters felt most vulnerable. The resisters themselves created the movement and presented it as a fait accompli to their sympathetic older allies, who expanded the movement's reach and helped to carry it forward in the months following October 16.

NOVEMBER 16 AND DECEMBER 4

Emboldened by the euphoria of October 16 and the rush of support that followed, New England Resistance organizers steadily planned their next actions. Although the Resistance chapters across the country planned to carry out new draft card turn-ins on December 4, the NER wanted to move more quickly. They set the date for November 16 and began planning almost immediately after the Pentagon march.

The intensity of the times cannot be overstated. The Resistance office, still in Memorial Hall at Harvard, swirled with activity as the organization tried to keep track of their "members," provide work for everyone who wanted it, supply information to nervous resisters regarding government reaction, galvanize support for future draft card turn-ins, and raise money to pay for it all. In the last newsletter distributed before November 16, Resistance leaders described plans for a service similar to that of October 16 to take place at the Old West Methodist Church on Cambridge Street in the West End. It would be called "A Service of Conscience and Memorial for

All Who Are Dead and Dying in Vietnam." The draft card turn-in would be followed by a march to the federal building in Post Office Square, where Resistance representatives hoped to deliver the collected cards to Paul Markham, the U.S. attorney general. The newsletter strongly urged all resisters to attend. "IT IS ESSENTIAL THAT EVERY OCTOBER 16 RESISTANT PLAN TO BE THERE. CUT CLASSES OR TAKE OFF FROM WORK IF YOU MUST. BUT BE THERE. RESISTANTS ARE NEEDED AS MARSHALS: THE FEDERAL AUTHORITIES MUST SEE OUR STRENGTH, AND THE PUBLIC MUST KNOW WHO WE ARE NOW." With a second act of mass civil disobedience coming so soon after the first, members of the NER hoped to send a message to both the government and their fellow citizens that said that more and more reasonable, responsible Americans were joining this growing movement. The confrontation between the federal government and the Resistance on November 16, they wrote, "WILL BE ON OUR TERMS, IN THE OPEN AND FOR THE PUBLIC TO SEE."[81]

When the day arrived, however, the event did not take place on their terms. First, a major snowstorm the day before greatly hindered mobility within the city and surrounding towns. Instead of the expected turnout of 5,000 supporters, fewer than 500 showed up. Second, and most important, a scuffle broke out between war supporters and resisters, and it—rather than the strength of the movement—attracted all of the press coverage.

As the service began, approximately 450 people sat in the pews with a significant number of FBI agents and reporters on hand as well. The Reverend William Alberts opened by inviting the FBI men to sit in the front pews rather than stand uncomfortably in the back; none of them responded. Father Larry Rossini, a Catholic priest at the downtown Paulist Center and one of the organizers of the event, later recalled being more apprehensive at this event than at the October 16 service. "It was a smaller crowd but there was more press. And the FBI was more obviously there. And I was very frightened. I did not know whether I was going to be arrested walking out of there and kind of put to shame by all these guys who were all Catholics. . . . There was an emotional sense of betrayal that I felt on my part." Several of the agents blended in with news cameramen as they scanned the pews with motion picture cameras. One resister later remarked that "you got the feeling that the people who were systematically photographing every face with the flood lights had to be FBI agents, but the people who were simply photographing the speakers or the [resisters] might well be working for the press."[82]

Outside the church, Jozef Mlot-Mroz, the Polish Freedom Fighter, burned a Soviet flag before a growing crowd of counterdemonstrators. He then marched into the church with a sign that said "Priests, Rabbis, Ministers, Start Fighting Communism. Don't Be Duped By the Reds." Harold Hector, the brawniest of the Resistance marshals, escorted Mlot-Mroz out of the church. A few minutes later, however, the persistent anticommunist returned—this time singing "God Bless America" at the top of his lungs. Again Hector removed him. Mlot-Mroz struggled with Hector, and when they reached the top of the steps outside the church, the freedom fighter fell. In a scene reminiscent of the South Boston beatings, at least fifteen men surged toward Hector and began pummeling him. Years later, Hector described what happened next:

> I'm fighting now. I'm just up there throwing punches, landing—I'm doing all right—but I was grabbed and pulled down the steps. Got to the ground, and I'm still punching, but there's too many guys. Just too many. They grabbed me, kicked me, every which way. . . . [I get up], the ground had little ice patches on it, so I was slipping and sliding. I was down on the ground and two guys held me and kicked me in the face and I went down. And I was trying to get back up and continue fighting and I was losing energy . . . I was just getting weak. . . . And a cop, patrolman [James P.] Barry, broke through the crowd. He came in, held his hand up and they knocked *him* down.

Officer Barry called for backup, and soon fifty uniformed police officers arrived, including a squad of helmeted policemen on horseback and two with German shepherds. They dispersed the crowd. When Hector finally got to his feet, he could feel the blood coursing from a gash on the side of his head. Several other participants suffered bloodied noses, some inflicted by Hector. The crowd cheered as police officers helped Hector into the police ambulance that took him to City Hospital.[83]

Inside the church, the draft resistance ceremony continued without incident. The Reverend Harold Fray acknowledged to those in attendance that although certain pitfalls accompanied any act of civil disobedience, the state of the war in Vietnam demanded that "acts of last resort" be seen as "appropriate modes of expression." Returning and burning draft cards, he argued, just might provide "the therapeutic shock required to revive our moral sensibilities numbed by the war." Fray told the audience that he was "convinced that the majority of these young men in the Boston area who are turning in and burning their draft cards do so as genuine acts of moral conviction and conscience." When the ministers issued the call for draft cards, 54 new draft resisters (far fewer than the 1,000 organizers had hoped for) quietly turned in their cards. Father Rossini and Reverend Albert joined Jack Mendelsohn, Rabbi Herman Pollach, and Professor Hilary Putnam to receive the documents and looked on as another eight burned their cards at the altar.[84]

Although this service did not measure up to the first one at Arlington Street in scale, it possessed much of the same electricity. Resisters walked up the center aisle silently, deliberately. Some of those who burned their cards paused to pray as they did it. "We really believed that these were movements of the spirit," Larry Rossini later commented about the Old West Church ceremony. "These were true religious events. This was not theater," he said. A strong sense of spiritual righteousness moved the participants. "The emotion of the thing was that this was like being the early Christians in a hostile environment doing what they absolutely believed had to be done because if somebody didn't stand up for what was happening, this craziness would never end and more and more people like this would get hurt." According to Rossini, not only was there a strong belief that they were right, but "there also was a sense that there really was a presence of the Spirit in these activities and that there was something important about the flame that was coming off the draft cards, that that was a light and that that was a candle and that those burning draft cards were bringing a light of understanding and belief into the world." The power of such sentiments greatly outweighed the concern that card burning might offend some of the resisters' fellow citizens.[85]

Besides, those few who chose to burn their draft cards fully expected to suffer the consequences. Bill Clusin, an MIT sophomore from Oak Park, Illinois, and one of the eight who burned his card at Old West, realized that the men who turned in their cards were more likely to be arrested but figured card burners might get picked up on the spot. Clusin felt that the government would be making a "very strong statement" if they arrested someone like him—an Eagle Scout and an outstanding student. So he decided to test them. "If they wanted to arrest me they could get evidence that what I had done was illegal," he recalled in subsequent years. "I was surprised that no one [who burned their cards] was arrested." When he made it back to Cambridge safely later that day, he began waiting to hear from the authorities. Since all eyes and cameras had been focused on him when he burned the card and when Noam Chomsky, with whom he had taken a course at MIT, shook his hand afterward, he fully expected to be arrested. It could happen at any time. When it had not happened after six months or so, he stopped worrying. The FBI never caught up with Bill

Clusin, instead choosing to pursue those men who turned in their draft documents.[86]

Another November 16 card burner tried to make it easier for the government to punish him for his crime. In a letter to his Paterson, New Jersey, draft board, Michael Levin, also a student at MIT, reported his crime, noting that he had broken the law in this way only after concluding that all of the other legal forms of protest in which he had taken part had accomplished nothing. "Time is running out," he wrote. He pledged that he would not carry a draft card, would refuse to be inducted into the military, and would aid as many young people as possible, "showing them the reasons why there is a right and moral thing to do, and offering any assistance . . . to shelter them from the legal consequences" of draft resistance. In this way, he concluded, "I hope that we can do what our government will not do—end this awful war." Levin deviated from standard Resistance strategy in promising to shelter other resisters "from the legal consequences." Nevertheless, Levin's letter captured the spirit of Resistance protest and demonstrated that at least some draft card burners were willing to accept the price set by society for the commitment of such sins.[87]

Meanwhile, immediately following the service at the Old West Church, and in the aftermath of the melee outside, approximately 200 resisters and supporters marched the mile-long route to the federal building under police escort. As they walked, counterprotesters heckled and pelted them with snowballs. When Lenny Heller (of Berkeley Resistance), Michael Ferber, and Howard Zinn spoke to the crowd outside the building, four others—Rev. Fray, Neil Robertson, and Alex Jack of the New England Resistance and Louis Kampf of Resist—went inside to deliver the draft cards and complicity statements signed by 140 people to Assistant U.S. Attorney William Koen.[88]

The next day, press accounts in all three Boston newspapers emphasized the fight outside the church and the burning of draft cards. Each carried multiple photographs (with at least one on the front page) of Harold Hector being beaten and with blood streaming down his face. The headlines were remarkably similar: "Fists, Insults Fly at Hub Viet Protest," read the *Boston Globe*; the *Record American* ran with "Fists Fly at Hub Anti-War Rally"; and "Punches Swing, Cards Burn in Anti-Draft Rally" greeted readers of the *Herald Traveler*. The *Record American* article reported a counterdemonstration of 2,000 people at the federal building, although this figure may have been a typographical error intended to say 200, a more accurate estimate, according to New England Resistance members. That paper also claimed that construction workers stepped in to help (not punch) Hector, another point strenuously challenged by the Resistance in their next newsletter. On the whole, the newspaper reports of the ceremony at the Old West Church conveyed very little of the Resistance's message. Its hopes of reaching more of the public through a confrontation with the government on the resisters' terms were not fulfilled. Falling well short of the predicted 1,000 new draft resisters (a number that presumably would have received more serious press attention), the demonstration could only be viewed as a setback. The *Record American* called it a "flop." For their part, New England Resistance organizers, reflecting on the day, said, "It was generally agreed that one month was not enough time to adequately engineer the confrontation." In the aftermath, the plan to wait until December 4 (like the rest of the country) to flout the government's will seemed like a better idea than it once did.[89]

When December 4 did arrive, some New England Resistance activists from Boston joined their comrades in New Haven for another draft card turn-in at Yale's Battel Chapel; others went to Manchester, New Hampshire, to join demonstrators from the CNVA and other groups in a large protest at the induction center there. The event in New Haven took place without incident. Twelve hundred people turned out and thirty-five new cards were turned in at the county courthouse following a march from the chapel. In Manchester, however, despite a promising start to the morning, things went horribly wrong. Approximately 300 to 400 demonstrators—a sizable crowd—arrived at the induction center before 6:30 in the morning, and as many as half of these, according to later estimates, may have been willing to commit civil disobedience by blocking either the inductees' bus or the entrance to the induction center. Two hours later, however, the center made an announcement that no draftees were going to be inducted that day; local radio stations repeated the news. Upon hearing this, most of the protesters left. Shortly after 9:00, when most people had already departed, about forty helmeted Manchester police officers suddenly arrived. They formed two lines guarding the steps of the induction center as a bus full of inductees arrived. The remaining thirty demonstrators ran quickly to link arms and block the steps, but it was useless. As the police pushed and shoved the protesters, the inductees double-timed it up the steps. Police then arrested twenty-six of the demonstrators. While they waited in the Hillsborough County Jail before posting bail, they could hear the irrepressible Jozef Mlot-Mroz leading fifty counterprotesters in chants of "Fee, Fi, Fo, Fum, we smell the hippie scum." Worst of all, the New England

Resistance later learned that the bus had been full of enlistees not draftees. "We can never permit blunders like [that] in the future," the next newsletter said.[90]

Thus the year ended with another disappointing setback. The promise of October 16, bolstered by a growing community of supporters, had been blunted in part by the negative reactions of parents and friends and by the disappointment of the two subsequent demonstrations. Resistance leaders began to conclude that they might have to settle in for a long, protracted battle with the government. As it turned out, the government would not force them to wait long before it made its next move. The long, uncertain dance between draft resisters and the Johnson administration soon came to a close, and the Justice Department's own actions helped to spark a new round of activism in the early months of 1968.

March 31, 1966. Four members of the New England Committee for Nonviolent Action burn their draft cards on the steps of the South Boston District Courthouse. *Left to right*: David Reed, David O'Brien, David Benson, and John Phillips. Moments later, a mob of several dozen high school students stormed up the steps and beat the four pacifists. The four men were later convicted of burning their draft cards, reclassified and called for induction by their local draft boards, and ultimately sent to prison for refusing induction. (©Bettman/CORBIS)

November 1966. Secretary of Defense Robert McNamara, confronted by students in Harvard Yard, speaks to the crowd from the hood of his car. The episode, illustrative of the erratic antiwar movement on Boston campuses at the time, electrified the Harvard community briefly, but it produced little sustained activism. (PeterSimon.com)

October 16, 1967. A crowd of several thousand turned out for the first major draft resistance rally on Boston Common, part of a nationwide challenge to the authority of the Selective Service and the Johnson administration's prosecution of the war. (Photo by T. A. Rothschild)

October 16, 1967. Noam Chomsky, MIT linguistics professor and author of the influential essay "The Responsibility of Intellectuals," addresses the crowd on Boston Common. (Photo by T. A. Rothschild)

October 16, 1967. Howard Zinn, Boston University professor of government and author of *Vietnam: The Logic of Withdrawal*, speaks to the crowd on Boston Common. (Photo by T. A. Rothschild)

October 16, 1967. Following the rally on the Common, draft-age men lead the march to the Arlington Street Church, where they later turned in their draft cards. (Photo by T. A. Rothschild)

October 16, 1967. The capacity crowd during the formal service of resistance inside the Arlington Street Church for the first draft card turn-in. The church setting was unique to the Boston event and helped attract national press attention. (Photo by Bob Hohler)

October 16, 1967. Contrary to the press's image of "shaggy-haired, bewhiskered youths" burning their draft cards, draft resisters more likely looked like these two men (identities unknown). Nevertheless, draft cards on fire led the news in Boston's three daily papers the next day, and resisters eventually limited their protest to turn-ins alone. (Photo by Bob Hohler)

July 1967. Attorney General Ramsey Clark conferring with President Johnson at the White House. In the wake of the first national draft card turn-ins, Clark was hesitant to bring the full force of the government to bear on individual draft resisters. He instead settled on a strategy of indicting five prominent proponents of draft resistance, people he believed could adequately defend themselves and air the issues in court. (LBJ Library photo by Yoichi Okamoto)

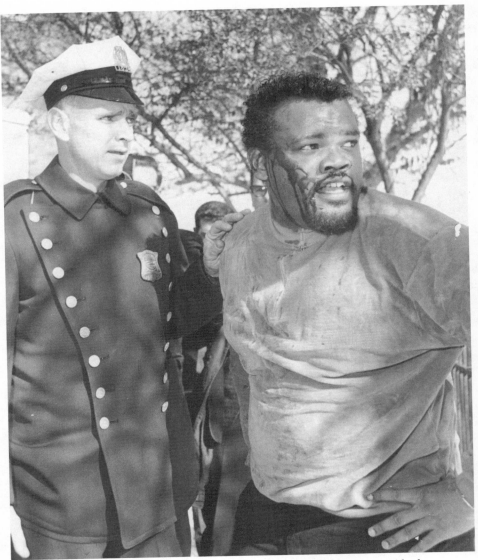

November 16, 1967. New England Resistance organizer Harold Hector outside the Old West Church, after being jumped by a mob during a draft card turn-in ceremony. (*Boston Record American* photograph)

January 29, 1968. Demonstrators organized by the New England Resistance and the Boston Draft Resistance Group picket in front of the federal courthouse in Boston in support of the "Boston Five": Dr. Benjamin Spock, William Sloane Coffin Jr., Mitchell Goodman, Marcus Raskin, and Michael Ferber. For the first time, members of the antiwar movement felt sure that the Johnson administration had abandoned its practice of ignoring dissenters. (*Boston Herald Traveler* photo by James K. O'Callaghan; courtesy of the Boston Public Library, Print Department)

February 1967. General Lewis Hershey, director of Selective Service, meeting with President Johnson at the White House. In contrast to Clark, Hershey responded to draft resisters—allegedly at the president's urging—by instructing the more than 4,000 local draft boards to reclassify as draftable any registrant whose draft card was returned and to call those registrants for induction. In a case arising from Boston, the U.S. Supreme Court later ruled this move unconstitutional. (LBJ Library photo by Yoichi Okamoto)

January 29, 1968. Ubiquitous counterprotester and self-proclaimed "Polish Freedom-Fighter" Josef Mlot-Mroz taunts Dr. Benjamin Spock as the latter arrives at the federal courthouse in Boston for his arraignment on charges of conspiring to aid and abet draft resisters. The indictment of Spock and four others galvanized the draft resistance movement over the next few months. (*Boston Herald Traveler* photo by James K. O'Callaghan; courtesy of the Boston Public Library, Print Department)

February 26, 1968. Dick Hughes and Jim Oestereich outside the Boston Army Base on the day of their induction refusal. Hughes later went to Vietnam and established the Shoeshine Boys Foundation, a network of houses set up to shelter and train children orphaned by the war in a skill. Oestereich won a class-action suit against the Selective Service in the U.S. Supreme Court. (Photographer unknown; courtesy of Jim Oestereich)

Ca. winter/spring 1968. Protesters line the streets around the Boston Army Base in support of draft resisters refusing induction. (Photographer unknown; courtesy of Fred Bird)

January 19, 1968. Howard "Chick" Marston Jr. with his father at the Boston Army Base on the day of his induction refusal, the first of several high-profile refusals following the indictments of the Boston Five. (*Boston Herald Traveler* photo by Warren Patriquin; courtesy of the Boston Public Library, Print Department)

March 26, 1968. President Johnson conferring with the "Wise Men," a group of foreign policy elder statesmen who had supported the president's war plans in the fall but who now advised him to deescalate the war. Internal memoranda show that the president and his advisers understood that further escalation of the war would result in, as Townsend Hoopes put it, "a domestic crisis of unprecedented proportions," part of which would include "increased defiance of the draft." (LBJ Library photo by Yoichi Okamoto)

March 31, 1968. An unidentified man crossing Boston's Commonwealth Avenue flashing the peace sign following President Johnson's announcement that he would not run for re-election. (PeterSimon.com)

March 6, 1968. Ray Mungo, former editor of the *BU News*, refusing induction outside the Boston Army Base. Despite his status as a well-known Boston political figure, the government never sought to prosecute him. (*Boston Record American* photograph)

April 3, 1968. Just three days after the president's speech announcing that he would not seek re-election, the largest antiwar demonstration and draft card turn-in to date took place on the Boston Common. This composite photograph conveys the size of the crowd as Howard Zinn speaks at the microphone. (*Boston Record American* photograph)

April 3, 1968. A young antiwar protester joins the Resistance. (*Boston Herald Traveler* photo by Ulrike Welsch; courtesy of the Boston Public Library, Print Department)

May 23, 1968. Three days into the first "symbolic sanctuary," Boston police and federal marshals removed draft resister Robert Talmanson from the Arlington Street Church. After the officials got him into the patrol car, Talmanson's supporters surrounded the car. The police decided to use force during the confrontation to remove the protesters. The tactic of sanctuary represented a shift in tactics toward outreach to GIS, thus upsetting the stereotype of the antiwar movement as being antisoldier. (*Boston Herald Traveler* photo; courtesy of the Boston Public Library, Print Department).

July 10, 1968. *Left to right*: convicted "conspirators" Dr. Benjamin Spock, Rev. William Sloane Coffin, Mitchell Goodman, and Michael Ferber speak to the press following their sentencing hearing. The convictions were later thrown out on appeal. (*Boston Herald Traveler* photo by James K. O'Callaghan; courtesy of the Boston Public Library, Print Department)

September 23, 1968. Marine corporal Paul Olimpieri, twice wounded in Vietnam, and his wife, Lynn, at the Harvard Chapel, where Olimpieri took sanctuary. After military police arrested Olimpieri less than forty-eight hours after he arrived, the marine renounced the sanctuary and claimed to have been used by the New England Resistance and the seminarians who hosted him. The Resistance concluded that the government had used Olimpieri as a plant to discredit the movement. (*Boston Herald Traveler* photo by James K. O'Callaghan; courtesy of the Boston Public Library, Print Department)

October 2, 1968. Army private Raymond Kroll with the New England Resistance's Nan Stone during Kroll's sanctuary at Marsh Chapel, Boston University. For four days, more than 1,000 people participated in what Howard Zinn called "an ongoing free speech exercise" at the chapel. The FBI arrested Kroll early in the morning on October 6; he later received a sentence of three months' hard labor. (*Boston Herald American* photo by George Dixon; courtesy of the Boston Public Library, Print Department)

Fall 1968. Ira Arlook organizing high school students, Newton, Massachusetts. Outreach to high school students was another new strategy following the tumultuous events of spring 1968. (Photo by Rob Chalfen)

December 1, 1969. Rep. Alexander Pirnie (R-N.Y.) picks the first capsule in the first national draft lottery as outgoing Selective Service director Lewis Hershey looks on. Richard Nixon, the new president, understood Americans' long-standing resentment of the Selective Service's unfair deferment system. A random selection process was one of his administration's priorities in his first year in office. (©Bettman/CORBIS)

February 17, 1970. The president and the First Lady host a special reception for General and Mrs. Hershey, marking the awarding of his fourth star and his "reassignment" as a presidential adviser on manpower. Nixon understood how polarizing the director of the Selective Service had become. (Photo by Jack Kightlinger; courtesy Nixon Presidential Materials Staff, National Archives)

Fall 1969. Mick Jagger wears the Resistance's omega on his shirt during a Rolling Stones performance at the Boston Garden. (PeterSimon.com)

PEAKS, VALLEYS, AND THE CHANGING HORIZON

7 A NEW BEGINNING
CONFRONTATION, RENEWAL, AND TRIUMPH

It is my firm belief that in the complex constitution under which we are living, the only safe and honourable course for a self-respecting man is, in the circumstances such as face me, to do what I have decided to do, that is, to submit without protest to the penalty of disobedience.

I venture to make this statement not in any way in extenuation of the penalty to be awarded against me, but to show that I have disregarded the order served upon me not for want of respect for lawful authority, but in obedience to the higher law of our being, the voice of conscience.

—M. K. Gandhi, Champaran, India, 1917

After spending Christmas 1967 with his parents and sister in his hometown of Buffalo, New York, Michael Ferber returned to Boston and his quiet Beacon Hill apartment at 71 Phillips Street on Friday, January 5, 1968. As he cleaned the place and sorted through his mail he mused about his plans for the upcoming semester. Work with the New England Resistance, which had become all-consuming at times during the fall, had tapered off since early December, and the group did not have another major event planned until the spring; he thought it might be time to "cool it a bit" anyway and focus again on the Ph.D. program that had brought him to Boston in the first place. Others could step up and take the lead in the Resistance—some already had—and that would give him time to pursue his studies. Late that afternoon, after settling in, he cracked open a beer and looked forward to a more relaxed couple of months. But then the phone rang:

"Hello?" Ferber answered.

"Mr. Ferber?"

"Yes."

"This is United Press International. Do you have any comments about the indictment?"

"What indictment?" Ferber responded.

"Well, haven't you heard? You've been indicted by a Federal Grand Jury for conspiracy with Dr. Spock, William Sloane Coffin Jr., Mitchell Goodman, and Marcus Raskin."

"No," a startled Ferber replied, he had not heard. He gave the reporter a comment, something defiant about the draft and resistance to it, and hung up. The telephone kept ringing that night and continued to ring off the hook over the weekend, forcing him to leave for a few days. He quickly realized that his plans to "cool it" had just evaporated.[1]

News of the indictments stunned the nation and especially the antiwar movement. Draft resisters expected to be prosecuted eventually, but over the previous two months the government seemed to be in no hurry. As more and more local boards reclassified resisters and called them for induction, it appeared that the Justice Department would wait for the resisters to refuse induction and then prosecute cases individually. Few movement participants anticipated indictments on conspiracy charges, and those who did expected the local, draft-age organizers to be charged. No one expected the government to go after older advisers like Spock, Coffin, Goodman, and Raskin; they, after all, followed the lead of the draft-age men who started the movement. Yet, although many resisters feared that the indictments marked but the first stage of a wider government crackdown, many more looked to the impending trial with hope—hope that the confrontation with the administration over the immorality and illegality of the war that they had sought from the start might now take place. That optimism, coupled with the growing number of resisters being called for and refusing induction in the winter and spring of 1968, fueled a new beginning for the draft resistance movement. If mistakes had been made in the fall and if interest in draft resistance had leveled off (and not everyone agreed on this point), the federal government provided an unintended boost to the movement by indicting the men the press dubbed the "Boston Five" and by reclassifying and attemping to induct resisters. By April, the organizations and supporters of draft resistance that were struggling to stay focused in December had transformed themselves into what one reporter called a draft resistance "industry," an industry that policy makers in Washington clearly had noticed.

THE HAMMER FALLS

All five of the indicted men learned of the charges against them from the press, including Dr. Spock, who saw his own photograph on the front page of a fellow subway passenger's newspaper that Friday as he returned to his Manhattan home. Over the weekend they struggled to answer reporters' questions without having seen the actual indictments, though they at times turned the occasion to their advantage. Spock told reporters that he had "no qualms" about going to prison. "This trial," the sixty-four-year-old pediatrician said, "will better dramatize the illegal and immoral war in Vietnam, and if this trial will further my efforts to stop it so much the better." Likewise, Ferber, the youngest in the alleged conspiracy, argued that the indictments betrayed fear on the government's part and that its action would "galvanize the peace movement." Like Spock and "thousands of others in the Resistance," he said, "I am fully prepared to go to prison."[2]

On Monday, January 8, each defendant received official notice of his indictment and, for the first time, saw the government's charges. The indictments were handed down by a Boston grand jury to Judge W. Arthur Garrity, a former U.S. Attorney for Massachusetts who later gained notoriety as the judge at the heart of Boston's busing crisis. In the indictment of each man, the grand jury stated that "from on or about August 1, 1967, and continuously thereafter," William Sloane Coffin Jr., forty-three-year-old chaplain at Yale, Michael Ferber, twenty-three-year-old graduate student, Mitchell Goodman, forty-four-year-old novelist and teacher, Marcus Raskin, thirty-three-year-old head of a Washington think tank, and Dr. Benjamin Spock "did unlawfully, wilfully, and knowingly, combine, conspire, confederate, and agree together and with each other . . . to commit offenses against the United States." Those offenses, the government contended, included: 1) counseling, aiding, and abetting "diverse" draft registrants to "fail, refuse, and evade" service in the armed forces; 2) counseling, aiding, and abetting registrants to "fail and refuse to have in their possession" their Selective Service registration certificates and their classification certificates; and 3) hindering and interfering "by any means" with the administration of the Selective Service.[3]

To support these charges, the indictment listed several "overt acts" committed by the defendants to further the alleged conspiracy. These acts included the four older men's signing and circulating the "Call to Resist Illegitimate Authority," Coffin's and Ferber's participation in the October 16, 1967, service at the Arlington Street Church (where they "accepted possession" of draft cards), the presence of all five in the demonstration at the Justice Department on October 20, and the abandonment of the brief-case full of draft cards there by Coffin, Goodman, Raskin, and Spock (Ferber had remained outside) and several others. These five men, the government asserted, conspired to "sponsor and support a nation-wide program of resistance to the functions and operations of the Selective Service System." The indictment acknowledged that the five were not the only ones who took part in these activities and repeatedly referred to "other co-conspirators, some known and others unknown to the Grand Jury," but by indicting only the five it implied that they were the ringleaders.[4]

Even to the layperson unacquainted with the intricacies of conspiracy law, the government did not appear to have a strong case. Use of the word "conspiracy" conjured up dark images of criminals meeting in secret, plotting elaborate schemes over a long period of time. In fact, all of the draft resistance activities detailed as part of the indictment occurred publicly and rarely included all five defendants. Ferber, for instance, had been introduced to Coffin for the first time at Arlington Street and had never even met the other three despite being with them for the Justice Department rally. As a result, some members of the draft resistance movement viewed the indictments as evidence that the government had rushed to assemble its case. It was a reasonable supposition. Even John Wall, the assistant U.S. Attorney in Boston who would prosecute the case, later admitted that when the case came to him from the Justice Department, it looked like it was "a jerry-built thing . . . put together at the last minute." Speculation on that point aside, the movement's reaction to the indictment determined the direction draft resistance would take in the coming months.[5]

At first, the responses within the draft resistance community to the indictments ranged from wariness over what the government might do next to satisfaction that their movement had elicited such a strong response from Washington. Those who felt anxious were concerned that the indictments of these five might be just the first in a wave of repression aimed at squashing draft resistance and the antiwar movement. Rev. Coffin cautioned that "there may be other indictments handed out, and a move to repress a great many people." If that happened, he said, then "it gets pretty serious." Indeed, predictions circulated that more than one hundred indictments would soon follow in San Francisco, New York, Chicago, and other cities where draft resistance was strongest. Moreover, some rumors suggested that the indictments were timed to coincide with an American ground invasion of North Vietnam and that refrigerator units loaded with blood plasma to support such a mobilization had been sighted ten miles south of the demilitarized zone. (By the end of the month, the world would learn that the opposite was true as North Vietnam launched attacks in a coordinated offensive on dozens of targets in the South during the Tet holiday.) The most persistent fear, however, stemmed from predictions that the government repression had only just started. When the five defendants met in New York the week after being indicted—the first time ever that they *did* get together in the same room to plot strategy on anything— Michael Ferber remembers Marc Raskin being particularly despondent. Raskin believed the indictments were the first move in a planned "decimation of the intelligentsia," soon to be followed by indictments of Noam Chomsky, Dwight MacDonald, Ashley Montagu, Susan Sontag, Howard Zinn, and on down the line.[6]

Not everyone in the antiwar movement agreed with Marc Raskin's dire predictions, but most were willing to grant that the government at least intended to scare people away from draft resistance and maybe from criticizing the administration altogether. Howard Zinn later said that he saw the indictments as typical of political indictments, in which the government goes after prominent opponents in order to send a message to everyone else. "Whenever the government has moved against radicals," Zinn later commented, "it has usually taken the top leadership and used it as a kind of lesson for all the rest." Louis Kampf of Resist agreed. The government went after a representative group as a way of "scaring the shit out of everybody," he said. An editorial in *Ramparts* called the indictments an "act of repression" representing a "fundamental break with previous handling of opposition to the Vietnam war." Such "heinous repression of freedom at home," they wrote, "forebodes a greater desperation" on the part of policy makers. As Hilde Hein recalled, the notion that these five formed a conspiracy—the etymology of the word reduces to "breathing together"— was absurd. If they could still be indicted for a conspiracy, she thought, "anybody could be indicted as a member of a conspiracy." Many participants in the movement grew anxious.[7]

In fact, the government did not have any additional "repression" planned, and if antiwar activists had been privy to the manner in which the Spock indictments originated, their concerns might have been eased. Investigation of the men who became known as the "Boston Five" did not start until December, after Attorney General Ramsey Clark and General Hershey issued their joint statement on the enforcement of Selective Service laws. As part of that communiqué, the Department of Justice announced the formation of a special unit in the Criminal Division that would handle draft cases. Clark chose John Van de Kamp, a former U.S. Attorney in Los Angeles, to head up the effort. Van de Kamp had been present at the Justice Department meeting between John McDonough and the delegation bearing draft cards, and he quickly put together a small team of lawyers to "look at if there was any overall conspiracy . . . any kind of national effort to persuade people, to *induce* them to evade the draft." Eventually, that investigation led to the preparation of an indictment of a long list of people found to be pushing for a national draft resistance movement. The attorney general rejected it; he wanted it whittled down to a group of the individuals who were most intimately involved.[8]

Who the government finally indicted as ringleaders is telling. Of the five men chosen for prosecution by the Justice Department, only Michael Ferber was of draft age; the other four were older and, more important, had joined the movement as supporters, not draft resisters. As Mitch Goodman remarked, "The kids invented the Resistance movement, we came along behind." According to John Van de Kamp, John McDonough, and John Wall, however, the government felt obligated to go after the older advisers who were "inducing," "soliciting," "inciting," or "encouraging" draft-age men to violate Selective Service laws. In the government's view, these men invited prosecution. The specific language Coffin used on the Justice Department steps, for example, seemed to come right from the statute books. "We hereby publicly counsel these young men to continue in their refusal to serve in the armed forces," Coffin said. "And we pledge ourselves to aid and abet them in all the ways we can." Indeed, they were asking for it. But more important, the Justice Department's interest in prosecuting these conspirators stemmed in large part from a concern that older, wiser men were urging younger, more impressionable men to break the law. That was not only illegal, it was offensive. Although Van de Kamp, McDonough, and especially Wall doubted the wisdom of the administration's Vietnam policies, none of them felt that they justified what these older advisers were trying to do by urging younger men to resist the draft. The department, as Van de Kamp later noted, wanted to send a message that although criticism of the war and the draft would be tolerated, "inducing or procuring evasion" would not. To protect America's youth and the integrity of the draft laws, such individuals would have to be prosecuted.[9]

If the Justice Department truly believed that coersion was behind the draft resistance movement, then they misjudged it. The young men who founded the draft resistance movement, who worked in Resistance chapters across the country, who planned draft card turn-ins and sent the yield to Washington did all of those things on their own, and they would have done so with or without the encouragement of older supporters. Only when the older men who circulated the Call to Resist sought to raise their own personal stakes did they ally with the younger men by suggesting that they be the ones to accept the returned draft cards and then convey them to the attorney general. Of course, the younger men were happy to accept the support of the older partisans; it gave the entire movement an added air of credibility that could only help the cause, and their fund-raising abilities proved invaluable, too. Ultimately, however, even a perfunctory review of the draft resistance movement should have indicated to government investigators that the resisters themselves were the leaders of the movement. These younger men were certainly guilty of aiding and abetting the mass violation of Selective Service laws. In this context, indicting Michael Ferber made sense. The government might also have indicted David Harris and Lenny Heller in California, Bill Dowling, Alex Jack, Neil Robertson, and Nan Stone in Boston, and other Resistance leaders from Chicago, New York, and Philadelphia. Instead, the government orchestrated the trial of Dr. Spock.

Resistance organizers likely would have refused the support of the older men and women if they had known that the government would choose to target them instead of the resisters themselves. This unexpected response from the administration undermined the Resistance goal of bogging down the court system and filling the jails with America's youth. Then again, maybe someone in the Justice Department knew that.

The answer to this prosecutorial riddle apparently lay at the top, with Attorney General Ramsey Clark. It turned out that no one outside the department—and very few within it—understood the complicated motives behind Clark's approval of this indictment. Years after the trial of the Boston Five, Clark acknowledged that he intentionally sought a draft resistance "control case" or "test case"; significantly, he wanted "a case that would justify deterring other aggressive actions" by the department against individual draft resisters. Two motives led him to this particular case. First, as he later said, "the law always has to consider how you test an unpopular law" like the Selective Service Act. The law, he said, "has an obligation to protect governmental institutions, even when they're engaged in erroneous policy." Sounding almost utopian, Clark argued that in any society "that wants to be democratic and free," important issues like the war and the draft should be "vigorously debated" as early as possible. A draft resistance test case, therefore, would "ventilate the issues, escalate them where they can be seen, [and] provide vigorous defense" for the defendants—or so he hoped. Second, Clark felt he had a duty to avoid injuring "innocent" people like ordinary draft resisters who were not engaged in acts of moral turpitude but were acting on conscience. Here, his own experience during World War II and the treatment of his friends who were conscientious objectors informed his decision to put only these five men on trial. As he later put it, "the saddest thing to see is a youngster out in the boondocks who's a pacifist. There's no sympathy there for him, no support there for him, he's got no way to defend himself . . . and it looks like the whole world is against him (perhaps his father feels he's a traitor, and his mother feels he's a coward, his buddies don't like him). He's got nothing and you come down on him with a prosecution that's just devastating." Clark badly wanted to avoid prosecuting men like this. The Spock defendants were mature, "had thought things through for a long period of time, and had firm—even passionate—understanding and commitment of what they were doing and why," he reasoned. They also had the resources to mount a more adequate defense than an isolated young resister might have. The Justice Department, Clark later commented, "could have ground up tens of thousands of youngsters and nobody would ever [have] notice[d] it." But here, Clark remarked, "with a famous baby doctor and a prominent chaplain of a major university, attention had to be paid." Reflecting on his plan years later, Clark still believed it had been a good one. "I think it was sound government, sound law, and sound morality," he said.[10]

By this time, Clark himself had turned against the war. Within the administration his well-known opposition to Johnson's Vietnam policies rankled colleagues. Clark believed that the president left him off the National Security Council because of it and later admitted that his relationship with Johnson and others became "very strained." The Foreign Intelligence Advisory Board charged that his resolute refusal to grant wiretaps of antiwar groups undermined "not only the war effort then but generally the national security of the country." By the time the administration left office, he had become a virtual outcast, not invited to any of the many going-away parties held in the final weeks. So, in early January 1968, when the grand jury handed down indictments of the Boston Five, Clark recalls, the president and Joe Califano, in particular, were "genuinely and actually surprised."

They did not think Clark would do it, especially on his own. The antiwar movement would have found the president's surprise hard to believe since they were certain that Dr. Spock could have been indicted only with Johnson's consent. (In later years, Secretary of State Dean Rusk countered Clark's claim that he was opposed to the war, describing the attorney general in his memoirs as having never said a word about his opposition to the war to Rusk or anyone else in the cabinet.)[11]

Although some individuals in the antiwar movement worried that the indictments represented the first act in a growing wave of repression, others speculated that the Justice Department had done them a favor by choosing five clean-cut, articulate defendants and by trying the case in Boston.[12] One week after being indicted, Michael Ferber told an audience, "maybe we have a friend in high places." He saw Boston as one of the best communities for the trial because of the strong church and academic support there. Similarly, the choice of defendants made one wonder about a benefactor. "Why else would they pick a healer of babies, the best known doctor in the country, a chaplain at Yale, a novelist, a research assistant who is in the National Security Council, and me?" Ferber asked. They could have gone after a group of bearded, long-haired draft resisters, but "none of us has so much as a moustache," he said.[13]

INDICTMENTS AS CATALYST

Indeed, rather than facing the trial with dread, many people in the movement looked forward to it with great anticipation and with high expectations for how it might further their cause. *Ramparts* magazine declared that "the Spock case will undoubtedly be one of the most important political trials in American history." Echoing that sentiment, Rev. Coffin told a reporter that he looked forward to "a really good confrontation with the government on the legality and morality of the war." Similarly, Rev. Dick Mumma, Presbyterian chaplain at Harvard, told other reporters that it pleased him "that the legal confrontation" would at last take place. "A lot of the hope I have in the human race is pinned on these five indicted men," he explained. Michael Ferber later reflected: "I felt really good for the Resistance. I felt *grateful* that we had Spock in trouble, and Coffin . . . I thought this was the best thing for draft resistance that we could do." Though he knew the trial might draw some attention away from the resisters themselves, the idea of draft resistance would get much more attention and it would be "a huge political problem for the government." In fact, he thought the administration was "really stupid to have done it." Putting

Dr. Spock in prison, he reasoned, should have been the last thing the government wanted. This confidence shaped Ferber's reaction to the indictment when he finally received it in the mail. Accustomed to grading freshman English papers at Harvard, Ferber sat down with the indictment and, with red pen in hand, edited it. He crossed out redundancies ("combine," "conspire," "confederate," and "agree"), marked the split infinitives ("to unlawfully, knowingly, and willfully, counsel, aid and abet"), and circled misspelled words ("co-conspirator," in which the "co-" seemed superfluous). In the margins, he wrote, "You should do better. See me." He gave the whole indictment a grade of C− and mailed it back to the U.S. Attorney.[14]

Although such open acts of bravado were rare, the indictments did elicit a new sense of defiance and solidarity from draft resisters and the antiwar movement in general. In the days immediately following the announcement of the indictments, Resist, the organization of older supporters that evolved out of the "Call to Resist Illegitimate Authority," issued a complicity statement: "We stand beside the men who have been indicted for support of draft resistance. If they are sentenced, we, too, must be sentenced. If they are imprisoned, we will take their places and will continue to use what means we can to bring this war to an end." Among the signers were Martin Luther King Jr., Noam Chomsky, Robert McAfee Brown, Dwight MacDonald, and Howard Zinn. In addition, Resist called for a nationwide academic strike during the trial and another march on Washington. Teach-ins were scheduled at universities around the country, and the Resistance predicted that by spring another 10,000 men would turn in their draft cards. For many opponents to the war, their challenge had been met and now choices needed to be made. "If these five go to jail and thousands of others do not follow them, we can forget about serious opposition to the war and civil liberties in this country," a *Ramparts* editorial warned. "We are all on the spot. . . . If these five men are conspirators, then we must become a nation of conspirators. If we do not stand with them, it is impossible to see where the repression at home, and the oppression abroad, will stop." The indictments served as catalysts for a closing of ranks, a renewal of that bold rebelliousness that launched the draft resistance movement.[15]

The groundswell of support for the five defendants and the draft resistance movement surprised even the most experienced political organizers. One week after the indictments came down, Resist organized an event at New York City's Town Hall with the idea that individuals could line up and sign the group's complicity statement on stage in a very public, dramatic fashion. As the day approached, Louis Kampf and other movement leaders worried that the turnout might be too small. But when the time came, people packed Town Hall and overflowed into the streets. The meeting never opened formally since people spontaneously began signing the statement and speaking into the microphone one at a time. "We couldn't keep people off the stage," Kampf recalled. "People just rushed up there wanting to sign up and made a lot of very heartfelt statements about overcoming fear." Even more significant, the money began pouring into Resist. Instead of scaring the draft resistance movement, and the larger antiwar movement, the government opened the financial floodgates. "Financially," Kampf says, the donations "gave us the wherewithal to really set up a serious organization and be able to look to the future."[16]

In the fervent atmosphere of draft resistance organizing at this time, however, passions sometimes collided. Bill Dowling, founder of the New England Resistance and essentially its de facto leader in the fall, recalls growing frustrated with the organization almost immediately in the weeks after the October 16 draft card turn-in. Instead of trying to organize hundreds or thousands more draft resisters, "to keep the pressure on, to fill the jails," Dowling observed, the Resistance grew more concerned with publicity and media exposure. As a result, the relatively straightforward task of organizing, which was their main concern before October 16, became more complicated. "Once we became glamorized," he later recalled, "people wanted to buy into the glamor, not the action so much." As a result, organizing meetings turned into lengthy debates over procedures, "who should have the right to make that decision, and what the correct policy is." Each meeting turned into what Dowling calls a "talk-fest." Dowling recalls slowly shifting his attention to the organizing in New Haven, where Resistance organizers were not influenced by the "media-ization" of the movement, and he withdrew from organizing in Boston by December.[17]

Michael Ferber recalls Dowling's departure differently and, more to the point, as a result of the Spock indictments. According to Ferber, Dowling remained active in Boston into January and viewed the indictments as an opportunity to increase the friction with the administration. Dowling suggested a massive sit-in at the federal courthouse in Boston on the day of the arraignment, scheduled for January 29, 1968. But some of his comrades had other ideas. Ferber, in particular, saw the occasion of the indictments as an opportunity to broaden the Resistance's base of support and to continue on the course of resistance already charted as they prepared for the confrontation with the government. Switching to new tactics at every new opportunity, just for the sake of creating ongoing discomfort for the administration, did not seem prudent, he thought. Ultimately, as Ferber recalls it, this disagreement regarding tactics produced a kind of showdown with Dowling. After discussing Dowling's plans with his codefendants—all of whom concluded that the mass sit-in would be supernumerary at best and counterproductive at worst—Ferber urged Dowling to reconsider. Dowling refused. Standing in the falling snow in the middle of Harvard Yard, Dowling told Ferber that he and others intended to go ahead with the sit-in anyway. Ferber warned that he would have to come out against Dowling if he did. Disgusted, Dowling turned and walked away. On January 29, the sit-in did not materialize. Bill Dowling dropped out of the Resistance in Boston, and he and Michael Ferber never spoke to one another again.[18]

Bill Dowling's estrangement from the New England Resistance notwithstanding, internal dissension rarely reached such levels, especially at this time, when the indictments actually galvanized more fervent support for the cause. More and more supporters turned out for rallies and teach-ins in the weeks following the indictments. Donations streamed in to the BDRG, the New England Resistance, and especially Resist, which began giving out monthly grants to draft resistance organizations nationwide.

Perhaps most telling, a new confidence could be discerned in public and in private. The tone of demonstrations clearly changed in January 1968. While the draft card turn-ins and demonstrations of the fall generally had been somber affairs, the rallies and turn-ins sponsored by the Resistance in the wake of the indictments were almost jubilant. This transition occurred most noticeably around the time of the arraignment of the Boston Five. On January 28, the night before the arraignments, two meetings took place that effectively marked the passage of one era to the next. Early in the evening, the First Church of Boston in the Back Bay held a service of support. Seven hundred people came to hear William Sloane Coffin Jr. in a contemplative service not unlike those of the fall. But later that evening, the Resistance sponsored a rally (much like a college pep rally) at Northeastern University in support of the defendants. Twenty-two hundred people showed up to hear an all-star series of speakers that included Dr. Spock, Coffin, Paul Goodman, David Dellinger, Tom Hayden, Paul Lauter, Bill Hunt, and Harvard professor H. Stuart Hughes. A mood of both defiance and near-celebration permeated the entire evening. A kind of closing of ranks within the antiwar movement seemed to occur as Dellinger told the hall that it was time for those in attendance to "decide whether we're going to stand with them [the defendants] and take the kind of risks they take" and as Hayden told the crowd, "The question of draft resistance is a line that you must cross if you are to be a serious participant in opposition to the war." Each speaker elicited enthusiastic bursts of applause throughout the night, but one young man, Richard Wolcott, received the most thunderous ovation when he spontaneously stepped to the podium and told the crowd that he would refuse to be inducted into the armed forces the next day. The crowd basked in a new sense of solidarity and seemed emboldened by it. By the end of the night, another $1,000 had been raised to support draft resistance and 350 people signed a complicity statement that would be sent to Ramsey Clark the next day.[19]

No day epitomized the draft resistance movement's new beginning like the day of the arraignment itself, January 29, 1968. By the time the five defendants arrived at the federal courthouse in Post Office Square, 1,200 to 1,500 supporters had been quietly picketing outside for more than an hour. They carried signs saying, "Join the New American Revolution"; "Resist"; "Napalm: Johnson's Baby Powder"; "Don't Enlist, Resist"; "Make Love, Not War"; "End the Draft, Let Men Live"; and most cleverly, "Dr. Spock Delivers Us Again!" A special detail of thirty police officers monitored the crowd while several FBI agents wove in and out of the picket line with their cameras. Naturally, Josef Mlot-Mroz and his group of Polish Freedom Fighters provided the alternative viewpoint. In the battle of the placards, Mlot-Mroz offered his standard themes along with some new signs aimed at the media: "Squash Communism Everywhere"; "Burn, Baby, Burn: Your Draft Card, Your Birth Certificate, and Your Citizenship Papers"; "Dr. Spock—Change Diapers, Not Foreign Policy"; "Don't Call Them Hippies, Peaceniks or Draft-Dodgers. Rather Call Them Hypocrites, Cowards, Anarchists & Bums!"; "Press-News-Media: It is High Time That You Gave U.S. the Truth About the Red Menace, $64,000 Question: Who is Controlling You?"; and "Why is the Press Always Slanted in Favor of the Reds & Pinkos, Vietniks and X-niks?" Twelve members of the conservative Young Americans for Freedom also counterprotested.[20]

Inside the courthouse, the five defendants appeared for a mere nine minutes before Judge Francis Ford. Only relatives of the defendants and reporters were allowed into the courtroom. Two newsmen from Tass, the Soviet news agency, sat in the back (the next day's *Izvestia* carried the headline "Crime in Boston: Crude Reprisal Against American Patriots"). When Deputy Clerk Austin Jones asked for their pleas, each man answered "not guilty." (Several observers noted that moments earlier, in an adjacent courtroom, 350 new citizens took the oath of citizenship, an oath that called on them to uphold the Constitution and to bear arms to defend it if necessary.) The judge set bail at $1,000 for each defendant and told them that they could travel anywhere they wanted within the United States. By the time the five emerged from the courthouse, the line of supporters had become so long that it stretched all the way around the massive Art Deco courthouse in a complete circle from Water Street to Devonshire, Milk, and Congress Streets. A crowd of supporters surrounded Dr. Spock as he stepped into the daylight, and counterprotesters shouted "Traitor!" and "Coward!" A snowball whizzed by Spock's head as many of the counterpickets stormed into the crowd, grabbed signs from supporters and stomped them on the ground. The draft resistance sympathizers did not respond, except for one who bloodied Josef Mlot-Mroz's nose and shoved him to the sidewalk after the freedom fighter called him a "red."[21]

Across town at the Arlington Street Church, where a "service of rededication" had been planned, the scene at first appeared much as it did on October 16. As the defendants arrived and held a press conference in the basement below, a teach-in took place in the sanctuary of the church. Close to 1,000 people jammed the church. Spock told reporters that "the war in Vietnam is on trial just as much as we are. There is no question in our minds that we're not guilty because the war is illegal." The press conference adjourned as the teach-in upstairs ended. As the Service of Rededication began, the defendants walked triumphantly into the sanctuary, where they were met with several minutes of deafening applause and cheering. After the invocation and the singing of *Once to Every Man and Nation*, Bill Hunt read excerpts from General Hershey's channeling memo. Denise Levertov then read a few of her poems; she was followed by Neil Robertson, who read writings of nonviolent struggle by Gandhi.

The heart of the service, however, centered on the responsive reading led by Bob Hohler, director of the Unitarian Universalist Laymen's League. The text of the readings and the congregation's responses appeared in the order of service that had been distributed to those in attendance and, notably, to the press. The readings and responses reflected the new era of draft resistance. They were critical of government policy and especially of the complacency of American citizens in the face of what they believed to be an obscenely immoral war. In a way, the readings were a vehicle for participants to confront their own past inadequacies in protesting the war and to simultaneously renew their commitment, "rededicating" themselves to constant vigilance in opposing the war. In part, the exchange included the following:

Leader: Why did we raise no cry of outrage when our government first sent planes to destroy the city of Vinh in North Vietnam?

Congregation: We believed the false reports and lies of our government. We felt secure because we had elected a President who promised peace. We buried ourselves in daily trivia and grew numb. We did not care. . . .

Leader: Where were we when four men burned their draft cards in South Boston in 1965 [*sic*]? When over 200 men said No to the government in this church and in Old West Church last fall?

Congregation: We were hiding behind our student and ministerial deferments. We were seeking jobs that were in the "national interest." We were able to afford medical and psychological excuses, while our black, poor, and working-class brothers were sent to die. We were working within the system. We were paying our taxes to make the system work.

Leader: The world will say that we were wrong and its judgement will be harsh upon us. The world will say that we should have disobeyed our leaders. History will remember us as "Good Americans" as we remember those who acquiesced to the slaughter of the Jews as "Good Germans." Our children will not accept the excuse that we were only doing our job.

Congregation: We were wrong. But if it is not too late, we are ready now to act.

Leader: It is not too late. For although there are many we have ignored there are many others we can help. . . . Today at the Boston Federal Court, five men were arraigned for conspiracy to aid and counsel others to resist the draft.

Congregation: We stand beside these men.

Leader: And tomorrow, and the day after, and every day until the war ends in Vietnam and our country turns to freedom and justice for all its people at home, thousands and thousands of young Americans will stand up and resist the machinery of war and racism.

Congregation: We pledge to work beside these young men. Their struggle is our struggle. Their fate is our fate. The world shall not say they stood alone.

When recited in unison, these passages, steeped in self-examination and dedicated to a renewed activism, were meant to produce a kind of catharsis among the participants that would reinforce the growing sense of solidarity within the draft resistance movement. In this house of worship, they were to feel cleansed.[22]

The confidence that this renewed solidarity engendered manifested itself in the next phase of the service. Father Phillip Berrigan, under indictment himself for pouring his blood on the files of a Baltimore draft board, issued the Call to Resist. In an apparent reference to the five indicted men seated in the first pew, Berrigan said: "Those of you coming forward to turn in your draft cards do not have to be encouraged by me if you're not already moved by the display of resistance here today." As the Boston Five looked on, Berrigan, the Reverend Richard Mumma, Rabbi Judea Miller of Temple Tilfereth in Malden, and David Dellinger stood in the chancel, prepared to commit the same acts for which the others had been indicted. Young men, led by Dellinger's son, Patchen (then a Harvard Medical School student), streamed up the center aisle of the church and turned over their draft cards. According to one reporter who witnessed the scene, "the overflow crowd rocked the large church with applause." From the balcony, supporters flashed the V-for-victory sign and smiled their approval. Denise Levertov, sitting next to her indicted husband, Mitch Goodman, wiped tears from her eyes as the young men turned in their cards.[23]

Ultimately, twenty-five men joined the Resistance that day, a much smaller number than in the fall, but they defied their government in a ceremony that New England Resistance leaders called "the most inspiring we have had yet." In a letter sent with the newly collected draft cards to Attorney General Ramsey Clark, Neil Robertson wrote: "You will please note that the Resistance has been neither intimidated nor deterred from its activity by the unjust indictments of the 'Boston Five.'" The questionable tactics and public-relations errors of the fall were absent on January 29. Resisters turned in draft cards—they did not burn them. No fistfights erupted on the steps of the church. Rather than intimidate the draft resistance movement, government "repression" offered proof to resisters that they had grabbed the administration's attention. Confrontation, whether in the form of the Spock indictments or, increasingly, in attempts to induct resisters gave the movement strength.[24]

REFUSING INDUCTION

By the time the Spock indictments came down, draft resisters across the country had been receiving notices from their local Selective Service boards informing them that their draft classifications had been changed to

1-A. Each draft board varied in its approach to resisters. Some tried to get them to reconsider. Others simply sent replacement draft cards (with the same classification) to the resister, while still others chose to ignore the defiance of such registrants. Most draft boards, however, declared resisters delinquent, reclassified them to 1-A (if they were not already 1-A), and placed their names in the pipeline for future induction.

In early 1968, the army called the first reclassified resisters for induction and, in doing so, offered the draft resistance movement new opportunities for confrontation. For the resister being called, the induction order raised his personal stakes considerably; noncompliance would certainly mean an indictment and probably prison time. Inductions were the ultimate test of a resister's commitment to the cause. Resisters found it much easier to turn in a draft card in an act of fellowship with dozens of other men than to stand up to the army—to their own government—all alone in an induction center full of willing, or at least acquiescent, conscripts. Both the New England Resistance and the Boston Draft Resistance Group recognized this and took pains to provide support to resisters on the day of their induction refusals.

In January the Resistance and the BDRG described the coming induction refusals as marking "a new beginning" for the movement. Given its experience with Early Morning Shows and Horror Shows, the BDRG felt comfortable confronting the army on its own turf, and to this confidence the New England Resistance added its ability to mobilize large numbers of supporters for big demonstrations. As the army called more and more resisters for induction, large rallies at the army base in Boston became commonplace and attracted widespread media attention. In a practical sense, induction refusals—for the New England Resistance in particular—solved one of the most significant dilemmas that the organization faced in the fall: the lack of day-to-day work for rank-and-file resisters. Equally important, Resistance leaders used induction refusals as motivational tools; these dramatic confrontations would demonstrate their determination to prove to the administration that it could not "silence the American people by resorting to intimidation and bogus conspiracy charges." In this respect, General Hershey's plan backfired. Instead of undermining the resistance movement, drafting resisters actually helped to sustain the confidence and optimism of the movement by providing a vehicle for ongoing struggle with the government. Resisters predicted that more "acts of repression" would follow as the government grew "progressively more frightened of its own people," and they argued that "history will regard these men [resisters] and the thousands that are prepared to follow them as the authentic patriots of our time." As the movement looked ahead to the Spock trial, induction refusals helped to maintain the renewed momentum that draft resisters felt. Although numerous draft resisters refused induction in the winter and spring of 1968, the four men who resisted induction on three separate days at the Boston Army Base—Howard Marston Jr., James Oestereich, Richard Hughes, and Ray Mungo—merit close attention, for their experiences as resisters demonstrate how varied life in the Resistance could be.[25]

HOWARD MARSTON JR.

The Selective Service had been calling draft resisters for induction at least since 1966, and maybe since 1965, but not until January 10, 1968—two days after the Boston Five received their indictments in the mail—did one resister's induction refusal become the focus of a mass antiwar/antidraft protest. Unlike on the lonely days of 1966 when a handful of CNVA supporters—John Phillips, David Reed, David O'Brien, Gary Hicks, and David Benson—picketed the Boston Army Base hundreds of people turned out on the cold winter day of Howard "Chick" Marston Jr.'s anticipated induction refusal.

In many ways, Chick Marston made an unlikely draft resister. Marston and two of his friends applied to their draft board (Local Board 72 in Gloucester) for conscientious objector status over a year before he turned in his draft card on October 16. Later, inspired by John Phillips's example, they burned their draft cards together on the side of the road on their way back from the Cambridge American Friends Service Committee office. One of Marston's friends, Jannik von Rosenvinge, had actually refused induction twice and had never been indicted. On one of those trips to the Boston Army Base, he had witnessed the death of a draftee. According to von Rosenvinge, even before the group of inductees entered the induction center, one young man (later identified as Joseph Didinger, son of nationally known architect Joseph C. Didinger) was "being kind of defiant, just talking strange." Inside, Didinger got into a verbal confrontation with Sergeant Brown, threw his file of papers on the floor, and disappeared, running, behind a long partition. The sound of crashing glass followed. Von Rosenvinge later recalled that he knew exactly what had happened. "He went right out the fucking window. Now we're on the third floor of the Boston Army Base . . . and I remember people moved over towards where he'd gone. And I went down the stairs and went around the corner and I got close enough to him to see that there was no life in him. And I walked away from that place." Doctors pronounced Didinger dead at the Chelsea Naval Hospital later that morning. Von Rosenvinge hitchhiked home and later renewed his application for conscientious objector status.[26]

By October 16, 1967, Chick Marston and his friends, their conscientious objector requests still pending, decided that as the war intensified they could no longer cooperate at all with the Selective Service System. "I figured the time had come for someone to do something," Marston said later. Although his father, Howard Sr., and two older brothers were veterans, they backed his decision to resist, as did his pacifist mother. Marston's father, in particular, was so supportive of his twenty-year-old son that he practically took over Chick's resistance.[27]

The younger Marston would have resisted quietly, but his father led him into a more public role as the elder Marston became the first parent in the Boston area to announce that he would prohibit his son, a minor, from being drafted. Chick later described his father, a surveyor from Rockport, as "the local left-wing nut." In the early 1950s he had led demonstrations in Rockport's Dock Square protesting the Top Mast Restaurant's refusal to serve African Americans. Later, in the sixties, he fired off letters to the *Gloucester Daily Times* charging that the American economy depended on war and the military industrial complex for its strength. The elder Marston was "a great character," his son later said, though he could be "a little overbearing and pushy." Those traits became apparent when Mr. Marston pushed his son into making his resistance into a cause célèbre and thus brought unforeseen consequences to his family.[28]

The New England Resistance and the Boston Draft Resistance Group thoroughly (if hastily) planned Chick Marston's induction refusal in advance. First, organizers held a press conference for the Marstons on January 8 to which they invited a couple from Dorchester who had lost a son in Vietnam. The mother of the slain soldier, speaking for herself and her husband, a marine veteran of World War II, offered the Marstons their complete support. "We feel the war is exceptionally cruel, immoral and absolutely unnecessary," she told the press. "It is a tragic waste" of both Vietnamese and American lives, she said. "We support our boys in Vietnam. We want them brought home alive, not dead—as was our only young son." Howard Marston Sr. followed at the microphone, telling the media that because Chick had not yet reached the age of twenty-one and was therefore a minor, he forbade him to go into the armed forces. In light of the Spock indictments, Marston noted, he realized he might be prosecuted for "counseling" his son in this way. "Friday's indictments only made us a little more eager to act," he said. "It's an illegal and immoral war." The press conference produced the desired effect. Newspapers, television, and radio announced that Chick Marston, with his parents' approval, would refuse induction two days later.[29]

Draft resistance leaders may have envisioned a "new beginning" with the onset of the first induction refusals, but resisters like Chick Marston still had to face some of the old hassles. When Marston arrived in Gloucester to wait for the train that would take him and his fellow draftees into Boston on January 10, the effect of the press conference immediately became apparent. A group of supporters (including John Phillips, recently freed from federal prison) passed leaflets while a group of hecklers shouted epithets at Marston and his comrades. One young man told a reporter that he came down just to see if a sniper would "shoot these idiots." Others shouted, "Let's see you burn your draft cards!" and "Go get a haircut," while one man said, "Somebody ought to offer a medal for putting a bullet through your heads." If the Marstons did not expect this kind of hostility, they were in for a shock when they got to the army base in Boston, where passions would continue to rage.[30]

Outside the Boston Army Base, a crowd of more than 300 people braved subzero temperatures to cheer on Chick Marston and Corey Brown, another man who planned to refuse induction that morning. The crowd had been generated largely by the efforts of the New England Resistance and the Boston Draft Resistance Group, and many of the participants wore white armbands with the black omega symbol of the Resistance. A large press contingent turned out to see the unusual sight of two parents accompanying their son to the base as he planned to refuse service in his nation's military. As the family approached the gates, they were mobbed by reporters and photographers. Howard Marston Sr. told the crowd: "I've been opposed to the war all along. I demanded that he not go. He thinks the same way. I told him not to go, and he was amenable." Chick himself said little. His father stressed that *he* was taking responsibility for his son's actions. "I would like to see mothers and fathers across the country forbid their children to enter the service," he said. "I would like to see thousands and thousands more resisters." The ubiquitous Josef Mlot-Mroz rushed up to the elder Marston and called him a "communist stooge."[31]

After Chick Marston and Corey Brown entered the base, demonstrators continued to endure the cold, perhaps because Mlot-Mroz had shown up with thirty of his fellow "freedom fighters" (his largest group yet), many of whom were armed with signs unloaded from the back of Mlot-Mroz's red

Cadillac, all inscribed with the same fervently anticommunist messages for which they were known. Fistfights were probably inevitable, and several broke out before police stepped in. Two brawny counterprotesters stuffed a Resistance picketer headfirst into a snowbank while several others threw eggs.[32]

Inside, base officials separated Marston from the other inductees and escorted him through the different stages of induction. After nearly six hours, however, Lieutenant Colonel Edward J. Risden, the base commander, sent both Marston and Brown home without asking them to take the oath of induction. Risden told the media that the army needed to conduct investigations into the men's loyalty to their country, but he would not be more specific. "I think that there probably was a reason [for the investigation], but I'm not at liberty to discuss it," he said. This development came unexpectedly; never before and never after did either draft resistance organization encounter this type of response from the base. Resistance activists expected Marston and Brown to emerge heroically from the base after rebuffing the army, but they would have to wait until January 19 for a second attempt.[33]

It is impossible to know exactly why Lt. Col. Risden sent Marston and Brown home but he may have been trying to buy some time while he sorted out his own conflicted feelings about Vietnam. Risden, a veteran of World War II and Korea, served two tours in Vietnam. In 1957 and 1958 he went to Vietnam as an adviser and returned feeling good about American efforts there. But after another tour in 1966–67—this one a combat tour—Risden came home disgusted. American forces didn't know why they were there or who they were fighting, he thought. Complicating matters, Risden became base commander at the Boston Army Base in February 1967, just weeks after his twenty-three-year-old son Joe had been drafted. Risden possessed a strong sense of duty and commitment, yet his anger about the war led him at times to be somewhat sympathetic to the antiwar movement. Eventually, he grew weary of it all and retired on April 1, 1968.[34]

Although a large crowd of backers again appeared at the army base when Chick Marston (and Corey Brown) returned on the 19th and finally refused induction, the support offered little comfort. The entire ordeal, which had been drawn out over more than two weeks, had taken its toll on Marston. He later admitted to being "on the verge of a nervous breakdown through it all." Unlike his father, who loved the spotlight, Marston "couldn't handle the cameras and the interviews." He would have preferred to resist quietly. While he fully expected to go to jail, the publicity added a completely new dimension to his activism, one that put a tremendous strain on his family. "I hated the whole thing," he later said. "Hated it."[35]

Most important, the public nature of his resistance brought constant harassment and torment to his entire family. According to Marston, the head of his draft board called to tell his family that he had information suggesting that their phones were tapped. Marston also claims that during this same period much of the mail the Marston family received had already been opened. Hate mail came addressed to "Chicken" Marston. In addition, Marston and his sister, Deb, recall the day that a local Boy Scout leader led his troop in a march up their street so they could throw rocks at the Marston house. All of this added up to a tense household. Marston's mother was a "nervous wreck," especially when faced with reporters seeking interviews. "She'd start shaking uncontrollably," her son later said.[36]

Eventually, the U.S. Attorney in Boston, after indicting Marston and bringing him to trial in the fall of 1968, dropped the case because the Selective Service had mishandled Marston's classifications. The legal challenge that Howard Marston Sr. wanted never materialized, and a technicality ended it all. The press and, for the most part, the draft resistance movement did not know the case had been dismissed. Just like that, the ordeal ended with no fanfare, though it left Chick Marston "close to a breakdown when it was all over." Thirty years later, he recalls being "lost for quite a while" and doing his best to leave that past behind. He finds it difficult to see how useful his resistance had been.[37]

Chick Marston's induction refusal did, however, help to further intensify the commitment of many resisters and activists to the draft resistance movement. Just as Marston's father dominated his draft resistance, the movement co-opted it for its own purposes.

JAMES OESTEREICH AND RICHARD HUGHES

In sharp contrast to Chick Marston's induction refusal experience, a month later Jim Oestereich and Dick Hughes cheerfully invited the New England Resistance and the Boston Draft Resistance Group to capitalize on their day of noncompliance. Neither Oestereich nor Hughes knew each other before February 26, 1968, their date of induction, but when both approached the BDRG and the NER for help (Oestereich had already done some work for NER), the groups teamed them up for promotional purposes. Two resisters always beat one. A leaflet produced jointly by the two organizations featured photographs of each man with a brief statement encouraging other inductees and draft-age men to join them. "I have chosen to take a stand against the Selective Service System which presently functions as an accomplice to *mass murder*," Oestereich wrote in the definitive style of so many resisters. "It is *very* clear to me and the thousands who stand with me that this war is wrong—and we will not return to our everyday lives until the war is over."[38]

Although they arrived at their evaluations of the war and their decision to resist with the same sense of clear-eyed moral righteousness, Hughes and Oestereich came from very different backgrounds. Oestereich, a seminarian at Andover-Newton Theological School, turned in his draft card at the Arlington Street Church on October 16. Soon after, his Cheyenne, Wyoming, draft board, acting on the instructions of General Hershey, changed his classification from 4-D, the ministerial exemption, to 1-A. As so many editorial writers did in the days after Hershey's memorandum to local boards, Oestereich questioned the legality of such reclassifications. After he consulted with Professor Vern Countryman at Harvard Law School, Oestereich contacted the American Civil Liberties Union, which, under the leadership of Melvin Wulf, jumped at the chance to challenge the reclassification in court. By the beginning of the new year, Oestereich brought suit against his local draft board in the U.S. District Court in Denver. The court dismissed the complaint, and the court of appeals quickly affirmed the lower court's decision. In late February, as the date of his induction approached, Oestereich and Wulf waited to learn if the Supreme Court would hear the case.[39]

Richard Hughes, a teaching fellow in the theater department at Boston University, on the other hand, did not turn in his draft card. His local board in Pittsburgh, Pennsylvania, granted his request for conscientious objector status (1-O) even though, as a former Catholic, he did not belong to any of the faiths traditionally recognized by the Selective Service for that deferment. In October 1967, however, Hughes apparently ran afoul of his local board when his new employer, the Theatre Company of Boston, applied for an occupational deferment for him. The board denied the request and kept his status as 1-O but then sent his file to the Selective Service state headquarters for "review and advice" for reasons that remain unclear. The state headquarters immediately recommended a challenge to Hughes's conscientious objector status, and without notifying him in advance, his local board reclassified him to 1-A at their next meeting (December 18, 1967). Even under General Hershey's new guidelines for handling draft resisters, Hughes had done nothing to compromise his draft status—no turned-in draft card, no draft board sit-ins, no polemical letters to his local board. Hughes could only guess that they objected to his attempt for an occupational deferment while he worked for a theater company. Meanwhile, throughout the fall, he became more and more "obsessed" with the war because, as he later remarked, "it was becoming a distraction from the acting world." He attended numerous teach-ins, got to know Howard Zinn well (in part because he dated Zinn's daughter, Myla, for a while), and read the *BU News*, all of which influenced his thinking about the war and the draft. When the actor Peter Ustinov spoke at Boston University and took questions from the audience, Hughes asked him if he had, in the course of his career, ever jeopardized his work because he felt he had to take a stand over a certain issue; the crowd booed the question, but Ustinov quieted them with a thoughtful answer, saying that although he had never been faced with such a dilemma, he sympathized with American students and the young actors who were. In the end, when the Pittsburgh draft board responded to Hughes's inquiry about his changed status with an induction notice, Hughes decided he would go to the induction but then refuse to be inducted.[40]

On February 26, 1968, a throng of some 350 people picketed the Boston Army Base in support of Oestereich and Hughes. They had marched from the Boston Common through Downtown Crossing, then all the way down Summer Street to the Boston Army Base. The crowd included ministers and seminarians from Andover-Newton, all in clerical collars; faculty and students from Boston University; and a large contingent from the BDRG and the Resistance. Howard Zinn spoke to the crowd as did the two resisters. Jim Oestereich arrived not knowing how the day would end for him. He and his lawyer feared that if he refused induction it might jeopardize his court case, but accepting induction was not an alternative. In the days leading up to the induction, Melvin Wulf contacted Supreme Court justice Byron White and asked for the induction to be stayed until the Court decided if it would hear the case. On the morning of February 26, they had heard nothing. In spite of this confusion, Oestereich made a strong public statement to the crowd outside the base, one that conveyed the urgency and moral rigidity endemic to the movement. "I have come to the Boston Army Base this morning," he said "to say that the securities of being a student, a minister, or a citizen in this land are worth nothing unless I can also affirm the duties and rights of moral and political protest when that country engages in disastrous and illegal actions against an underdeveloped nation of the world community." He said that he could no longer study, teach, or live in America "until we have brought enough pressure upon this government to force an end to this war and the initiation of a positive program for peace and equality in a world torn by our fatal misunderstandings and blind destructiveness." Consequently, Oestereich said, he renounced his "ministerial immunity" to stand with resisters like Dick Hughes, "who have chosen to risk their lives and their futures in the most concrete act remaining to us—the severing of our relationship with an illegal system in pursuit of an unjust war."[41]

Once inside, the pair of resisters followed instructions while doing their irreverent best to disrupt the proceedings enough to attract the attention of the other inductees. When base officials administered an intelligence test to the men, Oestereich raised his hand and said, "Uh, listen, I'm looking at this test, sir, but I don't see any questions about the legality of the Vietnam war. Shouldn't that be on here if that's where we're going?" Nonplused draftees looked at him as though he had lost his mind. Similarly, Dick Hughes elicited bewildered expressions as he filled out one of the numerous forms provided and asked: "If you're refusing induction, do you have to fill out question number. . .?"[42]

Not long after Oestereich entered the base, the base commander, Lt. Col. Risden, pulled him aside to tell him that word had just arrived from the Supreme Court that his induction had been stayed. Oestereich, ready for this eventuality, produced a statement for Risden to sign. The statement, prepared by his lawyer as a means of protecting him from any miscommunication or foul play, asserted that Oestereich had appeared as ordered, that he had not interfered with the induction of other registrants, and that Risden was now ordering Oestereich to leave the premises because of the injunction staying the order of induction. The demonstrators outside cheered when Oestereich emerged with the news. They then marched back into downtown, where they picketed the federal courthouse in Post Office Square briefly before breaking up.[43]

Inside, Dick Hughes went through the rest of the army's procedures and then refused induction. He stood with about forty other men in the room in which all inductees took the oath of service. An officer told them that the oath was binding and irrevocable. When he called each man's name, each stepped forward in symbolic acceptance of the oath. He left Hughes until the end, and when he called his name, Hughes stepped backward. The officer called his name again, and again the draftee refused to step forward. A soldier then took him out of line and explained that if he did not step forward he would be committing a crime. When Hughes again refused to comply, base officials asked him to write and sign a statement indicating that he had intentionally refused induction. Thanks to the FBI and the Freedom of Information Act, the statement that Hughes wrote has been preserved. On a blank piece of paper, Hughes began with a quote that he had memorized from the London newspaper the *Sun* regarding the recent American destruction of the South Vietnamese village Ben Tre:

> What meaning is left in language when the Americans claim to save a town by destroying it? [After the assault on Ben Tre, U.S. Air Force major Chester Brown of Erie, Pennsylvania, explained to the Associated Press that "it became necessary to destroy the town in order to save it," noting that he thought it "a pity about the thousands of civilians who were killed and left homeless."] Can President Johnson and Ho Chi Minh reach the stature to understand that any military gains will count for nothing in the face of horrors like Ben Tre, a town devastated by fighting? If not, history in the end will record of them that they made a desert and called it peace.

Hughes then extemporaneously wrote a statement that equaled the force of Oestereich's morning speech:

> I deeply believe this war is wrong. I deeply believe the present draft law is wrong. After what I consider to be sincere and painful self-examination, I see no other choice.
>
> I cannot, regretfully, reconcile this war and the draft law to my deepest desires: freedom to choose, human survival, and service to principle. I have searched for other alternatives. I have found none. There are none.
>
> Thus it seems evident to me that all of us, as a nation, must face the inevitable question, 'throughout history, and perhaps even now, have not the greatest crimes against humanity happened through silence?'
>
> I, Richard Hughes, on this day 26 Feb 1968 refuse induction into the Armed Forces of the United States. The above statement speaks for my motivations.
>
> [signed]
> Richard Michael Hughes.

When he finished, a base official escorted him to the door and allowed him to leave. The demonstrators were long gone (he had been inside almost all day), and the grey clouds overhead produced a light drizzle. Hughes later described this as "a very sad moment in a way." He walked down a rainy, empty street with only the tall street lights for companions. By the time a *BU News* reporter caught up with him later that night, Hughes had gained some perspective. He recognized the individual nature of resistance now. "It's important to realize that decisions like this [resistance] are tremendously personal," he told the reporter. "But you just have to know that the sin is not the choice, but in not choosing."[44]

Dick Hughes soon carried his draft resistance over into what Howard Zinn later called one of the "most imaginative" protests made by any antiwar activist in America. Rather than wait for the imminent indictment and prosecution for violation of Selective Service laws, Hughes picked up and left the country. But he did not go to Canada, as more than 30,000 American draft evaders did; nor did he go to Mexico or Sweden, nations to which another 2,000 Americans fled. He did what probably no other resister did: he went to South Vietnam. In March, having secured a visa from the South Vietnamese embassy in Washington (based on reporter credentials provided by the *BU News*), Hughes wrote a letter to the FBI and left it on his desk in his apartment. In the letter he said that he could be reached in Saigon, care of the Joint United States Public Affairs Office. He packed two changes of clothes and with a couple of friends drove someone's car across the country for pay. Hughes stopped in Pittsburgh to see his family but did not tell them where he planned to go. He sent them a postcard from Con Thien. Not long after his parents received the postcard, the FBI visited his father, who was then director of Lands and Buildings in the mayor's cabinet in Pittsburgh, at his office. When the FBI agents asked about his son's whereabouts (they apparently never entered Hughes's Boston apartment), Hughes's father gave them the postcard. The agents left without asking further questions.[45]

Although Hughes went to Vietnam as a reporter, he intended from the start to do some kind of social work. At first, he did do some reporting and helped establish Dispatch News, the agency that later aided Seymour Hersh in breaking the story of the My Lai massacre. But ultimately he settled into social work, establishing a home for orphaned boys in Saigon that eventually grew into the Shoeshine Boys Foundation, a network of houses set up in Saigon and Danang to house the boys and teach them the shoe-shining trade. The operation continued to grow every year. When Dick Hughes left Vietnam in August 1976, the last American to leave, his operation had grown to six homes in Saigon and two in Danang, housing a total of 300 kids. Over 1,500 boys passed through his centers in those eight years. In addition, the foundation owned two farms on which some of the boys worked and developed an extensive program aimed at reuniting children with their parents after the war ended. By the time the foundation disbanded, scores of children had been reunited with their families.[46]

According to FBI records, in November 1968, John Wall of the Boston U.S. Attorney's office informed the Selective Service and the FBI that he would not prosecute Hughes. He believed Hughes to be "sincere in his beliefs" and that he had been reclassified, probably unfairly, the year before. It did not matter because Hughes stayed in Saigon for another eight years.[47]

Jim Oestereich's story did not unfold quite as dramatically as Dick Hughes's, but it followed its own twists and turns. Since Oestereich was a seminarian preparing for a ministerial career, his decision affected his fellow seminarians as well as members of the United Parish in Lunenburg, where he served as youth minister. Although Oestereich received mixed reactions from fellow students at Andover-Newton, the faculty there supported him without equivocation. At a chapel forum on the issues raised by Oestereich's upcoming induction refusal, Dean George W. Peck announced that the faculty had voted unanimously to "express its faith in Mr. Oestereich's integrity" and to defend his right to object to the war and the draft in this way. The faculty and Dean Peck found Oestereich's reclassification to be particularly offensive, "utterly contradictory of what is finest in the American tradition." He urged even those who did not "take an unequivocal stand against the war" to speak out against this kind of "mindless repression." "We are dangerously close to a course of action with regard to men like Mr. Oestereich which is more in keeping with the Nazism we condemned at Nuremberg than with the liberty and respect for conscience of which this nation boasts," he said. "No war, however just, is worth that."[48]

Outside the city, at his suburban church in Lunenburg, however, Oestereich faced a situation not unlike the one Michael Jupin confronted in Winchester. Though the United Parish did not erupt when Oestereich turned in his draft card, it came apart at the seams when he refused induction. Three days after Oestereich had been sent home by the army, the church held a meeting to which more than 100 people came. According to newspaper reports, most people in the crowd were outraged by Oestereich's stand. Active duty military men, members of veterans groups, parents of servicemen, and many others spoke. Oestereich claims that some of the people there were members of the John Birch Society and that more than one had pistols tucked in their trousers. When one man made an analogy between the American Revolution and the Vietnam War, Oestereich told him that the analogy did not fit, unless he likened American involvement in Vietnam to the British role in the Revolution. The whole crowd, or so it seemed, groaned in response. As was the case for Jupin in Winchester, many of Oestereich's critics feared his influence on the young people in the congregation and wanted him removed immediately. The minority of those who spoke in Oestereich's defense, however, were members of the youth groups; they said that the seminarian had never tried to impose his views on them and that they rather admired the stand he took on the war.

Eventually, however, Oestereich concluded that he had to resign. The issue so polarized the parish that he feared his draft resistance might lead to the removal of the two ministers. Ultimately, though, his resignation did not save the church. It remained split until one minister began a "people's ministry" in nearby Fitchburg with those who supported Oestereich's position. Oestereich, meanwhile, waited for the Supreme Court to hear his case.[49]

RAY MUNGO

On March 6, 1968, Ray Mungo refused his induction into the service in a manner that stood in stark contrast to his predecessors. Mungo's notoriety as former editor of the *BU News* made him unique among resisters. He could easily mobilize large numbers of activists and attract the attention of the media in ways that no other resister could. The two draft resistance organizations grabbed on to Mungo's coattails and went along for the wild ride he orchestrated on his own. Chick Marston's induction refusal made the front page of Boston newspapers, but subsequent refusals, like the Oestereich/Hughes one, turned up deeper and deeper in subsequent papers; Ray Mungo's induction refusal put draft resistance back on the front page.

Outrageous leaflets publicized Mungo's act of noncompliance well in advance. They announced that Mungo would refuse induction into "Lyndon Johnson's Army" and simultaneously accept induction into "Sergeant Pepper's Brigade." Mungo promised a rock band, a parade, and a speech from Howard Zinn, followed by blueberry pancakes after the demonstration. Then, uncharacteristically for the Resistance, the leaflet predicted that "lots of pretty girls will publically say yes to guys who say no," "young girls will be violated!," and "resisters and inductees alike will goose the sergeants!" Moreover, it said, "Josef Mlot-Mroz's BOMB PEKING sign will flip over and say LBJ SUCKS just as the cameras zoom in." It also pledged that demonstrators would plant 8,000 marijuana seeds on the grass surrounding the base and noted that one resister had threatened to "dump two buckets of his own shit (he's been saving it for weeks!) in the path leading to the base." It concluded as irreverently as it began with two cryptic slogans: "Fuck the Apocalypse!" and "Rise up and abandon the creeping meatball!" This kind of mixing of protest with countercultural impiety did not represent current movement dynamics, although it did anticipate one direction in which the Resistance would go later in the year. But it certainly caught people's attention.[50]

Shocking or not, the advance publicity attracted more than 600 demonstrators to stand outside the Boston Army Base to see Ray Mungo say no to his country. Mungo, wearing a marching band jacket not unlike those worn by John, Paul, George, and Ringo on the *Sgt. Pepper's* album cover, appeared at his Lawrence, Massachusetts, draft board and took the train with twelve other inductees to Boston. Before the bus carrying the men from the train station could enter the base, however, Mungo got off and, to the cheers of his huge audience, climbed on the roof of a car. Instead of entering the base and going through the motions as had Oestereich and Hughes, Mungo tore up his induction notice and flung the pieces into the air. "I have nothing to say to the U.S. Army," he said. "I have nothing to say to the U.S. government. I have no intention of playing their games. But, oh baby, is this ever a refusal!" Although the rock band did not materialize (too expensive), and passing truckers leaned on their horns in an apparent protest as Mungo spoke, the event took on a carnival-like atmosphere. In the midst of Mungo's hippie-goofing, he attempted to interject his analysis of the war and his resistance to it by criticizing the president directly. "It is no longer necessary to say the war is wrong, brutal, economically inspired, imperialistic," he shouted. "It is important to point out that Johnson, Rusk, McNamara know these things too. It is even more important to realize that Johnson continues this war because his value system sees money and power and land and self-aggrandizement as naturally good and desirable things. He has thus forfeited his humanity, and we should be prepared to regard him at all times as a beast. The war itself is the greatest and most powerful statement against war." When he finished, the crowd marched from the base up Summer and Winter Streets, to Tremont and Boylston, to the Arlington Street Church, where the blueberry pancakes, like the band, did not appear. Marchers settled for doughnuts and coffee as they listened to Howard Zinn talk about the war. In the wake of the huge turn-out and raucous confrontation at the army base, Zinn told the demonstrators, the Resistance would continue to grow and would be successful in ending the war. "I am confident that very soon we are going to bring this war to a screaming halt," he said.[51]

In the late winter of 1968, with induction refusals taking place on an almost weekly basis—bolstered by a solid group of supporters—Zinn's prediction seemed reasonable to many members of the draft resistance movement. For one, the earlier uncertainty of the Boston draft resistance movement gave way to a more intense, hothouse atmosphere in which the actions of the New England Resistance and the Boston Draft Resistance Group clearly dictated the direction of the city's larger antiwar movement and continued to attract considerable publicity. In early February, the New England Resistance, buoyed by the indictments and recent publicity, finally moved into its own office on Stanhope Street in Boston, right behind Boston City Police headquarters. Meanwhile, the numbers of men seeking counseling at the BDRG office reached new highs while its counselor training courses continued to attract more people than it could handle. This climate of activism also proved fertile for the birth of new organizations related to draft resistance. John Phillips, not long out of prison, formed the Prisoner's Information and Support Service (PISS), an organization of ex-convicts (who had served time for draft resistance) aimed at demystifying prison experience for resisters. As more and more men were reclassified and called for induction, this kind of support became vital. March also saw the founding of the Committee for Legal Research on the Draft, a new agency established by law students and lawyers to provide attorneys handling draft cases with all of the technical information on the draft and military law they might need. Meanwhile, donations poured into Resist and thousands of men continued to sign the Call to Resist (15,000 by the end of March) and complicity statements admitting to "crimes" equal to those of the Boston Five (28,000 by the start of the trial).[52]

No doubt the movement intensified in part because of a sense among many resisters and their supporters that they could be facing prison time. Many, like Marc Raskin, felt that the Spock indictments portended greater repression. As Harvard philosopher Hilary Putnam later remarked, since no one knew who would be prosecuted next, "there was a great hurry to get something accomplished" on all fronts. Many of these organizations and efforts became the foci of activists' lives. Even social time usually occurred in the offices of these organizations or in coffee shops, in which conversation never drifted far from political concerns and the war. Members of the Resistance movement sensed their strength as the spring approached and simultaneously felt an urgency to use their strength to their advantage, and, they hoped, to bring the draft and the war to an end.[53]

WORRIES IN WASHINGTON

Draft resisters and their supporters might not have felt so rushed to press their confrontations with the government if they had known how much they had already affected Vietnam policy making. They could not know that as their movement gained momentum in the late winter of 1968, the Johnson administration was reconsidering its strategy in Vietnam, in part because it feared greater noncompliance with the draft.

Many other factors contributed to the reevaluation of policy in Vietnam. First, and most important, the Tet Offensive launched by the North Vietnamese on January 30 (the day after the Boston Five arraignment) stunned the administration and the nation. The military's and administration's claims that victory lay just around the corner were dashed by a well-orchestrated offensive that hit 36 of 44 provincial capitals and 64 of 242 district towns, as well as 5 of South Vietnam's 6 autonomous cities. In Saigon, one of those autonomous cities, the enemy even penetrated the walls of the American embassy compound. As more and more Americans began to wonder about the efficacy of a continued American presence in Vietnam, the president sent the chairman of the Joint Chiefs of Staff, General Earl Wheeler, to South Vietnam to assess the situation. Wheeler, like General William Westmoreland, commander of American forces in Vietnam, argued that the American and South Vietnamese had routed North Vietnamese and Viet Cong forces in the wake of their initial assaults, though fighting continued. Indeed, the enemy continued to display remarkable tenacity, particularly in urban areas. American and South Vietnamese forces were spread thin as they attempted to contain the fighting. As a result, on February 26 (the same day Dick Hughes and Jim Oestereich refused induction), Wheeler cabled Secretary of Defense McNamara with General Wesmoreland's additional troop requests, which amounted to another 206,000 men by the end of the calendar year. The next day, presidential aide Harry McPherson wrote, "We are at a point of crisis."[54]

That troop request forced the numerous former supporters of American policy in Vietnam, especially at the Pentagon, to reassess their strategy. It happened that Westmoreland's request came during a changing of the guard in the Department of Defense. Robert McNamara, no longer the resolute defender of the war who had stood on top of that car in Harvard

Yard only a year before, resigned in the fall of 1967 and stepped down officially on February 28, 1968. The troop request issue then fell into the lap of the new secretary of defense, Clark Clifford. When Clifford took office, President Johnson named an ad hoc task force on Vietnam to review the Westmoreland request and to examine the potential ramifications at home. The president made Clifford chairman of the committee. Although considerable debate ensued, most men on the committee began questioning for the first time America's ability to win the war—even with the additional 206,000 troops.[55]

Though draft resisters did not know it at the time, they had already influenced the Johnson administration in such a way that some of the president's advisers were left with no option but to oppose the troop request. Not only had the resisters drawn the attention of the FBI and the Selective Service after October 16, they had moved the president to recall Westmoreland from the field in mid-November for a public-relations campaign at home. This action, according to historian Melvin Small, was "spurred by the increasing levels of dissent." In six different press briefings and public statements, Westmoreland assured the nation that he was "very, very encouraged" and that American forces were "making real progress." In the aftermath of Tet, it became clear that the purpose of such pronouncements may have been to prevent further slipping of public support, but they also created a false sense of optimism and expectation.[56]

After the Tet Offensive shattered those expectations, one theme consistently appeared in memoranda on the troop request: declining public support for the war and predictions of more draft resistance. Phil Goulding, undersecretary of defense for public affairs, specifically warned in two separate memos (March 2 and March 4) of increased draft resistance if the additional troops were approved. "Until a few weeks ago, the people were being told that we were moving toward victory," Goulding wrote. "No one was suggesting extra troops, hardships, more spending, Reserve call-ups, high draft calls and increased casualties. Now, suddenly, the picture has changed and all of these emergency, hardship measures are required." Goulding dedicated a subsection of one of his memos to draft resistance under the heading "Problems We Can Anticipate in U.S. Public Opinion." "Increased draft calls will accentuate demonstrations, on and off campuses," he wrote. Noting that the Selective Service laws had just been changed, making graduate students eligible for the draft, Goulding said, "Now it gets worse. Again, it [the additional troops request] was not anticipated. Letters to Congress will pour in." This memo eventually made it to the president's desk as part of a package of memoranda on the troop request assembled by Clifford.[57]

Clark Clifford received similar warnings from other quarters. Townsend Hoopes, undersecretary of the air force, wrote a lengthy memo to the new defense secretary on March 14. "At the present level the war is eroding the moral fibre of the nation, demoralizing its politics, and paralyzing its foreign policy," he argued. "A further manpower commitment to SVN would intensify the domestic disaffection, which would be reflected in increased defiance of the draft and widespread unrest in the cities." Hoopes had turned completely against continued escalation of the war. He strongly urged Clifford to consider a negotiated settlement. He concluded: "Anything resembling a clear-cut military victory in Vietnam appears possible only at the price of literally destroying SVN, tearing apart the social and political fabric of our own country, alienating our European friends, and gravely weakening the whole free world structure of relations and alliances." Another aide wrote to Clifford that if the president were to grant Westmoreland's request, "it will be difficult to convince critics that we are not simply destroying South Vietnam in order to 'save' it, or that we genuinely want peace talks." "This growing disaffection," he continued, "accompanied, as it certainly will be, by increased defiance of the draft and growing unrest in the cities because of the belief that we are neglecting domestic problems runs great risks of provoking a domestic crisis of unprecedented proportions." These concerns over public opinion, coupled with unsatisfactory answers from military leaders regarding a timetable for victory, quickly turned Clifford from hawk to dove. Clifford soon agreed that the troop request should be denied and that the first steps toward a negotiated peace be taken, but he needed a little more help before he could take his case to the president.[58]

That extra boost came from a group of advisers whose opinions Johnson had sought and valued time and again. The Wise Men, as they were known, were generally older, elder statesmen all of whom had served their country faithfully in earlier administrations. They included Dean Acheson, secretary of state under President Truman; Averell Harriman, former ambassador to the Soviet Union; General Maxwell Taylor, chairman of the Joint Chiefs under President Kennedy; Supreme Court justice Abe Fortas; McGeorge Bundy, former national security adviser; George Ball, former undersecretary of state who before resigning the previous year had lobbied Johnson to end the war; Henry Cabot Lodge, ambassador to South Vietnam under President Kennedy; Douglas Dillon, former Treasury secretary; United Nations ambassador and former Supreme Court justice Arthur Goldberg; Omar Bradley, World War II commander and chairman of the Joint Chiefs during the Korean War; Arthur Dean, chief Korean War negotiator; John McCloy, assistant secretary of war during World War II; Cyrus Vance, former deputy secretary of defense; and General Matthew Ridgeway, the venerated Korean War leader. When Johnson had convened the Wise Men in November 1967, they assured the president that his present policies in Vietnam were sound. But at their next meeting—one recommended by Clifford in large part because he knew that several of these men were changing their minds about Vietnam just as he had—on March 25 and 26, 1968, the Wise Men offered new advice. Confronted for the first time with sobering data from the field and reports of potential domestic unrest, many of the Wise Men reconsidered their support of the war. Senator Mike Mansfield and Assistant Secretary of Defense Paul Warnke, in particular, raised concerns about an increase in draft resistance. Acheson, whose opinion carried the most weight with the president, argued forcefully against the additional troops and urged that withdrawal begin by summer's end.[59]

Of course, the president's advisers did not argue against Westmoreland's troop request solely because they feared more draft resistance. They considered many other factors. The importance of the Tet Offensive, especially, in these reconsiderations cannot be overstated; without Tet, public opinion would not have concerned policy makers in the way it did. The prospect of imminent victory—practically promised in response to draft resistance in the fall—disappeared, and the growing criticism at home limited the administration's options. As Acheson put it, "We can no longer do the job we set out to do in the time we have left [before the public's patience is exhausted], and we must take steps to disengage." The declining credibility of policy makers who had for too long presented optimistic projections to the nation hurt the hawks' case the most. But the draft resistance movement could claim some responsibility for creating the circumstances that led to the administration's loss of credibility in the first place. By March 1968, draft resisters' commitment and their increased defiance following the Spock indictments unquestionably resonated with those administration officials who pointed to a potential increase in draft noncompliance as a risk of continued escalation. In the end, it all added up to deescalation, though Johnson biographer Robert Dallek argues that the president's shift to a strategy of slow withdrawal "came not from what his briefers said . . . or what some of the Wise Men counseled." Instead, Dallek says, Johnson realized on his own that the war had stalemated and that it could not be won without "an escalation that would risk a domestic and international crisis unwarranted by the country's national security." Draft resistance surely would have been at the heart of that domestic crisis.[60]

SENSING THEIR STRENGTH

As far as resisters and draft resistance activists were concerned, the war continued unabated and resistance and confrontation continued to be the only reasonable responses. Following Ray Mungo's boisterous demonstration at the army base, however, momentum began to sputter. Just as draft resistance experienced six to eight intense weeks in the fall followed by a near month-long lull in December, the renewed Resistance of January and February slowed to catch its breath for a few weeks in March. Organizers found that maintaining that kind of energy could be very difficult for long periods of time and that a certain boom-bust cycle would occur organically.

Other variables contributed to the break in the action following Mungo's induction refusal. Most of all, the candidacies of Eugene McCarthy, who nearly beat the president in the New Hampshire primary on March 12, and Robert Kennedy, who joined the race several days later, attracted the attention of antiwar activists everywhere and, for the time being, took the spotlight off of draft resistance. This development concerned some movement members, but they hoped that the huge draft card turn-in and rally scheduled for April 3 would "restore the balance, and give some needed impetus toward continuing activity in the summer." Despite their recent successes in garnering publicity for the movement, the trademark impatience of draft resistance activists made them constantly question their methods and effectiveness. As Martin "Shag" Graetz, the editor of the BDRG newsletter, noted, "a strong feeling of 'What's Next?'" could be detected running through the movement at the time. As a result, the BDRG and the Resistance planned a series of workshops at the Arlington Street Church for April 4, following the big demonstration and turn-in on the common on the 3rd. A "new" renewal appeared to be in order.[61]

Then, on the night of March 31, without warning, Lyndon Johnson announced that he would not run for another term as president. Johnson's speech that night stunned the nation. The American people heard their president put the war (and peace) ahead of politics. First, he announced a bombing halt that he hoped would lead to negotiations with the North Vietnamese. "With our hopes and the world's hopes for peace in the balance every day," the president said, "I do not believe that I should devote an hour or a day of my time to any personal partisan causes or to any duties other than the awesome duties of this office." Johnson's approval ratings shot up dramatically in the wake of the speech as pundits, Democrat and Republican alike, applauded his selfless, patriotic act.[62]

Regardless of the complicated motives for Johnson's withdrawal, antiwar and draft resistance activists saw it as a vindication of their protests against the war. They believed that their unrelenting challenges to the administration's war policies had created a climate of friction intolerable to most Americans. The president had, after all, referred to "division in the American house tonight" and asked that the country guard against "divisiveness and all its ugly consequences." While many of the resisters' and activists' fellow countrymen—like Johnson himself—no doubt continued to fault them for this tension, more and more blamed the president and the war for the disruption in American life. A mid-March Gallup Poll showed that just 26 percent of the public approved of Johnson's handling of the war; 63 percent disapproved. "Lyndon Johnson's refusal to run for a second term," a New England Resistance statement said, "is a clear admission that the policy in Vietnam, already responsible for 20,000 dead American soldiers and countless Vietnamese, is indefensible." At last, it seemed to those in the movement, they were making progress. The antiwar and draft resistance community in cities like Boston rejoiced.[63]

A spontaneous celebration erupted in Boston on the night of Johnson's announcement. About 700 students poured out of dormitories and apartments at Harvard University and began an impromptu parade across the river to Boston University. They crossed the Harvard Bridge, turned down Commonwealth Avenue and began calling for BU students to join them. Another 400 people joined the march by the time it spilled into Kenmore Square. In a scene more reminiscent of a New Orleans street party, the crowd (some of whom were in their pajamas) sang "Ding, Dong, the Wicked Witch is Dead" and other songs to the accompaniment of trumpets, drums, cymbals, and the honking horns of cars. As the march grew to more than 2,000 people, they chanted, "Hey, Hey, what do you say? LBJ dropped out today!" They marched down the tree-lined mall of Boston's most picturesque avenue to the Public Gardens and the Common. Boston police helped stop traffic at the cross streets along the way but became anxious when the crowd arrived at the State House. Michael Ferber, Bill Hunt, and Neil Robertson of the Resistance heard one police officer calling for dogs on the radio. It was 2:30 in the morning, the march did not have a permit, and some of the police looked tense. As the three Resistance leaders arrived at the head of the crowd on the steps of the State House, one police captain, recognizing them from earlier demonstrations, turned on his radio and said, "Ah, thank God the anarchists are here! Now everything is under control." When someone handed Ferber a bullhorn, he said, "This is not a time for political speeches. This is a time for celebration."[64]

Although the party at the State House ended abruptly when the skies opened and literally rained on their parade, the movement's enthusiasm carried over to the April 3rd rally and draft card turn-in on the Common. As one reporter described it, the uncharacteristically mild, sunny weather, and the afterglow of Johnson's withdrawal "gave a carnival air to the rally" of over 5,000 people (the New England Resistance estimated the crowd at 12,000) gathered on Flagstaff Hill. Many of them carried single flowers, jonquils or roses, to symbolize their desire for peace. Over the course of the two-hour rally, they listened to speakers describe Johnson's "abdication" as a partial victory and criticize the McCarthy and Kennedy campaigns for failing to ask if America had any right to be in Vietnam at all. Out of the usual speakers (Howard Zinn, Noam Chomsky, Staughton Lynd, etc.), only Michael Ferber's remarks survive thanks to FBI agents who recorded it for use in his upcoming trial. The challenges that Ferber made to the "men waging the war" demonstrate just how confident and bold the events of the previous three months had made the Resistance. "Let them face that either the war stops and the draft stops, or they will find that this country can no longer be governed," he said. "Let them face the prospects of thousands and thousands of men refusing induction this spring and summer. Let them face riots on American Army bases, desertions in Europe, and mutinies in Vietnam. Let them face the exodus of hundreds every week to Canada and let them face, what is worst for them—the return of men by the hundreds from Canada to join the Resistance. If that is what they want to face, then we are ready, stronger today than ever to give it to them." When he finished, new draft resisters came forward to turn in their cards. At over sixty similar rallies across the country, more than 1,000 men gave up their draft cards; 235 of them did so in Boston.[65]

If state or federal regulations had required the Resistance to file quarterly performance reports as they did other organizations and businesses, draft resistance activists could rightfully have claimed that the first quarter of 1968 and the first few days of the second quarter were their most productive yet. In January, the indictments of Spock, Coffin, Goodman, Raskin, and Ferber galvanized the movement to heightened confrontation and engendered greater solidarity among its members; induction refusals from January through March sustained the momentum created by that solidarity; and the president's decision to drop out of the presidential race seemed to validate the movement's critique of the war while providing a glimmer of hope that peace could be achieved. As April approached, by every standard, the Resistance thrived as it never had. The movement continued to attract regular press attention, increasing numbers of men were turning in their draft cards and committing themselves to noncompliance, huge numbers of people came out to demonstrations to support those men, and public opinion was souring on the war. The antiwar movement seemed to be making headway, and draft resistance led the charge. Resist leader Louis Kampf gave all the credit for Johnson's decision and for the shifts in public opinion to the Resistance. "These young men were the vanguards of the peace movement," he told the *BU News*. "They got people like me involved. They galvanized the peace movement."[66]

What he did not know at the time, and what no one in the movement could know, was that the draft resistance movement's momentum peaked on April 3rd. For beginning on the very next day, the sunny, exuberant, self-assurance that resisters and their supporters had cultivated over the previous months began to unravel as events beyond their control pushed and pulled the movement in new directions.

SPRING 1968 A HOTHOUSE ATMOSPHERE

> Without civil morality communities perish; without personal
> morality their survival has no value.
> —Bertrand Russell, "Individual and Social Ethics,"
> *Authority and the Individual*, 1949

New England Resistance activists learned from previous experience that new resisters usually yearned for direction—and a sustaining sense of solidarity—in the aftermath of their first act of resistance. Consequently, on April 4, 1968, the day after their biggest draft card turn-in, Resistance leaders, as promised, held a series of workshops and teach-ins at the Arlington Street Church. After a full day of sessions, one last panel convened on the stage in the basement of the church to discuss strategy and ways of sustaining the strength of the movement. Based on the events of the previous several days and especially the previous thirty-six hours, the panelists and the more than fifty men and women in the audience felt optimistic. Much work remained to be done, they knew, but momentum now appeared to be on their side. Lyndon Johnson's decision not to run for reelection and the growing numbers of people turning out for Resistance rallies gave them reason to be upbeat. The mood did not last.

That same night in Memphis, Tennessee, Martin Luther King Jr. stepped out on to the second-floor balcony of the Lorraine Motel and an assassin's bullet cut him down. When the technician in charge of recording the Arlington Street Church panel's discussion for WBUR (the Boston University radio station) heard the news, he leaned out of his makeshift booth to the right of the stage and informed the crowd that King had just been shot. The audience and panelists gasped as one, as though someone punched each of them in the stomach simultaneously. Silence followed, then scattered weeping and prayer. And when the WBUR man emerged a few minutes later with the news that King was dead, the shock turned to outrage. The New England Resistance and the entire draft resistance movement in Boston would never be the same. Almost immediately after receiving word of King's death, the Resistance began to fragment.[1]

No social movement takes place in a vacuum; it constantly seeks to engage the broader society of which it is a part and likewise must react to significant developments in it. Over the next ten to twelve weeks, through April, May, and June, an almost constant string of dramatic events—local, national, and international—followed King's assassination. The cumulative effect of these developments created a powerful centrifugal force that started to pull the draft resistance movement in several new directions, away from its original mission and identity. Resistance activists continued to target the war in Vietnam, but in what seemed an increasingly apocalyptic climate, they started to expand their critique of the war to encompass a much broader indictment of American society.

The impatience and urgency that characterized the movement from its inception now served as fuel for its fragmentation. In the weeks following Johnson's "abdication," it became clear that the war and the draft would go on. Casualties mounted along with draft calls. Frustrated, Resistance activists began to think that the evils of both the war and the draft were rooted in more systemic problems. King's murder and other events seemed to confirm this view. Their "analysis" grew more complicated, if not more sophisticated. American society as a whole, not just the Johnson administration or the "war machine," was responsible for injustices and inequities at home and abroad. Resistance rhetoric, therefore, changed markedly from a critique based on the "immorality" and "illegality" of this particular war to wholesale charges of American racism and imperialism. And as Resistance members looked around the country—and the rest of the world—they saw other young people (students mainly) who, upon reaching the same conclusions, were moving beyond resistance, sometimes to revolution.

Although New England Resistance leaders did not see themselves as revolutionaries in the spring of 1968, they did feel that they were part of a worldwide student movement, something much larger than a mere challenge to the American system of conscription. In this climate, their agenda slowly diversified. They reached out to new constituencies, especially blacks and GIs, and slowly moved away from solely contesting the draft system. Paradoxically, this change in the tenor of the movement took place just as the Spock trial, the most prominent manifestation of the original resistance spirit, opened. For months, resisters and supporters had been looking forward to the big event—the "political trial of the century," some called it—with great anticipation. Yet rather than serving as a potential counterbalance to the force pulling the movement apart, the trial of the Boston Five only hastened its splintering. By July 1968, the first mass draft card turn-in of October 16, 1967, seemed a lifetime away.

KING'S DEATH AND A WORLD UPSIDE DOWN

Perhaps more than any other branch of the antiwar movement, draft resistance followed closely the examples of Martin Luther King Jr. and the civil rights movement. That King had been a national public figure since 1956 meant that most members of the draft resistance community became politically and socially aware as the civil rights leader reached the peak of his influence. They remembered the 1963 March on Washington and King's "I have a dream" speech. More important, many resisters and supporters cut their activist teeth in civil rights and, like the earlier movement, draft resistance (in Boston, especially) witnessed a convergence of religious and political activists working together for a common goal. Not only were churches important to both movements, but the New England Resistance modeled its strategy and tactics—always emphasizing nonviolence—after examples from the civil rights movement. Just as King sought in 1963 to end segregation in Birmingham by filling the jails there with children, draft resisters were prepared to bog down the court system and fill America's prisons with the draft-age kids of the middle class. King himself all but endorsed draft resistance in the last year of his life, and when the Boston Five were indicted, he said, "If Dr. Spock and Michael Ferber are jailed, then I should be jailed as well." As Gandhi had been to King, King was to the New England Resistance. According to Neil Robertson, King's death had a "massive impact" on the organization. Losing him so violently rocked the New England Resistance to its foundation.[2]

As riots erupted in cities across the country in response to the terrible news of King's death, the New England Resistance, through its one black leader, Harold Hector, immediately moved to assist the African American community in keeping order and safety in its neighborhoods. They stayed in touch with the Black United Front (BUF) in Roxbury and aided the organization with medical supplies, food, and water. When rumors spread that white firefighters entering Roxbury might be shot by snipers, members of the New England Resistance broke into the downtown campus of the University of Massachusetts and "liberated" all the fire extinguishers for BUF members' use. Although tensions were high, widespread rioting did not break out in Roxbury.[3]

At the same time, the New England Resistance took the lead in organizing a coalition march in memory of Dr. King and called for a three-day student-faculty strike in order to have teach-ins on racism in America. On April 5, more than 15,000 people, mostly white, marched from the Common past the State House through downtown streets to Post Office Square. (As they moved into the square, they noticed the flag atop the courthouse flapping at full staff. Chants of "Lower it! Lower it!" rose up through the canyon of office buildings—followed, minutes later, by cheers when someone lowered the stars and stripes to half staff.) It was one of the biggest marches the city had ever seen. Although the student-faculty strike did not come off as successfully, several well-attended teach-ins and workshops took place.[4]

The draft card turn-in scheduled as the culmination of the three-day strike offered the first indications that the Resistance program would be diversifying. "It took the death of Dr. King . . . to bring home to the New England Resistance the connection between the war in Vietnam and racism," a spokesman said. Resisters suggested that attacks on the draft also were attacks on institutionalized racism. "The Resistance intends to undermine the institution pampering the middle-class while it uses black bodies for an ugly war," they said. On April 10, another eighteen men turned in their draft cards at the Arlington Street Church. These were, of course, men who could have performed this act just a week before with hundreds of others on the Common, yet they did not; it took King's assassination to push them over the edge. Bob Shapiro, an antiwar activist at MIT, had considered turning in his draft card for months but always hesitated—until April 10. Even though he favored SNCC's approach to civil rights over King's, the murder of this nonviolent man "demanded some kind of very strong response," he later said. "The response I decided on was to become more active in the antiwar movement than I already was and to just basically say 'no' to the government."[5]

In life, Martin Luther King Jr. had deeply influenced the lives of many individuals in Boston's draft resistance community, but in death, King drove them to see what he had always hoped white America would see: that racism, poverty, militarism, and materialism were "interrelated flaws . . . evils rooted deeply in the whole structure of [American] society." The night of King's death, resident Resistance poet Jim Havelin wrote a poem that shows that draft resistance activists finally saw (if some did not already) the connections King was making:

When I Heard the News—
April 4, 1968 8:35 P.M.

I was told a little while ago

Martin Luther King has been shot
in Memphis in the face
by a white in a car . . .

ours is the age of the gun
we may die by it
ours is the age of the gun
we may try to throw it away
but it comes back to us
ours is the age of the gun . . .

police are searching
for a white assailant
he is all of us
he is all we have stood for
ours is the age of the gun

I cannot separate myself
from another corpse

We must have known
We must have expected
He must have
and he saw the bullet coming toward him
did he?
the bullet that has been coming so long
ours is the age of the gun

we may die by it.

Havelin's poem conveyed an anguish felt by almost everyone in the draft resistance movement. That anguish, coupled with a sense of guilt for having failed to connect racism with the war before, contributed to a new urgency that led the New England Resistance to completely alter its focus in the coming weeks.[6]

For the rest of April and into May, combating racism became the organization's newest priority. An editorial in the *Resistance* laid out the rationale for this shift: "Dr. King made the connection between racism and the war. He drew the lines between the slaughter in the city, teaching us that it is the same mind that napalms Hue and bivouacs in Detroit . . . thus we have seen that our struggle against the draft and the war must be as well a struggle against racism in the white community. We have all lost a leader." Even Resist, the organization of adult advisers, soon identified their "job" as "push[ing] the political offensive against the war and against racism." It was a remarkable transformation.[7]

Despite the Resistance's visceral reaction to King's death, however, the organization's interest in racial issues manifested itself primarily in print. For example, over three days at the end of April, more than forty men and women camped out in a parking lot in Boston's South End to protest urban renewal programs that resulted in demolition of low-cost housing and the relocation of families to other neighborhoods. Although some Arlington Street Church members joined forces with black leaders in the demonstration that became known as Tent City, few, if any, resisters took part.[8]

No sooner had Resistance leaders begun to emphasize new education programs on racism, however, when other events beyond their control again altered the climate in which they worked. On April 23, students at Columbia University protested against the school's "manifest destiny" policy, by which the university historically purchased property in the low-income neighborhood of Morningside Heights, demolished it, and built new university buildings (in the previous ten years, more than 7,000 residents—85 percent of whom were black or Puerto Rican—were displaced in this manner). In particular, Columbia's plans to build a gymnasium in the area set off protests that began with the occupation of the administration building, Hamilton Hall, and the holding of a dean in his office for more than twenty-four hours. Over the next week, more than 1,000 students occupied several more buildings (declaring them "liberated zones") as the protest escalated into a rebellion against the Vietnam War and Columbia's affiliation with the Institute for Defense Analysis, a weapons research organization. On April 30, between 2:30 and 5:30 A.M., New York City police officers stormed the occupied buildings, brutally beating many of the unarmed demonstrators. They arrested 712 students and left 148 injured. The rest of the student body reacted with outrage over police tactics. On May 6, when the university reopened, thousands of students took part in a general boycott of classes that shut down the school until May 16, when President

Grayson Kirk accepted their demands that formal charges against students be dropped. On May 21, students again occupied Hamilton Hall to protest the disciplining of four SDS leaders. Again, the police came. They arrested 138 people, and the university later suspended 66, taking care to notify the offenders' draft boards that they were no longer eligible for student deferments.[9]

The two major issues the Columbia students protested—one rooted in a racially insensitive expansion program and the other relevant to the war—mirrored the concerns of draft resistance activists in Boston. And although no one in Boston suggested the occupation of university buildings as a method of protest in April and May of 1968, the example of Columbia changed activists' sense of what was possible. "Liberated zone" soon became part of the New England Resistance vocabulary.

Even more astounding than the battles at Columbia were the strikes and riots led by students in several European countries. In Czechoslovakia, students and writers, who were outspoken supporters of Alexander Dubček's reform government, ushered in the Prague Spring, a new culture of free and uncensored expression. In Madrid, students and workers joined forces in calling for democratic, economic, and educational reforms. When the fascist government of General Francisco Franco brought in the civil guard to break up the protests, extensive rioting crippled the city through much of early May. And over the same period, furious rioting occurred in Berlin and elsewhere in West Germany following the attempted assassination of German student leader Rudi Dutschke.

But none of these uprisings stunned the world more than the general strike that evolved from student protests in France. In early May, contemporaneous with the Columbia uprising, students at the Sorbonne in Paris, inspired by protests at Nanterre, began street demonstrations to demand the reform of what one observer called the "totally outdated and medieval structure of the university." When police entered the Sorbonne for the first time in its 700-year history and beat and arrested hundreds of students, a full-scale uprising began. Most Parisians were shocked by the police brutality and sympathized with the students. Ten days of street demonstrations followed, culminating in the violent "Night of the Barricades" on May 10. That night, in anticipation of a police offensive, as many as 30,000 marchers followed French revolutionary tradition and ripped up paving stones in the Latin Quarter—the same stones used in 1848 and 1871—and overturned cars as they built more than fifty barricades in the winding streets surrounding the university. In the middle of the night, the police came with incendiary grenades and the same CS tear gas used by American forces in Vietnam. They clashed with the students all night. Three hundred and sixty-seven people were injured and 460 were arrested as the police went door to door, taking anyone with black hands, gas spots on their clothes, or visible wounds.

A tremendous number of French workers and professionals joined the general strike that resulted from the May 10 fighting. Eventually, some 9 million French citizens went on strike not just to support the students but to demand better wages, a roll back of government bureaucracy, and *la participation* in the daily decisions affecting their lives. On May 29, Charles de Gaulle fled to West Germany; it appeared that his government would fall, that students and workers had forged a revolution. But the old general came back the next day and in a powerful four-minute television address all but sucked the life out of the rebellion. He dissolved Parliament, called for general elections, and mobilized the military under local prefects. In response, an estimated 700,000 Gaullist supporters rushed to march on the Champs Élysées; the momentum had shifted. Ultimately, a combination of concessions to workers from the government—a 35 percent increase in the minimum wage and increased worker participation in industry—and the strain created by a lack of social services (for example, no mail, no garbage collection, and inconsistent public transportation) weakened the strike and caused the majority of the French population to give up on the students. Bitter over this betrayal, the students put up posters showing a student's bloody face above the message, "Bourgeois Vous N'avez Rien Compris (Bourgeoisie, You've Understood Nothing)."[10]

For the New England Resistance, the French students' uprising occurred against the backdrop of more depressing news from Vietnam and a series of local confrontations that helped fuel the organization's increasingly radical analysis of American society. Despite Lyndon Johnson's promise to seek negotiations with the North Vietnamese, fighting dragged on. Five hundred and sixty-two American GIs died in one week in the middle of May—the worst week of casualties yet—and another 2,225 were wounded. The judge in the upcoming trial of the Boston Five ruled that arguments about the immorality and illegality of the war would not be admitted because he thought them irrelevant to the charges. In addition, racial tensions continued to flare in Boston and in other parts of the country. Three hundred black students took over the Boston University administration building demanding more emphasis on African American history and increased financial aid to black students. In Roxbury, someone stabbed Jozef Mlot-

Mroz in the chest when he taunted a crowd of people boarding buses bound for the Poor Peoples March in Washington with a placard reading, "I am Fighting Poverty. I Work. Have You Tried It? It Works." He later recovered, but the incident demonstrated that violence was becoming commonplace. On the whole, the political climate appeared to be getting worse rather than better, and tensions seemed to rise almost daily.[11]

Draft resistance activists found inspiration in the student uprisings in Europe, and especially the general strike in France. They began to see themselves as part of a worldwide movement for revolutionary change. In a telegram to the students at the Sorbonne, New England Resistance leaders wrote: "The Resistance in America has been inspired by your victories and salutes your alliance with the workers of France. We share your determination to rid society of inequality and exploitation. Like you, we are recalling our country to its revolutionary heritage. The movement for human liberation is becoming international, and the future is ours. Vive la Résistance! Vive la Révolution!"[12] This kind of rhetoric marked a significant shift in objectives from the early days of October 16. At that time, no one raised the ambitious prospect of ridding society of "inequality and exploitation," nor did anyone describe noncompliance with the draft as part of a "movement for human liberation." But times had changed, and New England Resistance leaders increasingly saw the roots of American racism and imperialism embedded deep within the structure of their society. "Moral witness began to be spoken of less as something noble than as something educational or as a tactic," Hilary Putnam, the Harvard philosopher and New England Resistance supporter, later said. "One felt the need for what was called 'an analysis.' Originally one did not feel that need. I thought: 'the war [is] wrong and I'm not going to be complicit in an evil war.'" But after several months, when it became clear that draft resistance had not moved the country materially closer to withdrawal from Vietnam, and that more and more resisters were being called for induction—and would be prosecuted for refusing—then, Putnam recalled, "people started producing analyses and debating these analyses." For the first time, Marxist interpretations of the war and race relations began to dominate discussion, and soon the Resistance started to show its leftist leanings more overtly than ever before.[13]

SANCTUARY AT ARLINGTON STREET

As the Spock trial opened in late May, the New England Resistance's intellectual shift became more apparent. On the very first day of the trial,

Resistance leaders declared the Arlington Street Church a "liberated zone" and accepted two men, a convicted draft resister and an AWOL GI, into the first "sanctuary" there. They then issued a manifesto that clearly showed their shift in focus. First, they were critical of themselves: "We have failed to expose the *social origins* of American foreign policy, to identify the economic interests responsible for exploitation at home and abroad," they wrote. "As a result, our analysis has remained superficial and conciliatory." Therefore, the leadership explained, "the time has come for the Resistance to present a radical critique of the nature of our society." The critique that followed shaped Resistance activism for the rest of the year:

> The myth of American affluence conceals enforced want, prosperity undercut by the anxiety of constant indebtedness, and the emptiness of the lives of those who have attained wealth and power. Meanwhile, private industry poisons our atmosphere, pollutes our rivers, and squanders our resources. But even this pseudo-prosperity is based on a global system of exploitation which further corrupts the fabric of American society. Imperialism requires the maintenance of a gigantic military establishment, the distortion of men's lives through conscription or the fear of it, and the perversion of a desire for law and order into a rationalization for and defense of an intolerable *status quo*.

This focus on economic inequality, on "the emptiness" of people's lives, and on militarism smacked of Port Huron–era SDS rhetoric and its existentialist call for more authentic human relations. Some Resistance members may have thought of themselves as part of the New Left when the movement was born the previous fall, but the language of the New Left never dominated discussion as much as it did now.[14]

Although the intensity of the times and the radical examples of the NER's contemporaries may have most directly influenced the change in its agenda, a gradual change in leadership facilitated it. Of the ten people who signed the new manifesto, only three—Bill Hunt, Nan Stone, and Neil Robertson—had been involved with draft resistance since the previous summer. The other original "founders" of the New England Resistance were noticeably absent: Bill Dowling had departed because of disagreements over strategy; Alex Jack remained active in draft resistance but focused most of his energies on the biweekly newspaper the *Resistance*, which merged into the *Boston Free Press* at the time of the trial; and Michael Ferber had not been very active on the local level since his indictment. Like the other defendants, Ferber spent most of his time at speaking engagements around the country, which he felt obligated to accept as a way of helping other local Resistance groups. By the time of the trial, Jack and Ferber, the two men most responsible for injecting into the New England Resistance its Unitarian-based sense of morality (even though both were also products of the New Left), no longer exerted much influence on the day-to-day operations of the organization.

Two other men, Ira Arlook and Joel Kugelmass, assumed more responsibility and, with Bill Hunt, gradually pushed the organization further to the Left. Arlook and Kugelmass knew each other from Stanford and were friends of David Harris and some of the other original Resistance founders there. They came to draft resistance less from a New England–style civil disobedience perspective than from a California New Left slant. Connie Field, another of the manifesto's signers, later remarked that she, Arlook, and Kugelmass saw their work with the New England Resistance more as "movement work" than draft resistance work alone; they always felt part of something much bigger and interrelated, a movement that included other forms of antiwar work, civil rights, black power, the student movement, and eventually women's liberation. For them, especially, the broadening Resistance program made sense.[15]

With the new manifesto and the simultaneous opening of the first sanctuary at the Arlington Street Church, New England Resistance members appeared also to be growing more militant, particularly when compared with the well-mannered defendants in the Spock trial across town. The manifesto, for example, concluded with the statement, "We shall resist the enforcement of the laws we oppose" and the pledge not to "allow" the government to arrest the two men for whom they organized the sanctuary. Semantics aside, these sweeping statements certainly appeared to be more radical than any earlier pronouncements. What did resisting the "enforcement of the laws we oppose" mean? It sounded vaguely dangerous. Likewise, promising not to allow the government to take the two men in sanctuary implied that arresting officers might face physical resistance, and maybe violence. To some mainstream observers, this tone added to the apocalyptic nature of the times, and, as a result, Joel Kugelmass found himself defending the organization during the sanctuary. "We're not anarchists," he told a reporter, "because we're not interested in destroying the social system, but in building a new order. We want an order based on equality, such as equality between the sexes, races, economic equality, educational equality, not to blur the individual differences, but to give every individual a truly equal chance." Consistent with the new Resistance line, Kugelmass mentioned nothing about the draft or the war and focused on bigger issues. "We don't live in a democratic society," he said, "but in an oppressive shadow of democracy in which a few people determine the policies and programs of the country and give the majority of Americans the false impression that they have a say." Although the New England Resistance hinted at some of these themes in their publications in April and early May, it was not until the first sanctuary opened at Arlington Street that the change in the organization became obvious to observers.[16]

The possibility of sanctuary, the granting of asylum by a church to a draft resister or AWOL serviceman, had been in the air for months. As early as October 16, William Sloane Coffin Jr., in his Arlington Street Church sermon, urged churches and temples to grant sanctuary. But only as the Resistance searched for new tactics beyond draft card turn-ins did it become more likely. Once again, twenty-one-year-old Robert Talmanson, the CNVA activist who burned his card outside the federal courthouse in June 1966 and who later made the first efforts to start a Resistance chapter in Boston, found himself at the center of a new phase of draft resistance in the city. In the middle of May, the U.S. Supreme Court refused to hear Talmanson's appeal of his conviction for burning his draft card, so the first sanctuary began with him. Army private William Chase, a nineteen-year-old high school dropout and former garbage collector from Dennis, Massachusetts, joined Talmanson in sanctuary. Chase had served as a clerk in Cam Ranh Bay for nine months and on three occasions sought psychiatric discharges from the army; all were denied. Later, Chase went Absent Without Leave (AWOL) for twenty days, and when the army did not discharge him—instead ordering him to report to Fort Lewis, Washington—Chase again went AWOL and soon gravitated toward the Resistance looking for help.[17]

In some ways, Chase represented a sizable number of alienated servicemen. GI desertions continued to plague the American military in 1968 after record numbers fled the army and marines in 1967. According to historian Richard Moser, the rate of army AWOL cases jumped from 57.2 per thousand in 1966 to 78 per thousand in 1967. Total desertion from the army (absence over thirty days) climbed from 14.9 per thousand in 1966 to 21.4 in 1967. The marines fared little better, with desertion rates increasing from 16.1 per thousand to 26.8 per thousand from 1966 to 1967. Altogether, Moser reports, the military listed 40,277 men as deserters by June 30, 1967. Many of those men wound up in Sweden or in Canada (though Canada had an extradition agreement with the United States in such cases), but none had yet taken the course Bill Chase had in seeking the assistance of a civilian antiwar group to publicly announce his desertion as a way of protesting the war. In subsequent months, dozens of servicemen followed Chase's lead, possibly because they believed that the publicity might keep the military from channeling them to either the stockade or Vietnam. But Chase had no idea what would happen when he joined Talmanson at the Arlington Street Church. He knew only that he did not want to go back to Vietnam.[18]

The Reverend Jack Mendelsohn learned of his church's distinction as the first one in the country to offer sanctuary to a serviceman as he campaigned for Robert Kennedy in California. In fact, Mendelsohn's executive assistant, Victor Jokel, made the decision to host the first sanctuary at Arlington Street almost unilaterally. He did have the support of Ed Harris, the associate minister, and Bob Hohler, a "lay minister" of the church and executive director of the Unitarian Universalist's Laymen's League, but he did not consult with the Prudential Committee, which represented the parishioners. Ralph Conant, the chairman of the Prudential Committee, learned of Jokel's plans by chance but opted not to intervene because he wanted to avoid "unfortunate consequences of a confrontation with the New England Resistance movement." If not supportive of draft resistance, some members of the church—like Conant—were resigned to such activities taking place in their place of worship. The sanctuary eventually tested the limits of their patience.[19]

The tradition of sanctuary dated to ancient times and had been used extensively as late as the Middle Ages. In the Book of Kings, when King David's son and military commander, Joab, takes refuge from King Solomon's soldiers, he does so in a tent containing the Ark of the Covenant, a holy place. In 693, the King of West Saxons (England) declared that anyone who committed a capital crime could save himself from the penalty of death if he took asylum in a church. This sanctuary law lasted in England until 1623, when an act of Parliament abolished it. Still, when Victor Jokel opened the sanctuary at Arlington Street, he emphasized that no one expected it to have any legal force, nor did he think it should. Instead, he noted, "this historic concept, as renewed today, has the force of a moral imperative on the side of life and man at a time when, through well-meaning but tragic misguidance, the leadership of our country, gutting its ideals, indicts its patriots and acts as executioner for thousands of this generation of young men—American and Vietnamese of both sides."[20]

This first sanctuary marked an important turning point for the antiwar movement. First, it set off a wave of dozens of other sanctuaries in churches across the country, most of which granted asylum to deserting

American GIS. Over the next fifteen months, at least fifty-four men (forty-nine of whom were AWOL servicemen) took sanctuary in more than twenty cities and towns across the country, including Boston; New York; Philadelphia; Chicago; San Francisco; South Bend, Indiana; Columbus, Ohio; Providence, Rhode Island; and Honolulu, Hawaii. Second, it demonstrated for the first time (and quite clearly) that the antiwar movement and American servicemen were not necessarily antagonists. While some civilian opponents of the war no doubt regarded soldiers with suspicion, by the middle of 1968, more and more antiwar activists understood that men who enlisted or submitted to the draft did so for various reasons, most of which did not stem from strong convictions about the war, communism, or anticommunism. Finally, the sanctuary movement signaled the shift in the focus of the antiwar movement. Increasingly, as the civilian antiwar movement began to fragment in 1968 and 1969, and as GI dissent escalated, veterans groups such as Vietnam Veterans Against the War began to assume a more prominent role in the movement. The tactic of sanctuary ushered in that transition.

To many resisters and their community of supporters, sanctuary offered a creative redirection for the Resistance, something new (and newsworthy) to do in place of draft card turn-ins. Over the course of ten days, the participants treated the church more like a meetinghouse where, as in seventeenth-century New England, a community would meet to tend to all of its business, not just its religious instruction.

Within hours of its start, the Talmanson and Clark's sanctuary began to take on a life of its own. At times, it seemed like an ongoing teach-in. At other times, the crowd focused on preparing for the authorities who would inevitably come. On occasion it also took on the characteristics of a big party. On the first night, several hundred people turned out for dinner in the church basement. Organizers showed films of past draft card turn-ins, and musicians played the blues for the crowd. A couple of nights later the rock band Earth Opera (led by future bluegrass greats Peter Rowan and David Grisman) performed on the stage in the basement of the church. More than seventy people spent the first night in the church awaiting the police, and the crowds grew each night. Every day people could be found sleeping, eating, cooking, giving speeches, and having "endless conversations." Some roamed around trying to keep everyone's spirits up, trying to build solidarity. And reporters mingled throughout the building interviewing as many participants as they could. Joel Kugelmass later called it "a very beautiful thing" because of the range of people who got involved. In addition to diehard activists, he said, some members of the church helped, and several suburban women came in with sandwiches for everyone. By using the church, the New England Resistance immediately attracted new supporters. The sanctuary began to be "self-propagating," Kugelmass noted.[21]

No one knew exactly when the authorities would come, though U.S. Attorney Paul Markham had warned that although he hoped he would not have to use U.S. marshals to apprehend Talmanson, "if it comes to that we will have to do our duty." At about 3:30 P.M. on May 22, the third day of the sanctuary, Markham and the marshals arrived, walked up the front steps of the church, and entered the sanctuary. Father Anthony Mullaney of St. Phillips Rectory in Roxbury met the four men and told them that they were about to "violate a moral sanctuary." He especially stressed to Markham that if they passed the crowd of supporters and took Robert Talmanson, the U.S. Attorney and his marshals would be cooperating with a law that Mullaney and everyone else in the church believed to be immoral. The government men listened politely and then stepped past the priest. One could have heard a pin drop as the marshals approached Talmanson, then standing at the massive mahogany pulpit, and told him that they were placing him under arrest. Talmanson replied that he would not resist and fell limp into the arms of the marshals. There had been no violence, just the promised moral confrontation, and they carried Talmanson from the pulpit.[22]

Order began to unravel, however, as the marshals attempted to leave the church. For some reason, Markham and the marshals elected not to go out the way they came in and instead took Talmanson outside via a side door that led to an alley that runs down the right side of the church, bisecting the block between Arlington and Berkeley Streets. When the marshals emerged with Talmanson, they met the crowd of supporters, who had moved from the front of the church down the alley and now stood before them with their arms interlocked. The path to the marshal's car was blocked. For approximately forty-five minutes, the action stalled as Markham and the marshals plotted what to do next. Talmanson sat on the ground reading Chinese poetry with marshals standing on both sides of him. The protesters sang the "Battle Hymn of the Republic," "America," "We Shall Not Be Moved," and other civil rights songs. As a steady rain began to fall, shouts of "You're beautiful, man," and "We love you" buoyed the spirits of the arrested man.

At about 4:15 P.M., demonstrators could see that the marshals had a new plan. Fifteen Boston police officers suddenly emerged from the Ritz Carlton

Hotel's parking lot on Newbury Street, which bordered the alley in which the protesters were confronting Talmanson's captors. The police moved up the alley to offer support to their federal counterparts. They did not wear riot gear or carry tear gas guns. Eventually, some twenty-five police officers arrived at the Ritz parking lot aided by another six who walked down Newbury Street from Arlington to give them support. The marshals picked up Talmanson and once again tried to move him through the crowd, now numbering several hundred. When that failed, they quickly turned toward the parking lot and, with police officers forming a barrier between the marshals and the protesters, they whisked Talmanson to a waiting squad car. Along the way, several officers pushed protesters to the ground. Tensions quickly heightened.

Before the police and marshals could get Talmanson into the back seat, supporters ran to sit down in front of the police car. Michael "Walrus" Colpitts laid himself out across the hood (and later under the wheels) of the car, and two other protesters lay on its roof. By this time, the demonstrators were soaked to the skin, so when it became clear that there would be another delay in the action, a few ran into the church to get blankets and coats for the crowd. During the calm, a helicopter flew over the crowd. When one demonstrator yelled, "Look out! Here comes the napalm!" for a moment, amid the tension, even some of the police officers laughed.

Finally, however, the police made it clear that they meant business. A police wagon pulled up in front of the parking lot on Newbury Street. Then, all at once, the marshals pulled Talmanson from the surrounded police car and the police officers formed a phalanx that pushed through the crowd to bring the arrested man to the wagon. Officers pulled the woman from the top of the car by her hair, and as they moved through the crowd some of them clubbed and punched the sitting or standing demonstrators; others sprayed them in the face with mace. Some demonstrators were kicked or trampled. The police later denied using nightsticks on the demonstrators, but participant and eyewitness accounts confirmed that the twenty protesters who were hurt primarily had been clubbed and punched by police. One reporter for the *Boston Free Press*, an underground newspaper, evaluated tapes, still photographs, and witness accounts and concluded that the violence was "police-originated." The reporter noted that "although the police were tugged at, pushed and obstructed, at no time did any Resistance demonstrator strike or attempt to strike a police officer."[23]

Not every police officer participated in the beatings. John Phillips, one of the original South Boston draft card burners and no stranger to such frenzies, later recalled that he shook hands with Deputy Superintendent Joseph Saia "in the middle of the carnage that was going on underneath us" because Saia was so obviously trying to "control things, control his officers." Likewise, Dan Tilton, who had been sitting in front of the car, recalled that after a "beefy" policeman grabbed him and threw him (practically through the air) to the ground, another cop held Tilton down on the ground and said, "I don't want to be a part of this. Just stay where you are." Despite these examples of police restraint, many Resistance activists now feared that the Boston police had reached their limit. Historically, the New England Resistance had always been grateful that Boston police handled demonstrations and crowds better than their counterparts in other cities. Following the melee in the Ritz parking lot, however, activists suspected that Boston cops might start responding like Oakland or New York City police. In any case, the physical confrontation, coupled with the arrest of sixteen demonstrators, added up to a stunning end to Robert Talmanson's sanctuary and set an example that activists hoped would not be repeated when the army came for Bill Chase.[24]

From one perspective, the skirmish with police bolstered the level of attention already being paid to draft resistance because of the ongoing Spock trial. After the dust settled from the clash outside the church, Michael Ferber arrived in the middle of a meeting called by the New England Resistance to discuss how to handle the military authorities who would undoubtedly be coming for Bill Chase. "We are all over the city," Ferber triumphantly told the crowd after he had spent the day in court (where the prosecution showed films of the October 16 draft card turn-in) and walked through the Boston Common and the Public Garden, listening to the buzz. The title of one reporter's mid-June article, "The Boston Happening," referred not just to the trial. Draft resistance and discussion of it seemed to dominate the city's discourse.[25]

Editors at the *Boston Globe*, however, offered an alternative view of the sanctuary altercation in an editorial titled "Can We Keep Our Cool?" The *Globe*, like some resisters, feared that the violence hitherto seen in other parts of the country had now spread to Boston. "Is this result inevitable?" they asked. "Isn't it possible for demonstrators to make their points and police to carry out their duties without spilling blood? Or is violence so much a part of the American heritage that real, mutual non-violence still doesn't have a chance in our society?" It appeared that the apocalyptic mood that seemed to be sweeping the world wherever young people congregated might have migrated to Boston, too.[26]

Four days later, as Bill Chase and his supporters awaited his arrest, the Resistance suffered another blow. On May 27, just a week after agreeing to hear Jim Oestereich's suit against his Cheyenne, Wyoming, draft board, the U.S. Supreme Court ruled seven to one against draft resister David O'Brien. O'Brien, one of the four men beaten on the South Boston courthouse steps in March 1966, had seen his lower court conviction overturned by Boston's First Circuit Court of Appeals on the grounds that burning one's draft card constituted "symbolic" speech and that the 1965 law prohibiting the destruction of draft cards violated the First Amendment. The appellate court ruled that although O'Brien could be convicted for failure to carry his card, he could not be tried for burning it. The Supreme Court, however, disagreed and overturned the appeal. Chief Justice Earl Warren, writing for the majority, argued that when speech (the burning of the card) and "nonspeech" (nonpossession of the card) are combined in the same action, and the government has a reasonable interest in limiting the nonspeech element, then the "incidental limitation on First Amendment freedoms" is reasonable. The Court, therefore, did not disagree with the lower court's characterization of a draft card burning as "symbolic" speech but found that the Selective Service System had a substantial interest in "an efficient and easily administered system for raising armies." O'Brien undermined that interest, the Court asserted, once he failed to possess his draft card. Although O'Brien ultimately lost the case, the judge who heard his resentencing appeal did not return him to prison; instead, O'Brien took a hospital job to work off his sentence.[27]

For the rest of the draft resistance community, the only silver lining in the O'Brien ruling came from the lone dissenter, Justice William O. Douglas (Justice Thurgood Marshall did not participate in the case), who suggested that the Court order the case to be reargued on the broader issue of whether the military draft is permissible at all in the absence of a declaration of war. He also asked several rhetorical questions: "Is the war in Vietnam a constitutional war? Is it constitutional to have an 'executive' war? Is it constitutional to have an 'executive-declared' war? Is it not entirely up to Congress to declare war?" Antiwar activists, of course, wanted answers to these questions, too.[28]

Still, Justice Douglas's dissenting opinion offered small solace to draft resistance activists in Boston. After the promising start of the Talmanson-Chase sanctuary, they found themselves bloodied by police batons and discouraged by a court system that seemed to favor the government over its citizens. David O'Brien suggested that the Court's decision in his case, combined with the recent conviction of Father Philip Berrigan and three others in Baltimore (for pouring blood on draft files) and the ongoing trial of Dr. Spock, demonstrated that the United States and its courts were "moving toward an authoritarian state." Two days after the O'Brien decision came down, Bill Chase turned himself in to authorities at the federal building in exchange for a promise of psychiatric tests; it was an anticlimactic end for antiwar activists hoping to milk the sanctuary for more publicity. In addition, Resistance leaders put plans for future sanctuaries at the Arlington Street Church on hold when the church lost its insurance. (It turned out that an executive from Aetna Insurance witnessed the Talmanson arrest and ensuing commotion from his window in the Ritz Carlton Hotel and immediately called his office to have the company drop the Arlington Street Church's $1.4 million in fire insurance and public liability coverage). All in all, despite frequent mention in the press, the Resistance seemed to have gone a little flat as more and more members grew disillusioned, unable to plan for the future existence of the organization. There would be more sanctuaries and new attempts at antidraft organizing, but as Ira Arlook later commented, in the swirl of events that made 1968 such a watershed year, "no one had . . . a sense of how to keep [their] bearings with respect to the war. That was lost for a while." As an organization, the New England Resistance slipped almost rudderless into the murky summer waters of 1968.[29]

THE SPOCK TRIAL

As the New England Resistance wrestled with its plans for the future in the late spring of 1968, the trial of Dr. Spock, William Sloane Coffin, Michael Ferber, Mitchell Goodman, and Marcus Raskin took place in the federal courthouse downtown. The trial put draft resistance on the front pages of newspapers across the country for three and a half weeks, yet, in some ways, it could not have been more irrelevant to the local draft resistance effort. Certainly, it provided several opportunities for demonstrations, but, ultimately, it did nothing to help the Resistance sharpen its focus on the war. For several reasons, the trial turned out to be a chore for the defendants and a bore for an antiwar movement that expected fireworks.

In the years since it dominated the headlines, the Spock trial has remained largely hidden from history. In particular, it has lingered in the shadow of the more famous Chicago conspiracy trial (1969) and, consequently, receives no more than cursory treatment from only a handful of the period's historians.[30] This lack of attention seems to stem from the widely held perception that the Spock trial was a dull, uneventful affair dominated by too many lawyers seeking the acquittal of their clients on technicalities. But this perception is largely the product of more than thirty years of memory clouded in large part by the antiwar communities' disappointment in the trial and the disparaging remarks about the trial made by the Chicago defendants to justify their more confrontational approach.[31]

The most persistent criticism of the trial centered on the strategy of the defense. Like almost everyone in the antiwar movement, the five defendants looked forward to the trial as an opportunity to attack the administration's conduct of the war. When the indictments came down, each man made public comments about putting the war, and thus the administration, on trial. In this, they were unknowingly aided by an attorney general who had his own motives for prosecuting them (see Chapter 7). But the shifting and sometimes conflicting strategies employed by the defense both raised expectations for a political victory and guaranteed that those expectations could not be met.[32]

The accused considered three options for their defense. First, they could take a Gandhian approach. If they were not allowed to address the larger issues of the war and make their own charges that America violated the Geneva Accords and was committing war crimes, or raise constitutional issues regarding an undeclared war and the inequities of the draft, then they would stand mute and take their punishment. This idea resonated most with Coffin and Ferber, to whom further civil disobedience appealed on both a religious and a practical basis. They believed not only that accepting one's punishment followed more consistently the examples of Socrates, Thoreau, Gandhi, and King but also that the sight of Dr. Spock entering prison—handcuffed and in overalls—would prove extremely embarrassing to the administration. As Michael Ferber envisioned this approach, "The jury would be instructed to convict, the judge would sentence us, and we would march off to prison as heroes, with a huge antiwar movement making us into martyrs. Dr. Spock with his head held high marching into Danbury Prison. I thought it was great."[33]

The five defendants' second option would be to plead not guilty and then act as their own lawyers. The press coverage of a political trial, with Rev. Coffin, veteran and ex-CIA operative, interrogating government officials about the nature of the war in Vietnam or of Dr. Spock questioning government witnesses in his Connecticut Yankee accent might have amounted to a stunning public relations victory. As Jessica Mitford later pointed out, however, political trials often end with guilty verdicts and the best that defendants can hope for is a solid appeal; letting the defendants defend themselves could only undermine the appeals process.

Their third option—the one they chose—was to wage a full-scale civil libertarian defense. They embarked upon this course for several reasons. For one, if the government did indeed plan, in Marc Raskin's words, a "decimation of the intelligentsia," then mounting a sold defense might delay further onslaughts. In addition, all five men believed that they were *not* part of a conspiracy, at least in the ordinary sense of the word. They barely knew each other, after all, and never stood in the same room together until they met for the first time at the New York apartment of Leonard Boudin, Spock's lawyer. The attorneys also argued that the case would give them the opportunity to challenge the use of conspiracy law against peace groups, something that appealed to all of the defendants. Moreover, although they admitted to giving moral and symbolic support to draft resisters, the Boston Five denied that they had counseled or urged young men to resist the draft.[34]

The discussion of these three options, however, exposed mutually exclusive goals that were not acknowledged at the time. On the one hand, the defendants wanted a political trial, one in which they would be able to present evidence of the illegal and immoral nature of the Vietnam War. Since the judge presumably would not allow such latitude, using the trial to score a political victory would prove difficult. The first two court strategies—standing mute and accepting punishment or acting as their own attorneys—were probably the best available options for discrediting the administration. On the other hand, the defendants, counseled by their lawyers, also recognized that there might be some value in winning a civil libertarian victory, in which they would undermine the use of conspiracy laws and protect free speech. Such a goal would require a more technical defense, rooted in the law, and detached from the political context from which it sprang.

The Spock defendants and their lawyers did not clearly isolate the two objectives and, consequently, embarked on the virtually impossible course of pursuing both goals. For example, the decision to abandon the strategy in which the defendants would work as their own lawyers was based on a more civil libertarian assumption that these dissenters should not, ultimately, be imprisoned. This strategy, therefore, lessened their chances of winning political points in the court of public opinion. The potential loss of an appeal should not have mattered when the defendants' being sent to prison as martyrs would have hurt the administration politically.

The Boston Five, each acting individually, chose what turned out to be an eclectic mix of attorneys to represent them. Some were high profile, nationally known lawyers, while others practiced only in Boston and came to the case through the Civil Liberties Union. Marc Raskin, for instance, secured the services of Telford Taylor, a law professor at Columbia University best known as the chief American prosecutor in the Nuremberg war crimes tribunal. (Taylor, in turn, retained Calvin Bartlett, a thirty-five-year veteran of the Boston courts, to work with him.) Dr. Spock hired Leonard Boudin of the New York firm of Rabinowitz, Boudin, and Standard, known as much for its Left-leaning politics as for its capable representation. The firm, for example, represented the Cuban government in all litigation with the American government. In thirty years of work, Boudin (whom Jessica Mitford referred to as "a sort of Clarence Darrow of the appellate bar") represented many individuals who had been called to testify before the House Un-American Activities Committee and Senator Joseph McCarthy's committee investigating suspected communist subversives. Not long before the Spock case, he won the case of Julian Bond, the civil rights leader and state legislator from Georgia who, because of his outspoken opposition to the war in Vietnam, was removed from his seat by the Georgia House of Representatives. The Reverend Coffin, with the help of Yale law professor Abe Goldstein, hired James St. Clair, a highly regarded Boston attorney who had once assisted Joseph Welch as counsel for the army in the Army-McCarthy hearings and who later gained more notoriety as one of Richard Nixon's attorneys during the Watergate scandal. Michael Ferber and Mitchell Goodman availed themselves of the services of William Homans and Edward Barshak, respectively, both Civil Liberties Union of Massachusetts (CLUM) lawyers with long-standing interest in and experience with civil liberties cases.[35]

Despite, or because of, the formidable array of legal talent, the defense ceased to act in unified fashion once the lawyers took over. Of course, it made sense for the defendants not to use one lawyer so as to avoid *looking* like they were part of a conspiracy. Each lawyer also filed his own motions for his client and generally kept his trial strategy to himself. This failure to conduct a coordinated—if not unified—defense, however, put the defendants at a disadvantage when they were confronted with an efficient prosecution.[36]

Assistant U.S. Attorney John Wall, whom one observer described as "a cross between a fox terrier and a young bloodhound," presented the case. (Only one other person, Joseph Cella of the Justice Department, sat with

Wall at the prosecution's table.) Wall grew up in a working-class family in nearby Lynn. He put himself through Boston College while working nights at a Lynn tannery and later went to law school at Columbia University. He joined the organized crime division of the Justice Department in 1963 under Attorney General Robert Kennedy and, while in Washington, completed a master's degree in labor law at Georgetown. In 1964, U.S. Attorney Arthur Garrity hired Wall in Boston.

For two years, John Wall handled a variety of cases, primarily focusing on fraud, but when the assistant U.S. Attorney handling Selective Service cases left the office in 1966, Garrity assigned the cases to Wall—over his protests. Although Wall had served as a paratrooper in Korea between college and law school, he opposed American involvement in Vietnam and sympathized especially with religious objectors, like Jehovah's Witnesses, to the war. Garrity responded that unless Wall could tell him that he was morally opposed and could not in good conscience prosecute draft cases, he would have to take the assignment. Wall could not go that far. He considered himself a "Lyndon Johnson liberal Democrat" and would have preferred that the nation's resources be marshaled to "doing good" at home rather than "supporting dictators and butchers all around the world [simply] because they say they're anticommunist," but, "in those days," he later recalled, "it never occurred to me that 'hey, this [the draft] is *morally* wrong.'" He took the appointment to handle draft cases, and long before the New England Resistance rose to prominence, Wall prosecuted John Phillips, David O'Brien, David Benson, Gary Hicks, David Reed, and Robert Talmanson. All were convicted and sent to prison. In December 1967, Ramsey Clark called on John Wall to prosecute the Spock case.[37]

The prosecution of the case was made easier for Wall because of, among other things, the defense's shifting and conflicting goals. In speech after speech in the months leading up to the trial, several of the defendants described their motives and their defense strategies as aiming for either a political or a civil libertarian victory—or both. The day before they were arraigned, for example, Rev. Coffin told reporters on NBC's *Meet the Press* that they planned to raise the constitutional illegality of the war, but if the government wanted "to fight it along other lines," they would be prepared to do so, "lest the area of dissent be narrowed." Similarly, Michael Ferber, in a January speech at Harvard characterized the upcoming trial as a "large drama for the world to watch" and described a plan to prove that the war was illegal according to international law, the U.S. Constitution, and the Nuremberg principles. At the same time, however, he relayed that the defendants' lawyers believed that even if the judge did not allow them to "raise the fundamental questions," the defense "may, in fact, accomplish some good" in changing or "knocking down the conspiracy laws" or in "reforming the draft law." And Dr. Spock, in an April speech at the University of Kansas, outlined a hierarchy of defense strategies in which the most ideal would be one based on the Nuremberg standards, then on the constitutional illegality of the war; and if those two approaches failed or were not allowed, the defense would accept victory on First Amendment grounds. Spock did not mention that they might lose on all three fronts.

The articulation of these multivalent strategies notwithstanding, the public, and especially the draft resistance and other antiwar communities, expected a political trial, one in which the movement would directly confront the Johnson administration. Yet, in April, at a hearing on pretrial motions before eighty-five-year-old Judge Francis J. W. Ford, it became immediately clear that the Boston Five would not get one. Judge Ford's career spanned the entire century. He grew up in South Boston, graduated from Harvard with Franklin Delano Roosevelt in 1904, served on the Boston City Council under James Michael Curley during and after the First World War, and in 1933 became a federal prosecutor; five years later, Roosevelt appointed him to the judiciary. Throughout his tenure on the bench, critics charged that Ford's experience as U.S. Attorney "left him with at least some noticeable sympathy for the prosecution's point of view." Just as he religiously followed a daily lunchtime routine that included dining on a hard-boiled egg and an apple followed by a walk, he never wavered in his belief in the sanctity of the law. As the Boston Five would soon learn, when someone broke a law, no matter what the law, motive mattered not a whit to the judge.[38]

Moments after taking his seat in the courtroom for the pretrial hearing, Judge Ford announced that he would not allow the defense to invoke the Nuremberg principles during the trial. Moreover, he said, debates over the legality of the war and the draft were irrelevant to the facts of the case and would not be permitted. Just like that, with stunning dispatch, Ford quashed the defendants', and thus the antiwar movement's, principal hopes for their case. A direct (or indirect) legal challenge to the administration's policies in Vietnam would not take place, at least not in this trial.[39]

When the first day of the trial arrived a few weeks later, the defendants, though they "radiated confidence in the justness of their cause," according to one writer, quickly found themselves at great disadvantage when they saw the prospective jurors. Of the eighty-eight people milling about in the corridors outside the courtroom, only five were women. The defense protested vociferously. In a trial in which the most recognizable defendant was a world renowned baby doctor, the almost complete absence of women, those most likely to have read *Baby and Child Care*, was an outrage. Despite Leonard Boudin's protest, the trial began with an all-male jury.[40]

The government presented its case first. In methodical fashion, John Wall took the jury through the series of events that the prosecution saw as the framework for the conspiracy. He described the early October press conference announcing the "Call to Resist Illegitimate Authority," showed films of the October 16 draft card turn-in and burning at the Arlington Street Church, and entered into evidence enlarged photographs of draft cards collected there. Wall put John McDonough of the Justice Department on the witness stand to describe the conveyance of the draft cards to the attorney general and introduced the Fabrikoid briefcase, photostats of the cards, as well as the ashes from one of the cards (reconstructed by the FBI and secured between two pieces of glass) as government exhibits. The prosecution scrupulously presented evidence detailing the overt acts for which the defendants were indicted. Of course, the defendants had not denied that they committed any of these acts; indeed, they had performed them publicly with the hope of getting the government's attention. Still, they thought, these events hardly constituted a conspiracy. "The government has bitten off less than it can chew," one court observer said.[41]

Nevertheless, the legal standards for proving the existence of a conspiracy made it easy to convince the jury in this case. As John Wall eventually explained in his closing argument, members of a conspiracy do not have to know one another, nor does the conspiracy have to take place in secret. Each member of a conspiracy merely has to "have knowledge of the aims and purposes" of the conspiracy and "agree to those aims and purposes," he said. At that point, he asserted, each participant "becomes liable for all future and past acts" of the conspiracy. Furthermore, Wall argued, if the government proved that the Boston Five conspired to commit just one of the acts with which they were charged, then that would be sufficient for a guilty verdict; the prosecution did not have to prove that the defendants conspired to commit all of the acts listed in the indictment. To better illustrate his points, Wall used the plot of Stanley Kubrick's popular 1956 film, *The Killing*—in which the mastermind behind a plan to rob a racetrack employs several accomplices without telling them of the others involved. Each of the characters in the film knows that he is involved in a plot to rob the racetrack and, by participating, approves of the plan. As John Wall explained to the jury, even though these characters did not know each other, all were part of a conspiracy. Therefore, Wall finally stressed, the jury should regard as irrelevant the persistent claims of the Boston Five's lawyers that most of them barely knew each other and, in some cases, did not meet until after they were indicted. From the government's perspective, the actions of the five defendants met the legal standards for establishing a conspiracy. All of them knew that they were involved in a national effort to undermine the Selective Service System and affirmed it by taking part in the overt acts outlined in the indictment. Case closed.[42]

As the defense presented its case, most notably by putting the defendants on the stand, the prosecution's objective—consciously or not—seemed to shift from trying to prove conspiracy to trying to prove that the defendants were guilty of urging, convincing, inducing, even *pushing* draft-age men into draft resistance. This development seemed to catch the defense off-guard, for the indictment did not charge the Boston Five with the actual acts of counseling, aiding, and abetting draft-age men to resist the draft; rather, it charged them with *conspiracy* to counsel, aid, and abet. The government's new tactic suited its cross-examination of the defendants better than its focus on the existence of a conspiracy, which the defendants would only deny and which the government believed it already had proved. As the testimony of several of the defendants soon demonstrated, the strategy worked.

The Reverend William Sloane Coffin Jr. took the stand first and exposed the first hints not only that the court indeed would forbid the defendants to address the larger issues important to the antiwar movement but also that the defense's secondary civil libertarian stand would be disappointingly lawyerly and timid. James St. Clair, Coffin's attorney, took his client through the events described by the prosecution as comprising the conspiracy and asked Coffin why he took part in the October 20 Justice Department demonstration and draft card turn-in. Coffin replied that, first, he wanted to show "moral support" for the resisters; second, he hoped his actions would "force" the government to prosecute him and others for violation of the Selective Service Act, thus bringing about a trial in which the legality of the war and the draft could be challenged; and third, he hoped that his presence would help the draft resistance movement to "win the hearts and minds of the American people." But when St. Clair asked him if he believed the turning in of draft cards would undermine the Selective Service System, he answered, "Certainly not." "Why not?" asked St. Clair. "Because turning in of draft cards speeds up induction. . . . It leads to reclassification." Defense supporters squirmed. Did Coffin really believe that? Until a few weeks after October 20, no one knew that General Hershey would order punitive reclassifications and accelerated inductions for those who turned in their cards. And as Jessica Mitford pointed out, was the jury "really supposed to think that Mr. Coffin's purpose in handing over the draft cards was to clear the way for inducting the registrants into the armed forces," as St. Clair's line of questioning seemed to suggest?[43]

Under cross-examination, Coffin continued to equivocate and backtrack. He did not appear to be the same man who earlier suggested standing mute and defiantly marching off to prison. In the most dramatic example of this transformation, John Wall zeroed in on the power of Coffin's oratory to move young men to commit crimes. Wall began by establishing the fact that Coffin had worn his clerical robe during the October 16 service at Arlington Street Church and that he and other "moving speakers" had addressed the crowd from the pulpit there. But the chaplain argued that the resisters' came to the event knowing they would turn in their draft cards and that there was only "an outside chance" that his words may have moved someone to resist. The jurors, however, had seen films of Coffin's speech and his address at the Justice Department. Wall reminded them of Coffin's words:

> The National Selective Service Act declares that anyone "who knowingly counsels, aids, or abets another to refuse or evade registration or service in the armed forces . . . shall be liable to imprisonment for not more than five years or a fine of ten thousand dollars or both." We hereby publicly counsel these young men to continue in their refusal to serve in the armed forces as long as the war in Vietnam continues, and we pledge ourselves to aid and abet them in all the ways we can. This means that if they are now arrested for failing to comply with a law that violates their consciences, we too must be arrested, for in the sight of that law we are now as guilty as they.

Whether or not Coffin intended it, a reasonable person could easily envision a young man being inspired to turn in his draft card after hearing such language from a man of his stature. And Coffin's response that he never considered the power of his speeches to move people to resist the draft seemed disingenuous.[44]

In later years, Coffin acknowledged that he walked a fine line between counseling and aiding and abetting. "I felt very strongly that I personally had never counseled," he reflected, "because I didn't think it was my role as

chaplain at Yale University to counsel people to turn their draft cards in. . . .
For me as a pastor, that would have been wrong." Instead, he sought to
limit his participation to aiding and abetting those who had already made
up their minds. Still, he admitted, "aiding and abetting is an indirect form
of counseling." When others saw someone of Coffin's standing aiding and
abetting others, "the implication is that these guys [the resisters] are the
really conscientious ones" and anyone wanting to be thought of as conscientious would follow suit.[45]

John Wall thought Coffin made a terrible witness. "He did an awful lot
to win my case for me," the prosecutor said. Indeed, Wall believed that
Coffin could have swung the case and at least secured a hung jury if only he
had maintained his defiance and pleaded the rightness of his cause. Wall
previously witnessed Coffin at his oratorical best and admired the "musi-
cality and poetry of his words," but to his "dismay and disappointment,"
Coffin waged a "lawyer's defense," and that, Wall pointed out, "was not
what the movement needed at the time." If Coffin instead had "preached to
that jury and acknowledged legal responsibility . . . he'd have been magnifi-
cent," Wall later commented. "But to get up there and try to weasel . . . he
guaranteed at least his own conviction."[46]

Coffin's testimony showed the pitfalls of shifting from a political strategy
to a civil libertarian one, and soon supporters of the defense—and even the
defendants themselves—began to regard it as too lawyerly. As the government relentlessly asserted that the defendants, through their speeches and
actions, were inducing and inciting draft resistance among young men, the
defense responded that they were only stating their opinions, exercising
their First Amendment rights of free speech, and offering their support to
any man who had already decided to resist. In his closing arguments,
Leonard Boudin told the jury that the case raised questions of "freedom of
speech, of association, of assembly and even of the freedom of the press."
Thus the defendants, all of whom passionately opposed the war and all of
whom obviously had been actively working to stop the war (rather than
just talking about it), seemed now to be saying that they were only speaking, that they really were not doing anything of consequence. Their defense
rang hollow to most everyone in the courtroom. During the trial, William
Sloane Coffin told Daniel Lang of *The New Yorker*, "I wanted a trial of
stature. I wanted to test the legality of the war and the constitutionality of
the Selective Service Act. I wanted a trial that might be of help to selective
conscientious objectors. But this—what is it?"[47]

Perhaps the most electrifying moments of the trial occurred when

Dr. Spock took the stand and came closest to putting the war on trial. Spock methodically laid out his understanding of the history of the origins of American intervention in Vietnam, noting that the 1954 Geneva Accords called for "no further interference by foreign countries and [for] the Vietnamese government be decided by general elections in 1956." He noted former president Eisenhower's assertion that had such elections been held, 80 percent of the vote would have gone to Ho Chi Minh. Spock further charged the American government with illegal intervention when it introduced thousands of advisers into South Vietnam in the early 1960s, maintaining that "there was no valid declaration of war." After describing his public support for Lyndon Johnson in the 1964 election as a candidate of peace and his subsequent feeling of betrayal, Spock, unrepentant, declared that protesting against the war was the only thing a conscientious American could do. "We have been destroying a country which never intended us any harm," he said angrily. "We have been killing hundreds of thousands of men, women, and children." In other words, he went on, raising his voice, "my own belief is that this was a totally *outrageous* and *abominable* thing that the United States had been carrying on . . . [and] I felt strongly that the United States had lost its leadership of the free world and that the United States was now despised by hundreds of millions of people who used to believe in the United States around the world."

More to the point, unlike Coffin, Spock defiantly declared that he hoped his high-profile association with draft resistance would reach Americans of all stripes, including draft-age men who "were evading the issue of the rightness or the wrongness of the war, who preferred not to look into it," and that the latter would "listen to our views and . . . join us." Although he quibbled with Wall during cross-examination about whether or not he had set out to *persuade* young men to break the law, Spock's firm testimony fueled the most dramatic day of the trial. The report of Spock's testimony nonetheless made only page ten in the *New York Times*. The spark of the oldest, best known of the defendants, it turned out, proved insufficient to rescue an otherwise flat fortnight.[48]

Ultimately, then, the trial could only disappoint. Although the judge allowed the defendants to testify as to their "state of mind" at the time they took part in their draft resistance activities (as distinct from their motives), very little of that kind of testimony filtered through the media to the general public; only readers who carefully combed their daily newspaper for such details could get beyond the government-fostered image of older men manipulating younger ones to break the law. Consequently, the mainstream media did little to help the defendants. As several studies have shown, the media, even as late as June 1968, remained largely unpersuaded by the antiwar movement. Dr. Spock, exasperated after the trial, complained that *Pravda* reported on the trial more thoroughly than "any of the American papers."[49]

Many antiwar movement members believed that a defense predicated on claiming First Amendment freedoms minimized the importance of civil disobedience to their cause and reduced the friction necessary to sustain their efforts to end the war. The jury seemed to sense it, too. Michael Ferber's and especially Dr. Spock's testimony notwithstanding, the defense created the impression that the defendants were putting aside their principles to avoid conviction.

John Wall highlighted this contradiction in his closing arguments. He told the jury that, on the one hand, "the defendant Spock on the stand was a man who appeared to be telling the truth, appeared to be hiding nothing. . . . I submit on the evidence that the man convicted himself on the stand—that's for you to decide." Wall later added, "If Dr. Spock goes down in this case, he goes down like a man, with dignity, worthy of respect." At the same time, however, the prosecutor charged that "there [were] others in this case, other defendants, who didn't appear to be so candid."[50]

In closing arguments, the defense attorneys continued to press the free-speech line, although the two CLUM lawyers also attempted to make larger points. Ed Barshak, Goodman's counsel, reminded the jury that the ongoing war in Vietnam had been present in the "atmosphere of this courtroom" throughout the trial. And, ignoring the judge's orders regarding the discussion of the legality or morality of the war and the draft, Barshak asked the jurors to judge the conduct of the defendants against the context of the war and the divisions it created in American society. Bill Homans, representing Michael Ferber, finished his closing argument by raising the issue of individual morality and its place in a civil society. "Few are willing to brave the disapproval of their fellows, the censure of their colleagues, the wrath of their society," he said. "Moral courage is a rarer commodity than bravery in battle or great intelligence. Yet it is the one essential vital quality of those who seek to change a world that yields most painfully to change." He urged the jury to find his client not guilty.[51]

On June 14, 1968, after seven hours of deliberation, the twelve male jurors found William Sloane Coffin, Benjamin Spock, Mitchell Goodman, and Michael Ferber guilty of all charges except counseling draft-age men to turn in their draft cards. They acquitted Marcus Raskin, whom they suggested had been only minimally involved in the events outlined in the indictment. (Certainly, it helped Raskin's case when Justice Department officials and the prosecution repeatedly confused him with Arthur Waskow, another of the Call to Resist's authors and one of the men present at the Justice Department on October 20). On the whole, the convictions of the other defendants surprised few in the movement. No one really expected them to be acquitted. Although Ramsey Clark attempted to intervene by urging John Wall to seek only suspended sentences for the four convicted men, Judge Ford sentenced them to two years in prison and fined the three older men $5,000 each and Ferber $1,000 ("the student discount," Ferber quipped). The convicted men remained defiant, and Ferber, in particular, promised to remain working in the antiwar movement. A year later, an appeals court overturned the convictions, primarily because Judge Ford's charge to the jury had been so specific that the jury had to convict.[52]

By July 1968, the draft resistance movement no longer existed in its original form. Since the April 3rd draft card turn-in on Boston Common, events and conditions beyond participants' control overtook it. The personal risk taking that characterized draft resistance in its earliest stages receded as the movement turned in new directions. Over the summer a new pattern of activism began to develop. Rather than adopting a strategy of direct action to combat racism, for instance, the New England Resistance satisfied itself with incorporating the issue into its written and spoken rhetoric. The Boston Five likewise settled, if not by choice, on a strategy aimed at a civil liberties victory instead of adopting a more militant approach that, though it surely would have landed them in prison, would have done more to embarrass the Johnson administration. Finally, the new sanctuary movement created a sense of personal risk but only for the men taking asylum. Police beatings notwithstanding, sanctuary supporters risked little; instead, their presence served primarily to attract the press and, in turn, to introduce the public to the sight of GIS and antiwar activists collaborating to protest against the war. These were long-term strategies now, some with a hint of revolutionary possibility. Activists worked not simply for a draft resistance organization in Boston but for a worldwide student movement.

The new directions that the New England Resistance took were not unwelcome or seen as an admission of failure. Certainly there were activists who disapproved of abandoning more radical, confrontational tactics. On July 10, for example, shortly after the Spock trial sentencing, David Dellinger, an antiwar leader and himself a draft resister during World

War II, spoke to a rally on the Boston Common. He urged Resistance supporters to stay militant because he feared that if antiwar and antidraft sentiment grew too soft, they would no longer be deterrents to American policy makers. On the other hand, those who continued to be active with the New England Resistance were excited about the new directions of the movement. The movement needed a fresh approach. Outreach to GIs and high school students soon became top priorities; the building of a mass movement designed to fill the jails with America's middle-class sons, bog down the court system, and impair the draft soon became a memory. As a result, the New England Resistance dwindled from an organization once claiming more than 500 members to one made up of no more than 20 full-time activists. The new organizing required fewer people to carry it out.

9 BEYOND DRAFT RESISTANCE
NEW STRATEGIES AND DANGLING MEN

He has honor if he holds himself to an ideal of conduct though it
is inconvenient, unprofitable, or dangerous to do so.
—Walter Lippmann, *A Preface to Morals*, 1929

Twelve days after Judge Ford passed sentence on the
Spock defendants and David Dellinger voiced concern about the withering
antiwar challenge to the administration, another rally demonstrated that,
in Boston at least, Dellinger's fears were misplaced. Far from growing com-
placent, leaders of the New England Resistance and other groups with
whom they were allied made it obvious that they were growing only more
militant. Many now spoke of revolution.

Ostensibly, the Monday, July 22, 1968, demonstration on the Boston
Common had been organized as a forum for Eldridge Cleaver, the Black
Panther leader and presidential candidate of the Peace and Freedom Party.
But Bill Hunt, the longtime BDRG and New England Resistance leader, used
his time at the rostrum to ruminate on the revolutionary potential of draft
resistance. "The draft resistance movement," Hunt argued, "means the beginning of what may become a white revolutionary left in this country." The
convictions of Spock, Goodman, Coffin, and Ferber, he said, could be taken
as "a measure of the threat we pose to the system." This threat and the
movement Hunt envisioned were in their embryonic stages, however. As he
stood side by side with several Black Panthers, members of what he called
"the one authentic revolutionary force in America," Hunt acknowledged
the "galactic" distance, in terms of "dedication and risk," between the
Panthers and the Resistance. "When you hand in your draft card—to take
the most radical action performed by the white left so far—you face five

years in jail," he said. "But the members of your local draft board don't jump in unmarked patrol cars, armed to the teeth with the latest in western genocidal technology, and lay in ambush for you." This, Hunt said, is exactly what "the Oakland pigs" do to the Black Panthers. White draft resisters—and they were mostly white—did not face the same kind of physical threat that black revolutionaries encountered, he asserted. But Hunt saw in draft resistance the potential for developing a white revolutionary movement because it constituted an organized effort to eliminate a system through which draft-age men were "channeled, coerced, and brutalized." More broadly, he said, that brutalization also came in the form of the "banality and mental torment" of most people's daily lives. Emphasizing the Resistance's newly prominent theme of authentic human relations, Hunt asserted that as long as "the System" proved successful in getting whites to focus their "aggression" on blacks, hippies, and "commies" in Vietnam, no one would notice that they were "suffocating to death at home."[1]

Hunt pointed to "a new climate of insurgency" in Boston growing out of three forces: the draft resistance movement, the defense of resisters in sanctuary, and a new development, "the defense of free speech on the Common." In recent weeks, Boston, like San Francisco the year before, experienced an unprecedented influx of young people, most of whom spent all of their time on the Boston Common. The press called them "hippies," and the name seemed to fit. Indeed, the young people called themselves the "hip community"; they gathered on the Common, smoked pot, and listened to the music of Jimi Hendrix, the Jefferson Airplane, and the Grateful Dead, among other artists—and they did not do much else, except to make the residents of nearby Beacon Hill and the Back Bay uncomfortable.

In response to the hippie presence, the city had instituted a midnight curfew on the Common, and over the weekend of July 20–21, the Boston Police Department launched several raids on the hip community there. They arrested eighty-three people, all of whom came before municipal court judge Elijah Adlow on Monday morning, July 22. Adlow openly scorned the hippies as menaces to the city. "To look at these people," he sneered, "you'd think the fence fell down around the insane asylum." He accused them of turning the Common into a "festering sore" and asked, "Is our beautiful Boston going to become a disaster area?" Despite his personal contempt for the defendants, the judge gave probation to forty-four of them (whose cases were adjudicated in small groups) and declared six to be not guilty of the charges against them. He fined the remaining hippies $20 each.[2]

Several of those arrested and sentenced by the judge were leading figures in the New England Resistance. The Resistance had treated the police round-up as another manifestation of illegitimate authority in action and staged a sit-in. This demonstration signaled a new willingness or propensity on the part of the Resistance leadership to tackle issues outside their traditional scope of protest. Thus, just as the escalating war and the draft had created an urgency among draft resisters to challenge the administration nine months before, the Spock trial verdicts, the recent assassinations, police and military attacks on student protesters around the world, and the ongoing war drove the New England Resistance to expand its mission.

Bill Hunt's speech about the white revolutionary Left, therefore, characterized the hippies' challenge to the curfew as part of the growing "climate of insurgency" started by the draft resistance movement. More important, however, Hunt suggested that the crackdown by Boston police and Judge Adlow amounted to political repression. "The Man" sees the new climate of insurgency, Hunt charged, "and he plans to put a stop to it. . . . We all know what it means when a government declares a curfew. We've seen it used in every black rebellion, and we've seen it imposed in Saigon. It means denying the streets to the people, tightening up on the small space people have to organize and fight for social change." He urged his audience to resist the curfew. The Constitution, Hunt said, provides for free assembly. "We're going to tell Mayor [Kevin] White and Pig Adlow—tonight, tomorrow, for as long as it takes—that if we can't have free assembly, then there's going to be no peaceable assembly in Boston, Massachusetts." The targets of resistance thus widened from a narrow focus on the Selective Service and the Johnson administration to all authority—including local authority—deemed illegitimate.[3]

This rhetoric—the talk of revolution, identification with the Black Panthers, calling police officers and a judge "pigs"—echoed some of the points made in the Resistance "manifesto" printed in late May, but it expressed a new militancy. Staughton Lynd, the radical historian and one of the leading intellectual supporters of the Resistance, later lamented this shift. Hunt's praise for the Black Panthers and use of the word "pigs" in reference to the police signaled a "change from the thoughtworld of October 16, 1967, after which the New England Resistance had thanked the Boston police for being different from Berkeley's." Years later, Bill Hunt characterized his inflammatory rhetoric as a product of a very depressing time for the antiwar movement. The highest profile opponents of the war were either being killed (Martin Luther King, Jr., Robert Kennedy) or given prison sentences

(Spock, Coffin, Goodman, and Ferber). Despite Eugene McCarthy's early strength in the Democratic primaries, the party seemed poised to give the nomination to Vice President Hubert Humphrey. Indeed, rumors circulated that Lyndon Johnson still planned to secure the nomination through a "draft Johnson" campaign that would exploit the instability of the party at the coming convention in Chicago. Moreover, brute force had defeated student protests around the world, and, even in Boston, students had clashed with police at the first sanctuary. According to Hunt, "We all went through a fairly apocalyptic phase, and I remember saying things on the Boston Common that I wish I hadn't said (I don't think they had any great lasting effect), but I thought, you know, we just really need a revolution."[4]

New England Resistance organizers never wavered in their commitment to end the war, but they did grow frustrated that all of their hard work had not had much effect. American troop strength in Vietnam remained at peak levels, and thousands of Americans and Vietnamese continued to die. As a result, in addition to Resistance leaders expanding their opposition to the war to a more general critique of American society—their literature now attacked American "imperialism" and "capitalism"—they sought also to broaden the organization's mission by enlarging its constituency. They began new programs, the largest of which were aimed at helping disgruntled American servicemen find alternatives to service in Vietnam and informing high school students about the war and the draft. Open resistance to the draft no longer possessed much strategic value. Instead, these new measures followed the more typical New Left example of community organizing.

As the New England Resistance turned its attention to other tactics, the organization shrank in size. A core group of about twenty activists worked full-time on their new projects. And although each new sanctuary organized by the Resistance required hundreds of bodies to be successful, most rank-and-file resisters stopped participating in regular work at the Resistance office. When a federal grand jury began handing down indictments on draft resisters at the end of the summer, the vast majority of men who turned in their cards over the previous twelve months, for a variety of reasons, went unprosecuted. Those whom prosecutors did indict received little support from the New England Resistance, and a new organization called SUPPORT stepped in to make up for this absence. As 1969 dawned, organized draft resistance no longer existed in Boston, and the organization most associated with it faded from public view.

SO, YOU SAY YOU WANT A REVOLUTION

By the time the Spock sentences were announced, a sense of frustration permeated the New England Resistance office. The trial of the Boston Five had proved especially disappointing and anticlimactic. A growing militancy hung in the air. Bob Shapiro, the MIT student who turned in his draft card after Martin Luther King's assassination, began working steadily in the Resistance office just as this shift in atmosphere occurred. Years later, he recalled that by the time he joined the organization that summer, many of his colleagues there "termed themselves 'revolutionaries' and not just draft resisters." This change occurred, he said, because "we just felt like we were banging our heads against the wall." Neil Goldberg, an October 16 resister and a draft counselor at Boston University confirmed this in a July 1968 interview. "I now consider myself to be a full-fledged revolutionary instead of just a radical," he said. "As a radical I felt that it was possible to move the conscience of the country . . . [but] nothing we can do seems capable of stopping Johnson. It's not going to stop through moral protest." Therefore, Goldberg asserted, "the only way change can occur is by changing the structure" of American society.[5]

Jim Oestereich, the seminarian who had been moved to tears when he returned his draft card on October 16 exemplified this shift in perspective. In an August 1968 article in the *Resistance*, Oestereich wrote admiringly of the Black Panthers and noted that "white radicals" faced "the difficult job of moving from symbolic and token protests to organizing the revolution." To achieve this metamorphosis, the Resistance must, he argued somewhat vaguely, "totally organize against the oppressive institutions of this society" and move the country "toward a complete transformation of the American economy and political system." Ten months earlier, Oestereich could scarcely have imagined making such a statement, but now, as the prospects for peace continued to prove illusory, wholesale change seemed the only answer.[6]

Goldberg's and Oestereich's analyses betrayed a disappointment with the mass of their fellow citizens who had not been moved by the example of draft resisters to rise up in opposition to the war. But the two resisters also did not hold the rest of America responsible, individually or personally, for this failure. Instead of charging their fellow citizens—and especially fellow citizens opposed to the war—with possessing inadequate moral standards, Goldberg and Oestereich blamed "the system" for numbing the sensibilities of most Americans. Under a more just economic and political system, they seemed to contend, the American people would have immediately recognized the Vietnam War as immoral and illegal and quickly demanded its end. The American consumer-capitalist system, however, had alienated so many citizens that the Resistance message got through to proportionately few ordinary people. "Everywhere we find people who find their lives meaningless," Goldberg noted, "even those who work in the middle class. . . . This is because they have been exploited." The Resistance would have to go to the heart of the problem and overthrow "the system" responsible for this exploitation and alienation.[7]

As the Democratic National Convention loomed in the not-too-distant future some New England Resistance members saw in it an opportunity to press this point. On the eve of the convention, Joel Kugelmass wrote an article in the *Resistance* in which he celebrated two popular radical slogans: "Let the People Decide" and "The Streets Belong to the People." For Kugelmass, the time to "live by those slogans" had arrived. Specifically, he wrote, "it is time to take to the streets and start making decisions." Chicago, he predicted, "will be a mess, but it will be a beginning."[8]

Most antiwar activists who went to Chicago did not expect their confrontation with the party in power to lead to a restructuring of American society, much less a revolution. Despite Abbie Hoffman's and Jerry Rubin's widely publicized threats to dump LSD in the city's water supply and carry out other stunts with their fellow Yippies (short for Youth International Party), the overwhelming majority of protesters came simply to demonstrate against the Democratic Party, which appeared poised to nominate Lyndon Johnson's vice president, Hubert Humphrey, for president. Many of them supported Eugene McCarthy's candidacy and, thus, could in no way be considered revolutionaries.

Although a few members of the New England Resistance went to Chicago, most stayed home. Regardless, the chaos that erupted in Chicago shocked everyone in the organization. As a parallel drama unfolded in Prague, Czechoslovakia, with Soviet tanks crushing a student-led democratic uprising, millions of Americans witnessed the Chicago police use what Connecticut senator Abe Ribicoff referred to as "Gestapo tactics" on young people in the streets outside the convention center. As Bill Hunt and Rosemary Poole watched the beatings of unarmed antiwar protesters on television in Boston, they sank into a state of despair. Hunt remembered Poole musing about catching the next plane to Chicago, strapping dynamite to her body, and destroying the biggest building she could find. "People were just boiling with rage," Hunt later recalled. And that, he said, was "not the best mood" for making political decisions.[9]

In the fall, a year after the first draft card turn-in at the Arlington Street Church, the angry and frustrated Resistance leadership held a general membership meeting to reassess the organization's goals and strategies. At the October 18, 1968, meeting, the leadership presented a statement of theory, strategy, and organization. In some ways, it echoed the "manifesto" produced in May, but it went further: "The Resistance should immediately and clearly state that American society is characterized by institutions that are under the sovereign control of a corporative ruling class; that its economic system, capitalism, is exploitative; that the government of the U.S. is by nature oppressive and that its policy of containing communism and promoting foreign investment is economically, diplomatically, and militarily imperialistic." Consequently, the statement concluded, the Resistance should seek "nothing less than a total transformation of this society that will leave every remaining institution in the collective control of those whose lives depend on it."[10] With this statement the New England Resistance now openly identified itself with a socialist, if not anarchist, solution to not only ending the war but altering the fundamental economic and political structure of American society. As Dan Tilton, an older resister and office IWW historian, wrote around the same time: "It is time for the Resistance to state clearly that not only is capitalism insane, but more importantly that socialism is the only possible alternative."[11] Much had changed in a year.

All of this talk of revolution, however, did not translate easily into practice. As this intellectual shift took place over the summer, the New England Resistance engaged in numerous new projects beyond draft resistance, but none could be seriously characterized as revolutionary. On the one hand, demonstrations grew more radical and strident. The Soviet invasion of Czechoslovakia in August provoked intense protests on the Common, and the appearance of Hubert Humphrey led to a "Dump the Hump" rally at Downtown Crossing and a clash with Boston police at the Statler Hilton. Through events such as these, the Resistance continued to make its presence known and continued to confront the public with the Vietnam War, but it did not materially move Boston or America closer to revolution.

Discussion of overthrowing the existing structure of American society, consequently, added up to little more than what historian Terry Anderson has termed the "rhetorical revolution."[12] The *Resistance* newspaper, newly revamped over the summer, reflected this tension between rhetoric and action. In an explanatory editorial, one unnamed writer wrote of the organization's realization that a "fundamental restructuring of American society" would be needed to overcome American imperialism and racism. "Only through revolution can we end the manipulation and distortion of our lives," he wrote. "Only through revolution can we hope to realize the possibilities for human freedom latent in the advanced state of American technology." He then turned his attention to more practical matters, saying one major task for revolutionaries is the "elevation of consciousness," presumably their own and that of others. As a result, the New England Resistance now sought to "engage in other programs as well as draft resistance which reveal the illegitimacy of the authority over us and build a spirit of unified struggle."[13]

HIPPIES, SUBURBANITES, AND HIGH SCHOOLERS

At the start, the group moved to elevate the consciousness of their own members and supporters. In early July, they started the Resistance Free School as a way to promote open investigation of a variety of topics. The Free School offered an alternative to the usual university education, which, they argued, "cultivat[ed] individuals who consider Establishment needs over and above human needs." Most courses were taught seminar style and revolved around common readings, with meetings often held at the house or apartment of the instructor (often a Resistance leader). Some of the courses offered focused on lighter topics such as "Conversational French," "Rock and Jazz Drumming," and "Woodwork and Cabinet Making," but most addressed contemporary issues or political theory; these courses included "American Labor History," "Origins of Radical Thought," "Comparative Revolutionary Development," "Hippies and the New Left," "the Writings and Theories of Herbert Marcuse," "the Media and the Movement," and "Black Nationalism, White Racism, and Black Power," and others. Most of these courses did not last through the summer, and some met only once or twice before folding, but the notion of a free school that challenged prevailing assumptions about education exemplified the new Resistance goal of rebelling against the basic structure of American society.[14]

Against this backdrop the "hip community" arrived on Boston Common. Traditionally, most antiwar activists held hippies in contempt: rather than challenging American society, hippies seemed to be "dropping out" of society all together. As two BDRG activists said, they regarded hippies as "hopelessly individualistic" and as "people who didn't work." Moreover, the hippie lifestyle, especially the use of drugs, made them easy targets for government repression. Nevertheless, the Boston Common curfew issue brought the New England Resistance into an alliance with the hip community. On one level, they were attracted to the Common confrontation because of the free-assembly issue at stake, but on another level, the hippies appeared to be a step ahead of the draft resistance community in rebelling against the fundamental structure of American society. As Doug Rossinow has argued, the strongest link between the New Left and the counterculture "lay in the common quest for authenticity, not in consistent political goals." To charges that hippies were counter-revolutionary because they would not "get off their asses," Neil Robertson, one of the Resistance leaders arrested during the police sweeps of the Common, offered a defense: "The hippie is, de facto, leading a different life, a life that is resulting in increasing worry among the merchants of Charles Street, and the residents of Beacon Hill." To those residents of Boston's finest neighborhoods, "the hippie is a threat," Robertson argued. "He ain't buying and he ain't producing." In short, the hip community rejected everything about mainstream America.[15]

The leading spokesman of the Common's hip community, Ben Morea, made the Resistance-hippie alliance even easier to understand. Morea came to Boston from New York as a member of the Lower East Side collective, Up Against the Wall, Motherfucker. The name came from a line in a LeRoi Jones poem (the following line is: "This is a stick-up"), and the group represented an unusual hybrid of anarchist political theory and countercultural direct action programs. As Todd Gitlin notes, the Motherfuckers organized as an "affinity group," a cultural and political representation of what society would look like after the revolution. They were hippies, but they were also revolutionaries. In Boston, Morea told reporters, "The existence of our community represents both an alternative to the present system and a means for its destruction." The hip community, he said, "rejects old middle-class values, especially that of the consumer life," while simultaneously making possible "a fuller and more complete life." This kind of rhetoric dovetailed well with the New England Resistance's own arguments for overthrowing existing society. As Morea concluded, "we feel that the existence of the hip community itself is fighting the Establishment."[16]

For several weeks, many Resistance members were, as Bill Hunt later recalled, "quite carried away" with the hip community, but the relationship soon became a burden. First, the logistics simply were unmanageable. Hundreds of hippies wound up sleeping in the basement of the Arlington Street Church every night, and dozens of others turned the Resistance office on Stanhope Street into a "crash pad." As Neil Robertson eventually realized, "it was a mistake to try to organize hippies," who generally eschewed any kind of organization. Worse than that, during a clash in which a group of toughs beat up several of the Motherfuckers on the Common, a Vietnam veteran who had joined the fight against the hippies was stabbed. Police arrested Ben Morea for the stabbing, and preparations for his court case quickly overshadowed the ongoing confrontation over the Common curfew. When the Resistance held a press conference for Morea to refute the charges, a full contingent of Boston reporters covered it, but the next day, not one story on the subject appeared in the papers or on television. Ultimately, for the Resistance, the hippies on the Common became a distraction that lasted much of the summer. "We just kind of got swept up in it," one Resistance leader later said, and they soon found themselves wishing the Motherfuckers would just go away.[17]

In addition to establishing the Resistance Free School and the Resistance-hippie alliance, the New England Resistance expanded its programs into some of Boston's suburbs over the summer. Small groups of Resistance activists fanned out to nearby towns such as Malden, Watertown, Newton, and Belmont, as well as to those in outlying areas like Lexington, Concord, Hingham, and Attleboro, aiming to elevate the consciousness of young men and women who lived there. The quality and success of these programs varied from place to place, and few of them left any record of their work. The Concord project is the exception. There, in a town that boasted of its Revolutionary heritage and its association with Henry David Thoreau, a group of three activists formed the Concord Area Resistance Summer (CARS), a local organization that quickly grew to about fifty active members.

From the start, CARS distinguished itself from the larger, more brazen Boston organization that spawned it. Rather than focusing on demonstrations or draft card turn-ins, it took a more methodical approach to educating the community of young people about the war and the draft. On one level, organizers said, they sought to "make people remember the war, no matter how hard they are trying to forget it."[18] On another, they envisioned a three-point progression that entailed first raising the consciousness of individual young people in the community, which then would lead to the elevation of a community consciousness; that would then provide the foundation for a "lasting and viable organization within the community, oriented towards change through direct action."[19]

CARS ultimately sought to create a community organization that practiced direct action, but it relied on other means to carry out its program. Aside from one protest staged outside the Concord draft board offices toward the end of the summer, the group avoided demonstrations. As Susan Starr, a Concord resident who became a CARS mainstay, later remarked, "you don't demonstrate in the suburbs; people don't like it." Instead, CARS members, many of whom were Quakers coming from a tradition of draft counseling, did a lot of leafleting and canvassing—looking to counsel young men classified 1-A or high school men about to register for the draft. In addition, CARS adopted the Boston Draft Resistance Group's practice of taking counseling to pre-inductees via Early Morning Shows. They also hosted a dance and several poetry readings, staged some guerrilla theater, and held regular Monday night dinners at the Friends' meetinghouse. Finally, like the New England Resistance, CARS began its own Free School, aiming to reach as many people as possible.[20]

On the whole, however, CARS did not receive a warm reception in Concord or in the surrounding towns. Local police frequently harassed them, on at least one occasion arresting a member for distributing leaflets at a supermarket. Most people living in the suburbs, it seems, did not expect to be confronted with information about the Vietnam War, and when they encountered CARS activists, it annoyed many of them. One woman complained to police that a spontaneous guerrilla theater performance—in this case a play based on the lyrics to the Fugs' song "Kill for Peace"—spoiled her picnic by the historic Old North Bridge. At times, supermarket customers reacted with hostility to leafleters, and on more than one occasion, groups of high school students threatened CARS activists with their fists. At the end of the summer, the organization lamented that it had not reached more than approximately 300 young people outside the group. They could, however, take solace in knowing that they had radicalized a core group of local youth who had gravitated to CARS over the summer and who would take their politics with them to college in the fall. Furthermore, it appeared in September that a lasting community antiwar organization would take the place of CARS.[21]

CARS and the other suburban groups did set themselves apart from other similar organizations in its reliance on an overwhelmingly female membership. Five years after Betty Friedan articulated the grievances of millions of American women alienated within their roles as "homemakers," most women in affluent suburbs such as Concord continued to fill that role or, at most, held part-time jobs. Just as nineteenth-century middle-class women participated in voluntary associations and women's clubs, some middle-class women in the greater Boston area joined antiwar organizations like CARS. Although they did most of the "shit-work" that their female counterparts in the New England Resistance and BDRG did, women in CARS actually took on more obvious leadership roles as well. Susan Starr, for example, edited and wrote much of the monthly newsletter, "CARS Mechanics," and another woman, Beth Navon, was one of the three original organizers and exercised considerable influence within the CARS leadership.[22]

At the end of the summer, despite the mixed success of the suburban programs, the New England Resistance decided to make high school outreach and organizing one of its top priorities. Several factors instigated this new approach. First, over the summer, dozens of high school students from Boston and surrounding towns had called and stopped by the New England Resistance looking for information on the draft. In many cases Resistance staffers sent these people to BDRG for counseling, but the numbers made an impression. Second, the suburban programs had uncovered enough alienation among students to warrant continued action on this front. Third, and most important, Resistance leaders believed something had to be done to "offset the oppressive public education system." The Resistance attacked high schools as "instrument[s] of social channeling, devoted not to the development of individual creativity, but to standardization." To challenge the "inculcation of discipline and conformity" imposed on students in Bay State high schools, the Resistance resolved to take its antiwar and revolutionary messages to young people in these schools. By year's end, the New England Resistance operated high school organizing projects in several Boston schools and in more than twenty suburbs.[23]

The high school programs initiated in the fall met with more success than their summer antecedents in large part because of a change in tactics conceived by Ira Arlook. Rather than raising the issues of the war and social channeling to high school students through multiple programs, Arlook narrowed the focus to one tactic: bringing Vietnam veterans into the high schools to speak with students as part of an "anti-recruitment program." Since the first sanctuaries of May and June, the New England Resistance had steadily established good relations with Vietnam veterans who returned to the United States and began working, individually and collectively, against the war. Although historians typically treat the GI and veteran antiwar movement in isolation from its civilian counterpart, the draft resistance movement effectively formed a partnership between the two groups. Without the veterans, it is highly unlikely that school administrators would have granted permission to Resistance organizers to enter their facilities and talk with students. These same administrators, however, generally proved eager to arrange student audiences for veterans. Therefore, Arlook encountered little resistance in his efforts to organize assemblies at which a veteran would speak with students about his experiences in Vietnam. Frequently, these discussions would take place after Arlook played a Department of Defense propaganda film such as "Why Vietnam?" or "Your Tour in Vietnam" for the students; the veteran would then describe how his experience differed from the film portrayals.[24]

Once the Resistance had established "a little beachhead" in a high school, Arlook and other NER members continued to help sympathetic students reach out to their classmates through additional events and often by starting an "underground" newspaper in the school. Although there is no way to measure the effectiveness of the Resistance's high school organizing, Arlook and others believed they were successful at least in offsetting the work of the armed services recruiters. More to the point, they were certain that they were educating students about the oppressive nature not only of their high schools and the draft but of American society in general. Eventually, in the spring and summer of 1969, Arlook and others came to regard this kind of work as so important that they moved into some of these communities to do full-time school and neighborhood organizing. By then, the New England Resistance had abandoned all draft resistance efforts and internal divisions had rendered the organization defunct, but their efforts to connect veterans and high school students had provided a solid base for organizing in new directions.[25]

THE GI ALLIANCE

At the same time that the New England Resistance turned its attention to high school organizing, the group's work with GIs and veterans blossomed into a sanctuary movement that continued to garner headlines for the organization and, more important, laid the foundation for a new GI support program. It is puzzling that historians have virtually ignored the sanctuary movement and have given only cursory treatment to the alliance formed between civilian and GI antiwar activists. Perhaps it has been too easy to accept the stories that portray returning soldiers as mistreated by civilian opponents of the war. Images of long-haired protesters spitting on Vietnam veterans or calling them "baby killers" endure in the American consciousness despite a lack of documentation to support their veracity.[26] And certainly there is plenty of evidence that many American servicemen, some even opposed to the war, regarded the largely middle-class, student-led, antiwar movement with contempt.[27] In any case, long before the United States Serviceman Fund and GIs United Against the War were founded, and even longer before Vietnam Veterans Against the War rose to prominence, the draft resistance movement established strong relations with servicemen and veterans. The Resistance benefited from the moral authority that a soldier brought to the antiwar movement, and the GIS and veterans profited from the organizational skills of the civilians.

After the first sanctuary at the Arlington Street Church in late May 1968, enlisted men "came out of the woodwork" looking for help from the New England Resistance. In June, Resistance activists organized sanctuaries in churches in Providence, Rhode Island, and Wellesley, Massachusetts, both of which ended with authorities dragging their quarry over blockades of supporters. In early August, the Friends' Meeting House in Cambridge granted asylum to another GI who remained there for more than two weeks before the authorities came to get him. Sanctuary soon swelled into a movement even beyond New England. By midsummer draft resistance groups and other antiwar organizations hosted sanctuaries in Ohio, New York, Pennsylvania, and California. Resistance organizers quickly recognized the value of sanctuary in reaching a new constituency: enlisted men.[28]

This new interest in the plight of American GIS represented a significant shift in Resistance attitudes toward military men. The draft resistance movement (and, indeed, the antiwar movement in general) had long assumed that anyone strongly opposed to the Vietnam War would never enter the military. Though, as Nan Stone later noted in a speech she gave on numerous occasions, it eventually became obvious to members of the Resistance that young men enlisted or submitted to the draft for many reasons, "most of which have nothing to do with agreement with U.S. foreign policy." Specifically, Stone said, the Resistance learned that servicemen usually had one of four motives for enlisting. Many men feared that being drafted would leave them with no choice regarding the branch of service in which they would serve; recruiters promised "choice, not chance" if one enlisted before being drafted. Some men, especially those from poorer families, enlisted as a step toward economic advancement. And others were attracted by recruiting campaigns that promised opportunities to learn specific vocational skills and to see the world. American society, finally, indoctrinated men, especially working-class men, with the notion that joining the service was a good way to learn loyalty, courage, and citizenship. Organizations such as the Boy Scouts (who taught militarylike discipline) and the American Legion (a veterans organization that gave out annual citizenship awards to young men), Stone argued, fostered this sense of obligation in many young men.[29]

It took Bill Chase, the AWOL soldier to whom the Arlington Street Church granted sanctuary, to get the Resistance to think about soldiers differently. Chase, who had served in Vietnam for nine months, described the war and military service in ways that few civilians could. Resistance activists soon developed a new appreciation for GIS and their own channeling experience and likewise began to understand the few options available to working-class men in a new light. That draft resisters had suffered the antagonism of many working-class men now seemed to make sense; the privileges that came with being a middle-class college student included insulation from the kind of physical harm that working-class soldiers in Vietnam faced every day. Even if a GI opposed the war, he sometimes could not tolerate college students protesting against a war about which they knew so little. Sanctuary and other outreach to GIS fostered a new understanding—and eventually an alliance—between civilian and military dissenters.[30]

By the fall of 1968, sanctuary and GI outreach became the most prominent antiwar work done by the New England Resistance. Sanctuary had strategic value in that it continued to attract media and public attention to the war and also to American servicemen who opposed it. In addition, Resistance activists hoped that sanctuaries would attract some of the high school students the organization was trying to organize at the same time. Moreover, Resistance organizers believed that the GIs who took sanctuary would actually be helped by it once they had been apprehended by authorities; the attention captured by each sanctuary, they reasoned, would prevent the military from railroading the deserters into the stockade. When they did wind up in the stockade, Resistance activists visited them regularly and tried to arrange legal and financial assistance. Most important, sanctuary preserved the confrontational nature of Resistance opposition to the war. Resisters hoped that the specter of U.S. marshals, FBI agents, or military police apprehending an American serviceman amid a crowd of nonviolent, peaceful demonstrators would affect public opinion.

Every sanctuary held in the Boston area and across the country over the summer took place in a church, but the New England Resistance entered the fall hoping to extend the reach of sanctuary into more secular institutions. Three sanctuaries—at Harvard, Boston University, and MIT—grabbed the public's attention and brought hundreds of people into contact with the Resistance for the first time.[31]

On September 22, marine corporal Paul Olimpieri, twenty-one years old and twice wounded in Vietnam, took sanctuary in the Andover Hall Chapel at Harvard Divinity School. It was the first time that a college or university had offered sanctuary to an American serviceman. In comments to the media, the seminarians, several of whom were members of the New England Resistance, noted that although they were part of an academic community, they had little to teach about their civilization "to a man who has already experienced some of the worst our society has produced." Instead, they concluded, "we have a great deal to learn from him."[32]

More important, however, the sanctuary organizers, reflecting the Resistance's more recent critique of the American social, political, and economic system described Olimpieri's sanctuary not simply as an act of protest against the war but as a challenge to an oppressive society. "We know that divinity schools are open to the privileged few who qualify, and closed to others," they wrote in a press release. "Today, in opening this chapel to a man oppressed by a militarist society, we are looking forward to a day when privilege no longer closes its doors to the oppressed." Likewise, in a separate statement, the New England Resistance described Olimpieri's sanctuary in the context of a new alliance among "those forces struggling to create a society in which men can be free." Both draft resisters and GIs like Olimpieri were "completely opposed to subjugation and bondage." Consequently, they said, "we mean to seize and maintain control of our lives and the use to which they are put."[33]

For his part, Paul Olimpieri limited his criticism to the military and to the war. The son and younger brother of marines, he had grown up in Fairfield, Connecticut. In April 1966, with the threat of the draft hanging over him, Olimpieri enlisted in the Marine Corps and soon landed in Da Nang. On the first day of his sanctuary at Harvard, he told reporters that he believed he had been "brainwashed" on the "use of physical torture" in boot camp. And by the time he left for Vietnam, he "couldn't wait to see action." "I considered myself a superhero," he said, "ready to free a country that was threatened by a Communist takeover." When he arrived in Vietnam, however, he decided that the "South Vietnamese Army [was] a joke" and that most South Vietnamese civilians did not want American forces there. After suffering wounds to his chest, arm, and ear in two separate firefights, Olimpieri found himself in a military hospital with "plenty of time to brood." Although his country thanked him for his pains with two Purple Hearts, he soon turned against the war.[34]

Stationed temporarily at Quonset Naval Air Station in Rhode Island, Olimpieri had read about the earlier sanctuaries in Boston and Providence. Sometime after going AWOL on August 30, he contacted the New England Resistance, who provided him with preliminary legal advice before referring him to a lawyer. After consulting with the attorney, Olimpieri decided to make his protest publicly, and the resisters at Harvard Divinity School soon won the privilege of granting him sanctuary. By the time they took him in, Olimpieri had adopted a new look, sporting a month's worth of new dark hair with a matching thin moustache and goatee. He wore sandals with an olive-drab marine jacket (to which he cheerfully pinned an Omega button). On the day he arrived in Cambridge, he figured the authorities would wait until he became classified officially as a deserter on September 30 before arresting him.[35]

A decorated war hero like Olimpieri brought a certain moral authority to the draft resistance movement that those who had not seen combat could not provide. Olimpieri's stories captivated his supporters. With each conversation, they learned more about the realities of fighting in Vietnam and about the realities facing working-class men faced with few alternatives to the draft. Equally important, however, Olimpieri condemned the war and the marines. He described a Marine Corps run by "lifers who are sadistic, sick people who couldn't make it on the outside." Moreover, he criticized the American presence in Vietnam. "I don't think we have the right to decide which form of government the Vietnamese should have," he said on the first day of his sanctuary. "If they don't want communism, they can win without our help like we won our revolutionary war." By claiming sanctuary, Olimpieri concluded, he sought "to tell other military personnel and civilians what is really going on" in the marines and in Vietnam. "I'm not a coward (I was awarded two Purple Hearts), but I still believe the military and the war are bad."[36]

Perhaps comments such as these led military authorities to grab Olimpieri before he attained deserter status. In the quickest end to a sanctuary to date, military police entered Andover Hall at 5:55 A.M. on Tuesday, September 24 (less than forty-eight hours after Olimpieri arrived) and, aided by Harvard police, removed Olimpieri from the chapel.[37]

The next day, within twelve hours of his arrest, Olimpieri stunned Boston's antiwar community by renouncing the seminarians at Harvard and the New England Resistance. In a press conference at the Charlestown Navy Yard, Olimpieri, flanked by his wife, brother, and a new attorney, told reporters that he had made a mistake. Clean shaven, and wearing a newly pressed uniform, he claimed that he had been "used by various groups to publicize their political goals, whatever they may be." Upon reflection, he no longer wanted to be associated with those groups. "I am just beginning to realize that things can be done through the proper channels," he concluded. "I found this out the hard way, and I hope that other servicemen will learn from my mistake."[38]

To a community that had grown used to watching resisters and supporters march off to jail defiant and unrepentant, Olimpieri's change of heart came as a shock. Few believed it conveyed his true feelings. "Paul would never say anything like this," one Resistance spokesman said. "The Marines obviously used some sort of coercion." The New England Resistance immediately issued a statement denying the charge that they had somehow used Olimpieri for their own ends; they noted that they had even tried to talk Olimpieri out of sanctuary and claimed that "he was well aware of the risks." But Olimpieri told reporters that he—not the marines—called the press conference and wrote his statement. The Resistance simply could not reconcile the old Paul Olimpieri with the new one. He refused to see his Resistance attorney and to communicate with the organization. It was a terrible setback.[39]

The surprising end to the Harvard sanctuary exposed some shortcomings of the sanctuary strategy. Unlike draft card turn-ins in which a large number of people assumed an equal amount of risk, sanctuaries placed most of the risk on the man or men taking asylum from the military. No one expected the authorities to ignore such open defiance of the law, and although members of the Resistance community attempted nonviolently to block the inevitable arrest, the man who took sanctuary faced the punishment alone. In addition, in spite of hopes that the public nature of sanctuary would somehow protect the arrested man from unfair treatment by the military, once the police took him away, he became virtually inaccessible. Furthermore, although sanctuary continued to promote public confrontation with the government, it did not do so on the same scale as the original draft resistance strategy.

These failings notwithstanding, several more sanctuaries—usually prompted by an individual serviceman seeking an alliance with the Resistance—took place in the fall of 1968. Just one week after the Harvard sanctuary ended, a new one started across the Charles River at Boston University. It started with the Committee of Concern for Vietnam (CCV), a small group of students in the BU School of Theology led by Alex Jack, Bob Winget, and George Collis. On October 2, at the usual daily service in Marsh Chapel, the CCV announced that it had offered sanctuary to two servicemen: Ray Kroll, an eighteen-year-old army private, AWOL from Fort Benning, Georgia, since July; and Private Thomas Pratt, a twenty-two-year-old marine more recently AWOL from Quonset Naval Air Station, and a friend of

Paul Olimpieri. Both Kroll and Pratt had sought out the New England Resistance after hearing about earlier sanctuaries. The Resistance, in turn, put them in touch with the ccv.[40]

With the Harvard sanctuary fresh in their minds, NER members did their best to demonstrate that they were not manipulating these two soldiers. On the first day of the sanctuary, Ray Kroll, a soft-spoken young man of slight build, told reporters, "The Resistance and the School of Theology are not using me in any way for anybody's gain except mine." Thomas Pratt said, "I chose sanctuary so I could make a stand, so I could tell people how the servicemen feel about the war." He knew the risks, he said. "I am ready to face the consequences."[41]

But like his friend Paul Olimpieri, Pratt soon changed his mind. At the end of the first day in Marsh Chapel, during which the number of students "protecting" Kroll and Pratt had not yet reached 100, Pratt left with his parents. He claimed to be "disenchanted with the circus setting" and said that he had only wanted to make a protest against the war. Two days later, in the custody of the marines, Pratt held a press conference similar to Olimpieri's, claiming he had been "used by the Resistance for their own purposes" and expressing his hope that the marines would give him "another chance."[42]

Members of the New England Resistance now began to suspect that they were being played for fools. That two marines—indeed two *friends*—both stationed at Quonset Naval Air Station, took sanctuary separately only to attack the people who had helped them smacked of betrayal at best and intentional sabotage at worst. Ray Kroll, who remained at Marsh Chapel, lashed out at Pratt and Olimpieri. "I have little doubt in my mind that both Paul Olimpieri and Thomas Pratt were plants," he told reporters. He suggested that the military sent the two to infiltrate the Resistance as agents provocateurs.[43]

Some Resistance members still believed that the marines had coerced the two men into recanting their previous statements, but in the tense atmosphere of the time, few of them doubted that the government might try to subvert their efforts by planting informants in the organization. An informal game called "Who's the fed?" developed around this time, especially among the inner circle of longtime NER activists. Barrie Thorne, a Ph.D. candidate in the Brandeis sociology department and a member of both the Boston Draft Resistance Group and the Resistance, recalls the day when she heard about the game and realized no one ever played it in front of her. Most people knew that she was writing her doctoral dissertation on the draft resistance movement, but in suspicious times, some of them apparently viewed her graduate work as a perfect front for an informant. She frequently conducted casual interviews with draft resisters and supporters and gathered leaflets and other written materials, and she always took field notes. Alex Jack confirmed that he had heard people's suspicions about her. And even Thorne acknowledged that her activities sometimes looked suspect. At one point, she got into the habit of sneaking off to write her notes in private. One night as she and several other Resistance workers finalized the production of the *Resistance* newspaper, she went to the bathroom and scribbled notes as she sat on the toilet. When someone opened the door accidentally, she later recalled, it was the "quintessential moment of shame and discovery." She had been "caught," she said, "literally with my pants down!"[44]

Fears of government penetration of the Resistance did not, however, slow the momentum of the BU sanctuary, which was beginning to shape up as the nation's largest to date. The crowd of supporters steadily grew each day from fewer than 100 to more than 1,300 as expectations of Ray Kroll's arrest heightened. Like the Arlington Street Church sanctuary, the gathering took on a life of its own. Howard Zinn later characterized it as an "ongoing free-speech exercise . . . sort of like a twenty-four-hour-a-day teach-in." At an open microphone, clergy gave sermons and resisters, academics, and anyone who wanted to spoke to the crowd. The Resistance showed films about the war, and several bands played music at night. In the basement, approximately twenty doctors and residents and six nurses staffed a makeshift medical center. At one point, an optimistic Zinn commented to a reporter that if the sanctuary continued to be successful, and "if people continue to appear seeking sanctuary," then the BU sanctuary "may be permanent."[45]

The FBI, however, had other ideas. At 5:30 in the morning on Sunday, October 6, sanctuary supporters sleeping in the pews and in the aisle between them awoke to a voice shouting, "This is the FBI. We will give you 15 seconds to clear the aisle." The students turned to see 120 federal agents streaming into the chapel. The agents moved through the crowd moving—and sometimes tossing—students into the pews. The sanctuary participants remained nonviolent. "No one in that place lifted a finger to resist them," Joann Ruskin, a BU junior said immediately after the raid. "It was the most beautiful thing." If the FBI agents were not rough with the crowd in the chapel, they were not as kind to Ray Kroll. Photographs on the front page of the *Boston Globe* and *BU News* the next day show four FBI agents whisking him down the steps of Marsh chapel. The two agents on either side of him held his arms tightly; Kroll winced as one of the agents, smiling, twisted the deserter's fingers. Two other agents squeezed his neck from behind and then pushed him and the entire group of agents through a path cleared by Boston police toward a waiting car. As Kroll attempted to go limp one last time, Ted Polunbaum, a *Newsweek* reporter, heard one agent say to Kroll, "Stand up or we'll kill you, you bastard."[46]

Everyone involved in the sanctuary expected it to end in Ray Kroll's arrest, but when it finally happened, it stunned many of them anyway. The FBI and the Boston Police Department had demonstrated their power. The students knew that they had power, too, but Kroll's "bust" reminded them that the state had more and knew how to use it. Although the BU confrontation with authorities did not repeat the violence of the clash at Arlington Street, in some ways, the end of this sanctuary proved more depressing.

In an article in the *BU News*, Alex Jack, the veteran activist and New England Resistance founder, expressed a new level of despair. The experience of this sanctuary (which he had planned) led him to openly urge revolution. "The Sanctuary at Marsh Chapel has shown, simply, that there can be no sanctuary . . . from oppression, from racism, from militarism . . . no place is sacred," he wrote. "No rights are inviolable. No people or humanity is sacrosanct." If the government felt it had to, he wrote, it "will slaughter us all." The only solution to this condition, he argued, was the creation of a new society in which "exploitation is structurally impossible, where power is returned and exercised by the people, where there is no distinction between religion, politics or art, where in short there are no sanctuaries because no one is oppressed." Only a revolution could create the society he described, and Jack urged others to join him. "We are the children of the most monstrous and destructive society in history, a society that has no conception of or respect for human needs, a society that will annihilate the planet before sharing its wealth, a society without sanctuary for any of its victims." Lastly, he called for his generation to "rise up and utterly destroy this universe."[47]

Alex Jack's radical stance and participation in the organization of the Marsh Chapel sanctuary got him dismissed from the BU School of Theology. When the sanctuary first opened, the university and theology school administrations expressed surprise and made it clear that "the university . . . will abide by the laws of the land." In fact, the sanctuary constituted just one episode in a growing list of conflicts between the School of Theology and its students. Debates over curricula and grades and the students' roles (or lack thereof) in these issues had been simmering for some time, and a rift between students and faculty was widening. In contrast to the Harvard Divinity School's reaction to the Andover Hall sanctuary, when the BU sanctuary took place, not one School of Theology professor came to the chapel to show support for it. When it ended, the school singled out Alex Jack for punishment. They based his suspension on his failure to inform the school of the sanctuary plans and for failure to seek permission to use the chapel for that purpose. Only Ray Kroll, who received a sentence of three months' hard labor and who was docked two-thirds of his pay for the three months, received a harsher punishment.[48]

Unlike Alex Jack, however, most rank-and-file participants did not regard the BU sanctuary as a failure. Many believed that it had brought good publicity to the antiwar movement and bad publicity to the war and the government. Louis Kampf of Resist argued that, like draft card turn-ins, sanctuaries drew people together and gave them "a sense of responsibility to each other." Too often, he noted, that sense of responsibility was fleeting. But "if resistance to the war . . . is to be deepened," and "if our sense of purpose is to be taken seriously," rather than worrying about elections (which few in the movement did, given the candidacies of Hubert Humphrey, Richard Nixon, and George Wallace), "resistance and peace groups might better spend their time developing strategies for building communities of resistance." No one knew how to do this, exactly, but continued outreach to GIs and providing symbolic sanctuary to those who wanted it, Kampf implied, could be key ingredients. Soon, some of Louis Kampf's own students responded to his call.[49]

To outside observers, in spite of the ignominious ends of the Harvard and Boston University sanctuaries, the sanctuary movement no doubt appeared to be growing as it spread from one school to another, each one larger than the last. Three weeks after Ray Kroll's arrest, students at the Massachusetts Institute of Technology organized another sanctuary, but this one took on a secular tone. For the first time, instead of hosting the AWOL GI in a church or chapel, the MIT Resistance—an offshoot of the New England Resistance—provided asylum in the student center.

Although the draft resistance movement in Boston had attracted some students from MIT over the past year, the university itself had seen very little antiwar protest before the sanctuary. Compared to Harvard and BU, the campus at MIT was one of Boston's quietest. This relative calm could be attributed in part to MIT's connection with the war effort. In 1968, for instance, MIT earned the distinction of being the only university on a list of

100 organizations receiving the largest dollar value contracts from the Defense Department. In 1969, the Pentagon effectively underwrote 80 percent of MIT's budget.[50] Two operations—the Lincoln Laboratory and the Instrumentation Laboratory—spent most of this money. The Lincoln Lab occupied facilities provided by the air force at Hanscom Field in nearby Lexington and specialized in advanced research in electronics, radar and radio physics, and information processing. Scientists used technology developed at the Lincoln Lab to design several major early-warning air defense systems and ballistic missile defense systems in use in the late 1960s. At the Instrumentation Lab (or I-Lab, as it was known), researchers developed the Multiple Independent Reentry Vehicle (MIRV), probably the most noted (and eventually the most controversial) program at the university. The MIRV was a high-accuracy ballistic missile that could carry multiple nuclear warheads capable of annihilating several targets as far apart as 100 miles. It became perhaps the most obvious symbol of the university's ties to the Pentagon.[51]

In addition to designing new technologies for modern warfare, faculty in other departments actively supported the American war effort in Vietnam. Many within the university community, for instance, knew that the Central Intelligence Agency openly funded MIT's political science department in the early 1960s and that the two maintained a formal relationship through the late 1960s. In fact, the department kept a villa in Saigon where graduate students worked on pacification projects and other American political/military programs for their dissertations.[52]

At the same time, however, a small number of dissidents—some students and faculty—had actively opposed the war for a long time. Most notably, Noam Chomsky and Louis Kampf—even before signing the "Call to Resist Illegitimate Authority" and long before they became key figures in the formation of Resist—taught a course outside their departments on their own time called "Intellectuals and Social Change." The course covered both contemporary foreign policy and domestic issues and challenged students to consider the role of intellectuals in taking sides on the important questions of the day. By fall 1968, almost all of the individuals responsible for organizing the MIT sanctuary had taken that course. In addition, a small group of students who had worked with the New England Resistance over the summer formed the MIT Resistance. From the beginning of the fall semester, these students plotted to hold a sanctuary on campus.

John M. "Mike" O'Connor, an army friend of Ray Kroll, took sanctuary at MIT on October 29, 1968. O'Connor, nineteen, came from Goldsboro, North

Carolina, where he enlisted in the army to avoid being jailed on a marijuana possession charge. In April 1968, he went AWOL from Fort Eustis, Virginia, for fifty days and spent two months in the stockade there as a result. He was released in August and again went AWOL on September 14. O'Connor had attended Kroll's sanctuary at Boston University and wanted to join it, but Resistance organizers persuaded him to wait for another chance.[53]

Resistance organizers from MIT wanted their sanctuary to symbolize a new level of militancy by separating the concept of sanctuary from its long-standing religious context. Resistance organizer Bob Shapiro reserved an immense space, the Sala de Puerto Rico, in the student center. In part, he chose this space simply as a practical matter; the Sala was the only large place on campus that could be reserved without disrupting the plans for other nonpolitical events.[54] Seven hundred people showed up the first night (a Tuesday), and by Saturday night, November 2, more than 1,200 supporters spent the night, most of them sleeping in sleeping bags, waiting for the FBI.[55]

The appeal of the MIT sanctuary derived in part from Mike O'Connor's magnetism. As the editors of MIT's student newspaper, the *Tech*, noted after his arrest, O'Connor, perhaps more than any other GI in a Boston area sanctuary, seemed to know what he was doing. On the first day of the sanctuary, he made it clear to his supporters and the media that he understood the probable consequences of his actions. By taking sanctuary, he acknowledged, he would probably spend more time in the stockade than if he simply turned himself in. "To me it is worth it," he asserted. "I feel that if I can convince 100 people that the war is wrong, that it is an injustice against the basic freedoms of our country, then I will gladly serve the extra time." Rather than leave the country, O'Connor said, "if there is something wrong with [the country], we should try to change it." Then, in an obvious reference to Paul Olimpieri and Thomas Pratt, O'Connor said that he realized that he would probably be forced to retract all of his statements upon his arrest. He told the crowd, however, that his was a "statement of the heart," that they should remember it, and that with their help he would be able to withstand any coercion. In the event that he did "weaken and make any statements against this community," he urged his supporters to disregard them and "remember me for what I write and say while I am free."[56]

The MIT sanctuary developed over several days in much the same fashion as the Arlington Street Church and Marsh Chapel sanctuaries. On the second day of the event, some faculty brought their classes to the Sala de Puerto Rico as an expression of solidarity; Louis Kampf, for instance, taught his Proust class there. That night, several bands played and organizers showed a few short films produced by Newsreel, the underground film collective. Abbie Hoffman made an appearance at one point. Through it all the numbers of people taking part ebbed and flowed until Thursday night, when more than 1,000 people claimed a space in the Sala. As participants reviewed their guidelines for greeting the authorities, a large number of people suggested that the sanctuary abandon its nonviolent approach. Members of the Living Theater, fresh from a performance at Kresge Auditorium, tried to talk some of the students into occupying some of the administration offices. Fearing a violent clash when the authorities arrived, O'Connor asked for a vote on the issue of nonviolence, saying that if the crowd voted for a direct confrontation, he would turn himself in to the army; they voted for nonviolence. Still, anxiety grew steadily over the next few days. Three technically adept students worked out seven different telephone and walkie-talkie systems to give a warning of any raid that might take place; meanwhile, another sympathizer armed with a ham radio patrolled the Charles River by boat looking for federal agents or military police.[57]

By Friday and especially Saturday, most people were physically and emotionally exhausted. Mike O'Connor in particular seemed to be suffering from the effects of too little sleep. Resistance organizers could not believe that the FBI or the army had not yet come to arrest O'Connor, so on Sunday night, on the sixth day of the sanctuary, they declared victory and sent everyone home. O'Connor went to sleep in a small room on the fourth floor of the student center while Resistance leaders placed the sanctuary in the best light possible. They had been successful, they argued, in protecting O'Connor for six days; he had explained his position on television and radio and in the papers; and the event raised the political consciousness of a campus formerly considered passive. In reality, few of the sanctuary participants knew what to do when the authorities did not show up.[58] A week later, on November 10, military police from Fort Devens finally arrived and arrested O'Connor. Thus, as Neil Robertson wrote soon after, the MIT sanctuary "ended in confusion after a gradual atrophy." After a January trial, a military court sentenced O'Connor to four months of hard labor and forfeiture of two-thirds of his pay over that time; the judge then added the four months remaining from his previous suspended sentence for going AWOL the second time.[59]

Mike O'Connor's sanctuary thoroughly transformed the activist climate at MIT. Noam Chomsky, who initially thought the sanctuary would fall flat and attract little student support, later remarked that to his "amazement" the sanctuary "just galvanized the whole campus." It "completely changed the mood of the whole university," he recalled. "It's never changed since, or never gone back." Indeed, in the wake of the sanctuary's end, many students commented on the new consciousness of students. Bill Berry, an MIT Resistance organizer, argued that MIT students suddenly began questioning their roles in society. He gave a hypothetical example of a student who would now be more likely to turn down a lucrative job at General Dynamics, where he would be creating new and more efficient destructive technology, to do scientific work that would help society. Previously isolated students now felt exhilarated by the sense of community that they experienced with faculty and their fellow students. Nevertheless, a handful of critics also began to criticize the tactic of sanctuary.[60]

The MIT sanctuary turned out to be the last significant sanctuary in the Boston area. Although students at Brandeis University offered sanctuary to another soldier in early December, the authorities' willingness to all but ignore it and let it sputter out on its own again undermined the protest value of the event. By January, the Resistance began to shift its focus on GIS away from sanctuary to lower-profile outreach. Organizers admitted that beyond the publicity that sanctuaries garnered, and the growing numbers of students on Boston campuses who turned out for such events, they actually played into the hands of the military. The public nature of the GI's protest had no mitigating effect on his punishment; indeed, it may have made his plight worse.[61]

The New England Resistance decided, therefore, to expand its GI outreach program. On Friday nights, Resistance members walked a few blocks from their Stanhope Street office to the Greyhound bus terminal on St. James Street where they sought out soldiers traveling for the weekend and gave them copies of *Vietnam GI*, the antiwar newspaper published in Chicago and aimed at providing GIS with a more critical analysis of the war than they could get from the army's official publication, *Stars and Stripes*. A few people also spent their Friday nights at Logan Airport for the same reason. In addition, Resistance activists tried to make contact with disgruntled soldiers to offer counseling on how to get discharges or apply for conscientious objector status. They handed out flyers inviting GIS to Resistance parties and the organization's office.[62] In one of the most ambitious activities of the outreach program, Nan Stone and Joel Kugelmass made several visits to bars and clubs in the Combat Zone (Boston's red-light district), where they could usually expect to encounter plenty of alienated servicemen and frequently someone who had gone AWOL. Stone and Kugelmass then offered help in the form of lawyers and counselors. Since their antiwar experience had taught them something about the reach of the federal government, Stone and Kugelmass usually encouraged AWOLS to turn themselves in with the help of movement lawyers. In a few rare instances, Stone and others in the Resistance participated in a sort of underground railroad with other antiwar organizations as a way of getting deserters out of the country.[63]

This shift to GI outreach demonstrated a measure of maturity in the Resistance. "As we all became a little more astute about what we were doing," Nan Stone later recalled, "we did get much more of a sense of how guys could end up in the military and even in Vietnam without believing in the war." Many servicemen, they learned, felt they had no choices. Gradually, in the second half of 1968 and into 1969, Resistance activists stopped looking at servicemen as potential enemies.[64]

This change in constituency, however, had two unintended consequences: the virtual abandonment of the hundreds of men who returned their draft cards in late 1967 and the first half of 1968 and the ultimate decline of the New England Resistance. When the Resistance turned away from draft card turn-ins to devote more and more time and resources to high school organizing and the sanctuary movement, it made no formal announcement. Newsletters and the *Resistance* newspaper no longer carried information on draft card turn-ins and instead included articles laced with revolutionary rhetoric and critiques of imperialism and capitalism. For the rank-and-file draft resister, the future seemed less clear, and the group to whom one might ordinarily look for guidance had moved in a new direction. As a result, several draft resisters created a new organization to meet that demand.

SUPPORT AND FORGOTTEN DRAFT RESISTERS

The U.S. Attorney's office in Boston, consistent with Ramsey Clark's wishes, waited until after the Spock trial ended to indict ordinary draft resisters. Between August and December 1968, a grand jury handed down forty-eight indictments of men who had refused induction when called. As Michael Zigmond, who had turned in his card at the Old West Church on November 16, 1967, and was among these indicted men, later recalled, "Now that people had refused induction, the movement . . . wasn't all that interested in them. Their political act had happened and what happened to them afterwards was of no particular political interest, I think." Zigmond approached the New England Resistance and Resist about providing some kind of support for the indicted men but got little in the way of a response. "My attitude was, maybe it isn't political, but it's sort of the other side of the Veterans Administration System," Zigmond reflected. "You know, we've served our time in the front lines, we refused induction, people ought to care about us now. Whether it's political or not doesn't matter." Frustrated by the indifference of movement leaders, Zigmond and his wife, Naomi, along with a few other indictees formed an organization called SUPPORT to raise money for legal expenses and travel expenses incurred by family members visiting resisters in prison.[65]

Michael Zigmond was somewhat older than most Resistance organizers. Two months before turning in his draft card, Zigmond turned twenty-six, making it very unlikely that he would ever be drafted. Moreover, he had earned his Ph.D. from Carnegie Tech and at the time of his resistance held a postdoctoral fellowship at MIT. The war and his immunity from it weighed heavily on him, however (see Chapter 4), and he decided to risk his safe status by returning his draft card to the Justice Department. His Arlington, Massachusetts, draft board quickly reclassified him and called him for induction. On the Friday of Memorial Day weekend 1968, Zigmond, accompanied by his wife and parents, arrived at the Boston Army Base and found that he was the only person scheduled for induction that day (a tactic often used on troublemakers so they would not have the opportunity to proselytize to other draftees). Although he had allergies, flat feet, and terrible vision, he passed the physical. He did better on the IQ test. During the psychological examination, Zigmond reported feeling a little depressed and anxious. When the doctor asked why, Zigmond responded, "Because at the end of this day I'm going to commit a felony." And so he did.

As his wife, Naomi, and his parents watched through a glass picture window, Zigmond refused to step forward on three separate occasions. Two FBI agents interviewed him after the ceremony and released him. The whole affair took all day.[66] As the Zigmond family walked the long walk from the induction center to the Boston Army Base exit, they heard a trumpet begin to play the familiar refrain of "Taps." Nearby, an old soldier slowly started to lower the American flag. But when he saw the Zigmonds walking—instead of stopping to observe the sacred ceremony—he began shouting at them. They walked on. The man yelled. The trumpeter played to the end.[67]

In the fall of 1968, Michael and Naomi Zigmond assumed more prominent roles in the Boston antiwar movement by starting SUPPORT, which drew its membership from several organizations such as the American Friends Service Committee, Resist, the BDRG, Mass. Pax, the New England Resistance, and the Prisoners Information and Support Service. The impulse to form SUPPORT came in part from the members of these groups attending the late summer trials of a few men who had refused induction. "Some of those who had been surrounded by 5,000 supporters on the Boston Common were left standing alone," a SUPPORT newsletter charged. "Court rooms (which hold about 35 people) were filled only with difficulty." Those who did attend trials realized that many of the men being tried were very young and often poor and frequently did not understand the judicial process and rarely had more than one supporter in the courtroom. SUPPORT got started by coordinating groups of people to go to each draft resistance trial. "The resistance movement must now decide whether the government will be allowed to continue to carry off non-cooperators quietly," they said as the number of indictments climbed through the fall. The objective, since the media did not cover the trials at all, would be to make each one a focus for political action and, consequently, a story worth covering.[68]

In contrast to the growing activist program of the Resistance, SUPPORT offered a fairly narrow array of services, but for the indicted men, what they did offer was very important. Each week, the Zigmonds and their one paid staff person, Carol Neville, combed the newspaper for announcements of indicted men. Then, in most cases, SUPPORT lined up someone from the indictee's own community to contact the young man and offer information on legal and financial assistance. Often resisters could enlist the aid of an attorney through the Committee for Legal Research on the Draft, an organization started by Harvard Law School students. Supporters assigned to each case also were responsible for coordinating support for the indictee in his own community by circulating petitions, organizing rallies, and encouraging others to attend the man's trial. SUPPORT's work did not stop with a conviction, however; while in prison, resisters could expect frequent letters and postcards from supporters, and, maybe most important, SUPPORT supplied travel money to families who wanted to visit their sons in prison.[69]

The irony is that most of the men who benefited from SUPPORT's assistance had not taken part in the draft resistance movement at any time over the previous year. By December 1968, Zigmond realized that all but four or five of the men indicted since August were men whose draft boards had denied their conscientious objector requests and who, in turn, decided to refuse induction rather than violate their consciences. This distinction did not distract SUPPORT from its work in any way, however. It seemed clear that indictments would eventually be issued for men who had openly defied the draft as part of the resistance movement and who subsequently refused induction. Moreover, SUPPORT activists knew just how important their work was to the families they had already helped. One couple who had received money to travel to Allenwood, Pennsylvania, to visit their imprisoned son wrote a letter to Michael and Naomi Zigmond that conveyed their gratitude: "[We're] certain that just knowing that there are people like yourself on the outside that have not forgotten about him is enough to give him the courage and reassurance that he so needs right now." Letters like that inspired continued activism regardless of the resister's movement credentials or lack thereof.[70]

In the end, however, it turned out that the U.S. Attorney in Boston secured proportionately few indictments—and even fewer convictions—of draft resisters who turned in their draft cards at any of the gatherings organized by the New England Resistance in 1967–68. Nearly thirty-five years later, the reasons for this are not altogether clear. After the flurry of indictments at the end of 1968, no Boston area draft resister was indicted in all of 1969. Assistant U.S. Attorney and Spock trial prosecutor John Wall recalls "an avalanche of [draft] cases" overwhelming his office, and he suggests that many cases simply "fell through the cracks." The department just did not have the resources to pursue every draft resister. That may have been the case, but the evidence shows that several variables probably factored into the ultimate resolution of each draft resister's case. The final determination of each resister's future usually derived from decisions made by either the resister himself, his draft board, or a judge.[71]

Until now, many members of the draft resistance community have believed that once the New England Resistance abandoned draft card turn-ins as its primary tactic for confronting the government, most resisters who had lost their deferments as a result of their protest sought to have them renewed. Sociologist Barrie Thorne reported in 1971 that although "there were no certain figures, only cumulative hearsay and general impression," most people in the movement guessed that at least half—and as many as three-fourths—of Boston's draft resisters "had gone back on their pledge of non-cooperation." These figures seem inflated when one considers, as Michael Ferber and Staughton Lynd have, that between the fall of 1968 and the spring of 1970 some 400 men had refused induction in Boston; as of

March 1970, none of those men had been indicted, "a fact," Ferber and Lynd have noted, "for which no one has offered a good explanation." These 400 men no doubt included some of those who had begun their draft resistance odyssey by turning in their draft cards at a New England Resistance organized ceremony, but most of them probably refused induction on their own.

Draft resisters who completed the 1997 survey conducted for this study provide the first clear indication of how the cases of Boston's draft resistance community turned out. Table A.20 shows what happened to draft resisters after they turned in their draft cards. Most local draft boards followed General Lewis Hershey's instructions and reclassified draft resisters once they received their draft cards. Out of 102 survey respondents, 77 (75.5 percent) report being reclassified to 1-A; 56 (54.9 percent) of these men later received orders to report for induction into the armed services. Nine men (6 of whom were twenty-six or older and 1 of whom was a veteran) heard absolutely nothing from their draft boards. Only 15 (14.7 percent) avoided reclassification by seeking or accepting a duplicate draft card or a new deferment, but another 11 of the men who *were* reclassified 1-A also secured new deferments before they could be called for induction (see Table A.21). Since government officials chose not to prosecute men for turning in their draft cards, they generally waited until a draft resister refused induction before pursuing an indictment. Table A.22 presents data on the Boston draft resisters who received induction notices after having their classifications changed to 1-A. Thirty of 53 respondents went through with their original plans and refused induction, while another 14 who might have refused induction failed their pre-induction physicals. Only 9 of the men called for induction avoided their own personal showdowns at the Boston Army Base by seeking and receiving new deferments before their induction dates. In addition, 26 men escaped reclassifications and/or induction calls by accepting duplicate draft cards or new deferments.

Resisters compromised on their original commitment to refuse induction for a variety of reasons, but generally their decision came down to two considerations. First, many realized that even if every man who turned in his draft card in late 1967 and early 1968 refused induction, it would not stop the war. As one resister commented on his survey: "I had hoped, naively, that I would be one of hundreds of thousands, on October 16 or later, who refused to serve, and that my act would, with others, lead to a quick end to the war. Eight months later, I reluctantly concluded it wasn't going to happen." David Clennon, the Yale graduate student who turned in his draft card at Arlington Street Church, likewise recalls the doubt that many resisters had about their original strategies by the middle of 1968. When he was called for induction in June 1969, he used his fragile psychological state to secure a note from his psychiatrist that effectively won him a new deferment. At the same time, Clennon acknowledges that he "began to doubt whether I could handle 32 months in prison." Self-interest was the second most common reason for resisters' seeking new deferments. In Clennon's case, more than a year of anxiety followed his draft card turn-in (which led him to the psychiatrist in the first place). As another resister wrote, "People were no longer doing this (turning in cards) and there seemed to be a general feeling that it was pointless to go to jail over it. . . . Fear of going to prison was also a major factor."[72]

Today, many of the draft resisters who chose not to refuse induction still have mixed feelings about their decision and some regret it altogether. David Clennon has called his new deferment "a real copout." Although he had "taken this big step and . . . stood my ground for about a year, year and a half," he said, he then "copped out and took the middle-class road to get out of the draft." Similarly, Larry Etscovitz, the Boston University student who spontaneously turned in his draft card at the Arlington Street Church on October 16, admits giving in to his fear when he accepted a 1-Y deferment at his pre-induction physical. He now regards his initial act of resistance as "an inviolate moment in an otherwise very gray scenario of self-preservation in moving from one extreme to another." When he turned in his card, he says, "I felt I was committed to an irrevocable course of protest." But the government kept "dangling carrots" in front of him to make it easy to back out. These offerings—of duplicate cards, new deferments, etc.—"became more and more enticing as my tolerance for being in a state of chaos got less. I got scared," he says. "Let's just be straight about it. I got scared . . . and I regret it to this day. I really do."[73]

What the men who avoided an induction-ceremony confrontation did not know was that with each passing year, prosecutors found it increasingly difficult to bring draft resistance cases to trial and to win them when they did. Table A.23 shows that in 1966, the U.S. Attorney in Boston won 16 convictions or guilty pleas from a total of 26 indicted draft resisters, which amounts to a 62 percent success rate. But by 1968, the situation had changed dramatically. The department won only 8 convictions or guilty pleas out of 50 indictments (a 16 percent success rate). This drop can be attributed in part to an increase in the number of indicted men who left the country (17)—almost all of the indicted men refused induction individually, not as part of a draft resistance movement, which strongly discouraged immigration. It also resulted in part from mistakes made by draft boards. Sometimes, bureaucratic errors were sufficient to keep a case from being prosecuted (or to get it dismissed), but it seems reasonable to attribute the dearth of prosecutions (only 12 of the 30 men surveyed who refused induction were prosecuted) to the fact that several draft resistance cases had attracted the attention of the Supreme Court, which was expected to rule on several issues germane to such cases. Indeed, several major judicial decisions, three of which stemmed from Boston draft resistance cases, were handed down in late 1968 and 1969.

Not long after a Cheyenne, Wyoming, draft board reclassified Jim Oestereich, the Andover-Newton seminarian, to 1-A, Oestereich engaged the services of the American Civil Liberties Union. The ACLU filed suit against the Selective Service in federal court to prevent Oestereich's induction on the grounds that his local board had punished him through a punitive reclassification without due process. The judge dismissed the complaint and the court of appeals affirmed it, in part because the Selective Service Act of 1967 stated that there should be no pre-induction judicial review of the classification record of any registrant. In May, however, the Supreme Court agreed to hear the case. In October, Oestereich's attorney, the ACLU's Melvin Wulf, argued the case before the Court. Wulf asserted that General Hershey used the draft to punish dissenters of national policy and, consequently, deterred many draft-age Americans from expressing any view at all. In addition, Wulf reiterated his original charge that punitive reclassification was unconstitutional.[74]

On December 16, 1968, in what was hailed as a landmark decision, the Court ruled in favor of Jim Oestereich. The Court focused on Oestereich's status as a ministerial student and the draft exemption that his draft board had granted him. As distinct from the 2-S student *deferment*, which theoretically postponed a registrant's obligation to serve in the armed forces, the 4-D classification *exempted* the registrant from military service for as long as he was a divinity student or minister. "Once a person registers and qualifies for a statutory exemption," Justice William O. Douglas wrote for the Court, "we find no legislative authority to deprive him of that exemption because of conduct or activities unrelated to the merits of granting or continuing that exemption." Douglas described the conduct of the Cheyenne draft board as "basically lawless" and asserted that Oestereich's reclassification and induction order were no different in constitutional implications than if the board called a minister or another "clearly exempt person" for induction "(a) to retaliate against the person because of his political views or (b) to bear down on him because of his religious views or his racial attitudes or (c) to get him out of town so that the amorous interests of a Board member might be better served."[75] A few weeks later, Douglas commented, "There is no suggestion in the current draft law that the Selective Service has free-wheeling authority to ride herd on registrants, using immediate induction as a disciplinary or vindictive measure."[76] The draft resisters, it seemed, had won at last—and at least—a legal and moral victory.

In fact, however, the Court did not rule that punitive reclassifications were inherently unconstitutional (as Melvin Wulf had argued). The decision applied only to the reclassification of registrants with ministerial exemptions. The Court's judgment said nothing about reclassification of other registrants resulting from protest activity. In Boston, Jim Oestereich learned of the decision on the morning of the 16th when a United Press International (UPI) reporter called him at the American Friends Service Committee office. Oestereich, who had been filled with so much emotion when he turned in his draft card, and who had been basically run out of Lunenburg, where he had been a youth minister, now had something to cheer about. Others cautioned against getting too optimistic. Michael Zigmond reminded readers of the SUPPORT newsletter that the Oestereich decision amounted to "victory on the narrowest possible grounds." He feared that piecemeal victories such as this might undermine some of the outrage that fueled the movement. "Any victory is important," he wrote. "Yet we must be careful. Too many of us are still uncomfortable in our new anti-establishment roles, all too ready to return to our old lives at the slightest hint of a bombing halt or a favorable court decision."[77]

Still, the Oestereich decision offered a glimmer of hope that the Court might yet clamp down on the Selective Service's use of the draft as punishment for protesters. A year later, two decisions effectively expanded the Oestereich ruling to all draft resisters. In Gutknecht v. United States the Court ruled in the petitioner's favor in a case in which Gutknecht's draft board accelerated his induction schedule, effectively trying to take him out of order (he was already classified 1-A) after he left his draft card on the steps of the Federal Building in Minneapolis on October 16, 1967.[78] And in the decision for Breen v. Selective Service Board No. 16, issued the same day as the Gutknecht decision, the Court decided that the draft board had acted unconstitutionally when it reclassified Timothy Breen, a student at Boston's Berklee College of Music, for failure to possess the draft card he had returned at the Arlington Street Church on October 16. "We fail to see any relevant practical or legal differences between exemptions and deferments," Justice Hugo Black wrote, thus extending the Court's judgment in *Oestereich* to cover all registration classifications.[79] Collectively, the three decisions held that punitive reclassification by local draft boards was unconstitutional.

A third court ruling in a Boston case further undermined the Selective Service's channeling system. In the case of *United States v. Sisson*, U.S. District Court judge Charles Wyzanski, who had presided over many draft resistance cases in the previous four years, issued a ruling that said the Selective Service law's identification of practitioners of only certain religions as eligible for conscientious objector status discriminated against nonreligious objectors. John Sisson, a resident of Lincoln, Massachusetts, held a 2-S student deferment until he graduated from Harvard in 1967. His West Concord draft board reclassified him 1-A in November and called him for induction in April 1968. At the time, Sisson worked for the *Southern Courier*, a civil rights movement newspaper associated with Harvard in Montgomery, Alabama. In February 1968, while still in Alabama, Sisson had written to his draft board requesting an application form for conscientious objector status but decided not to complete it because he did not fit the religious profiles required for that classification. At his trial he said he refused induction because he believed that "the United States military involvement in Vietnam is illegal under international law as well as under the Constitution and treaties of the United States" and that his "participation in that war would violate the spirit and letter of the Nuremberg Charter." On the basis of his knowledge of the Vietnam War, Sisson concluded, "I could not participate in it without doing violence to the dictates of my conscience." His was the most common argument among draft resisters. Many resisters came to their stand in the fall of 1967 or spring of 1968 after having their conscientious objector applications denied because they were not Quakers. The Sisson decision at last acknowledged their stand.[80]

Judge Wyzanski, who many court observers believed had long been seeking a case like this, issued an arrest of judgment in the guilty verdict against Sisson in deciding that the defendant could not be criminally convicted in the case because he was a legitimate conscientious objector. In a lengthy opinion, Wyzanski raised the question of selective objection to war, a pivotal issue for the draft resistance community, and repeatedly pointed to Sisson's sincerity. "On the stand, Sisson was diffident, perhaps beyond the requirements of modesty," the judge wrote. "He was entirely without eloquence. No line he spoke remains etched in memory. But he fearlessly used his own words, not mouthing formulae from court cases or manuals for draft avoidance." Wyzanski highlighted Sisson's sense of social obligation in working for the *Courier* and applying to the Peace Corps, and in prose that heartened all draft resisters, outlined in detail Sisson's moral development: "Sisson's table of ultimate values is moral and ethical. It reflects quite as real, pervasive, durable, and commendable a marshaling of priorities as a formal religion. It is just as much a residue of culture, early training, and beliefs shared by companions and family. What another derives from the discipline of a church, Sisson derives from the discipline of conscience. . . . He was as genuinely and profoundly governed by his conscience as would have been a martyr obedient to an orthodox religion." In short, Wyzanski said, the 1967 draft law discriminated against "atheists, agnostics, and men like Sisson," who were motivated in their objection to conscription "by profound moral beliefs which constitute the central convictions of their beings."[81] The United States appealed to the Supreme Court, but the Court let the decision stand without hearing the appeal.

With these important cases working their way through the federal court system, it is not surprising that prosecutors in Boston relaxed the pace of draft resistance indictments after December 1968. Even before the *Breen* and *Gutknecht* decisions, it would have been reasonable to assume that the *Oestereich* ruling would make winning any of these cases more difficult. Ultimately, of the thirty men in this study's sample who refused induction, only twelve were prosecuted and only five of them were convicted.[82] Therefore, for a variety of reasons—from illegal behavior on the part of local draft boards and self-preservation on the part of resisters—only five (roughly 4 percent) of the 121 draft resisters who responded to the survey went to prison. This record is virtually identical to the national average, in which 8,750 (4.2 percent) out of 209,517 accused draft offenders were convicted.[83]

The proportionate few who lost in court soon faced the alienating experience that all draft resisters feared: spending two to five years in federal prison. Most of them traveled an indirect route from court to the Charles Street jail to one or more jails en route to prison, usually in Allenwood, Pennsylvania, or Petersburg, Virginia. Federal marshals transporting David O'Brien to Petersburg drove him through Arlington National Cemetery, a final resting place, they told him, for "real Americans." Convicted resisters were no longer surrounded by the communities that hosted them. The general feeling of alienation intensified at this point, as resisters went through a process called admission and orientation, or A and O. This indoctrination often took place among the general population in the maximum security section of the prison; for resisters sent to Allenwood, for example, A and O took place at the nearby maximum security facility at Lewisburg. Once assigned to their minimum security dormitories (sometimes called the "Honors Dorm") the new prisoners found themselves in enormous, overcrowded rooms that housed as many as 120 prisoners, usually with rows of alternating beds and lockers, sometimes with a shower at either end of the hall. In Petersburg, the fact that the walls were painted with bright spring colors prompted resisters to coin the term "pastel fascism"[84] to describe the legal and political system that channeled them into those painted cells.

In most cases, draft resisters were among another 20 to 30 men imprisoned for similar convictions. Often, as at Allenwood, this community of resisters included the Amish and Jehovah's Witnesses, and sometimes members of the Nation of Islam. Depending on their daily responsibilities and routines, these men tended to gravitate toward one another, although, as psychologist Willard Gaylin found in his study of imprisoned war resisters, prison officials discouraged any sense of community. Consequently, wardens and guards tolerated prejudice-induced tension and violence that minimized any sense of unity.[85]

Just as many Americans regarded resisters as cowards and sissies, other prisoners assumed that most resisters were weak and submissive and, therefore, easily intimidated. The bullying that occurred often came from sexual predators, and few things scared the new prisoners more than the prospect of being raped. None of the men who participated in this study and went to prison reported being raped, but a few experienced some close calls. For example, soon after Gary Hicks, one of the original Boston CNVA resisters, arrived at Petersburg, another inmate sat down next to him at a cafeteria table and asked him how well he could fight. When Hicks said, "pretty well," the predator asked, "good enough to make the difference between being called Mr. and Mrs.?" Hicks answered, "Probably." The next day, when the same inmate propositioned Hicks in the cafeteria, Hicks put a fork to his throat and walked him out of the cafeteria in front of all of the other inmates. He spent two weeks in solitary confinement for the confrontation, but no one bothered him again. Others reported similar difficulties, while some described intimidation at the hands of the guards; still others had few problems at all.[86]

Violence notwithstanding, resisters' experiences in prison were shaped much more by the routine of work, exercise, and self-study. The types of jobs assigned them varied from prison to prison, but most involved manual labor. At Allenwood, which functioned primarily as a working farm and cattle ranch, most prisoners worked outside. Elsewhere, an inmate might work in the laundry or the kitchen. Some resisters managed to learn a trade. Dan Brustein, who, on October 16, turned in a letter pledging to not register for the draft when he reached his eighteenth birthday (and eventually went to prison in Ashland, Kentucky, for fulfilling that pledge), learned carpentry and cabinet making. Others, like Gary Hicks, found time beyond their work responsibilities to study. Hicks eventually got his G.E.D.[87]

Imprisoned draft resisters had mixed feelings about their communication with the world beyond the prison walls. Prison officials did little to relax the sense of isolation from the outside world by, say, making televised news reports available, but prisoners could receive mail from an authorized list of people and could receive visitors. In some ways, ordinary mail sustained the resisters more than visits from parents or loved ones. Some found that "doing time" was more difficult when they had frequent visitors. According to Brustein, "The day you have visitors, anticipating the visit and then the day or two after the visit, reliving the visit, just makes the time a lot harder." A number of men simply refused to accept visitors for that reason. Likewise, some refused to accept mail, and especially the piles of Christmas cards that would arrive from well-meaning supporters in the peace community, in part because it set them apart from the other inmates and could lead to tension.[88]

Most of all, time passed slowly. Resisters managed the physical experience of prison fairly well, but the psychological experience drained them. Some, like Gary Hicks, tried to escape. During a riot at Allenwood, Hicks made a run for it and immediately got lost in the woods surrounding the prison. Prison officials picked him up within twenty-four hours, and he wound up with an extra eighteen months added to his sentence. More significant, he spent the remainder of his time, nearly three years, at Lewisburg, Allenwood's maximum security counterpart. He finally got out in June 1970. Hicks's experience was atypical, but all of the imprisoned resisters reported psychological strain. Dan Brustein, who in later years became a physician, recalls that when he learned about post-traumatic stress disorder in medical school, he realized that he had suffered from it. Even though he had not been the victim of physical violence, long after his release from prison, he had flashbacks and suffered from insomnia, often arising from persistent feelings of isolation and vulnerability left over from prison life.[89]

Had they known about it, the imprisoned men may have been surprised to learn that by late 1968, the Justice Department's record of success against draft resisters had crumbled, and they may have been even more surprised to know that as resisters finally began to win their cases in court, the draft resistance movement in Boston came to an end. A lack of finances and the organization's internal divisions eventually led to the Resistance's disintegration. First, by moving away from draft card turn-ins and the middle-class men who participated in them, the Resistance gave up its main source of funding: suburban liberals. And even if the working-class families of GIs were inclined to donate money to the Resistance, they had few resources to share with the antiwar movement. In August 1968, the Resistance had to send out a special letter soliciting more funds. "At a time when we must expand our operations, we are in danger of bankruptcy," the letter said, noting that the organization was $2,000 in debt and operated on a $3,500 monthly budget. By January, the monthly budget had dropped to $2,000, but debts now tallied close to $3,000. One year before, the Resistance was Boston's leading antiwar organization, but now, as they acknowledged in their January 1969 newsletter, few knew what had happened to them. The "desperate financial straits" they found themselves in would not improve.[90]

In the spring, the New England Resistance finally folded. The end came after Penney Kurland (who had been active with the Resistance since the BU sanctuary) returned from the national Resistance conference in Bloomington, Indiana, where she had met many other women from other Resistance groups across the country. They shared their experiences and realized that they were all being marginalized within their organizations in the same ways. When they left Bloomington, they pledged to one another that they would confront the men in their organizations on the gender inequities in the movement. In Boston, this confrontation between the men and women of the New England Resistance led to the collapse of the organization. Although some men expressed contrition over the way the group had treated women, the women decided that the formation of their own resistance was more important than continuing with their present course. The six or eight women still in the NER left the organization and went on to form Boston's first consciousness-raising groups, some of which merged into the Bread and Roses women's collective, one of the most influential women's liberation organizations in the country. The New England Resistance soon voted to become a chapter of Students for a Democratic Society but by summer was forced to move out of the Stanhope Street office. Neil Robertson, Steve Pailet, and Ira Arlook drove taxi cabs to raise money to pay off the remaining Resistance debts. On August 2, 1969, in the saddest footnote to the history of the New England Resistance, a passenger shot and killed Pailet in a robbery, a crime the police never solved.[91]

Even before the New England Resistance dissolved, most of the remaining activists felt burned out. The organization's revolutionary rhetoric from the previous summer had given way to cautious approval for positive court decisions. The intensity of 1968 had taken its toll on the movement. In 1969, Richard Nixon took over a war that showed few signs of ending.

The last half of 1968 and the early months of 1969 could be viewed as a period of fitful searching for new strategies to end the war, but the fact is, Boston's draft resistance community, though diminished in size, made several important advances. First, its alliance with servicemen and its emphasis on GI dissenters ushered in a new phase of antiwar protest in which GIS and veterans—with whom the public associated a moral authority that they never granted civilian protesters—eventually came to dominate the movement against the war. The sanctuaries organized by the Resistance attracted considerable publicity to antiwar servicemen, and GI outreach helped sustain soldiers who opposed the war. Second, the network of supporters pulled together by SUPPORT kept alive dreams of a real resistance community that sustained resisters and their families in their time of need, especially during trials and once resisters were sent to prison. Finally, the Resistance could take some credit for protecting the civil liberties of draft-age men when federal courts and the Supreme Court ruled against the government's misuse of the draft.

EPILOGUE

In the battle for freedom . . . it is the struggle *for, not so much the attainment of, liberty, that develops all that is strongest, sturdiest, and finest in human character.*
—Emma Goldman, "What I Believe," 1908

In 1969, a new president took office promising to end the war in Vietnam. During the election campaign he promised "peace with honor." But despite initiating a gradual troop withdrawal program and altering the draft selection process to a lottery system, Richard Nixon actually expanded the war during his first year in office. Within weeks of taking up residence in the White House, Nixon widened the air war to include thousands of secret sorties over Cambodia. A year later, he sent ground forces into Cambodia, thus triggering protests more widespread and intense than any directed at his predecessors. There would be no peace with honor. By the time the United States signed the Paris Peace Accords in January 1973, the Nixon administration had seen another 20,553 American soldiers die along with 107,000 South Vietnamese troops and more than half a million enemy soldiers; civilian casualties from 1969 to the end of 1972 may have reached one million.

For the men and women who made up Boston's draft resistance community from 1966 to 1969 the end of their organization did not signal an end to their activism. Although Nixon initiated a draft lottery and began troop withdrawals, and although the larger antiwar movement certainly experienced some lulls, most former draft resistance activists found plenty of opportunities to express their opposition to the war long after the Resistance disbanded. Campus protest continued to grow throughout the greater Boston area, and the October 15, 1969, Moratorium—a national day of protest in which citizens all across the country stayed home from work and school to register their opposition to the war—attracted 100,000 people to a rally on the Boston Common. It was the largest demonstration in the city's history. On the same day, doctors in white lab coats collected signatures for antiwar petitions outside the historic Old South Church, and

400 lawyers gathered at Faneuil Hall to protest the war. As several historians later wrote, for one day, at least, it became patriotic to demonstrate.[1]

As Resistance activists moved on to other forms of protest, or drifted away from the movement, they took some satisfaction in the fact that, try as it might, the government had not been able to ignore them. Their impact on policy making in both the Johnson and the Nixon administrations is undeniable. In addition, their lives since the 1960s make clear that most former resisters and their supporters have defied the stereotype of the sixties activist who in the 1980s became a yuppy concerned only about the accumulation of personal wealth. Few of these former activists practice civil disobedience today, but their worldviews remain largely consistent with those of their youth.

NIXON TAKES NOTICE

In his memoirs, Richard Nixon wrote that he regarded draft resisters as cowards, but he also admitted that they influenced the way he approached the war.[2] When he reassigned the aging General Hershey and instituted a lottery system for the draft, he did so in part, as one historian has noted, to "lessen the steam behind student protest."[3]

Nixon assumed the presidency prepared to remove Hershey as quickly as possible. Just weeks after the election, Congressman Donald Rumsfeld had told Nixon aide Pete Flanigan that it would be "a terrible, terrible mistake if he were not replaced." Before the first month of his term had ended, Nixon approved Hershey's removal and assigned the job to Flanigan. Several weeks later, H. R. Haldeman, Nixon's chief of staff, followed up with Flanigan: "The President is anxious to move as quickly as possible on General Hershey because of the significance this will have with the youth community." By late summer, however, Flanigan had not figured out how to push Hershey out, and the general proved stubborn. Although the president did not want to simply fire the old man, and perhaps create the impression that he had given in to the protesters, White House memoranda makes it clear that, as one aide noted, Hershey had to go as part of a plan that will "maximize the President's interest and publicity, as well as serve the purpose of putting *some* water on war protest." Flanigan finally fashioned a deal in which Nixon awarded Hershey a fourth star and "reassigned" him as special adviser to the president on manpower. The White House announced Hershey's new duties on October 10 and scheduled his reassignment to take effect in February 1970.[4]

In April 1969, as Pete Flanigan tried to figure out how to get Hershey out of the way, he also urged the president to institute "some sort of cosmetic reform" of the existing induction system. Most significant, Flanigan called for a lottery system to be implemented as soon as possible, until an all-volunteer force could be created. Nixon clearly understood the political wisdom of this proposal and thus went before Congress on May 13, 1969, to, among other things, ask for the power to create the lottery system. Again, internal memoranda confirm that the administration connected draft reform to undercutting antiwar protest. As Congress moved slowly on the draft issue, Nixon's urban affairs adviser, Daniel Patrick Moynihan, predicted a new "season of student unrest, disorder, and turmoil" as the fall approached. To reduce the impetus for such protest, Moynihan suggested, Nixon should make his proposed reforms on the draft a national issue. An academic himself, Moynihan pointed out that in resisting or evading the draft, middle-class students were allowing the poor and minorities to take their places. The very people that the college protester most wants to "see served by society," Moynihan observed, were the ones who went to war. "The inevitable result," he wrote, "is a generation of college youth afflicted by intense and persistent emotional crises," which led them to protest the whole system. Therefore, he concluded, draft reform "would go a very long way to eliminating the intense anxiety which the present system imposes on college men," particularly if it got a good airing on the nation's cam-puses.[5] In the fall, Congress passed legislation enacting the draft lottery. With the outgoing Hershey looking on, the Selective Service held the first national lottery on December 1, 1969.

The new administration moved quickly to insure that it would not face the same kind of dissent expressed by the draft resistance movement. However, after a brief pause in demonstrations through the summer of 1969, it again faced dissent, but from a widening array of organizations—some of which included veterans of the draft resistance movement.

LIFE AFTER THE RESISTANCE

Draft resistance activists did not simply disappear or retreat to live in communes after 1968. Indeed, according to the 1997 Boston Draft Resistance Survey, as draft resistance tapered off, at least two-thirds of the Boston draft resistance community stayed active in antiwar work that continued to pressure the Nixon administration.[6] Some former draft resisters and their supporters joined other antiwar organizations, such as the Indo-china Peace Campaign, the Coalition for Peace and Justice, the Fifth Avenue Peace Parade Committee, the U.S. Servicemen's Fund, and many others. John Phillips and Suzy Williams, both of whom had been attacked on the South Boston Courthouse steps in 1966, joined what became known as the "Ultra-Resistance," raiding draft boards, often in broad daylight, and destroying thousands of 1-A files.[7] Others, less bold, worked for town referendums against the war. Eventually, the Massachusetts legislature passed a bill in April 1970 that would allow Massachusetts men to refuse combat if Congress did not first declare war as required by the Constitution. The new law empowered the state attorney general to bring any such cases directly to the U.S. Supreme Court for rulings. In turn, the bill's sponsors hoped to get the Court to rule on the constitutionality of the Vietnam War. But in November 1970, the Court refused to hear the first Massachusetts case based on this law. As Nancy Zaroulis and Gerald Sullivan have noted, "Thus failed one more attempt to end the war through the system."[8] And so, some people continued to work outside the system. One respondent to the 1997 survey wrote that even though he felt "completely exhausted, physically, emotionally and financially, after the movement," he continued to withhold payment of his income taxes until fall 1972.[9]

In addition to maintaining their commitment to antiwar activism, some members of the draft resistance community went on to other social and political activism. Almost all of the women who participated in the 1997 survey (21 of 25, or 84 percent) went on to join the women's movement. They formed the city's first consciousness-raising groups and eventually founded the influential Bread and Roses collective.[10] A handful of draft resistance activists followed Ira Arlook into the working-class communities of Lowell, Lynn, Lawrence, New Bedford, Fall River, and Boston's Mission Hill neighborhood to do community organizing.[11] A few joined the Progressive Labor Party, a Maoist offshoot of SDS largely credited with the demise of the BDRG and the Harvard SDS.[12] And not one respondent to the 1997 Boston Draft Resistance Survey aligned himself or herself with the Weathermen, the most extreme SDS splinter group. Critics of the 1960s generation generally inflate the importance of the Weathermen, an organization that, thanks to several successful bombings, attracted considerable media attention from 1969 to 1971. They likewise overstate the extent to which many radicals dropped out of society to live together in communes. Here again, the survey upsets these misconceptions. Of 185 respondents, only 20 (10.8 percent) stated that they moved into a commune after their draft resistance days. Few, it turned out, were prepared to drop out altogether.

For those who wanted to return to a more quiet life of work and family, it has not always been so easy. In Rockport, Massachusetts, friends and acquaintances turned their backs on both Chick Marston and Jannik von Rosenvinge, spitting on them and calling them names. "To this day, people still call me a communist," Marston reports. Von Rosenvinge grew so tired of the provincial abuse that he moved out of the area.[13]

Although some draft resistance activists have certainly mellowed in their political and ideological stands over the last thirty years, very few hung on to the American political pendulum as it has swept from Left to Right. Table A.24 shows that when the movement waned, there were no Republicans among the survey participants. Today, eight (4.8 percent) of them are Republicans. More significant is that the large number of men and women who identified themselves as anarchists, socialists, or communists has decreased, though nearly one-third continue to use these labels. Consequently, there has been an attendant increase in the proportion of "liberal Democrats" in the survey population.[14]

Over the years, an overwhelming majority of Boston's draft resistance community have chosen to participate at one time or another in other social causes and protest activism. Table A.25 shows the extensive variety of this work. Although no single issue has galvanized this group of people to protest as fervently as the Vietnam War once did, a significant number of them have taken part in the environmental movement, in the antinuclear movement, and in protests against American involvement in El Salvador and Nicaragua in the 1980s. Only 16 of 185 survey respondents (8.6 percent) have not participated in any type of social or political activism since the Vietnam War. Evidently a certain faith in the power of social movements and grassroots organizing persists among former draft resisters and their supporters.

That said, there are some indications that they are ambivalent about social movements, too. Though it is no doubt unfair to compare other forms of activism with antiwar activism (because the sense of crisis—and commitment—can be so intense during wartime), the survey results clearly demonstrate that the level of involvement has generally been lower than during the war (see Table A.25). The average number of individuals from this sample who characterize their activism as "somewhat involved," for example, is more than three times the number who described themselves as "very involved," and twice the number of those "moderately involved."[15] Of course, there are numerous reasons for these decreases. As one person wrote on his questionnaire, his paucity of involvement today derives "not from [lack of] conviction, but lack of time."[16] It is a common sentiment among former draft resistance activists.

Maybe more important is the slight undercurrent of cynicism regarding social movements among former members of the draft resistance community. One survey respondent wrote that while she believes activism *could* effect real change in America one day, she also thinks that the "collective will necessary to mobilize people now" is absent. "Apathy, self-centeredness, runs too deep," she said. Mike Jupin, the associate rector who caused such a stir at his Winchester church in 1967 says now that his experience opposing the war in Vietnam led him to develop "a certain amount of cynicism about political processes and the difficulty of bringing about change." For one, he says, arguments made on both sides of issues "are much less intellectual than they are emotional," which makes it difficult to move others. More important, he says now, however, is that he learned how "incredibly resistant to change" is any system. "It's just very difficult," he laments. "I'm not nearly the activist that I once was."

This skepticism notwithstanding, most former resisters and their supporters still possess a strong faith in the ability of ordinary people to effect change in American society. Table A.26 shows that an overwhelming majority of this group agrees that social movements can be potentially effective vehicles for social change in contemporary America. One former resister commented that, although the United States is currently experiencing a period of "moral and political crisis," and although "the potential for social movements now seems low," he firmly believes that "nothing else will bring us toward being a country of justice and peace."[17] This sentiment was echoed by another former resister, now a minister, who sees social movements as the most obvious manifestation of what he calls "the struggle." The objectives of the struggle—which engages "people of good will from all communities"—are "human liberation and . . . acting against that which oppresses people."[18] Naturally, some among the draft resistance community are not as sanguine. One former draft counselor wryly remarked, "Chomsky says movements *do* have an effect [in shaping society], but TV and the mall seem to have more effect."[19] Moreover, another former Resistance supporter argued, "the media does not like movements today." He believes that the social movements of the 1960s benefited from positive media coverage—an assumption that some of his former colleagues would challenge—that cannot be expected today. "Social change is boosted by the marriage of movement and media, and I just don't see that happening any time soon," he concluded.[20] Overall, however, a vast majority of respondents agree with the former resister who described social movements as "the only hope" for American society.[21]

Finally, the career choices of former draft resistance advocates in many ways seem to reflect their concerns with social issues or facilitate their examination and discussion of them (see Table A.27). Far and away the most popular current occupation of this group is in academia and teaching. More than 30 percent of respondents to the 1997 survey indicated that they currently teach at colleges and universities or in a local school system. Professions in which the welfare of others is a primary concern also dominate the list of occupations. For instance, in addition to the noticeable number of physicians, psychiatrists, and psychologists (9 percent) in the group, a number of respondents work and often run nonprofit or charitable organizations: Nan Stone is the director of a regional AIDS service organization; Ray Mungo is a social worker; Gary Hicks is a tenant organizer; and others list their occupations as patient advocate, child welfare worker, community arts program director, and cooperative housing organizer. Likewise, another 10 percent are involved in artistic endeavors, whether as actors (David Clennon, Dick Hughes, and Harold Hector), film makers (Connie Field and Tim Wright), or artists and writers. There is an apparent leaning away from mainstream work in the business world, and although there are a significant number of doctors and lawyers in this group, most of the professional categories lean toward the liberal arts. As many of those who attended the 1997 reunion remarked, their work has turned out to be a natural extension of the activism of their youth. They remain engaged with major issues of the day and are concerned about the young, the poor, and the alienated.

LOOKING BACK

The positive view of social movements that most former resisters and supporters maintain today no doubt stems in part from a sense that they waged a struggle that was at least partially successful thirty years ago. Not only do they disagree overwhelmingly with conservative critics who charge that the 1960s generation was primarily "destructive," or that the antiwar movement was ineffective and actually prolonged the war (thus causing more deaths), but the vast majority believe that the draft resistance movement ended the draft and helped to end the Vietnam War (see Table A.28).

The validity of these claims remains subject to debate. In his historical survey of American draft law violators from 1658 to 1985, Stephen Kohn describes the Vietnam War–era draft resistance movement as the one that "finally succeeded." He credits draft resisters with causing the "collapse" of the nation's draft system. Likewise, Lawrence Baskir and William Strauss conclude in their landmark study of the Vietnam War generation that if the Resistance did not bring the war to an end or bog down the court system with draft cases, it at least jammed prosecutors' offices.[22] The analysis of Boston's draft resistance movement presented in this book, as indicated especially in Chapter 9, did not reach the same conclusion: in this one city, at least, proportionately few draft resisters faced the threat of prosecution. Nevertheless, George Q. Flynn, the leading historian on the modern draft and Lewis Hershey's biographer—and certainly not an antiwar movement partisan—confirms that the Nixon administration decided to reform and ultimately end the draft in reaction to the draft resistance movement and its success in publicizing the conscription system's inequities.[23] At a time when most Americans believed the draft should continue after the war ended (and fewer than one-third favored an all-volunteer force),[24] Nixon moved to institute the lottery and later terminated the draft altogether. For a variety of reasons, that decision to move to an all-volunteer armed force remains a dubious legacy of the Nixon presidency.

There can be little doubt that the potential for more draft resistance caused great concern in the Nixon administration and contributed to calls to abolish the draft altogether. The organized draft resistance movement may have long since peaked, but individual resistance continued and even expanded in 1969 and 1970. "There are signs that active draft resistance is building," White House advisers on the draft and the all-volunteer force wrote to the president. "A substantial number of young men are not report-ing for physical examinations or showing up for induction. If resistance continues to grow, increased prosecution efforts by the Justice Department may be necessary to avert the breakdown of the draft system." Two months later, following the Cambodia invasion, Martin Anderson, head of the task force on the all-volunteer force, confirmed that passive resistance to the draft was building "at an alarming rate" nationwide and that word was spreading that "the government is almost powerless to apprehend and prosecute them."[25]

The elimination of the draft has been criticized by those who regard mil-itary service as one of the few duties of citizenship in America that fosters a sense of civic responsibility in those who participate. Historian John Cham-bers, for instance, argues that Nixon unintentionally "further reduced the symbolic importance of American citizenship." Elimination of the draft, he notes, "diluted a preeminent feature of political membership—the sense of shared sacrifice and patriotic commitment to a common goal." When asked if they agreed or disagreed that compulsory military service would help to bring a greater sense of civic responsibility in contemporary America, the vast majority of the draft resistance survey participants agreed,[26] but the question produced a bounty of qualifying statements. Most of those who commented acknowledge that there has been an attenuation in attitudes of social responsibility over the last generation and would favor a system of compulsory service for young Americans that, like the plan proposed by Robert McNamara in 1967, included nonmilitary options. In addition, several resisters commented that the all-volunteer force that evolved out of the end of the draft is no more equitable than the deferment-riddled system of conscription they fought to abolish. Fewer wealthy and better-educated men and women enter the military than poorer and less educated men and women, who are drawn to serve by promises of educational and employment opportunities otherwise unavailable to them. (Consequently, the former do not bear the same burdens for their country as the latter.) Thus, whether the draft resistance movement caused the collapse of the draft or not, the draft's elimination has had consequences that some former resisters find troubling.[27]

The assertion that draft resistance helped shorten the war is another matter of some contention. Claims that a draft resistance movement that essentially folded in 1969 helped to stop a war that continued until January 1973 are suspect. As Thomas Powers wrote in the years immediately following the war, opponents of the war had to come to grips with the reality that the American government abandoned its policy in Vietnam not because the antiwar movement had persuaded most Americans to oppose the war—or because the war was simply wrong—but because the Vietnamese would not yield after more than a decade of fighting. Indeed, this issue is at the heart of Adam Garfinkle's argument that the antiwar movement failed totally in its efforts to move public opinion against the war and that it succeeded only in prolonging the war. But Garfinkle does not address draft resistance specifically or issues of manpower allocation at all in his analysis, and, more important, he does not consider the issue of conscience in civil society.[28]

When draft resisters and their supporters took their level of protest to new heights in 1967 and 1968, the Johnson administration was forced to finally take notice. Johnson soon launched a public relations campaign, employing General Westmoreland to reassure the nation that the war would soon end in victory; when the enemy stunned the American public with the Tet Offensive, the administration's credibility withered. At the same time, as the Selective Service made matters worse by punitively reclassifying resisters, and as the Justice Department prepared to prosecute these men, key officials in the Pentagon and the State Department warned of a surge in draft resistance if the president granted Westmoreland's request for 206,000 additional troops. That is the most obvious evidence that the draft resistance movement helped to rein in the war effort.

And here Garfinkle may yet be right: by fueling the Johnson administration's "credibility gap," by preventing the fulfillment of that troop request and, more significant, by causing foreign policy officials to worry about the antiwar movement, perhaps the antiwar movement quite indirectly contributed to a longer war. We can never know, of course; there is no historical evidence to suggest that the United States would have defeated the North Vietnamese if only there had been more united domestic support. At the end of the day, then, whether or not the antiwar movement prolonged the war is not a particularly meaningful issue. A more important question is a moral one: to what extent is a citizen responsible to his country when the government is engaged in a violent war that he deems "illegal," "immoral," or "obscene"? Should he remain passive, as Garfinkle's argument seems to suggest, in hopes that the war will end sooner than if he took to the streets in protest? As one resister asked rhetorically, "What would have happened without the movement? Would we have nuked Vietnam? Destroyed half the world in our anticommunist obsession? Despite rampant revisionism, history has born[e] us out. Communism self-destructed without us having to bomb Russia, China, etc. Governments evolve without war." It is significant that he emphasizes the draft resistance movement's role in deterring an even wider war in Vietnam or elsewhere. Even among those who believe their efforts in the Resistance did not help end the war, most agree that, as another resister wrote in his survey, the Resistance "served only as a counterbalance to keep the war from being wider . . . from being more vigorously fought."[29]

Noam Chomsky argues that one of the greatest legacies of the Vietnam-era antiwar movement is that it set an example for others to follow. When Ronald Reagan began to build a "counterinsurgency" program in El Salvador, just as John F. Kennedy had done in South Vietnam, his administration eventually had to back off, Chomsky says, because "there was just an uprising all over the country—nobody was going to tolerate it." Soon, the Reagan administration moved to a program of "clandestine terror," a tactic that Kennedy and Johnson, operating at a time when most Americans did not generally question their government's foreign policy, never had to consider. That, Chomsky concludes, is a major change.[30]

Many former resisters and supporters, reflecting on the significance of the draft resistance movement, speak about its personal impact rather than its political one. Chris Venn, who ultimately went to prison following an accumulation of run-ins with the law over draft resistance and fighting police in Berkeley's battle for People's Park, says that turning in his draft card has "defined who I am ever since." Although his mother criticized him for his draft resistance, saying he would never get the GI Bill or the kinds of home loans afforded veterans, Venn always regarded the "standing up for principles, [and] understanding the consequences of it" as the most valuable lessons of draft resistance. Ray Mungo likewise wrote in 1970 that regardless of what happened with his battles with the draft he hoped "never to regret having handled it as I did—uncompromisingly but kind of cavalierly." "It's something I'm doing," he concluded, "maybe the only thing, for my self-respect." Others, like David Stoppelman, who also did prison time, now regrets the effect his draft resistance had on his family and is not so sure that resisting the draft was the right thing to do. Finally, a significant number remain angry that the government ever put them in such a predicament. Jannik von Rosenvinge, who watched a draftee plunge to his death through the third-floor window of the Boston Army Base in 1966, notes that "it's only been many, many years later that I've found that I can look back and think what a horrible thing that was to do to kids. . . . We all fought that war," he said recently. "We're all veterans of that war."[31]

In spite of such lingering bitterness, most activists regard their draft resistance work as invaluable in that it taught them how make difficult choices based on principle and that acting on them did not signal "the end of the world." They could survive. "Although I'm older now and . . . we pay our taxes and we have this average sort of urban lifestyle," Jim Oestereich says now, "I know that tomorrow, if I had to hit a barricade, I know how to do it. And I'd know how to make the decision, and I'd know how to live with it. Those are things I didn't know before [resisting the draft]." Jack Bishop, the rector at Winchester's Parish of the Epiphany during the Mike Jupin controversy, regards that crisis as "the turning point" in his life. "It's awfully hard to move forward without constant reference to 1967 and what it meant to me as a priest," he said. "It certainly pointed out that if one is going to take a personal stand, that that's going to require an awful lot of energy: spiritual, mental, emotional, and physical—the whole works." Perhaps the survey comments of one other resister come closest to conveying how most activists feel today about their draft resistance experience: "Would I do it again? Depends on the circumstances. I did not like being illegal, but I still thought the war and the draft were wrong, wrong enough to demand civil disobedience. I like to think that I would still be willing to break a bad law. But I don't know . . . you get awfully comfortable. Like E. M. Forster, I hope I would have the guts to betray my country."[32]

Finally, a common sentiment among members of the Boston draft resistance community is that the movement introduced them to some of the finest people they have ever met and taught them something about the essential qualities of a good human being and a decent society. Their reflections on their participation in the movement to end the war in Vietnam echo Emma Goldman's assertion that the struggle for freedom, not freedom itself, is what forges the finest qualities of human character. As Penney Kurland-Lagos, a former NER member, put it, "The emphasis on values, feelings, human rights, justice, the collective spirit have formed how I view the world, how I raise my children, and hopefully, how I treat others in both my personal and professional life." Bill Bischoff, a former Harvard graduate student, veteran, and resister remembers it the same way: "It was gratifying to be associated with as many people of high moral caliber and intellectual caliber as I was involved with. I really, in later years, I've missed that."[33]

The draft resistance movement's confrontation with the government extends a legacy of conscience and civic engagement that dates to the earliest days of the republic and continues to this day. As has happened to dissenters so often in American history, draft resisters and their supporters faced ridicule, condemnation, and physical violence in their quest for world peace and sane policy; in spite of such obstacles, they built not only a movement but a community of people who stood for an alternative definition of patriotism. They were frequently frightened, and they did not always succeed where they wanted to, but their experiences nevertheless serve as examples for those who may decide to confront the war machines of the future.

APPENDIX A TABLES

TABLE A.1. Selective Service Classifications of Resisters in New England, Fall 1967

Classification	No.	%
1-A (Available for service)	35	17.5
1-D (Reserve or ROTC)	1	.5
1-O (Conscientious objector)	4	2.0
1-S (Student)	1	.5
1-W (Conscientious objector)	1	.5
1-Y (Physical or mental)	23	11.5
2-A (Occupational)	2	1.0
2-S (Student)	85	42.5
3-A (Hardship or dependent)	6	3.0
4-A (Prior active service)	13	6.5
4-D (Minister or divinity student)	13	6.5
4-F (Not qualified for military service)	11	5.5
5-A (Over-age)	3	1.5
Refused to register	2	1.0
Total	200	100

Source: New England Resistance Master File, Alex Jack Papers

TABLE A.2. Resisters' Parents' Level of Education

Highest Level of Education Achieved	Fathers		Mothers	
	No.	%	No.	%
Some grade school	6	5.1	3	2.6
Completed grade school	4	3.4	3	2.6
Some high school	6	5.1	9	7.7
Completed high school	18	15.4	26	22.2
Some post–high school training	10	8.5	9	7.7
Some college	16	13.7	19	16.2
Completed college	13	11.1	27	23.0
Some graduate school	7	6.0	4	3.4
M.A. or M.S.	7	6.0	11	9.4
Professional degree	16	13.7	5	4.3
Master's plus additional grad work	3	2.6	0	0.0
Doctorate	11	9.4	1	0.9
Total	117	100	117	100

Source: 1997 Boston Draft Resistance Survey

TABLE A.3. Resisters' Parents' Occupations

Occupation	Fathers		Mothers	
	No.	%	No.	%
Semiskilled or unskilled	5	4.3	2	1.7
Skilled	13	11.3	1	0.9
Farmer	2	1.7	0	0.0
Clerical or sales	15	13.0	20	17.2
Proprietor	13	11.3	2	1.7
Professional	67	58.3	31	26.7
Homemaker	0	0.0	60	51.7
Total	115	99.9[a]	116	99.9[a]

Source: 1997 Boston Draft Resistance Survey
[a]Percentages do not total 100 due to rounding.

TABLE A.4. Resisters' Class Status

Class Description	No.	%
Working class	12	10.0
Lower middle class	13	10.8
Middle class	53	44.2
Upper middle class	40	33.3
Upper class	2	1.7
Total	120	100

Source: 1997 Boston Draft Resistance Survey

TABLE A.5. Religious Affiliations of Resisters and Their Parents

Denomination	Fathers		Mothers		Resisters	
	No.	%	No.	%	No.	%
Agnostic	8	7.1	5	4.3	30	25.4
Atheist	10	8.8	6	5.2	20	16.9
Baptist	0	0.0	1	0.9	0	0.0
Congregational	6	5.3	5	4.3	3	2.5
Episcopal	16	14.2	17	14.7	7	5.9
Jehovah's Witness	0	0.0	0	0.0	0	0.0
Jewish	27	23.9	29	25.0	18	15.3
Lutheran	1	0.9	1	0.9	1	0.8
Mennonite	0	0.0	0	0.0	0	0.0
Methodist	8	7.1	10	8.6	4	3.4
Presbyterian	11	9.7	10	8.6	3	2.5
Quaker	0	0.0	0	0.0	4	3.4
Unitarian-Universalist	10	8.8	12	10.3	15	12.7
Roman Catholic	11	9.7	14	12.1	5	4.2
Other	5	4.4	6	5.2	8	6.8
Total	113	99.9[a]	116	100.1[a]	118	99.8[a]

Source: 1997 Boston Draft Resistance Survey
[a]Percentages do not total 100 due to rounding.

TABLE A.6. Veteran Status of Resisters and Their Parents

	Fathers		Mothers		Resisters	
Veteran Status	No.	%	No.	%	No.	%
Veteran	48	39.7	3	2.5	8	6.6
Nonveteran	73	60.3	118	97.5	113	93.4
Total	121	100	121	100	121	100

Source: 1997 Boston Draft Resistance Survey

TABLE A.7. Political Leanings of Resisters and Their Parents

	Fathers		Mothers		Resisters	
Political Identity	No.	%	No.	%	No.	%
Conservative Republican	15	13.0	6	5.2	1	0.9
Moderate Republican	27	23.5	28	24.1	1	0.9
Moderate Democrat	21	18.3	28	24.1	6	5.1
Liberal Democrat	41	35.7	46	39.7	48	41.0
Socialist/Communist	4	3.5	4	3.4	29	24.8
Anarchist	1	0.9	1	0.9	17	14.5
No preference	3	2.6	3	2.6	7	6.0
Other	3	2.6	0	0.0	8	6.8
Total	115	100.1[a]	116	100	117	100

Source: 1997 Boston Draft Resistance Survey
[a]Percentage does not total 100 due to rounding.

TABLE A.8. Parents with Shared Political Leanings

Political Identity	Number of Couples	Percentage of Couples
Both Republican	29	32.2
Both Democrat	56	62.2
Both Socialist/Communist	4	4.4
Both anarchist	1	1.1
Total	90	99.9[a]

Source: 1997 Boston Draft Resistance Survey
[a]Percentage does not total 100 due to rounding.

TABLE A.9. Parents' Views of Their Sons' Draft Card Turn-Ins

Parent	N/A	Strongly Disapprove	Disapprove	Noncommittal	Approve	Strongly Approve	Total
Father	35	24	23	16	13	10	121
Mother	22	19	27	21	21	11	121
Total	57	43	50	37	34	21	242

Source: 1997 Boston Draft Resistance Survey
Note: Although 121 draft resisters responded to the questionnaire, only 86 answered questions regarding their fathers; only 99 answered questions about their mothers. Therefore, the percentages that appear in the text are based on $N=86$ and $N=99$.

TABLE A.10. Parish of the Epiphany (Winchester, Massachusetts) Reaction to Rev. Michael Jupin's Draft Card Turn-in

Reaction	No. of Parishioners	% of Parishioners
Approval	73	55.7
Disapproval in favor of disciplinary action	25	19.1
Disapproval but not in favor of punishing Jupin	22	16.8
Other	11	8.4
Total	131	100

Source: Written responses, Parish of the Epiphany, October 29, 1967, The Reverend Jack Bishop Papers

TABLE A.11. Supporters' Occupations

Occupation	No.	%
Students	33	48.5
Academics	10	14.7
Other	25	36.8
Total	68	100

Source: 1997 Boston Draft Resistance Survey

TABLE A.12. Supporters' Parents' Occupations

Occupation	Fathers		Mothers	
	No.	%	No.	%
Semiskilled or unskilled	1	1.7	2	3.1
Skilled	4	6.8	0	0.0
Farmer	1	1.7	0	0.0
Clerical or sales	5	8.5	9	14.1
Proprietor	15	25.4	4	6.3
Professional	33	55.9	23	35.9
Homemaker	0	0.0	26	40.6
Total	59	100	64	100

Source: 1997 Boston Draft Resistance Survey

TABLE A.13. Supporters' Class Status

Class Description	No.	%
Working class	6	9.1
Lower middle class	4	6.1
Middle class	31	46.9
Upper middle class	24	36.4
Upper class	1	1.5
Total	66	100

Source: 1997 Boston Draft Resistance Survey

TABLE A.14. Religious Affiliations of Supporters and Their Parents

Denomination	Fathers No.	%	Mothers No.	%	Supporters No.	%
Agnostic	6	10	5	7.8	16	24.6
Atheist	5	8.3	3	4.7	22	33.8
Baptist	1	1.7	2	3.1	0	0.0
Christian Scientist	1	1.7	0	0.0	0	0.0
Congregational	2	3.3	2	3.1	0	0.0
Episcopalian	4	6.7	5	7.8	1	1.5
Jewish	18	30	19	29.7	10	15.4
Lutheran	0	0.0	1	1.6	0	0.0
Methodist	1	1.7	4	6.3	0	0.0
Mormon	1	1.7	1	1.6	1	1.5
Presbyterian	6	10	5	7.8	1	1.5
Quaker	0	0.0	1	1.6	1	1.5
Roman Catholic	8	13.3	7	10.9	4	6.2
Unitarian	5	8.3	6	9.4	7	10.8
Other	2	3.3	3	4.7	2	3.1
Total	60	100	64	100.1[a]	65	99.9[a]

Source: 1997 Boston Draft Resistance Survey
Note: Of the 60 fathers, 49, or 81.7%, identified themselves with a religious denomination. Similarly, 56 of 64 mothers (87.5%) identified themselves with a religious denomination. In contrast, of 65 supporters, 27, or 41.5%, identified themselves with a religious denomination.
[a]Percentages do not total 100 due to rounding.

TABLE A.15. Veteran Status of Supporters and Their Parents

Veterans	No.	%
Supporters	11	25.0[a]
Fathers	29	42.6[b]
Mothers	1	1.5
Both mother and father	1	—

Source: 1997 Boston Draft Resistance Survey
[a]Out of 44 male supporters, 11 were veterans.
[b]Out of 68 fathers, 29 were veterans.

TABLE A.16. Supporters' Self-Identifications

Label	No.	%
Hippie	5	7.4
Politico	23	33.8
Activist	51	75
Revolutionary	23	33.8
Member of counterculture	27	39.7
Part of New Left	47	69.1

Source: 1997 Boston Draft Resistance Survey

TABLE A.17. Political Affiliations of Supporters' Parents

Political Affiliation	No.	%
Mother and father both Republican	18	35.3
Mother and father both Democrat	29	56.9
Mother and father both Communist/Socialist/anarchist	4	7.8
Total	51[a]	100

Source: 1997 Boston Draft Resistance Survey
[a]Of 68 supporters, the parents of 51 (75%) both belonged to the same political affiliation.

TABLE A.18. Supporters' Political Affiliations

Political Affiliation	No.	%
Conservative Republican	—	—
Moderate Republican	—	—
Moderate Democrat	1	1.8
Liberal Democrat	28	49.1
Communist/Socialist	22	38.6
Anarchist	6	10.5
Total	57	100

Source: 1997 Boston Draft Resistance Survey

TABLE A.19. Supporters' Prior Activism

Type of Activism	No.	%
Students for a Democratic Society	23	33.8
Campus or community peace activism	38	55.9
Campus or community Vietnam Summer	14	20.6
Campus or community civil rights activism	42	61.8
No activist experience	7	10.3

Source: 1997 Boston Draft Resistance Survey
Note: Percentage is based on population of 68 respondents.

TABLE A.20. Outcomes of Resisters' Draft Card Turn-Ins

Outcome	No.	%
Reclassified to 1-A, but no induction notice	21	20.6
Reclassified to 1-A *and* sent induction notice	56	54.9
Resister retrieved original draft card before sent to Department of Justice	2	2.0
Resister asked draft board for new draft card	3	2.9
Draft board sends duplicate card unsolicited	4	3.9
Resister applied for and received new deferment	6	5.9
Resister left the country	1	1.0
Resister heard nothing from SSS or Department of Justice	9	8.8
Total	102	100

Source: 1997 Boston Draft Resistance Survey

TABLE A.21. Action Taken by Resisters Reclassified to 1-A but Who Did Not Receive Induction Notices

Action	No.	%
Applied for and/or accepted a new deferment	11	52.4
Joined Oestereich lawsuit	2	9.5
Left the country	1	4.8
Heard nothing further from SSS or Department of Justice	7	33.3
Total	21	100

Source: 1997 Boston Draft Resistance Survey

TABLE A.22. Action Taken by Resisters Reclassified to 1-A and Who Did Receive Induction Notices

Action	No.	%
Refused induction	30	56.6
Failed physical or other induction test	14	26.4
Applied for new deferment after reclassification	9	17.0
Total	53	100

Source: 1997 Boston Draft Resistance Survey

TABLE A.23. Draft Resistance Indictments and Prosecutions in Boston, 1966–1968

	1966	1967	1968
Indictments	26	25	50
Fugitives	3	4	17
Convictions or guilty pleas	16	12	8
Acquittals and dismissals	2	3	18
Dismissals for compliance	5	6	2
Pending	—	—	5

Source: SUPPORT Newsletter, January 1970, 4, Michael Zigmond Papers

TABLE A.24. Political Affiliations of Draft Resistance Community Then and Now

Political Affiliation	Immediately after Draft Resistance		Today	
	No.	%	No.	%
Conservative Republican	0	0	2	1.2
Moderate Republican	0	0	6	3.6
Moderate Democrat	5	3.0	9	5.4
Liberal Democrat	46	27.5	72	43.1
Socialist/Communist	71	42.5	39	23.4
Anarchist	32	19.2	14	8.4
No preference	10	6.0	13	7.8
Other	3	1.8	12[a]	7.2
Total	167	100	167	100.1[b]

Source: 1997 Boston Draft Resistance Survey.
[a]The labels survey respondents used to identify their politics today include: "Progressive populist," "social democrat" (2), "pro-people/community," "revolutionary," "autonomist," "Green" (2), and "maverick humanist."
[b]Percentage does not total 100 due to rounding.

TABLE A.25. Resisters' and Supporters' Level of Activism in Other Causes and Movements after Draft Resistance

Cause, Movement, or Organization	Very Involved	Moderately Involved	Somewhat Involved	Not Involved
Other Vietnam antiwar activities	67	42	33	42
Student movement	22	23	24	118
Women's movement	17	25	43	103
Gay and lesbian rights movement	8	16	23	138
Farm workers movement	2	11	49	123
Labor organizing	14	10	26	135
Pro-choice movement	9	16	41	119
Pro-life movement	1	5	6	173
Environmental movement	14	34	45	92
Common Cause	0	6	20	159
Antinuclear movement	16	15	53	101
Nuclear freeze	7	7	36	135
Contemporary draft resistance	0	3	17	165
Contemporary peace movement	9	17	44	115
1980s Central American antiwar movement	23	22	40	100
Anti-Apartheid movement	11	19	47	108
Moral Majority	0	1	0	184
Christian Coalition	0	0	0	185
Socialist movement	9	14	23	139
Democratic Party	9	24	42	110
Republican Party	0	1	1	183
Libertarian Party	0	1	2	182
Local electoral campaigns	12	27	46	100
State electoral campaigns	8	19	37	121
National electoral campaigns	12	18	36	109

Source: 1997 Boston Draft Resistance Survey
Note: In addition to the causes listed in this table, respondents listed a total of 24 other causes, with the following receiving multiple mentions: race relations (4); Native American rights (2); antipoverty/welfare rights (6); children's rights (2); community organizing (4); health care (2); Palestine liberation (2); prison rights (3); and Green Party (2).

TABLE A.26. Resisters' and Supporters' Current Views on the Effectiveness of Social Movements

Subject	Strongly Agree	Agree	Disagree	Strongly Disagree
Social movements were very effective vehicles for social change in 1960s	90	81	11	0
Social movements are potentially effective vehicles for social change in contemporary America	80	98	3	1
Social movements based on moral witness are potentially effective	64	92	17	3
Social movements based on nonviolence are potentially effective	72	98	6	2

Source: 1997 Boston Draft Resistance Survey

TABLE A.27. Resisters' and Supporters' Current Occupations

Occupation	No.	%
Professor or other academic job	47	25.8
Teacher or librarian	12	6.7
Physician/psychiatrist/psychologist	16	8.8
Nonprofit/charity/activist	13	7.1
Artist/actor/author/filmmaker	19	10.4
Attorney or judge (1)	10	5.5
Ministers or priests	9	4.9
High tech	8	4.4
Skilled labor	5	2.7
Clerical or sales	5	2.7
Self-employed	6	3.3
Farmer	1	0.6
State/local government	3	1.7
Professional—other	17	9.3
Retired	5	2.7
Unemployed	6	3.3
Total	182	99.9[a]

Source: 1997 Boston Draft Resistance Survey
[a]Percentage does not total 100 due to rounding.

TABLE A.28. Resisters' and Supporters' Current Views on the 1960s and the Success and Failure of the Draft Resistance Movement

Subject	Strongly Agree	Agree	Disagree	Strongly Disagree
1960s generation was a destructive generation	5	1	53	120
Antiwar movement was ineffective and actually prolonged the war	1	3	53	124
Draft resistance movement brought about the end of the draft	30	79	55	4
Draft resistance movement helped to end the Vietnam War	80	93	4	3

Source: 1997 Boston Draft Resistance Survey

APPENDIX B STATEMENT ON METHODOLOGY

This book's primary goal is to recover the history of a social movement that to date has been largely overlooked by historians. More narrowly, it seeks to capture the experiences of draft resisters and their supporters in a way that preserves individual stories while also making generalizations possible. Consequently, two of the most important sources used in this study were a questionnaire and dozens of oral history interviews.

QUESTIONNAIRE

The sheer number of participants in Boston's draft resistance movement made a questionnaire necessary. Hundreds of people made up this grassroots movement, and in an attempt to understand their collective experience—as opposed to focusing on experiences of a small number of "representative" participants—a blending of sociology and history became necessary.

The first step in this process required the gathering of as many names of draft resisters and other resistance movement participants as possible. After combing through the newsletters and internal memoranda of several key organizations (for example, the New England Resistance, the Boston Draft Resistance Group, Resist, SUPPORT, etc.), a "Master File" of draft resisters dating to circa January 1968, underground newspapers, mainstream newspapers, and other sources, I compiled a list of close to 600 names.

Locating all of these people thirty years after the fact proved to be one of the biggest challenges of the project. I put together a database that listed all of the names that I had found and any other information that I knew about each person, such as what organization(s) he or she worked with, university(ies) attended, hometown, etc. Beginning with Michael Ferber and many of the other former leaders of the New England Resistance, I circulated copies of the database to dozens of movement participants looking for leads. At the same time, an article by James Carroll in the *Boston Globe* elicited calls from many other activists who also helped to provide leads—and added more names to the list. Meanwhile, using an internet site called Switchboard.com, which carries the nation's telephone listings, I began to systematically move through the list of names, using all the information at my disposal, to get solid addresses for as many people in the database as possible. This method proved to be tremendously successful, especially in cases in which the activist I was seeking had an unusual name; it was much more difficult to find someone with a common name using this resource. Frequently, I mailed a letter to five or six people with the same name, hoping I would catch the right one. Sometimes it worked, and other times it did not (see the introduction). Finally, after almost a year of this kind of detective work, I turned to the alumni offices at approximately forty colleges and universities, who confirmed that they had addresses for some of the people whom I still had not found.

In the end, I decided to administer the questionnaire when I had a list of 310 people for whom I or their alumni offices had a solid address. Of the 310 who received the questionnaire, 185 (59.7 percent) completed and returned it. This is an excellent response rate, though caution is warranted in making generalizations about an actual population of what may have exceeded 1,000 people. One obvious consideration was to expand the number of respondents to the survey. For several reasons, however, this was neither necessary nor practical. First, it is unlikely that another year of detective work would have uncovered solid addresses for, say, another 200 people. As noted above, finding individuals who participated in a relatively short-lived social movement thirty years after the fact is very difficult. As a result, a truly random sample is impossible. Second, even if it had been possible to send the questionnaire to an additional 200 and get responses from 100 of them, most of the results from the 1997 survey are so striking that it is not likely that the statistics gleaned from this second group would materially alter the broad conclusions I had already made. For example, 62 percent of resisters' parents (Table A.8) were Democrats; 84 percent of resisters' fathers identified with a religious denomination (Table A.5) and, consistent with that figure, 82 percent of supporters' fathers identified with a religious denomination (Table A.14); and in the wake of returning their draft cards to the Justice Department, more than 75 percent of draft resisters reported having their draft status punitively reclassified. It is unlikely that another 100 completed questionnaires would yield results sufficiently at odds with original responses like these that it would warrant a modification of my conclusions. Finally, and perhaps most important, although the survey is important, it is just one of many pieces of evidence that has been used to write this book. On the whole, the anecdotal evidence mined from speeches, newsletters, underground newspapers, etc., supports the conclusions made from the survey results.

It is worth noting that the questionnaire aimed to capture the experience not just of draft resisters but also of those who worked in the movement in various capacities to support their efforts. Consequently, certain portions of the questionnaire (see Appendix C) were tailored for certain types of individuals. Rare was the person who was able to answer every question on the survey. Everyone was asked to complete the sections pertaining to their backgrounds and personal histories, as well as questions about what they have done since the end of the draft resistance movement.

The diverse nature of the population made it necessary to tabulate the data gleaned from the questionnaire in several different ways. As the tables in Appendix A show, data tabulated for Chapters 4 and 9 dealt only with resisters and data tabulated for Chapter 6 pertained only to supporters. For the epilogue, I tabulated data for the entire population. It is important to note that of the 185 respondents, 121 were draft resisters. That is, these respondents had either turned in a draft card, burned a draft card, or refused induction. The remaining 64 respondents, therefore, participated in the draft resistance movement in a variety of what can be called, for lack of a better term, support roles. They include members of the BDRG, other draft counselors, ministers, sanctuary participants, older advisers (such as those in Resist), etc. At the same time, however, I made the decision to include four of the 121 resisters in the supporter population as well. Three of the four individuals were older men (in their early to mid-thirties) who primarily acted in roles that I defined as support roles, but who turned in their draft cards as well. The fourth person is a woman who was extremely active in the movement, who also burned a colleague's draft card at the Arlington Street Church. In these few unusual cases, it seemed appropriate to include their data in analyses of both resisters and supporters.

See Appendix C for a copy of the questionnaire and a sample cover letter.

ORAL HISTORIES

To supplement the data mined from the questionnaire responses and numerous manuscript sources, interviews with a wide range of participants was also necessary. Most of those interviewed completed the questionnaire (usually before the interview, though a few interviews were conducted as exploratory discussions for the purpose of conceptualizing the questionnaire), but some did not—either because they chose not to or because they were located long after the questionnaire was administered.

All of the interviews have been recorded on audio tape and will be deposited at the Swarthmore College Peace Collection in Swarthmore, Pennsylvania, where they will eventually be available to other researchers. At the start of each interview, each interviewee was asked to complete an informed consent form and a deed of gift form agreeing to the eventual transfer of the tape to Swarthmore.

In conducting these interviews, I sought to touch on many of the issues raised in the questionnaire, but I also tried, to the extent possible, to elicit spontaneous storytelling from each interviewee. As any oral historian can testify, some interviews go brilliantly and others do not. Memories can be crystal clear and they can be very hazy. And recollections that seem crystal clear can be quite inaccurate. In all cases, I have tried to corroborate stories told in interviews with other sources, printed or oral. At times, however, I have used material gleaned from only one interview, but I have done so only in rare cases in which the account seemed reliable. To my regret, there are at least a few remarkable stories that I have elected to leave out of the present narrative for lack of corroboration.

In the end, I have sought to fuse the historian's traditional archival research with the sociologist's approach to examining large demographic groups. And although I am satisfied that this was the most useful and fruitful course to take, I must acknowledge its inherent limitations. In questionnaires, for instance, there are always questions that should have been asked but were not, and the issue of those who did not return the questionnaire always lingers. One hopes that even if every person to whom the questionnaire was sent had completed and returned it, the results would not be substantially different than those presented here, but it is worth pondering. For example, when I assert in the epilogue that most former draft resistance activists have continued to be active and have not "sold out," it is possible that some persons did not return the survey exactly because they did "sell out." It is impossible to know. The best one can do is to try to avoid overstating conclusions based on such data and to seek supporting evidence elsewhere. The variety of sources used in this book has made that possible.

APPENDIX C LETTER TO SURVEY RECIPIENTS AND QUESTIONNAIRE

UNIVERSITY OF NEW HAMPSHIRE

Department of History
College of Liberal Arts
Horton Social Science Center
20 College Road
Durham, New Hampshire 03824-3586
(603) 862-1764   FAX: (603) 862-0178

10 June 1997

Mr. John Doe
P.O. Box XXXX
Boston, MA 02134

Dear Mr. Doe,

My name is Michael Foley. I am a Ph.D. candidate here at the University of New Hampshire and am currently writing a dissertation on the history of draft resistance in Boston during the Vietnam War. I found your name among the records of the New England Resistance which indicate that you turned in your draft card at the Old West Church on November 16, 1967. I am contacting you through your alumni office in hopes that you will be willing to take part in my study.

It is my belief that the draft resistance movement has not received sufficient attention in our histories of the antiwar movement. Yet it was a vital part of the larger movement. My goal is to use Boston as a case study for the draft resistance movement and to focus on the participants more than on a traditional description of events. To that end, I have been working with records from different organizations associated with draft resistance in Boston; but to get a better understanding, I will be interviewing some participants and sending questionnaires to as many participants as I can locate.

As you will see from the questions on the survey, I am interested in understanding all varieties of experience. It is important that historians explore how different people from different backgrounds came to the same movement, how they experienced that movement, and how it ultimately affected their lives. I realize that, for some people, participation in the draft resistance movement was a deeply personal, sometimes painful, experience. If this was the case for you, I hope that you will still consider at least completing this questionnaire. One of the problems with many studies of social movements is that they rely too heavily on the experience of leaders and others who have predominantly positive feelings for the movement. I want to understand the whole draft resistance story (the good and the bad), so I hope to have a high response rate to this survey.

Finally, let me add that your responses to questions on this survey will remain absolutely confidential. I will not, under any circumstances, use any survey respondent's name in my oral or written interpretations of the survey results. Furthermore, I will not respond to any requests from the media or the government for information that I collect.

I hope that you will enjoy participating in this study, and would appreciate it if you would return the completed questionnaire within five days, if that is possible (otherwise, please return it as soon as you can). I have included a postage paid envelope for that purpose.

The success or failure of this project is heavily dependent upon the cooperation of people like you. It is my sincere hope that you will take a few minutes (generally no more than 30 minutes) to participate in a study that I hope will help recover an important part of our history, one that can teach us lessons important to our future. Please call me with any questions or comments you have regarding this questionnaire or the dissertation research as a whole. My number is 603.437.0513. Thanks very much.

Sincerely,

Michael S. Foley

Note: This questionnaire and dissertation have been approved by the University of New Hampshire Institutional Review Board for the Protection of Human Subjects in Research.

ADDITIONAL ENDORSEMENTS:

Michael Ferber, Professor of English, University of New Hampshire

I have been working closely with Michael Foley for over a year, and I am confident he will do a serious, thoughtful, responsible job of his research into draft resistance. He is entirely sympathetic with what we tried to do in 1967-70--I think he would have been one of us--but he has the scholarly detachment to pose certain questions of our movement and to place it in certain contexts that I, at least, would not have been able to do. You'll like him if you meet him. He'll write a good book. Please give him what help you can.

Michael Ferber

June 1997

Howard Zinn, Professor Emeritus, Boston University

May 10, 1997

Michael S. Foley
113 Bayberry Lane
Londonderry, NH 0305

Dear Mr. Foley:

I am happy to endorse your project in researching the draft resistance movement in Boston during the Vietnam war. I think it will be a valuable addition to our knowledge of the anti-war movement in that period of American history.

Sincerely,

Howard Zinn

Boston Draft Resistance During the Vietnam War: A Questionnaire

Please respond to all questions that apply to your experience. You may include comments at any point.

Draft Resistance Activity

1. With which draft resistance organizations did you work?
   (Circle as many as apply)
   1. None (resisted as an individual)
   2. Boston Draft Resistance Group
   3. New England Resistance
   4. RESIST
   5. SUPPORT
   6. Prison Information and Support Service
   7. Committee for Non-Violent Action
   8. American Friends Service Committee
   9. A campus-based draft counseling group
   10. East Coast Conspiracy to Save Lives
   11. Other: _____

2. Of these groups, was there one with which you worked more than the others?
   Which one?
   1. None (resisted as an individual)
   2. Boston Draft Resistance Group
   3. New England Resistance
   4. RESIST
   5. SUPPORT
   6. Prison Information and Support Service
   7. Committee for Non-Violent Action
   8. American Friends Service Committee
   9. A campus-based draft counseling group
   10. East Coast Conspiracy to Save Lives
   11. Other: _____

3. In what kinds of draft resistance activities did you participate?

	Yes	No
1. Draft counseling (e.g., out of an office such as BDRG or AFSC, or on a college campus)	1	2
2. Turned-in draft card	1	2
3. Burned draft card	1	2
4. Refused induction	1	2
5. "Early Morning Shows"	1	2
6. "Horror Shows"	1	2
7. Community outreach (e.g., door-to-door canvassing of potential draftees)	1	2
8. GI outreach	1	2
9. Sanctuaries	1	2
10. Draft board raids (to steal or destroy files)	1	2
11. Other _____	1	2

Please answer the following questions only if you turned-in your draft card, burned your draft card, and/or refused induction. Otherwise, please proceed to question # 20.

4. What was your draft status at the time you turned-in or burned your draft card?
    1. Did not turn-in or burn my draft card
    2. 1-A. Draft eligible
    3. 1-A-O. Conscientious objector available for noncombatant duty only
    4. 1-O. Conscientious objector available for civilian work only
    5. 1-S. Deferred to end of school year
    6. 1-Y. Physical or mental deferment
    7. 2-A. Occupational deferment
    8. 2-C. Agricultural deferment
    9. 2-S. Student deferment
    10. 3-A. Deferred because of dependants
    11. 4-B. Officials deferred by law
    12. 4-C. Alien deferment
    13. 4-D. Minister or ministerial student
    14. 4-F. Not qualified for any service
    15. 5-A. Overage

5. When and where did you turn-in or burn your draft card? Please circle.
    1. Did not turn-in or burn my card
    2. October 16, 1967 at the Arlington Street Church
    3. November 16, 1967 at the Old West Church
    4. December 4, 1967 at Battell Chapel, Yale University
    5. January 29, 1968 at the Arlington Street Church (day of the Spock arraignments)
    6. April 3, 1968 on the Boston Common
    7. November 14, 1968 on the Boston Common
    8. Independently mailed my card to the Justice Dept., Selective Service, or draft board
    9. Other (specify) _____
    10. Other _____

6. How did you first hear about this event?
    1. Did not turn-in or burn my card
    2. Friend or acquaintance told me about it
    3. Family member told me about it.
    4. Heard about it through news reports (television, radio, newspaper)
    5. Saw a poster or leaflet
    6. Happened upon it as I was walking by
    7. Other (specify) _____

7. What happened to you after you turned-in or burned your draft card?
   (Please circle all that apply)

	Yes	No
1. The FBI interviewed me.	1	2
2. The FBI interviewed one or both of my parents about me	1	2
3. The FBI interviewed other members of my family about me	1	2
4. The FBI interviewed friends about me	1	2
5. The FBI interviewed my employer about me	1	2
6. Draft board changed my draft status to 1-A (draftable), but I never received an induction notice	1	2
7. Draft board changed my draft status to 1-A (draftable), and I later received an induction notice	1	2
8. I retrieved my draft card from the people to whom I had given it.	1	2
9. I asked my draft board to issue another draft card to me.	1	2
10. I applied for and received a deferment.	1	2
11. I left the country	1	2
12. I accepted induction	1	2
13. I refused induction	1	2
14. Other _____	1	2

8. If you later applied for or accepted a deferment, which deferment
   did you receive?
   1. Did not later apply for a deferment
   2. 1-A-O. Conscientious objector available for noncombatant duty only
   3. 1-O. Conscientious objector available for civilian work only
   4. 1-S. Deferred to end of school year
   5. 1-Y. Physical or mental deferment
   6. 2-A. Occupational deferment
   7. 2-C. Agricultural deferment
   8. 2-S. Student deferment
   9. 3-A. Deferred because of dependants
   10. 4-B. Officials deferred by law
   11. 4-C. Alien deferment
   12. 4-D. Minister or ministerial student
   13. 4-F. Not qualified for any service
   14. 5-A. Overage

9. If you later left the country, please name the country to which you moved.
   1. Did not leave the country   2. Canada   3. Mexico   4. Sweden   5. Other
   _____

10. If you later accepted induction, please name the branch of service into which you were
    inducted.
    1. Did not accept induction   2. Army   3. Navy   4. Air Force
    5. Marine Corps   6. Coast Guard   7. National Guard

11. Based on the following scale of 1 to 5, please rate your father's reaction to events listed.

	Not Applicable	Strongly Disapprove	Disap-prove	Non-Committal	Approve	Strongly Approve
	1	2	3	4	5	6
1. When I turned in/ burned my draft card	1	2	3	4	5	6
2. When I retrieved my draft card or asked my draft board for a new one	1	2	3	4	5	6
3. When I applied anew for a deferment	1	2	3	4	5	6
4. When I left the country	1	2	3	4	5	6
5. When I accepted induction	1	2	3	4	5	6
6. When I refused induction	1	2	3	4	5	6

Comments:

12. Based on the following scale of 1 to 5, please rate your mother's reaction to events listed.

	Not Applicable	Strongly Disapprove	Disap-prove	Non-Committal	Approve	Strongly Approve
	1	2	3	4	5	6
1. When I turned in/ burned my draft card	1	2	3	4	5	6
2. When I retrieved my draft card or asked my draft board for a new one	1	2	3	4	5	6
3. When I applied anew for a deferment	1	2	3	4	5	6
4. When I left the country	1	2	3	4	5	6
5. When I accepted induction	1	2	3	4	5	6
6. When I refused induction	1	2	3	4	5	6

Comments:

13. Which of the following descriptions best characterizes the moment at which you turned-in or burned your draft card?
    1. It was not spontaneous; I had planned to turn in my card that day.
    2. It was somewhat spontaneous; I had been thinking about turning in my card, but was not committed to it until the moment I did it.
    3. It was completely spontaneous; I had not been considering turning in or burning my card until the moment I did it.

Please comment (further description of your decision):

14. If you later asked for your card back, or accepted a new one from your draft board, or sought a deferment, please rank the following factors that may have contributed to this decision.

	Not Important	Somewhat Important	Important	Very Important
1. Disapproval of parent(s) regarding open confrontation with the government	1	2	3	4
2. Disapproval of significant other regarding open confrontation with the government	1	2	3	4
3. Knew people who had been drafted or enlisted; didn't want to "betray" them	1	2	3	4
4. Turned in/burned my card impulsively; thought better of it soon after	1	2	3	4
5. Possibility of prosecution	1	2	3	4
6. Possibility of being drafted	1	2	3	4
7. Concern for how it might affect career	1	2	3	4
8. Concerned about being perceived as unpatriotic or cowardly	1	2	3	4
9. No longer viewed resistance as a useful antiwar strategy	1	2	3	4
10. Other _____	1	2	3	4
11. Other _____	1	2	3	4

Please comment (further description of your decision):

15. If you later left the country, please rank the following factors that may have contributed to this decision.

	Not Important	Somewhat Important	Important	Very Important
1. Disapproval of parent(s) regarding open confrontation with the government	1	2	3	4
2. Disapproval of significant other regarding open confrontation with the government	1	2	3	4
3. Possibility of prosecution	1	2	3	4
4. Possibility of being drafted	1	2	3	4
5. Concern for how it might affect career	1	2	3	4
6. No longer viewed resistance as a useful antiwar strategy	1	2	3	4
7. Other _____	1	2	3	4
8. Other _____	1	2	3	4

Please comment:

16. If you later accepted induction, please rank the following factors that may have contributed to this decision.

	Not Important	Somewhat Important	Important	Very Important
1. Disapproval of parent(s) regarding open confrontation with the government	1	2	3	4
2. Disapproval of significant other regarding open confrontation with the government	1	2	3	4
3. Knew people who had been drafted or enlisted; didn't want to "betray" them	1	2	3	4
4. Possibility of prosecution	1	2	3	4
5. Just seemed like the right thing to do	1	2	3	4
6. Concern for how it might affect career	1	2	3	4
7. Concerned about being perceived as unpatriotic or cowardly	1	2	3	4
8. Hoped to organize antiwar activity within the military	1	2	3	4
9. No longer viewed resistance as a useful antiwar strategy	1	2	3	4
10. Other _____	1	2	3	4
11. Other _____	1	2	3	4

Please comment:

17. If you later refused induction, please indicate which of the following actions applied to your case (by circling) and the approximate date of each:

Approximate Date
1. Refused induction   _____
2. Prosecuted   _____
3. Acquitted   _____
4. Convicted   _____

18. If you were convicted of charges of violating draft laws, please describe your sentence.

19. If you were sentenced to prison time, please indicate in which prison(s) you served and approximate dates.

Please answer the following questions only if you worked as a draft counselor. Otherwise please proceed to question 25.

20. For which draft counseling organization did you work?
    1. Boston Draft Resistance Group
    2. American Friends Service Committee
    3. Central Committee for Conscientious Objectors
    4. A campus draft counseling organizations (please specify) _____
    5. A church counseling center (please specify) _____
    6. Other (please specify) _____

21. Using the following descriptions of demographic groups, please rate from 0 to 100% the approximate proportion of men whom you counseled.
    1. White college students _____
    2. Minority college students _____
    3. Middle-class white men not in college _____
    4. Middle-class minority men not in college _____
    5. Working class white men not in college _____
    6. Working class minority men not in college _____
    7. Other _____

22. What did your parents think of your participation in the movement as a draft counselor?

	Not Applicable	Strongly Disapprove	Disap-prove	Non-committal	Approve	Strongly Approve
Mother:	1	2	3	4	5	6

	Not Applicable	Strongly Disapprove	Disap-prove	Non-committal	Approve	Strongly Approve
Father:	1	2	3	4	5	6

23. If reaching draft-age men who were not college students was part of your organization's goal, please note the extent to which you believe the draft counseling efforts of your organization were successful on that count.

Not a Goal	Unsuc-cessful	Somewhat Successful	Suc-cessful	Very Successful
1	2	3	4	5

24. If you participated in Early Morning Shows or Horror Shows with BDRG, were you ever arrested? If so, please indicate how many times you were arrested and the result of these arrests (i.e., were you fined, prosecuted, etc.)
    Number of times arrested _____
    1. Charges dropped   2. Fined   3. Prosecuted   4. Acquitted   5. Convicted
    6. Sentenced to jail time   7. Sentenced to community service
    8. Did not participate in such events

Background Information: The following questions apply to ALL survey participants.

25. Date of Birth: _____

26. Sex: Male   Female

27. Race/Ethnicity:
    1. White
    2. African-American
    3. Hispanic
    4. Asian-American
    5. Other _____

28. The following is a list of levels of education. Please indicate the highest level of education attained by your parents and yourself at the time of your involvement with draft resistance.

	Father	Mother	Self
1. Some grade school	1	1	1
2. Completed grade school	2	2	2
3. Some high school	3	3	3
4. Completed high school	4	4	4
5. Some post high school training, but not college (e.g., technical school)	5	5	5
6. Some college	6	6	6
7. Completed college	7	7	7
8. Some graduate work	8	8	8
9. M.A. or M.S.	9	9	9
10. Professional degree (J.D., M.D., etc)	10	10	10
11. Masters degree plus work for higher degree	11	11	11
12. Doctorate (Ph.D., Ed.D, etc.)	12	12	12

29. What kind of job did your father have at the time you became involved with draft resistance? First, give a brief name or title for her work such as electrician, engineer, accountant, etc.
Father: _____

30. In addition, please circle the answer category which best fits your father's occupation at that time:
1. Semiskilled or unskilled worker (truck driver, factory worker, etc.)
2. Skilled worker (foreman, cook, machinist, carpenter, etc.)
3. Farmer (owner-operator or renter)
4. Clerical or sales position
5. Proprietor, except farm (i.e., owner of a business)
6. Professional (teacher, chemist, doctor, etc.) or managerial position (department head, postmaster, police chief, etc.)
7. Don't know

31. What kind of job did your mother have at the time you became involved with draft resistance? First, give a brief name or title for her work such as electrician, engineer, accountant, etc.
Mother: _____

32. In addition, please circle the answer category which best fits her occupation at that time:
1. Semiskilled or unskilled worker (truck driver, factory worker, etc.)
2. Skilled worker (foreman, cook, machinist, carpenter, etc.)
3. Farmer (owner-operator or renter)
4. Clerical or sales position
5. Proprietor, except farm (i.e., owner of a business)
6. Professional (teacher, chemist, doctor, etc.) or managerial position (department head, postmaster, police chief, etc.)
7. Don't know

33. Which description would best characterize your family at the time you became involved with draft resistance?
1. Working class
2. Lower middle class
3. Middle class
4. Upper middle class
5. Upper class

34. Below is a list of political preferences. Please indicate which most closely describes the position of your parents and yourself prior to your involvement with draft resistance.

	Father	Mother	Self
1. Conservative Republican	1	1	1
2. Moderate Republican	2	2	2
3. Moderate Democrat	3	3	3
4. Liberal Democrat	4	4	4
5. Socialist/Communist	5	5	5
6. Anarchist	6	6	6
7. No political preference	8	8	8
8. Other _____	8	8	8

35. Did either of your parents belong to a trade union?

	No	Yes	
Father	2	1	Name of Union: _____
Mother	2	1	Name of Union: _____

36. Did either of your parents participate in any kind of social activism before your participation in draft resistance? Please describe:

_____
_____
_____
_____
_____

37. At the time you became involved in draft resistance were you a veteran of the armed services? Were either of your parents veterans at that time?

You:	1. Yes	2. No
Mother:	1. Yes	2. No
Father:	1. Yes	2. No

38. If you or either parent was a veteran, please indicate of which branch?

You:	Not a Veteran	Army	Navy	Air Force	Marine Corps	Coast Guard	National Guard
	1	2	3	4	5	6	7
Mother:	Not a Veteran	Army	Navy	Air Force	Marine Corps	Coast Guard	National Guard
	1	2	3	4	5	6	7
Father:	Not a Veteran	Army	Navy	Air Force	Marine Corps	Coast Guard	National Guard
	1	2	3	4	5	6	7

39. If you or either parent was a veteran, please indicate in which American wars any of you saw active combat duty in any of this country's wars (up to and including Vietnam)?

	Not a Veteran	No Combat Duty	World War I	World War II	Korea	Lebanon (1957)	Dominican Republic (1965)	Vietnam
You:	1	2	3	4	5	6	7	8
Mother:	Not a Veteran	No Combat Duty	World War I	World War II	Korea	Lebanon (1957)	Dominican Republic (1965)	Vietnam
	1	2	3	4	5	6	7	8
Father:	Not a Veteran	No Combat Duty	World War I	World War II	Korea	Lebanon (1957)	Dominican Republic (1965)	Vietnam
	1	2	3	4	5	6	7	8

40. At the time you became involved in draft resistance, were you or either of your parents members of any veteran's organizations? If yes, which ones?

You:	2. No	1. Yes	3. American Legion	4. VFW	5. Other _____
Mother:	2. No	1. Yes	3. American Legion	4. VFW	5. Other _____
Father:	2. No	1. Yes	3. American Legion	4. VFW	5. Other _____

41. What was your occupation at the time you became involved with draft resistance? First, give a brief name or title for your work such as electrician, engineer, accountant, etc.

_____

42. In addition, please circle the answer category which best fit your occupation at that time:
   1. Semiskilled or unskilled worker (truck driver, factory worker, etc.)
   2. Skilled worker (foreman, cook, machinist, carpenter, etc.)
   3. Farmer (owner-operator or renter)
   4. Clerical or sales position
   5. Proprietor, except farm (i.e., owner of a business)
   6. Professional (teacher, chemist, doctor, etc.) or managerial position
       (department head, postmaster, police chief, etc.)
   7. Student
   8. Don't know

43. If you were a student, please indicate *where* you were studying at the time you became involved with draft resistance.

_____

In which year of school were you at the time you became involved with draft resistance?

1. High School
2. College Freshman
3. College Sophomore
4. College Junior
5. College Senior
5. Graduate Student (Master's program)
6. Graduate Student (Doctoral program)
7. NOT a student at the time

Please circle your major or field of expertise at that time

1. English   2. Philosophy   3. Sociology   4. History   5. Anthropology
6. Political Science   7. Psychology   8. Business 9. Biology   10. Physics
11. Chemistry   12. Engineering 13. Linguistics   14. Foreign Language
15. Religion/Theology 16. Law   17. Medicine
18. Other _____

44. Below is a list of religious preferences. Please circle the ones which most closely describe the preference of your parents and yourself at the time you became involved with draft resistance. Circle all that apply.

	Father	Mother	Self
1. Roman Catholic or Orthodox Catholic	1	1	1
2. Baptist	2	2	2
3. Episcopal	3	3	3
4. Lutheran	4	4	4
5. Methodist	5	5	5
6. Presbyterian	6	6	6
7. Unitarian	7	7	7
8. Quaker	8	8	8
9. Mennonite	9	9	9
10. Jehovah's Witness	10	10	10
11. Jewish	11	11	11
12. Agnostic	12	12	12
13. Atheist	13	13	13
14. Other (specify) _____	14	14	14

45. Please circle those activities in which you were involved prior to draft resistance:

On Campus:
1. Performing arts
2. National Student Association
3. Student government
4. Fraternity/sorority
5. Academic clubs or honor societies
6. Religious groups or activities
7. School newspaper
8. Athletics
9. SDS
11. Peace organizations or activities
12. Vietnam Summer
13. Civil rights organizations or activities
14. Other political organizations (e.g., Young Democrats, Young Republicans, Friends of SNCC, etc.)
15. Others (please describe) _____

In the Community:
1. Religious groups or activities
2. Civil rights organizations or activities
3. Peace organizations or activities _____
4. Vietnam Summer _____
5. Volunteer work
6. Others (please describe) _____

46. Please rank the following factors in terms of how important each one was to your decision to get involved with draft resistance.

	Not Important	Somewhat Important	Important	Very Important
1. Religious beliefs	1	2	3	4
2. Friends or acquaintances	1	2	3	4
3. Past social activism	1	2	3	4
4. News reports of draft resistance	1	2	3	4
5. Parents	1	2	3	4
6. Organizations of which you were a member (please name) _____	1	2	3	4
_____	1	2	3	4
_____	1	2	3	4

47. Did any of your *close* friends become involved with draft resistance at the same time or after you did?
1. Yes   2. No

48. During the time that you were involved in draft resistance only, would you have identified yourself as:

1. A hippie	1. Yes	2. No
2. A politico	1. Yes	2. No
3. An activist	1. Yes	2. No
4. A revolutionary	1. Yes	2. No
5. Part of the counterculture	1. Yes	2. No
6. Part of the New Left	1. Yes	2. No

49. Please circle the number for the response that most accurately reflects your view of the following statement regarding women in the draft resistance movement.

	Don't Know	Strongly Agree	Agree	Disagree	Strongly Disagree
1. Although women were not draft eligible they played an important role in the draft resistance movement	1	2	3	4	5
2. Women often attained positions of leadership in draft resistance organizations	1	2	3	4	5
3. Women sometimes attained positions of leadership in draft resistance organizations	1	2	3	4	5
4. Women often participated in determining important policy and procedure issues in draft resistance organizations.	1	2	3	4	5
5. Women were marginalized in the draft resistance movement and mostly limited to clerical work	1	2	3	4	5
6. Women were encouraged to participate in draft resistance organizations primarily as a way of attracting more men to the movement.	1	2	3	4	5

50. What did you do immediately following your experience with draft resistance? If you went in the service or served time in prison, please indicate what you did immediately after you left the service or got out of prison. Please circle all that apply.
    1. Went to/finished graduate school
    2. Remained active in antiwar movement
    3. Became active in women's liberation movement
    4. Joined a commune
    5. Joined Progressive Labor
    6. Joined Weatherman
    7. Employed as _____
    8. Other (please specify) _____

51. Please list all the political or "movement" organizations, including local groups, to which you belonged from the end of your draft resistance work until the end of the war in 1975.

52. Please check the appropriate space to indicate your level of involvement in the following movements or political activities since your participation in draft resistance.

	Very involved	Moderately involved	Somewhat involved	Not involved
1. Other Vietnam Antiwar Movement activities	1	2	3	4
2. Student Movement	1	2	3	4
3. Women's Movement	1	2	3	4
4. Gay and Lesbian Rights Movement	1	2	3	4
5. Farm Workers Movement	1	2	3	4
6. Labor Organizing	1	2	3	4
7. Pro-Choice Movement	1	2	3	4
8. Pro-Life Movement	1	2	3	4
9. Environmental Movement	1	2	3	4
10. Common Cause	1	2	3	4
11. Anti-Nuclear Movement	1	2	3	4
12. Nuclear Freeze	1	2	3	4
13. Contemporary Draft Resistance	1	2	3	4
14. Contemporary Peace Movement	1	2	3	4
15. 1980s Central American Antiwar Movement	1	2	3	4
16. Anti-Apartheid Movement	1	2	3	4
17. Moral Majority	1	2	3	4
18. Christian Coalition	1	2	3	4
19. Socialist Movement	1	2	3	4
20. Democratic Party	1	2	3	4
21. Republican Party	1	2	3	4
22. Libertarian Party	1	2	3	4
23. Local Electoral Campaigns	1	2	3	4
24. State Electoral Campaigns	1	2	3	4
25. National Electoral Campaigns	1	2	3	4
26. Others (please describe)	1	2	3	4
_____				
_____	1	2	3	4
_____	1	2	3	4

53. Are you presently employed? No _____ Yes _____ (if yes, please list your job below).

54. Please list all *major* jobs you have had from the present back to 1969.

	Years of Employment	
Job	*From*	*To*

55. Please circle the number which best characterizes your political stance:

	You Immediately *After* Draft Resistance	You Today
1. Conservative Republican	1	1
2. Moderate Republican	2	2
3. Moderate Democrat	3	3
4. Liberal Democrat	4	4
5. Socialist/Communist	5	5
6. Anarchist	6	6
7. No political preference	7	7
8. Other	8	8

56. Please list all political or movement organizations, including local groups, to which you currently belong. (Please include any ostensibly nonpolitical organizations through which you participate in political activities, e.g., churches.)

57. Are your currently involved in any social movements?
> 1. Yes   2. No

If yes, which ones?

58. How did your experience in the draft resistance movement affect decisions that you made later in life? Please circle the number for the response that most accurately reflects your view of the following statements.

	Strong Effect	Some Effect	No Effect	Not Applicable
1. My participation in draft resistance and/or related social movements affected my choice of mate(s).	1	2	3	4
2. My participation in draft resistance and/or related social movements affected my choices about work.	1	2	3	4
3. My participation in draft resistance and/or related social movements affected my choices about having children.	1	2	3	4
4. My participation in draft resistance and/or related social movements affected my choices about religion. (If your religious affiliation has changed from the denomination marked in question 44, please indicate your current religious affiliation)	1	2	3	4

59. Please circle the number for the response that most accurately reflects your view of the following statements.

	Strongly Agree	Agree	Disagree	Strongly Disagree
1. In the 1960s, social movements were very effective vehicles of social change.	1	2	3	4
2. Social movements are potentially effective vehicles of social change in contemporary America.	1	2	3	4
3. The 1960s generation was a destructive generation	1	2	3	4
4. Social movements based on moral witness are potentially effective vehicles for social change in contemporary America	1	2	3	4
5. Social movements rooted in non-violence are potentially effective vehicles for social change in contemporary America	1	2	3	4
6. The draft resistance movement brought about the end of the Vietnam era draft.	1	2	3	4
7. The draft resistance movement contributed to bringing the Vietnam War to an end.	1	2	3	4
8. The antiwar movement was ineffective and actually prolonged the war	1	2	3	4
9. Compulsory military service would help to create a greater sense of civic responsibility in contemporary America	1	2	3	4

Please comment in more detail:

Current Information (optional)

In contacting many survey participants, I have been aided by numerous college alumni relations departments. As a result, I do not have current addresses for many respondents. My hope is that you will be willing to complete this section, particularly if you are open to being interviewed, but let me again assure you that information from individual surveys will be completely confidential. I plan to use only the aggregate results of this survey; I will not, under any circumstances, connect names to individual survey responses, nor will I share such information with anyone else.

Interviews generally take no more than 2 hours. In most cases, interviewees will be identified on tape and in transcripts, however, anonymity can be arranged if desired.

60. Are you willing to be interviewed?
    1. I am willing to be interviewed   2. I am not willing to be interviewed

61. Name: _____

62. Address: _____
    _____
    _____
    _____

63. Phone: _____

64. E-mail: _____

THANKS VERY MUCH FOR COMPLETING THE QUESTIONNAIRE!

Again, any help you could provide in locating other individuals who participated in draft resistance in Boston would be greatly appreciated. Please list any addresses you can provide.

_____
_____
_____
_____

Also, do you have any draft resistance related archives (including pamphlets, leaflets, newsletters, photographs, diaries, correspondence) that you would be willing to share with me?

ADDITIONAL COMMENTS:

NOTES

ABBREVIATIONS

AJP   Alex Jack Papers, personal collection

ASCA   Arlington Street Church Archives, Arlington Street Church, Boston, Mass.

BDRG   Boston Draft Resistance Group

BSP   Benjamin M. Spock Papers, Bird Library, Syracuse University, Syracuse, N.Y.

BTP   Barrie Thorne Papers, Michigan State University, East Lansing, Mich.

CFDCR   Case Files, U.S. District Court Records, National Archives, Waltham, Mass.

CFP   Charles S. Fisher Papers, personal collection (now at Swarthmore)

CNVA   Committee for Non-Violent Action

HMP   Howard Marston Jr. Papers, personal collection

JBP   The Reverend Jack Bishop Papers, personal collection

JOP   James Oestereich Papers, personal collection

LBJL   Lyndon B. Johnson Presidential Library, Austin, Tex.

MFP   Michael Ferber Papers, personal collection (now at Swarthmore)

MZP   Michael Zigmond Papers, personal collection

NER   New England Resistance

NPM   Richard Nixon Presidential Materials, National Archives, College Park, Md.

NYT   *New York Times*

RCP   Robert Chalfen Papers, personal collection

RHP   Richard Hughes Papers, personal collection

RSP   Robert Shapiro Papers, personal collection

SCPC   Swarthmore College Peace Collection, Swarthmore, Pa.

SSS   Selective Service System

WHCF   White House Central Files

WHSF   White House Special Files

INTRODUCTION

1. Although Sandi Cooper covers European pacifists before the Great War, her use of "patriotic pacifism" is germane to the subjects of this study. See Cooper, *Patriotic Pacifism*.

2. See, for example, Powers, *Vietnam*; Zaroulis and Sullivan, *Who Spoke Up?*; Small, *Johnson, Nixon, and the Doves*; DeBenedetti, *American Ordeal*; Wells, *War Within*; Jeffreys-Jones, *Peace Now!* With the exception of Wells, each of these historians weaves brief discussions of draft resistance with discussions of the rest of the

antiwar movement. Wells (*War Within*, 191–95, 268–70) gives the most attention to draft resistance, but even he understates its impact. Although he credits draft resistance with affecting the rest of the antiwar movement and American policy in Vietnam, he provides comparatively few details about the lives and motivations of rank-and-file draft resisters and, instead, relies on a few interviews with former Resistance leaders. For a broader trajectory of the peace movement since the 1930s, see Wittner, *Rebels against War*. And for a national overview written by an active leader in the antiwar movement, see Halstead, *Out Now!*

Of course, as syntheses, these studies cannot capture every subset or geographical difference present in the antiwar movement. This book, therefore, will join Heineman, *Campus Wars*; Swerdlow, *Women Strike for Peace*; Moser, *New Winter Soldiers*; and Hunt, *Turning*, in answering Christian Appy's call for more complexity and nuance at the local level of the antiwar movement. See Appy, "Give Peace Activism a Chance," 142.

3. Gitlin, *Sixties*, 291–92; Terry Anderson, *Movement and the Sixties*. Rossinow, *Politics of Authenticity*, gives only the briefest mention of draft resistance within a larger discussion on New Left masculine identity; Isserman and Kazin, *America Divided*, give two paragraphs to draft resistance; Burner, *Making Peace with the 6os*, treats draft resistance in one paragraph; Farrell, *Spirit of the Sixties*, captures the influence of religiosity in social movements of that decade—an important point— but discusses draft resistance in only a handful of paragraphs; Morgan, *6os Experience*, treats it in a few paragraphs; Burns, *Social Movements of the 1960s* gives a little more attention to the Resistance than most but mischaracterizes it as "probably the most suffused [of New Left organizations] with countercultural values and lifestyle." The book cover's dominant image is also a man burning a draft card; Miller, *Democracy Is in the Streets*, focuses primarily on Students for a Democratic Society and draft resistance is all but ignored; Matusow, *Unraveling of America*, like Terry Anderson, addresses draft resistance in only a couple of pages; Blum, *Years of Discord*, dates draft resistance earlier than it actually occurred and makes it seem more like an SDS effort than it was; Farber, *Age of Great Dreams*, gives a brief, incorrect representation of draft resistance ("A group called the Resistance urged young men to burn their draft cards in public. Thousands did."); Terry Anderson, *Sixties*, ignores draft resistance altogether.

4. Caute, in *Year of the Barricades*, 127–35, provides a breezy summary of draft resistance in 1968 and directs almost all of his attention to the Spock trial rather than to the tactic of resistance. See also Fraser, ed. *1968*; Witcover, *Year the Dream Died*.

5. See, for example, Collier and Horowitz, *Destructive Generation*, and Garfinkle, *Telltale Hearts*.

6. An unscientific sampling of fourteen current college textbooks reveals the emphasis on the more controversial burning of draft cards and draft dodging. Only James Henretta et al., *America: A Concise History* (Boston: Bedford Books, 1999), actually name the Resistance and its omega symbol. Even so, they emphasize draft card burnings and make it seem as though the Resistance supported draft dodgers: "Several thousand young men ignored their induction notices risking prosecution

for draft evasion. Others left the country, most for Canada or Sweden. The Resistance, started at Berkeley and Stanford and widely recognized by its omega symbol, supported these draft resisters." Other textbooks either ignore or barely mention draft resistance. For example, George Brown Tindall and David E. Shi, *America: A Narrative History*, 4th ed. (New York: Norton, 1996), 2:1441, mentions draft resistance but lumps it together in a paragraph mostly about draft dodging; James West Davidson et al., *Nation of Nations: A Narrative History of the American Public*, 3rd ed. (Boston: McGraw-Hill, 1998), 2:1105, emphasizes burnings but makes no mention of resistance; John A. Garraty, *The American Nation* (New York: Harper Collins, 1995), 2:833, discusses the draft only, not draft resistance; Carol Berkin et al., *Making America: A History of the United States* (Boston: Houghton Mifflin, 1999), 2:957–58, addresses draft evasion, not resistance; Mary Beth Norton et al., *A People and a Nation: A History of the United States*, 5th ed. (Boston: Houghton Mifflin, 1998), 2:941, discusses draft dodging and protests at draft boards but not draft resistance; Gary Nash et al., *The American People: Creating a Nation and a Society*, 4th ed. (New York: Longman, 1998), 2:981, mentions Muhammad Ali and a "campaign" against the draft without being more specific; Paul Boyer et al., *The Enduring Vision* (Lexington, Mass.: D. C. Heath, 1996), 2:986, 983, briefly mentions draft resistance (though incorrectly states that hundreds of protesters at the Spring Mobe in New York on April 15, 1967, threw their cards into a bonfire. In reality, fewer than one hundred lit their cards with cigarette lighters and dropped them in a coffee can that people passed around); Alan Brinkley, *American History: A Survey*, 10th ed. (New York: McGraw-Hill, 1999), 1070, and Alan Brinkley and Ellen Fitzpatrick, *America in Modern Times: Since 1890* (New York: McGraw-Hill, 1997), 513, make the distinction between resistance and draft dodging but emphasize draft dodging; American Social History Project, *Who Built America?: Working People and the Nation's Economy, Politics, Culture and Society* (New York: Pantheon, 1992), 2:569, does not discuss draft resistance but, consistent with its emphasis on the experience of working people, stresses the inequitable draft deferment system; David Burner et al., *Firsthand America*, 4th ed. (St. James, N.Y.: Brandywine, 1996), 2:958, emphasizes draft card burning and the Berrigan brothers; John M. Murrin, *Liberty, Equality, Power*, 2nd ed. (Orlando: Harcourt, Brace, 1999), 2:1006, focuses on draft card burnings; and Thomas Bailey et al., *The American Pageant*, 11th ed. (Boston: Houghton Mifflin, 1998), 953, mentions draft card burnings only.

7. Tollefson, *Strength Not to Fight*; Gottlieb, *Hell No, We Won't Go!*; Haig-Brown, *Hell No, We Won't Go*. Epitaph quote from Michael Ferber. John Hagan's recent book, *Northern Passage*, not only uses the word "resisters" in its subtitle, but its cover is dominated by a photograph of a draft card in flames.

More encouraging is that sources on draft resistance are slowly making their way into the documentary readers that history professors so frequently use in upper-level courses on the Vietnam War and the 1960s. For examples of documentary readers that include the subject of draft resistance, see Gettleman et al., eds., *Vietnam and America*; Bloom and Breines, *Takin' It to the Streets*; and Robbins, *Against the Vietnam War*. Even so, the same cannot be said for the standard syntheses on the war, which generally include one chapter out of ten or more on the antiwar movement. Just as draft resistance is marginalized in college textbooks, it receives less attention than draft card burnings and draft evasion in these surveys of the war. For syntheses of the Vietnam War, see Young, *Vietnam Wars*; Schulzinger, *Time for War*; Herring, *America's Longest War*; Buzzanco, *Vietnam and the Transformation of American Life*; Kolko, *Anatomy of a War*; Moss, *Vietnam*; Karnow, *Vietnam*; and Emerson, *Winners and Losers*. In addition, no entry on draft resistance appears in either Buhle et al., *Encyclopedia of the American Left*, or Kutler, *Encyclopedia of the Vietnam War*. Likewise, entries on the antiwar movement, conscientious objectors, and selective service in Kutler barely mention draft resistance (see 30–46, 148, and 493–94), though the subject receives one paragraph in the entry on the Supreme Court.

8. Not knowing there would ever be any need to do so, I did not keep track of the number of duplicate letters that I sent out, or even how many names in my database received this treatment. I did, however, begin to track the responses fairly soon after I began receiving them. Out of a total of 51 responses, 36 were neutral, written simply to inform me that I had not found the correct person. In addition to the neutral responses, another five responses were positive, expressing interest in the project and wishing me well with the work.

9. Baskir and Strauss, *Chance and Circumstance*, xvii.

10. Hauser, *Muhammad Ali*, 142–43; Remnick, *King of the World*, 285.

11. Hauser, *Muhammad Ali*, 144–45, 154–55; Remnick, *King of the World*, 286–87; Marqusee, *Redemption Song*, 173–80, 218–25; "TV of Clay Fight Banned in 3 Cities," *New York Times*, March 19, 1966, 22.

12. Maraniss, *First in His Class*, 150–51, 165, 167–68, 173–75, 179–80, 190–93, 198–99.

13. MacPherson, *Long Time Passing*, 381–82.

14. Fallows, "What Did You Do in the Class War, Daddy?" reprinted in Capps, ed., *Vietnam Reader*, 213–21.

15. Shafer, "Vietnam-Era Draft," 57–76.

16. Edward P. Morgan ("From Virtual Community to Virtual History," 87, 102) blames contemporary media coverage: "While it may have offered encouragement to the disaffected young, media coverage and its favored forms of deviant behavior were having the opposite effect on much of the rest of the nation. In 1967 and 1968 the general public was becoming increasingly antiwar *and* increasingly alienated from the antiwar movement." He also notes that the persistence of this condition harmed future mass protest mobilizations that could find inspiration in the history of the antiwar movement.

17. "Resist!" *Resistance*, March 1–15, 1968, 9.

18. *Old Mole*, no. 28, December 5, 1969, 1, 9.

CHAPTER ONE

1. The description of the South Boston incident is pieced together from several sources: "7 War Protesters Beaten in Boston," *NYT*, April 1, 1966, 5; "Pacifist Group, Card Burners, Struck, Kicked," *Manchester Union-Leader*, April 1, 1966, 1; "Boston Draft Card Burnings, Beatings Jar Mayor, Police," *Boston Globe*, April 8, 1966, 1;

"Draft Protester Thanks FBI Agent," *Boston Globe*, June 1, 1966, 1; "The Wrong Place," *Time*, April 8, 1966, 28; Phillips interview; Williams interview; Hicks interview; O'Brien interview; and transcript of *U.S. v. O'Brien*, CR-66-91-S, 1966, CFDCR.

2. "Boston Draft Card Burnings," 8; editorial, *Boston Globe*, April 8, 1966, 14.

3. "Wrong Place," 28.

4. "7 War Protesters Beaten in Boston," 1; David O'Brien claims that Condon began inciting the crowd during O'Brien's statement to the press, but I have not been able to corroborate this claim in any other sources (O'Brien interview).

5. Editorial, *Manchester Union-Leader*, April 2, 1966, 1.

6. Letter, *Boston Globe*, April 12, 1966, 36.

7. Letter, ibid., April 24, 1966, A4.

8. Letter, ibid., April 25, 1966, 12.

9. Editorials, ibid., April 8, 1966, 14; April 23, 1966, 12.

10. Letter, ibid., April 29, 1966, 12.

11. Letters, ibid., April 26, 1966, 16; April 28, 1966, 16.

12. "Marchers Pelted in Boston Protest," *NYT*, April 7, 1966, 5; "Boston Pacifist Parade Pelted," *Manchester Union-Leader*, April 7, 1966, 1; "Boston Draft Card Burnings," 8; Jerome Grossman speech, ACLU annual meeting, October 2, 1993, videotape by Roger Leisner, Radio Free Maine.

13. In a Gallup Poll, 54 percent approved of Johnson's handling of the war, 31 percent disapproved, and 15 percent had no opinion ("LBJ Viet Policy Still Endorsed," *Boston Globe*, April 20, 1966, 25).

14. Bellow, *Dangling Man*, 9.

15. Nash, *Urban Crucible*, 59, 171, 221–22, 294.

16. Thoreau, "On the Duty of Civil Disobedience," 230–31.

17. McDougall, *Fugitive Slaves*, 44–48; Tyler, *Freedom's Ferment*, 538–40; Stewart, *Holy Warriors*, 154–59.

18. Zinn, *People's History of the United States*, 366.

19. Flynn, *Lewis B. Hershey*, 234.

20. Gordon Hall, "Viet Protest Influenced by Left," *Boston Globe*, October 15, 1965, 5.

21. "Cheers, Jeers, Eggs, Paint Greet Marching Thousands," *Boston Globe*, October 17, 1965, 1; "Some Students Demonstrate FOR LBJ's Policy," *Boston Globe*, November 3, 1965, 26; Noam Chomsky, letter to author, December 6, 1996.

22. Ferber and Lynd, *Resistance*, 23.

23. "Draft Card Burning Is Shocking—Saltonstall," *Boston Globe*, October 19, 1965, 4. If the tremendous increase in parcels sent to the Pentagon for forwarding to GIs in Vietnam is any indication, the International Days of Protest did little to persuade most Americans that they should protest the war. Thousands of packages and letters arrived at the Pentagon in the weeks following the demonstrations, creating a logistical problem for the military. Newspapers that featured a "Women's Page" ran helpful hints on what to send to soldiers ("send anything that can be mixed with water because the water there has a foul taste and the boys can't drink it") ("Viet Gifts Clog Pentagon," *Boston Globe*, November 7, 1965, 50; "Draft Protest

Backfires As G.I. Mail Swells," ibid., November 8, 1965, 1; "Helpful Hints: What to Send G.I. in Viet Nam," ibid., November 8, 1965, 11).

24. "Ted Back, Predicts Long, Tough War," *Boston Globe*, November 11, 1965, 10; "Veteran's Day Voices Rise against Pacifists' Protests," ibid., November 11, 1965, 19; "Answering the Anti-Warriors," ibid., October 21, 1965, 2.

25. "Some Students Demonstrate FOR LBJ's Policy," 26; "B.U. Viet Support Signed by 6,000," *Boston Globe*, November 19, 1965, 6.

26. Howard Zinn, "Don't Call Students Communists When They Protest against Viet Nam War," ibid., October 24, 1965, A4.

27. Letters, ibid., October 24, 1965, A4; November 1, 1965, 4.

28. "Link Reds to Protests," ibid., November 20, 1965, 7; "Pro-Viet Nam Fervor Infuses Longest Parade Here in 27 Years," ibid., November 12, 1965, 6.

29. Powers, *Vietnam*, 186; DeBenedetti, *American Ordeal*, 129–30.

30. Tracy, *Direct Action*, 99–104; DeBenedetti, *American Ordeal*, 31, 35; Zaroulis and Sullivan, *Who Spoke Up?*, 9.

31. Tracy, *Direct Action*, 107, 113–14.

32. Phillips interview; O'Brien interview; John J. Phillips letter to CNVA-West, February 24, 1966, Boston CNVA folder, New England CNVA Papers, SCPC.

33. Phillips interview.

34. Williams interview; Phillips interview; O'Brien interview; "Dear Fellow American" and "We Support Our President," leaflets, Boston CNVA folder, New England CNVA Papers, SCPC.

35. *NYT*, March 26, 1966, 2; "Pacifists Stage Boston March," *Manchester Union-Leader*, March 26, 1966, 1; "Punchers at Court," *Boston Globe*, April 10, 1966; Phillips interview; Williams interview; Boston CNVA Newsletter, undated (c. early April 1966), Boston CNVA folder, New England CNVA Papers, SCPC.

36. Flynn, *Lewis B. Hershey*, 217, 234.

37. Richard Gillam, "The Peacetime Draft: Voluntarism to Coercion," in Anderson, ed., *Military Draft*, 101.

38. Chambers, *To Raise an Army*, 254–60; Baskir and Strauss, *Chance and Circumstance*, 19; William H. McNeill, "The Draft in the Light of History," in Anderson, ed., *Military Draft*, 59–65.

39. Zaroulis and Sullivan, *Who Spoke Up?*, 9; Ferber and Lynd, *Resistance*, 4.

40. Ferber and Lynd, *Resistance*, 5; Flynn, *Lewis B. Hershey*, 170.

41. Flynn, *Lewis B. Hershey*, 176–77.

42. Baskir and Strauss, *Chance and Circumstance*, 21; Flynn, *Lewis B. Hershey*, 182, 201.

43. Chambers, *To Raise an Army*, 256.

44. Flynn, *Lewis B. Hershey*, 218, 221.

45. Ibid., 181; Mary McGrory, "Everybody's Grandfather," *Boston Globe*, April 18, 1966, 14.

46. Baskir and Strauss, *Chance and Circumstance*, 16.

47. Davis and Dolbeare, *Little Groups of Neighbors*, 154; Bellow, *Dangling Man*, 125.

48. Flynn, *Lewis B. Hershey*, 234–36, 243.

49. Powers, *Vietnam*, 86; Zaroulis and Sullivan, *Who Spoke Up?*, 54; Baskir and Strauss, *Chance and Circumstance*, 25.

50. Flynn, *Lewis B. Hershey*, 234, 241; DeBenedetti, *American Ordeal*, 166.

51. "Eggs Hurled at Hub Marchers in War Protest," *Manchester Union-Leader*, March 27, 1966, 1; *NYT*, March 27, 1966, 32; Chomsky interview; the New York figure is reported in DeBenedetti, *American Ordeal*, 149–50.

52. Phillips interview; O'Brien interview.

53. "Pacifist Group, Card Burners, Struck, Kicked," 10; Phillips interview; Williams interview.

54. Phillips interview; Williams interview; Hicks interview; O'Brien interview; transcript of *U.S. v. Hicks*, CR-66-103-J (1967), CFDCR. The FBI's collection of that evidence included whisking Hicks away for an interview in their car in which he made it clear that he knew what he was doing.

55. Transcript of *U.S. v. O'Brien*, CR-66-91-S (1966), CFDCR.

56. John J. Phillips letter to Lyndon B. Johnson, February 8, 1966, introduced as evidence in *U.S. v. Phillips*, CR-66-94-W (1966), CFDCR.

57. Exhibits A and C, *U.S. v. Reed*, CR-66-168-C (1966), CFDCR.

58. Transcripts, *U.S. v. Hicks*, CR-66-103-J (1967), CFDCR; Hicks interview.

59. Duffet, *Against the Crime of Silence*, esp. 180–85.

60. Wells, *War Within*, 142.

61. "450 Convicted in '66 as Draft Violators," *NYT*, January 6, 1967, 2.

62. DeBenedetti, *American Ordeal*, 167.

63. Transcripts of *U.S. v. O'Brien*, CR-66-91-S (1966), CFDCR.

64. The life of the Boston CNVA always was tenuous. Even before the trials of the draft card burners, a June newsletter desperately appealed for funds and complained of "the lack of support by those whom we thought were our supporters" (newsletter, June 7, 1966, Boston CNVA folder, New England CNVA Papers, SCPC).

CHAPTER TWO

1. *Face the Nation*, transcripts, April 16, 1967; Garrow, *Bearing the Cross*, 557. Garrow writes that during King's appearance on *Face the Nation*, he "pointed out that he advocated draft resistance, not draft evasion." In fact, King did not state this outright, though it can be inferred. The discussion went like this:

> King: ". . . I do not at this point advocate civil disobedience. I think we have to do a lot of groundwork in massive education before that. I have only urged young men to study their possible status as conscientious objectors. And there is nothing evasive or illegal about this. It is actually guided by and endorsed by the Selective Service Act, which is a perfect constitutional right."
>
> Martin Agronsky (CBS News): "Dr. King, am I to understand, then, that you do not advocate resistance of the draft by any American?"
>
> King: "Well, it depends on what you mean by resistance."
>
> Agronsky: "Refusing to serve." King: "Well, I have certainly advocated this, because I myself would be a conscientious objector if I had to face it."

2. "We Won't Go Statement," *Harvard Crimson*, April 15, 1967, 8; "Harvard Group Pledges Not to Enter Military," ibid., April 17, 1967, 1.

3. Hunt interview.

4. Ibid.

5. "Impact of the War and the Draft," *Harvard Crimson*, Registration issue, 1966, 7; 71 percent of the Class of 1965 went on to graduate school and 8 percent went into the military ("The Year of the Draft," ibid., September 30, 1966, 4).

6. "Students Vote NO on Class Ranks in HUC Poll on Selective Service," ibid., October 13, 1966, 1. The article noted: "Most of the students who repudiated the policy of ranking students in compliance with Selective Service requests indicated that they objected for reasons of 'educational policy' rather than any opposition to student deferments in general."

7. The student who made this remark was well informed. One million North Vietnamese *did* stream into South Vietnam following the establishment of Ngo Dinh Diem's government in South Vietnam. Just as Diem's rise to power was orchestrated by the American Central Intelligence Agency, so too was this exodus of Catholics, who fled North Vietnam at the urging of—and with assistance from—American operatives there. American agents used propaganda to portray the Viet Minh (in the North) as hostile to Vietnamese Catholics while portraying Diem, himself a Catholic, as a kind of savior. See CIA operative Edward Lansdale's report excerpted from the *Pentagon Papers* in Gettleman et al., eds. *Vietnam and America*, 81–96.

8. "McNamara Mobbed, Jeered by 800; Monro and Watson Are Appalled," *Harvard Crimson*, November 8, 1966, 1; McNamara, *In Retrospect*, 254–56. In his recollection, McNamara claims that he kept his driver from pushing forward, saying, "Stop! You'll kill someone!" He also suggests that after taking the two questions, "the danger was only increasing," so he simply "concluded his remarks, jumped off the car, [and] rushed through a Quincy House door." In fact, it seems clear that he concluded his remarks only when reinforcements arrived to provide safe passage.

9. "M'Namara Urges Two-Year Service for All U.S. Youth," *NYT*, May 19, 1966, 1.

10. "O'Konski Asserts Draft Takes Poor," *NYT*, June 24, 1966, 1–2; Remnick, *King of the World*, 289.

11. Flynn, *Draft*, 189–91.

12. Appy, *Working-Class War*, 27.

13. Ibid., 31.

14. Ibid., 31–33.

15. Flynn, *Draft*, 191, 194–95. It is curious that Flynn, probably the leading historian on the draft, disputes the notion that the draft was unfair. In fact, he argues that "the draft worked against social inequalities." Yet Flynn's own statistics show that in 1967, 60 percent of high school graduates served; 50 percent of non–high school graduates served; and 40 percent of college graduates served.

16. Ferber and Lynd, *Resistance*, 55–56. Before the "We Won't Go" conference took place, another national meeting produced a statement of noncooperation. Over two hundred people, mostly with roots in pacifist organizations, met in New York in late October and issued a signed pledge called "Saying 'No' to Military

Conscription, for Draft-Agers Who Have Shunned, or Broken Their Ties to, the System." David Reed, just weeks away from his trial and inevitable imprisonment, authored the earliest drafts of the statement, which began: "We, the undersigned men of draft age (18–35), believe that all war is immoral and ultimately self-defeating. We believe that military conscription is evil and unjust. Therefore, we will not cooperate in any way with the Selective Service System." Significantly, some of the signers included members of the CNVA (Reed, Chuck Matthei, Lou Waronker), future draft resisters (Don Baty, Rick Boardman, George Jalbert, Marty Jezer), and future members of the New England Resistance (Alex Jack, Ray Mungo, Robert Talmanson) (Ferber and Lynd, *Resistance*, 49–50).

17. Ferber and Lynd, *Resistance*, 59.

18. The Port Huron Statement has been excerpted in dozens of anthologies. See, for example, Bloom and Breines, *Takin' It to the Streets*, 61–74.

19. Sale, *SDS*, 313.

20. Ibid., 312–15; Ferber and Lynd, *Resistance*, 60.

21. Hunt interview.

22. "Faculty Debate on 2-S Opens at Meeting Today," *Harvard Crimson*, December 6, 1966, 1; "Faculty Avoids Deferment Debate, Tables Resolution Attacking 2-S," ibid., December 7, 1966, 1.

23. "The Draft: The Equity of a Lottery," ibid., February 25, 1967, 2.

24. Flynn, *Draft*, 198; "Draft Panel Calls for a Crackdown," *NYT*, March 4, 1967, 7.

25. National Advisory Commission on Selective Service, *In Pursuit of Equity*, ch. 3, pp. 38–42.

26. Ibid., 73–75.

27. Davis and Dolbeare, *Little Groups of Neighbors*, 58.

28. "Text of President Johnson's Message to Congress on the Selective Service System," *NYT*, March 7, 1967, 32; "Johnson Plans Draft by Lottery," ibid., March 7, 1967, 1; Flynn, *Draft*, 202–3.

29. Ferber and Lynd, *Resistance*, 62–63.

30. Mike Ferber and David Harris, "On the Resistance," leaflet distributed by the U.S. National Student Association, MFP.

31. Sale, *SDS*, 319–20.

32. "Signers of 'We Won't Go' Petition Organize Draft Resistance League," *Harvard Crimson*, April 26, 1967, 1; "Anti-Draft Group Seeks to Mobilize Harvard around Resistance Issue," ibid., May 5, 1967, 1.

33. "King Calls for Vietnam Summer Volunteers," *Harvard Crimson*, April 24, 1967, 1; John Herfort, "Vietnam Summer," ibid., Pre-Registration issue, 1967, 8; DeBenedetti, *American Ordeal*, 182–83; Keniston, *Young Radicals*. When King and Spock canvassed two homes in Cambridge, they were heckled by a group of young men with signs and a tape player blaring a recording of "God Bless America." One heckler carried a sign that said, "King Get the Hell out of Chicago and Harvard."

34. Wright interview.

35. Hunt interview; Hector interview.

36. Wright interview; Hunt e-mail to author, January 13, 2001.

37. Hector interview.

38. Ferber and Lynd, *Resistance*, 169–70; "Peace Movement Strives to Reach Working Class," *Harvard Summer News*, July 11, 1967, 5; Fisher, "Midwives to History," ch. 2, p. 16.

39. Leaflet announcing May 4, 1967, meeting, CFP.

40. Flynn, *Draft*, 204–5.

41. Memo to LBJ from Joseph Califano, June 29, 1967, Joseph Califano Papers, Box 55, LBJL.

42. Typescript of an article that appeared in *New Left Notes*, May 12, 1967, CFP.

43. "Vietnam Summer: Project Profiles," AJP; BDRG Newsletter, February 1, 1968, MFP; Fisher, "Midwives to History," ch. 2, p. 16; Bill Hunt, "Boston Draft Resistance Group," *New England SDS Conference Newsletter*, c. August 1967, CFP; "Peace Movement Strives to Reach Working Class," 5.

44. "Peace Movement Strives to Reach Working Class," 5.

45. BDRG Newsletter, February 1, 1968, MFP; "Anti Draft Organizing at Pre-Induction Physicals," undated memo, CFP.

46. BDRG Newsletter, March 1968, BTP; Fisher, "Midwives to History," ch. 2, p. 21.

47. Wright interview; "Anti Draft Organizing at Pre-Induction Physicals."

48. BDRG Newsletter, June 29, 1967, CFP.

49. Ibid.

50. Ferber and Lynd, *Resistance*, 172.

51. BDRG Newsletter, undated (c. August 1967), MFP.

52. Ibid.

53. Ferber and Lynd, *Resistance*, 170.

54. Ibid., 172–73.

55. Thorne, "Resisting the Draft," 311.

56. Fisher, "Midwives to History," ch. 3, p. 9; Thorne, "Resisting the Draft," 88; Ferber and Lynd, *Resistance*, 173.

57. Thorne, "Resisting the Draft," 91.

58. Fisher, "Midwives to History," ch. 3, p. 21; Thorne, "Resisting the Draft," 85, 112.

59. Thorne, "Resisting the Draft," 299–300.

60. Hector interview.

61. Fisher, "Midwives to History," ch.3, p. 22.

62. Thorne, "Resisting the Draft," 88.

63. *New England SDS Conference Newsletter*, CFP; Ferber and Lynd, *Resistance*, 65.

CHAPTER THREE

1. This quote often appeared in New England Resistance documents.

2. Harris, *Dreams Die Hard*, 181.

3. Ferber and Lynd, *Resistance*, 81. Ferber and Lynd quote Sweeney as citing McNamara's comments on the poor and minorities in a speech in Montreal (May 1966), though the text of that speech did not include any such reference. Such comments, however, would be consistent with McNamara's views on Project 100,000

(see Chapter 2). See "The Text of Address by McNamara to American Society of Newspaper Editors," *NYT*, May 19, 1966, 11.

4. Harris, *Dreams Die Hard*, 175–76; Ferber and Lynd, *Resistance*, 2–3, 88–90; Wells, *War Within*, 125.

5. Harris, *Dreams Die Hard*, 176.

6. Ferber and Lynd, *Resistance*, 90.

7. Walzer, "Democracy and the Conscript," 16; Staughton Lynd, essay, *Liberation*, April 1967.

8. Gallup, *Gallup Poll*, 2074.

9. Ferber and Lynd, *Resistance*, 104–5.

10. Dowling interview.

11. Jack interview; Ferber and Lynd, *Resistance*, 106.

12. Ferber interview, February 10, 1997; Ferber and Lynd, *Resistance*, 105.

13. Ferber interview, February 10, 1997; Ferber and Lynd, *Resistance*, 105–7.

14. Stone interview, March 28, 1997; Robertson interviews, August 24 and December 22, 1997; Ferber and Lynd, *Resistance*, 107.

15. Doug Rossinow (*Politics of Authenticity*) has produced a splendid study of the University of Texas at Austin that also identifies Christian existentialism and liberal Christianity as central forces in the formation of the New Left there. Much of what I found independently in Boston is similar, though the impulses varied by degree and depended on the chronology of events. In the fall of 1967, existentialism, anarchism, and Judeo-Christian ethics were palpable influences on the Resistance. By late 1968, although those influences remained, the tenor of the movement shifted away from religious trappings to more political ones. It also, at that point, moved to a broader New Left critique of American society (as opposed to strictly trying to end the war). See Chapters 7 and 8.

16. Ferber and Lynd, *Resistance*, 82–86; Hunt interview.

17. Advertisement for October 16 draft card turn-in, *BU News*, October 11, 1967, 5.

18. Ferber interview, April 21, 1998.

19. Hunt interview.

20. "A Call for Boston Clergy and Laity to Support Draft Resistors," undated (c. late September 1967), MFP.

21. "Seminarian Refuses Ministerial (4-D) Exemption," press release included with "Call for Boston Clergy and Laity"; Ferber and Lynd, *Resistance*, 106.

22. Jack, *Gandhi Reader*.

23. Ferber interview, April 21, 1998; Tilton interview.

24. Douglas Kellner, introduction to Marcuse, *One-Dimensional Man*, xxxv.

25. Ferber interview, April 21, 1998.

26. BDRG Newsletter, no. 1, June 29, 1967, 1, CFP.

27. Ibid., undated (c. August 1967), MFP.

28. Mark Kleiman, "Resistance and Non-Cooperation," *New Left Notes*, June 26, 1967, 8; "Draft and Resistance," ibid., July 16, 1967, 4–5.

29. Steve Hamilton, "October 16 . . . A Moral Witness?," ibid., October 2, 1967, 3.

30. Shalom interview.

31. Hunt interview.

32. "The Resistance Begins in Boston," press release, MFP. Eventually, Harvard SDS reluctantly endorsed the Resistance—but only after Michael Ferber attended three of their meetings seeking help (Ferber and Lynd, *Resistance*, 109).

33. James Reston, *NYT*, May 5, 1967; Tom Wicker, "In the Nation: Muhammad Ali and Dissent," ibid., May 2, 1967, 46; "October 16!" NER Newsletter, undated (c. September 1967), MFP.

34. "October 16!" second NER Newsletter, undated (c. October 1, 1967), MFP.

35. "October 16!" NER Newsletter, undated (c. September 1967), MFP; Ferber and Lynd, *Resistance*, 107.

36. Ferber and Lynd, *Resistance*, 108.

37. Jack interview; Mendelsohn interview; Ferber and Lynd, *Resistance*, 107–8.

38. "The Century and the Quest," centennial pamphlet (c. 1961), ASCA; "Arlington Street Church," brochure, undated (c. late 1960s), ibid.; Mendelsohn interview; Howe, *Unitarian Conscience*, 126. The original copy of the Mexican War resolution hangs today in the James Freeman Clark Room in the Arlington Street Church.

39. Moss telephone conversation; Mendelsohn interview; Hohler interview.

40. Mendelsohn interview.

41. "A Call to Resist Illegitimate Authority," *New York Review of Books*, October 12, 1967, 7. See also "320 Vow to Help Draft Resisters," *NYT*, September 27, 1967, 13, and Ferber and Lynd, *Resistance*, 122–23. Other "Call to Resist" signatories included poets Lawrence Ferlinghetti, Grace Paley, Robert Lowell, and Denise Levertov; artist Raphael Soyer; ministers James Bevel, Robert McAfee Brown, and Dick Mumma; and scholars and writers Gar Alperovitz, Mitchell Goodman, Gabriel Kolko, Christopher Lasch, Paul Lauter, Staughton Lynd, Dwight MacDonald, Ashley Montagu, Conor Cruise O'Brien, Linus Pauling, Philip Roth, Edgar Snow, and Susan Sontag.

42. "War Foes Are Promised Churches as Sanctuary," *NYT*, October 3, 1967, 5; "Harris Poll Shows a Decline to 58 percent in Support for War," *NYT*, October 3, 1967, 5.

43. Putnam interview.

44. On the history of Flagstaff Hill, see John Harris, *Historic Walks in Old Boston* (Chester, Conn.: Globe Pequot Press, 1982), xv, 9, 11, 17.

45. Police dogs appeared in a photograph that ran with "Vietnam War Called 'Immoral,'" *Boston Record American*, October 17, 1967, 3; The slogans noted are from photographs that appeared in "Resist the Draft," *Avatar*, no. 11, p. 5; "Resistance: Boston Style," *Avatar*, no. 11, p. 4; and "Youths Burn Draft Cards on Boston Church Altar," *Boston Globe*, October 16, 1967, evening edition, 1–2; and from photographs taken by Tom Rothschild (contact sheets in author's possession).

46. "67 Burn Draft Cards in Boston," *Boston Globe*, October 17, 1967, 1, 12; mimeographed copy of Harold Fray statement made on Boston Common, October 16, 1967, Hunt Papers.

47. Ferber and Lynd, *Resistance*, 112–13.

48. Clennon interview, June 12, 1997.

49. "Youths Burn Draft Cards on Boston Altar," 1–2; "67 Burn Draft Cards in Boston," 1, 12.

50. Clennon interview, June 12, 1997.

51. "Youths Burn Draft Cards on Boston Altar," 2; "October 16!," second NER Newsletter, undated (c. October 1, 1967), MFP; Skip Ascheim, "Resistance: Boston Style," *Avatar*, no. 11, p. 4.

52. "4000 Defy Draft in Common Rally," *Boston Record American*, October 17, 1967, 3.

53. Jim Harney, address delivered at Arlington Street Church, October 16, 1967, mimeographed copy circulated by New England Resistance, MFP.

54. Zinn, *You Can't Be Neutral on a Moving Train*, 116.

55. Michael Ferber, "A Time to Say No," in Mitford, *Trial of Dr. Spock*, 262–65. Ferber's sermon also appeared in several religious journals at the time, such as *Respond*, the magazine of the Unitarian Universalist's Laymen's League; portions of it have more recently been reprinted in Bloom and Breines, *Takin' It to the Streets*, 245–48.

56. Coffin, *Once to Every Man*, 242. This is Coffin's version of the story. Jack Mendelsohn, who remembers the incident slightly differently, recounted it at the Arlington Street Church thirty-year reunion service on October 18, 1997. According to Mendelsohn, as Coffin entered the church with his robe over his arm, he shook Mendelsohn's hand and shaking his head, said, "You Unitarians . . . So *thin* in your theology, so *thick* in your social ethics!"

57. In addition to Coffin's memoir, *Once to Every Man*, see Hall, *Because of Their Faith*.

58. William Sloane Coffin Jr., "Church and Synagogue: Sanctuary of Conscience," in Mitford, *Trial of Dr. Spock*, 266–69.

59. Jack interview; "280 New Englanders Turn in Draft Cards," *Harvard Crimson*, October 17, 1967, 1. A comment by Alex Jack on the sixteenth century might have been more appropriate since Williams is most noted for his scholarly work on the Radical Reformation.

60. George H. Williams, "Vietnam: October 11 and October 16, 1967," mimeographed copy of address circulated by New England Resistance, MFP.

61. Williams, "Vietnam: October 11 and October 16, 1967." I believe this portion of Williams's address is accurate. The quote, "I deplore the burning of draft cards," appeared in several news reports, including "67 Burn Draft Cards in Boston," 12, and "280 New Englanders Turn in Draft Cards," 1. Rev. William Sloane Coffin Jr., who spoke just before Williams during this ceremony, recalls Williams saying something that actually led to the burning of *more* draft cards:

> Suddenly, I heard his [Williams's] voice rise. I saw an excited finger shaking in the direction of the single candle on the table below. "There," he shouted in words I recall as follows, "there is Channing's own candlestick, the one he used night after night to illumine the progress of his writing. I am certain that were he also here for this occasion, its flame, illuminating as it does the faces of you resisters, would seem to him almost pentecostal. For you, gentlemen, are the very pillar of fire this nation needs to lead it out of the darkness now covering its people." (Coffin, *Once to Every Man*, 242–43)

To date, I have been unable to corroborate this recollection of the Williams address.

62. Zaroulis and Sullivan, *Who Spoke Up?* 134; Jack interview; Stone interview, March 28, 1997; Coffin, *Once to Every Man*, 243; "The Draft Resisters: In Search of a New Morality," *Yale Alumni Magazine*, December 1967, 47.

63. NER Newsletter, October 25, 1967, MFP; Coffin, *Once to Every Man*, 244.

CHAPTER FOUR

1. In the spring of 1968, the New England Resistance used this quote liberally in its newspaper, *Resistance*, and in other literature.

2. Edward P. Morgan's recent important article on the media and the antiwar movement, "From Virtual Community to Virtual History," is useful here. Morgan notes that "in terms of political or interpretive *content*, media reports were confined to a spectrum of 'respectable' opinion that virtually excluded content of a radical or even potentially radical nature," like draft resistance (95).

3. Wayne Hansen, "Resist the Draft," *Avatar*, no. 11, p. 5; Hunt interview.

4. Coffin, *Once to Every Man*, 244.

5. "Youths Burn Draft Cards on Boston Church Altar," *Boston Globe*, October 16, 1967, evening edition, 1; "67 Burn Draft Cards in Boston," ibid., October 17, 1967, 1; "67 Burn Draft Cards at Hub Peace Rally," *Boston Record American*, October 17, 1967, 1; "291 Youths Burn, Turn in Draft Cards," *Boston Herald Traveler*, October 17, 1967, 1; Earl Marchand, "The Youths Tell Why," ibid., October 17, 1967, 1.

6. Marchand, "Youths Tell Why," 26.

7. "The Resistance," editorial, *Boston Globe*, October 17, 1967, 16; "Paradox of Protest," editorial, *Boston Record American*, October 20, 1967, 34.

8. Letters, *Boston Globe*, October 21, 1967, 6; October 24, 1967, 20; Letters, *Boston Record American*, October 20, 1967, 34; October 21, 1967, 18; Letters, *Boston Herald Traveler*, October 19, 1967, 10; October 20, 1967, 18; October 21, 1967, 4; October 23, 1967, 12; October 25, 1967, 34; October 27, 1967, 20.

9. "Students to Stage Pro-Vietnam Rally," *Boston Herald Traveler*, October 24, 1967, 8; "Johnson Hails Wakefield Rally," ibid., October 27, 1967, 3; "100,000 Expected for Viet Rally," ibid., October 28, 1967, 1; "Rally Boss Paul Bans Birchers," ibid., October 29, 1967, 62; "50,000 Hail Red, White 'n Blue," ibid., October 30, 1967, 1; "25,000 Shout Support of War Effort," *Boston Globe*, October 30, 1967, 1; "'We Wanted to Be Heard in Vietnam,'" ibid., October 30, 1967, 8.

10. John Sullivan, "Tears Flow at Huge Pro-Viet Rally," *Boston Record American*, October 30, 1967, 2; "Teenagers Voice Solid Support," *Boston Herald Traveler*, October 30, 1967, 8; "'We Wanted to Be Heard in Vietnam,'" 8.

11. Wyatt, *Paper Soldiers*, 7; Small, *Covering Dissent*, 2. See also Gitlin, *Whole World Is Watching*. Gitlin applies Antonio Gramsci's theories of hegemony in explaining the role of the media in covering opposition to government policies. He argues that in a liberal capitalist state, the media, owned by elites and operated by the upper-middle-class and middle-class college graduates they hire, "quietly invoke the need for reform—while disparaging movements that radically opposed the system that needs reforming." During the Vietnam War, for example, the mainstream press portrayed the young people working on Eugene McCarthy's presiden-

tial campaign as "respectable opposition," in contrast to the "radical, confrontational Left." Gitlin's view is consistent with that of Edward S. Herman and Noam Chomsky, who use a "Propaganda Model" to argue that the media serves "to mobilize support for the special interests that dominate the state and private activity." The media, through its "manufacture of consent," acts as a propaganda arm of the government (Herman and Chomsky, *Manufacturing Consent*).

12. Clennon interview, June 12, 1997.

13. On chance of immediate arrest, see Stone interview, March 28, 1997.

14. Alex Jack, "The Case For Burning," undated position paper (c. September–October 1967), AJP; "100 Seminarians and Ministers Turn In 4-D Ministerial Exemptions," NER Newsletter, October 25, 1967, MFP.

15. Coffin interview; Jack Mendelsohn, "The Church and Draft Resisters," sermon, October 22, 1967, ASC; "67 Burn Draft Cards in Boston," 12.

16. Stone interview, March 28, 1997; see also Evans, *Personal Politics*, 179–85, and Thorne, "Women in the Draft Resistance Movement," 179–95.

17. NER Master File, AJP; the Master File that has survived is not complete. The extant version includes 203 resisters from October 16 and 59 others from three smaller turn-ins between November 16, 1967, and January 29, 1968. Significantly, it contains no names from the one other major Boston draft card turn-in, which took place on April 3, 1968. Of 262 records, 215 include the age of the resister. The average age is 22.3 years old and the median age is 22. Of 226 resisters for whom an occupation was listed, 173 (76.5 percent) were students. They attended a total of 31 schools, but 45 (26 percent) came from Harvard, 33 (19 percent) from Boston University, and 26 (15 percent) from Yale. No more than 8 students came from any other single school. Statistics gleaned from the 1997 Boston Draft Resistance Survey roughly confirm these figures. Of 121 resisters who responded to the survey, the average age was 23.2 years old; the median was 23. Eighty-nine (73.6 percent) of the 121 were students, 24.7 percent of whom came from Harvard, 16.9 percent from Boston University, and 14.6 percent from Yale.

18. From the 1997 Boston Draft Resistance Survey, out of 121 respondents, 31 (25.6 percent) indicated that they had at least one parent who participated in some form of social activism or social protest before they (the resisters) got involved with draft resistance. This figure includes 18 (14.9 percent) resisters who had a parent who was a union member.

19. Out of 121 draft resisters, 113 listed the political affiliation of *both* parents. Thus, the 80 percent figure was calculated by dividing 90 (number of couples with the same political leanings, as shown in Table A.8) by 113 = 79.6 percent.

20. From the 1997 Boston Draft Resistance Survey, out of 121 resisters, 25 (20.7 percent) saw themselves as "politicos," 25 (20.7 percent) saw themselves as "revolutionaries," and 82 (67.8 percent) saw themselves as "activists."

21. From the 1997 Boston Draft Resistance Survey, out of 121 resisters, 61 (50.4 percent) had been involved with civil rights on either campus and/or in their communities, 64 (52.9 percent) had been involved with peace issues either on campus and/or in their communities, and 19 (15.7 percent) had participated in

Vietnam Summer on campus and/or in their communities. Out of 121 resisters, 36 (29.8 percent) were members of SDS. Ferber interview, February 10, 1997. See also Staughton Lynd, "The Movement: A New Beginning," *Liberation*, May 1969, 14. Lynd theorizes that much of the connection between civil rights and the Resistance derived from white radicals being forced out of civil rights with the onset of the Black Power movement: "We were looking for something white radicals could do which would have the same spirit, ask as much of us, and challenge the system as fundamentally as had our work in Mississippi."

22. From the 1997 Boston Draft Resistance Survey, 29 out of 121 resisters (24 percent) had no previous activist or protest experience. Sixty-six resisters out of 121 respondents (55 percent) had close friends in draft resistance when they got involved; 55 (45 percent) did not.

23. From the 1997 Boston Draft Resistance Survey, out of 112 respondents, 15 men (13.4 percent) say they turned in or burned their cards spontaneously; 37 men (33 percent) say they had been considering turning in their cards beforehand but did not decide to actually do it until the moment arrived; meanwhile, 60 men (54 percent) made their decisions to resist in advance; Jack interview; Bischoff interview; Hector interview.

24. Coffin interview.

25. Respondent no. 40, 1997 Boston Draft Resistance Survey; Brustein interview.

26. For a notable exception, see the outstanding essay by James Fallows: "What Did You Do in the Class War, Daddy?"

27. Zigmond interview; Clennon interview, June 12, 1997.

28. Etscovitz interview.

29. Oestereich interview.

30. Hunt interview; Coffin interview.

31. For critical appraisals of the sixties generation and the antiwar movement, see Collier and Horowitz, *Destructive Generation*, and Garfinkle, *Telltale Hearts*; see also Stephen Ambrose's foreword in ibid.

32. From the 1997 Boston Draft Resistance Survey, out of 121 resisters, 60 (49.6 percent) saw themselves as part of the counterculture and 20 (16.5 percent) saw themselves as "hippies" at the time they resisted the draft. Likewise, 25 (20.7 percent) saw themselves as "politicos" and 25 (20.7 percent) as "revolutionaries." Eighty (66.1 percent) considered themselves members of the New Left. David Farber, "The Counterculture and the Antiwar Movement," in Small and Hoover, eds., *Give Peace a Chance*, 21; Collier and Horowitz, *Destructive Generation*, 15; Ambrose, foreword in Garfinkle, *Telltale Hearts*, v.

CHAPTER FIVE

1. Coffin, *Once to Every Man*, 247–48; Mailer, *Armies of the Night*, 86.

2. Mailer, *Armies of the Night*, 88–90.

3. Alex Jack, "Press Ignores Trial Issue," *Boston Free Press*, undated (c. July 11, 1968), 11, RCP.

4. McDonough interview. McDonough explained his skepticism about the value of civil disobedience in this interview:

I am skeptical, quite skeptical, about civil disobedience. You see, its logical consequence has to be anarchy. Now, one says, "well, but this is only small, only relates to this particular matter, whether it's abortion or something else, and *we*, because we hold this set of views, are entitled to disobey the law because we hold those views of our own, are superior morally to the law, and command our first allegiance." There's no logical stopping point for that, so I find it difficult intellectually to defend it. However appealing the cause may be, it is, I would think, justified only under the most extreme circumstances—not likely to occur in our society.

5. Wells, *War Within*, 194–95; Coffin, *Once to Every Man*, 247–51; McDonough interview.

6. Clark interview, April 29, 1998; Van de Kamp interview.

7. Wells, *War Within*, 194–95; Coffin, *Once to Every Man*, 247–51; McDonough interview.

8. Califano, *Triumph and Tragedy of Lyndon Johnson*, 198–99; Memo to Ramsey Clark from LBJ, October 20, 1967, WHCF, Box 26, LBJL; Small, *Johnson, Nixon and the Doves*, 113; FBI memo, October 23, 1967, and FBI teletype, October 21, 1967, William Bischoff's Freedom of Information Act Papers, author's files.

9. Memo to Ramsey Clark from Walter Yeagley, assistant attorney general, October 3, 1967, attached to memo from Clark to LBJ, October 4, 1967, Christopher Papers, Box 8, LBJL.

10. Ibid.; Minutes of meeting, October 3, 1967, Tom Johnson's Notes of Meetings, Box 1, LBJL; Wells, *War Within*, 184, 201.

11. Terry Anderson, *Movement and the Sixties*, 178.

12. Stephen Pollack to Ramsey Clark, October 22, 1967, Clark Papers, Box 29, LBJL.

13. The story of the march on the Pentagon has been told by many historians and participants. Perhaps the most engaging and least objective of these accounts is told by Norman Mailer in *Armies of the Night*. See also Zaroulis and Sullivan, *Who Spoke Up?*, 136–42; DeBenedetti, *American Ordeal*, 197–98; Wells, *War Within*, 195–203; Terry Anderson, *Movement and the Sixties*, 178–79.

14. DeBenedetti, *American Ordeal*, 188–89. For more on the march on the Pentagon, see Mailer, *Armies of the Night*, and Wells, *War Within*, 195–204. For more on media coverage of the demonstration, see Small, *Covering Dissent*, 70–84.

15. "FBI Questioning Campus War Foes," *NYT*, October 25, 1967, 8; "FBI Queries Students Who 'Resist' Draft," *Harvard Crimson*, October 25, 1967, 1. Out of 121 former resisters surveyed, 62 (51.2 percent) remember their FBI encounter, while 21 (17.4 percent) recall their parents receiving a similar visit.

16. NER Newsletter, October 25, 1967, MFP.

17. Ferber and Lynd, *Resistance*, 149.

18. NER Newsletter, December 15, 1967, MFP; Venn interview. In an interesting postscript, Chris Venn himself did not ultimately stay on the defensive against being arrested. In 1969, after moving from Boston to San Francisco, he took part in the demonstrations to save People's Park in Berkeley. When the police fired tear gas

canisters into the protesters, Venn lobbed one back at the police. The police continued to advance, and, as Venn ran down the street away from them, an Alameda County sheriff's deputy shot him in the buttocks with bird shot. Venn managed to escape and had most of the bird shot removed by a sympathetic doctor. But the FBI tracked him down a few days later and arrested him for violating his probation. This time he spent a year in the federal penitentiary in El Reno, Oklahoma. For more on People's Park, see Rorabaugh, *Berkeley at War*, 155–66.

19. Ferber and Lynd, *Resistance*, 149; Robertson interview, August 24, 1997.

20. NER Newsletter, December 15, 1967, MFP; Robertson interview, August 24, 1997.

21. Bruen interview; Jupin interview; Oestereich interview; Marston interview.

22. Richard Hyland, "The Resistance: An Obituary," *Harvard Summer News*, August 8, 1969, 3–4; NER Newsletters, December 15, 1967, and October 25, 1967, MFP; Ferber and Lynd, *Resistance*, 251–52.

23. Tilton interview; Bruen interview; Hector interview.

24. "FBI for the Resistance: Questionnaire," leaflet, MFP; Ferber and Lynd, *Resistance*, 153–54; Jack interview; Wayne Hansen, "The Resistance Turns the Tables," *Avatar*, no. 12, p. 4.

25. Hansen, "Resistance Turns the Tables"; NER Newsletter, undated (c. early November 1967), AJP.

26. Jack interview.

27. Stone interview, March 28, 1997; Hunt interview; Hector interview.

28. Hyland, "Resistance: An Obituary," 3–4; Stone interview, March 28, 1997.

29. Meeting minutes, October 23, 1967, Tom Johnson's Meeting Notes, Box 1, LBJL (emphasis added); Ramsey Clark to LBJ, October 21, 1967, Box 29, Clark Papers, LBJL; Minutes, Congressional Democratic Leadership meeting, October 31, 1967, Meeting Notes File, Box 2, LBJL; Goodwin, *Remembering America*, 404–5. Goodwin recalls a meeting at the LBJ ranch in which Johnson invoked the "mental institutions" and "McCarthyite" references. His quotations are nearly identical to those found in the meeting notes for the meeting on October 31 with congressional leaders (which I found at the LBJ Library). It is not clear which are correct—or if both are correct—but I am relying on the meeting notes as my source. The mention of the Communist Party supporting draft resistance is, however, unique to Goodwin's story.

30. Goodwin, *Remembering America*, 400; Wells, *War Within*, 183–84; Dallek, *Flawed Giant*, 367.

31. Donner, *Age of Surveillance*, 259–61; Dallek, *Flawed Giant*, 490; Wells, *War Within*, 204, 210; DeBenedetti, *American Ordeal*, 204–5.

32. The cards collected from across the country on October 20, 1967, and left at the Justice Department were introduced as evidence in the trial of the Boston Five the following June and, as evidence in a federal trial, should be part of the public record today. Inexplicably, however, they are not among the records of the trial at the National Archives in Waltham, Massachusetts. Court officials speculate that the evidence was sent back to the FBI, but numerous Freedom of Information Requests and appeals have turned up nothing. They have probably been destroyed.

33. Califano, *Triumph and Tragedy of Lyndon Johnson*, 198–200; Flynn, *Lewis B. Hershey*, 259; Flynn, *Draft*, 215–16. Through various sources, including interviews with Hershey, Flynn has confirmed Johnson's involvement in the decision to draft resisters. Additional primary source documentation linking the president to this issue has not yet been uncovered. The staff at the Lyndon Baines Johnson Presidential Library have begun releasing audio tapes of conversations held in the Oval Office and over the telephone during Johnson's presidency. My hope is that when the tapes for October 16 to 31, 1967, are opened, we will finally hear this conversation between Hershey and LBJ.

34. Local Board Memorandum no. 85, October 24, 1967, Califano Papers, Box 55, LBJL; Hershey to Members of SSS, October 26, 1967, National Security—Defense Files, ND 9-4, Box 148, LBJL.

35. For letters, see National Security—Defense Files, ND, Box 151, November–December 1967, LBJL; "Demeaning the Draft Act," editorial, *Boston Globe*, November 9, 1967, 14; Eugene Byrd telegram to LBJ, December 11, 1967, Hershey Folder, Macy Papers, LBJL. On the Ann Arbor protest, see Chapter 1.

36. Flynn, *Lewis B. Hershey*, 260–61.

37. Ibid., 262; Moss to Hershey, November 17, 1967; Hershey to Moss, December 13, 1967; and Moss to Hershey, December 15, 1967, Califano Papers, Box 56, LBJL. A good example of Hershey's dense prose comes from the December 13, 1967, letter to Moss:

> As I stated before, the charges which you have levied against the operation of the System are based on your underlying contention that actions or inactions inimical to the national interest because their objective is to defeat the purpose of the selective service law should be construed solely as violation of the criminal law and prosecuted as such, and that they cannot serve as a basis for local board action in carrying out the mandate of the law that a deferment is nothing but a temporary delay in consummating a man's statutory obligation to serve his country and that such delay can be granted only where it is clearly demonstrated that the national interest can be best served by such temporary delay.

38. Memo to LBJ from Larry Temple, November 16, 1967, attached to memo to LBJ from Califano, November 18, 1967, Califano Papers, Box 56, LBJL; Memo to Califano from Larry Levinson, November 8, 1967, Califano Papers, Box 55, LBJL; Memo to LBJ from Matt Nimetz, November 16, 1967, attached to memo to LBJ from Califano, November 18, 1967, Califano Papers, Box 56, LBJL; Memo to LBJ from Joe Califano, November 14, 1967, Califano Papers, Box 55, LBJL.

39. Hershey interview by Middleton, 17–18, LBJL; Clark interview, January 6, 1998; Ramsey Clark to Charles L. Schultze, draft letter, November 14, 1967, Califano Papers, Box 55, LBJL.

40. Clark interview, January 6, 1998; see also Wells, *War Within*, 233–36.

41. Clark interview, January 6, 1998; Wells, *War Within*, 234; Califano, *Triumph and Tragedy of Lyndon Johnson*, 201.

42. Flynn, *Draft*, 217–18; Califano, *Triumph and Tragedy of Lyndon Johnson*, 201–2.

43. "Joint Statement by Attorney General Ramsey Clark and Director of Selective Service Lewis B. Hershey," December 9, 1967, Califano Papers, Box 55, LBJL; Flynn, *Draft*, 217–18; Califano, *Triumph and Tragedy of Lyndon Johnson*, 201–2.

44. John Van de Kamp describes the joint statement as a victory for the Department of Justice (Van de Kamp interview); Clark interview, April 29, 1998.

45. Clark interview, April 29, 1998; Van de Kamp interview; McDonough interview. For more on the Justice Department's response to draft resistance, see Foley, "Confronting the Johnson Administration at War."

46. Neil Sheehan, "Hershey Upholds Induction Policy," *NYT*, December 12, 1967, 16; Califano, *Triumph and Tragedy of Lyndon Johnson*, 202–3; Flynn, *Lewis B. Hershey*, 265; Flynn, *Draft*, 218.

47. Califano, *Triumph and Tragedy of Lyndon Johnson*, 202–3; Flynn, *Lewis B. Hershey*, 265; "Hershey's Order Is Affecting Few," *NYT*, December 17, 1967, 15.

48. Lewis Brodsky (SSS Public Affairs Officer) e-mail to author, April 29, 1998, author's files; from the 1997 survey of Boston draft resisters, 77 (63.6 percent) out of 121 resisters were reclassified to 1-A.

49. The Resistance National Newsletter no. 2, December 1, 1967, MFP; NER Newsletter, October 25, 1967, MFP.

50. Clennon interview, June 12, 1997; Bruen interview; NER Newsletter, October 25, 1967, MFP; figures from the 1997 survey of Boston draft resisters.

51. Jack interview; Hunt interview.

52. Ray Mungo interview; Mungo, *Famous Long Ago*, 87.

CHAPTER SIX

1. Clennon interview, June 12, 1997.

2. Kirkland conversation. Notes of all telephone conversations cited are in author's files.

3. Kirkland conversation; Bower conversation; Dehmlow conversation.

4. Clennon interviews, June 12, 1997, and June 17, 1998.

5. Clennon interview, June 12, 1997.

6. Clennon interview, June 17, 1998; Bower conversation; Dehmlow conversation.

7. Clennon interview, June 17, 1998; Bower conversation.

8. Clennon interview, June 12, 1997; Bower conversation; Dehmlow conversation.

9. Clennon interview, June 12, 1997.

10. From the 1997 survey of Boston draft resisters, 116 resisters responded to the survey, though only 86 responded to the question about their fathers' reactions to draft resistance (35 were left blank or marked N/A) and 99 responded to the question about their mothers' reactions.

11. Mungo interview.

12. Venn interview; Robertson interview, August 24, 1997.

13. NER Master File, AJP; Respondent no. 105, 1997 Boston Draft Resistance Survey. This propensity to resist without discussing it with parents may account for

the high proportion of responses marked "not applicable" with respect to parental reaction; Clennon interview, June 17, 1998.

14. Clennon interview, June 12, 1997; Jack interview; Zigmond interview.

15. Mungo interview; Clennon interview, June 12, 1997; Respondent nos. 50 and 150, from the 1997 Boston Draft Resistance Survey; Hector interview; Field interview; Matteson interview.

16. Marston interview.

17. NER Newsletter, undated (c. early November 1967), AJP.

18. Bishop interview; Jupin interview; "The Draft, Conscience, and the Church," *Three Crowns of the Epiphany*, October 22, 1967, 1–2, JBP.

19. Bishop interview; Jupin interview.

20. Rev. Jack Bishop, "Winchester: Crisis in Conscience," unpublished paper, December 18, 1967, 3, JBP.

21. Bishop interview; Bishop, "Winchester," 2.

22. Bishop, "Winchester," 2–5; Bishop interview.

23. J. Michael Jupin, sermon, October 29, 1967, 1–2, JBP.

24. Ibid., 3–4.

25. Ibid., 4–5.

26. Written responses (numbers 89 and 124), Parish of the Epiphany, October 29, 1967, JBP, copies in author's files.

27. Written responses (numbers 105, 113, 13, 14, 117), Parish of the Epiphany, October 29, 1967, JBP.

28. Written responses (number 32), ibid.

29. Bishop, "Winchester," 6–7; "Decries Clergy's Advocation of 'Lawlessness,'" letter, *Winchester Star*, November 2, 1967, 5; "For Clergymen Who Live As They Believe: Admiration," letter, ibid., November 9, 1967, 7; "Our Obligation to Hear Critics of Administration," "Illegal Acts Lose Sympathy for the Peace Cause," and "'Gross Injustice' of War Justifies Counter Actions," letters, ibid., November 16, 1967, 6.

30. Bishop, "Winchester," 8; Bishop interview; "Corporal Francis J. Muraco Killed in Action in Vietnam," *Winchester Star*, November 30, 1967, 1; Tom Greenwood, "A Fallen Hero's Power to Inspire," *Boston Globe*, November 11, 1998, A23. In 1969, the town of Winchester named a new elementary school after Francis Muraco.

31. Anson Phelps Stokes, "The Church and War," statement, November 26, 1967, JBP; "Bishop Anson Stokes Asks Epiphany for 'Unity in Concern,'" *Winchester Star*, November 30, 1967, 1.

32. Fred Foye, "Bishop Defends Anti-Vietnam Cleric," newsclip (possibly *Boston Record American*), JBP; John K. Colony and William H. Buracker letter to parishioners of the Parish of the Epiphany, December 7, 1967, JBP; "On Christian Obedience," position paper of the National House of Bishops, 1964, JBP. The letter from the vestry said, "[I]t is the consensus of your Vestry that Mr. Jupin can continue effectively at Epiphany." In fact, the vestry did not reach a complete consensus; two days later, the one person who voted against the continued employment of Mike Jupin became the third member of the vestry to resign.

33. Bishop, "Winchester," 9–11; Bishop interview.

34. Bishop, "Winchester," 13–14; Bishop interview; Jupin interview.

35. "The Limits of Protest," editorial, *Boston Globe*, November 28, 1967, 20; "The Resistance," editorial, ibid., October 17, 1967, 16.

36. Bishop interview; Jupin interview.

37. In the 1997 Boston Draft Resistance Survey, 44 of the 68 supporters who responded were male; 24 (or 35 percent) were female. However, in the activist database I assembled before administering the questionnaire, I identified 127 non-resisters, of whom 68 (or 54 percent) were women.

38. See Carroll, *American Requiem*.

39. In the 1997 Boston Draft Resistance Survey, 26 of 68 (38 percent) supporters came from homes in which at least one parent took part in some form of social activism. This figure includes 13 supporters (19 percent) who came from homes in which at least one parent was a union member.

40. In the 1997 Boston Draft Resistance Survey, 19 supporters identified themselves as both Liberal Democrats and members of the New Left; 1 supporter identified himself as both a moderate Democrat and a member of the New Left. Therefore, 20 of 68 supporters (29 percent) considered themselves Democrats and members of the New Left. Likewise, 20 of the 47 supporters (42.6 percent) who identified themselves as part of the New Left also were Democrats.

41. NER Newsletter, undated (c. early November 1967), AJP.

42. BDRG Newsletter, February 1, 1968, MFP; Fisher, "Midwives to History," ch. 9, p. 10.

43. See Evans, *Personal Politics*; Thorne, "Gender Imagery"; Thorne, "Women in the Draft Resistance Movement"; and Rossinow, *Politics of Authenticity*.

44. For a more detailed analysis of gender dynamics in Boston's draft resistance movement, see Foley, "'Point of Ultimate Indignity?'"

45. Stone interview, March 28, 1997; Jack interview; Robertson interview, August 24, 1997.

46. Evans, *Personal Politics*; Thorne, "Gender Imagery," 56.

47. NER letter, March 20, 1968, courtesy William Clusin (copy in author's possession); Thorne, "Women in the Draft Resistance Movement," 190.

48. Ellen DuBois interview, June 11, 1997.

49. Stone interview, October 8, 1997; Field interview.

50. Rossinow, *Politics of Authenticity*, 297–333. Rossinow describes the quest for an authentic masculinity as one of the pillars of the New Left; while the machismo of draft resistance neatly fits that characterization, and had many of the same effects on women's participation, as Rossinow describes, one can persuasively make the case that the quest for an authentic masculinity was not so much a goal of draft resistance as a by-product of the movement's tactics (which emphasized male risk-taking).

51. Schenk interview; Mungo interview; Katz interview; Dana Densmore, "Year of Living Dangerously," in DuPlessis and Snitow, *Feminist Memoir Project*, 73; Poole interview; Field interview; Stone interview, March 28, 1997.

52. Field interview; Tilton interview; Stone interview, March 28, 1997.

53. One BDRG newsletter (March 1968, BTP) noted: "Sasha Harmon is our office manager; if you have an afternoon free and would like to lend a hand collating, stapling, folding, phoning, etc.-ing, call and ask her what's up." This instruction seems to have been aimed at all readers of the newsletter, male and female alike, but it also makes clear that Harmon, a woman, was in charge of these responsibilities.

54. DuBois interview, November 27, 2000; Wright interview.

55. Harmon interview, October 14, 1997; Matteson interview.

56. DuBois interviews, June 11, 1997, and November 27, 2000; Haasl, "'I Want to Knock Down the World,'" 24–29; Densmore, "Year of Living Dangerously," 73; Dunbar-Ortiz interview.

57. Harmon interview; Wright interview; Katz interview. Male dominance of New Left meetings is taken up by Evans, particularly regarding the earlier New Left, in *Personal Politics*, 115.

58. Field interview; Tilton interview.

59. Katz interview; Stone interview, October 8, 1997. An example of women as public representatives of the New England Resistance is Nan Stone, "GI Support Speech," undated, Stone Papers, copy in author's files.

60. Poole interview; Kurland Lagos interview.

61. Fay interview; see also Booth, Goldfield, Munaker, *Toward a Radical Movement*, reprinted in Crow, ed., *Radical Feminism*, 58–63.

62. DuBois interview, November 27, 2000. Rossinow (*Politics of Authenticity*, 230) has made the "beloved community" analogy to draft resistance but refers to it as a "distinctly male beloved community."

63. DuBois interview, November 27, 2000.

64. Ibid.; on sexual exploitation in SDS and Weathermen, see, for example, Evans, *Personal Politics*, 152–54, 177–79; Matusow, *Unraveling of America*, 340–41; Gitlin, *Sixties*, 371–72, 395; and Rossinow, *Politics of Authenticity*, 265–67.

65. Poole interview.

66. Dunbar-Ortiz interview.

67. Poole interview; Kurland Lagos interview; Matteson interview; Fisher, "Midwives to History," ch. 2, p. 16 (copy in author's files).

68. Todd Gitlin (*Sixties*, 385–86) describes Dorhn as combining "lawyerly articulateness with a sexual charisma—even more than her chorus line looks—that left men dazzled"; Poole interview; Wright interview.

69. Hunt interview.

70. Paul Goodman, "Appeal," *New York Review of Books*, April 6, 1967, 38.

71. Chomsky, *American Power and the New Mandarins*, 315, 324–25, 334–35. See also a good summary of the influence of Chomsky's essays (though followed by a less-than-substantive critique) in Tomes, *Apocalypse Then*, 152–55.

72. Vogelgesang, *Long Dark Night*, 127–28.

73. Ibid., 135–36. See also Tomes, *Apocalypse Then*, 131, 134–35, 156–58, 175.

74. Lauter interview; Kampf interview; Resist Newsletter No. 1, November 1967, Series 2, Box 28, BSP. Paul Lauter has recently deposited Resist's papers at Trinity College, Hartford, Connecticut. On Hershey's October 26 memo, see Chapter 5.

75. Chomsky, *American Power and the New Mandarins*, 380; Resist Newsletter No. 2, December 18, 1967, Series 2, Box 28, BSP.

76. Lauter interview; Kampf interview.

77. Lauter interview; Kampf interview; Hein interview.

78. Hein interview.

79. Lauter interview; Kampf interview.

80. Kampf interview; Hein interview.

81. NER Newsletter, undated (c. early November 1967), AJP.

82. Rossini interview; Clusin interview.

83. "Fists, Insults Fly at Hub Viet Protest," *Boston Globe*, November 16, 1967, evening edition, 1; "Fists Fly at Hub Anti-War Rally," *Boston Record American*, November 17, 1967, 1; "Punches Swing, Cards Burn in Anti-Draft Rally," *Boston Herald Traveler*, November 17, 1967, 1; NER Newsletter, December 15, 1967, MFP; Hector interview.

84. "Fists, Insults Fly," 32; "Punches Swing," 36.

85. Rossini interview.

86. Clusin interview.

87. Michael Levin letter to Local Board No. 36, December 19, 1967, courtesy Michael Levin (copy in author's files).

88. "Fists, Insults Fly,"1; "Fists Fly," 1; "Punches Swing," 1; The Resistance National Newsletter No. 1, November 24, 1967, MFP.

89. "Fists, Insults Fly," 1; "Fists Fly," 1; "Anti-Viet Protest at Church Fizzles," *Boston Record American*, November 17, 1967 (late edition), 5; "Punches Swing," 1; The Resistance National Newsletter No. 1, November 24, 1967, MFP.

90. "Bonehead Play of the Year," CNVA Newsletter, January 15, 1968, 2; NER Newsletter, December 15, 1967, MFP.

CHAPTER SEVEN

1. Michael Ferber, speech at Town Hall, N.Y., January 14, 1968, transcribed in FBI memorandum, Exhibit 33a, *U.S. v. Coffin et al.*, CR-68-1, CFDCR; Wells, *War Within*, 231.

2. "U.S. Indicts Dr. Spock, 4 Others," *Boston Globe*, January 6, 1968, 1.

3. Indictment, *U.S. v. Coffin et al.*, CR-68-1, copy in MFP. The complete text of the indictment also appears in the appendix of Mitford, *Trial of Dr. Spock*, 253–57.

4. Indictment, *U.S. v. Coffin et al.*, CR-68-1, copy in MFP.

5. Wall interview.

6. Ferber speech at Town Hall, New York, January 14, 1968, transcribed in FBI memorandum, Exhibit 33a, *U.S. v. Coffin et al.*, CR-68-1, CFDCR; "Indictments Protest Planned in Capital," *Boston Globe*, January 8, 1968, 1; Ferber interview, June 16, 1998.

7. Howard Zinn interview; Kampf interview; "The Repression at Home," editorial, *Ramparts*, February 1968, 2; John Fuerst, "Resistance and Repression," *New Left Notes*, January 15, 1968, 1; Robert Pardun, "The Political Defense of Resistance," *New Left Notes*, January 15, 1968, 1; Hein interview.

8. Van de Kamp interview; Clark interview, January 6, 1998.

9. Van de Kamp interview; McDonough interview; Wall interview; Mitford, *Trial of Dr. Spock*, 31, 271.

10. Clark interviews, January 6 and April 29, 1998. Also see Wells, *War Within*, 234–37.

11. Wells, *War Within*, 236; Clark interview, January 6, 1998; Rusk, *As I Saw It*, 473–74.

12. The reasons that the men were tried in Boston remain unclear more than thirty years later. John Van de Kamp saw Boston as "more neutral grounds" than Washington, where the press would seize on the political showdown between Spock and President Johnson. John Wall believed, however, that it was because the government would be more likely to impanel a conservative jury than in D.C. or New York, and thus would get a conviction more easily. Many movement participants interpreted the decision as Wall did (Van de Kamp interview; Wall interview; Ferber interview, June 16, 1998; Mitford, *Trial of Dr. Spock*, 220).

13. Ferber speech at Town Hall.

14. "The Repression at Home," editorial, *Ramparts*, February 1968, 2; "Draft Indictments Spur Calls for Strikes, Sit-Ins," *Boston Globe*, January 7, 1968, 1; "Indictments Protest Planned in Capital," *Boston Globe*, January 8, 1968, 1; Ferber interview, June 16, 1998; Coffin, *Once to Every Man*, 263; Mitford, *Trial of Dr. Spock*, 4.

15. "Draft Indictments Spur Calls for Strikes, Sit-Ins"; Ferber speech at Town Hall; "Repression at Home," 2.

16. Kampf interview.

17. Dowling interview.

18. Ferber interview.

19. Transcript of FBI tapes of David Dellinger's and Tom Hayden's speeches at the Northeastern University rally, January 28, 1968, Spock FBI files, copies in author's possession; Resistance National Newsletter No. 5, January 31, 1968, MFP.

20. "Dr. Spock Pleads Innocent," *Boston Globe*, January 29, 1968, evening edition, 1; "Dr. Spock's Trial Set in March," *Boston Globe*, January 30, 1968, 1; photograph, *BU News*, January 31, 1968, 9; Bud Collins, "The New Generation's New Heroes," *Boston Globe*, January 31, 1968, 13.

21. "Dr. Spock Pleads Innocent," 1; "Dr. Spock's Trial Set in March," 1; "Izvestia Gives Hub Big Play," *Boston Globe*, January 30, 1968, 2; Collins, "New Generation's New Heroes," 13; "1,200 at Anti-War Rally as Spock, 4 Others Plead," *Boston Herald Traveler*, January 30, 1968, 1; "Peace and Punches Mar Spock Hearing," *Boston Record American*, January 30, 1968, 3; "25 All Burned up over Spock Hearing," ibid., January 30, 1968, 3.

22. "Dr. Spock Pleads Innocent," 1; "Dr. Spock's Trial Set in March," 1; "1,200 at Anti-War Rally as Spock," 1; Order of Service of Rededication, leaflet, January 29, 1968, Series 2, Box 11, BSP.

23. "Dr. Spock's Trial Set in March," 1; "1,200 at Anti-War Rally as Spock," 1; "25 All Burned Up," 3.

24. "Dr. Spock's Trial Set in March," 1; "1,200 at Anti-War Rally as Spock," 1; "25 All Burned Up," 3; NER Newsletter, February 8, 1968, MFP.

25. "Statement of the Boston Draft Resistance Group," undated leaflet (c. January 10, 1968), CFP.

26. Von Rosenvinge interview; "Fall Kills Draftee Awaiting Army Test," *Boston Globe*, January 4, 1966, evening edition, 1–2. According to the *Globe*, Didinger hung from the ledge of the third-floor window before falling to the pavement below. Von Rosenvinge recalls it as a more deliberate plunge out the window.

27. "3 Cape Ann Men Join Draft Protest," *Gloucester Daily Times*, October 20, 1967, Scrapbook, HMP; Marston interview.

28. "Draft Resistance Involves Quiet Rockport," editorial, *Gloucester Daily Times*, April 6, 1968, 4.

29. "Boston Draft Protest Set," *Boston Globe*, January 8, 1968, 9; "Marston, 20, Says He Will Refuse Induction in Army," *Gloucester Daily Times*, January 8, 1968, Scrapbook, HMP.

30. "Marston Praised and Criticized for War Protest," *Gloucester Daily Times*, January 10, 1968, Scrapbook, HMP; "Gloucester Draftee Resists," *Salem News*, undated newsclip, Scrapbook, HMP.

31. "Army Base Picketed by Anti-Draft Group," *Boston Globe*, January 10, 1968, evening edition, 1; "Army Delays on Resisters," *Boston Herald Traveler*, January 11, 1968, Scrapbook, HMP; "Howard E. Marston, Sr., Speaks on His Son's Refusal to Be Inducted into the Army," NER leaflet, CFP; "'Stop Draft!' Cries Follow Indictments," *BU News*, January 17, 1968, 3; "Parents Back Boy Fighting Draft," newsclip from unknown newspaper, Scrapbook, HMP.

32. "26 in Hub Inducted as 2 Protesters Are Sent Home," *Boston Globe*, January 11, 1968, 1; "Dr. Spock Invites Marstons to Dinner," *Gloucester Daily Times*, January 11, 1968, Scrapbook, HMP; "Peacenik 'Inducted' into Snow," photograph, *Boston Record American*, January 10, 1968, Scrapbook, HMP; "Youths Lose Chance to Refuse Draft," *Boston Record American*, January 11, 1968, 5.

33. "Army Delays on Resisters," *Boston Herald Traveler*, January 11, 1968, Scrapbook, HMP; "26 in Hub Inducted as 2 Protesters Are Sent Home," 1; "Dr. Spock Invites Marstons to Dinner"; "2 Get Chance to Spurn Induction at Last," *Boston Globe*, January 20, 1968, 3.

34. Risden (son of Lt. Col Edward J. Risden) conversation (notes in author's files).

35. Marston interview.

36. Ibid. (with sister Deborah Jelmberg).

37. Marston interview.

38. Oestereich interview; Hughes interview; "We Won't Go" leaflet, February 26, 1968, JOP.

39. Oestereich interview; *Oestereich v. Selective Service System*, 393 U.S. 233 (1968).

40. Hughes interview; copy of Richard Hughes's SSS File, Local Board 14, from Hughes FBI file, RHP; Richard Hughes, e-mail to author, July 8, 1998.

41. Oestereich interview; Hughes interview; Oestereich statement, February 26, 1968, JOP.

42. Oestereich interview; Hughes interview.

43. Oestereich interview; copy of statement prepared for base personnel, February 26, 1968, JOP; "200 Peace Pickets Protest 2 Inductions," *Boston Globe*, February 26, 1968, evening edition, 4.

44. Hughes interview; "Teaching Fellow Refuses Induction," *BU News*, February 28, 1968, 1; statement written at request of army personnel at Boston Army Base, February 26, 1968, FBI file, RHP. For more on the destruction of Ben Tre, see "The Slaughter Goes On," *New Republic*, February 24, 1968, 13.

45. Zinn interview; Hughes interview.

46. Hughes interview; "Vietnam Street Children Getting Better Care, American Says," *NYT*, August 9, 1976, 2.

47. Hughes interview; FBI memo on Hughes induction refusal, FBI file, RHP.

48. Oestereich interview; statement by Dean George W. Peck, February 23, 1968, JOP.

49. "Youth Leader Defends Position on Refusal to Enter Armed Forces," *Fitchburg Sentinel*, March 1, 1968, 16; Oestereich interview.

50. "Spock's Flocks Rock!" leaflet on Mungo induction refusal, CFP.

51. "600 Back Draft Resister Here," *Boston Globe*, March 6, 1968, evening edition, 1; "600 March as Ex-BU Editor Refuses Draft," *Boston Globe*, March 7, 1968, 2; *Avatar*, no. 21, March 15–28, 1968, 1; "BU Draftee Rips up Induction Papers," *Boston Record American*, March 7, 1968, 2; "The American Ethic Must Fail," *BU News*, March 13, 1968, 10.

52. NER Newsletter, February 8, 1968, MFP; BDRG Newsletter, March 1968, BTP; "Ex-Cons Talk!" *Avatar*, no. 20, March 1–13, 1968, 7; "Ex-Cons Talk!," ibid., no. 21, March 15–28, 1968, 7; "An Interview with Louis Kampf," ibid., no. 22, March 29–April 11, 1968; Ferber and Lynd, *Resistance*, 124.

53. Putnam interview.

54. Dallek, *Flawed Giant*, 506–13; Isaacson and Thomas, *Wise Men*, 700–703; Hoopes, *Limits of Intervention*, 159–61; Harry McPherson Notes, Meeting of Advisors on Vietnam, February 27, 1968, Meeting Notes File, Box 2, LBJL.

55. Hoopes, *Limits of Intervention*, 171–81.

56. Small, *Johnson, Nixon, and the Doves*, 121–23.

57. Phil G. Goulding memo to Clark Clifford, "Possible Public Reaction to Various Alternatives," part of package: "Alternative Vietnam Strategies Back-Up Material," ca. March 2, 1968, Clifford Papers, Box 2, LBJL; Phil G. Goulding memoranda to Clark Clifford, "Problems We Can Anticipate in U.S. Public Opinion," March 4, 1968, Box 1, LBJL.

58. Townsend Hoopes memo to Clark Clifford, March 14, 1968, 8, 12, Box 1, LBJL; "The Case against Further Significant Increases in U.S. Forces in Vietnam," memo, undated, LBJL. The March 14 Hoopes memo is heavily excerpted in Hoopes, *Limits of Intervention*, 187–96.

59. Hoopes, *Limits of Intervention*, 214–18; Isaacson and Thomas, *Wise Men*, 700–703; memo from Mike Mansfield, "Reports of requests for an additional 200,000 men in Viet Nam," included in Meeting with Special Advisory Group, Cabinet Room, March 26, 1968, Meeting Notes File, Box 2, LBJL; Small, *Johnson, Nixon, and the Doves*, 147, 270 n.

60. Isaacson and Thomas, *Wise Men*, 700–703; Dallek, *Flawed Giant*, 512.

61. Editorial, BDRG Newsletter, April 1968, 2, BTP.

62. Dallek, *Flawed Giant*, 529–30.

63. Wells, *War Within*, 253; Gallup, *Gallup Poll*, 3:2114; "Johnson's Speech Fails to Divert Resistance Rallies," *BU News*, April 3, 1968, 11.

64. Ferber and Lynd, *Resistance*, 155; "Students Celebrate LBJ Move with Harvard Square Parade," *Boston Globe*, April 1, 1968, 11; "Johnson Quits; Thousands Cheer," *BU News*, April 3, 1968, 1; Michael Ferber, remarks at 30th anniversary reunion of Boston draft resistance, Arlington Street Church, October 18, 1997.

65. "Foes Hold Anti-Viet Protest on Common," *Boston Globe*, April 3, 1968, evening edition, 6; "Common Mobbed; 235 Turn in Draft Cards," *Boston Globe*, April 4, 1968, 2; Ferber and Lynd, *Resistance*, 222; Ferber speech on Common, FBI Memo, April 25, 1968, File Boston 25–25171, Exhibit, *U.S. v. Coffin et al.*, CR-68-1, CFDCR; Thorne, "Resisting the Draft," 149–50. Ferber and Lynd contend that more than 500 cards were turned in; I have not been able to corroborate that figure. Contemporaneous Resistance statistics put the number at "more than 200."

66. "Johnson's Speech Fails to Divert Resistance Rallies," 11.

CHAPTER EIGHT

1. Stone interview, March 28, 1997.

2. "Card Turn-In Opposes Racism," *Resistance*, April 8, 1968, 1; Robertson interview, August 7, 1998.

3. "Roxbury Riot Prevented," *Resistance*, May 1, 1968, 2, RCP; Stone interview, March 28, 1997; Kugelmass interview; Hunt interview.

4. "15,000 March Here—Mostly White," *Boston Globe*, April 5, 1968, 10; "Anti-Draft Group Calls for Student-Faculty Strike," ibid., April 8, 1968, 3.

5. "Anti-Draft Group Calls for Student-Faculty Strike," 3; "Card Turn-In Opposes Racism," 1; Shapiro interview.

6. Martin Luther King Jr., "A Testament of Hope," originally published in *Playboy* 16 (January 1969), reprinted in Washington, *Testament of Hope*, 315; Jim Havelin, "When I Heard the News," *Resistance*, April 6, 1968, 6, RCP.

7. "King Dies," *Resistance*, April 8, 1968, 1, RCP; Resist Newsletter No. 12, June 1968, Series 2, Box 28, BSP.

8. "23 Arrested in So. End Protest," *Boston Globe*, April 27, 1968, 1; Hohler interview.

9. Avorn et al., *Up against the Ivy Wall*; Terry Anderson, *Movement and the Sixties*, 199.

10. There are several good books on the tumultuous year of 1968. For descriptions of events in Europe, I have relied especially on two: Fraser, ed., *1968*, 203–30, and Caute, *Year of the Barricades*, 81–85, 185–210, 211–58. In addition, see Herbert Marcuse, "On the French Revolt," *Boston Free Press*, no. 5, p. 5, AJP.

11. "562 GIs Killed—Worst Week," *Boston Globe*, May 17, 1968, 1; "One-Man Picketer, Mlot-Mroz, Critically Stabbed in Roxbury," *Boston Globe*, May 10, 1968, evening edition, 1.

12. "To the Union des Etudiants Français at the Liberated Sorbonne," telegram to

French students from the Resistance, reprinted in *Boston Free Press*, first edition (c. late May 1968), 7, RCP.

13. Putnam interview.

14. "A Manifesto: The Resistance and the Draft," *Boston Free Press*, first edition (c. late May 1968), 2, RCP. For more on existential impulses in the New Left, see Rossinow, *Politics of Authenticity*.

15. Field interview.

16. Daniel P. Juda, "The Draft a Rallying Point for N.E. Resistance Group," *Boston Sunday Globe*, June 2, 1968.

17. "Two War Resisters Get Church Asylum," *Boston Globe*, May 20, 1968, evening edition, 1; "Anti-War Pair Spend Second Day Sheltered in Church," ibid., May 21, 1968, 15; "'I Know They Will Be Coming . . . I Know I Will Be Going to Jail,'" ibid., May 24, 1968, 27. For a fuller description of the Arlington Street sanctuary and subsequent Boston-area sanctuaries, see Foley, "Sanctuary!"

18. Moser, *New Winter Soldiers*, 75–77; Resist Newsletter No. 14, July 29, 1968, 8, BSP.

19. Mendelsohn interview; Ralph W. Conant, "Report of the Chairman of the Prudential Committee to the Annual Meeting of the Corporation," June 12, 1968, ASCA.

20. Joseph M. Harvey, "Talmanson Used Ancient Tradition in Seeking Sanctuary in Church," *Boston Globe*, May 26, 1968, 28; Victor Jokel, "The Meaning of Asylum," *Resistance*, June 15, 1968, 4, RCP.

21. "Anti-War Pair Spend Second Day Sheltered in Church," *Boston Globe*, May 21, 1968, 15; "Pair in Church 'Sanctuary' Say Next Move up to U.S.," ibid., May 22, 1968, 15; Kugelmass interview.

22. "Deserter, Card Burner in Church," *Boston Globe*, May 21, 1968, 9; "Anti-War Pair Spend Second Day Sheltered in Church," 15; "Pair in Church 'Sanctuary' Say Next Move up to U.S.," 15; "Police Haul Draft Resister from Church," ibid., May 23, 1968, 1; "Entire 4 Hour Melee Detailed by 2 Reporters," *Boston Globe*, May 24, 1968, 27; Keith Maillard, "Confrontation," *Boston Free Press*, third edition, 6–7, AJP.

23. "Police Haul Draft Resister from Church," 1; "Globe Reporter Saw Clash from Start to Finish," *Boston Globe*, May 23, 1968, 11; "Draft Resister Lost in Poetry," ibid., 2; "Entire 4 Hour Melee Detailed by 2 Reporters," 27; Maillard, "Confrontation," 6–7; Harris interview by Navias, ASCA Oral History Project; "Participant Accounts," *Boston Free Press*, third edition, 8.

24. Phillips interview; Arlook interview; Tilton interview.

25. Arlene Croce, "The Boston Happening," *National Review*, June 18, 1968, 602.

26. "Can We Keep Our Cool?" editorial, *Boston Globe*, May 24, 1968, 20.

27. *U.S. v. O'Brien*, 391 U.S. 367 (1968); O'Brien interview.

28. *U.S. v. O'Brien*, 391 U.S. 367 (1968); "Draft Card Burning Upheld As Crime in 7-1 Court Ruling," *Boston Globe*, May 27, 1968, evening edition, 1.

29. Croce, "Boston Happening," 601; "Chase Gives Up; Promised Mental Aid," *Boston Globe*, May 30, 1968, 17; "NER Position Paper," undated (c. January 1969), BTP; Mendelsohn interview; Minutes, Special Meeting of the Prudential Committee, May 28, 1968, ASCA; George Whitehouse, interview with Joan Goodwin, May

16, 1994, ASCA Oral History Project, 17; Ralph W. Conant, "Report of the Chairman of the Prudential Committee to the Annual Meeting of the Corporation," June 12, 1968, ASCA; Arlook interview.

30. The few things that have been written about the trial are contradictory. Tom Wells argues that the trial was good for the movement because of the media coverage, which gave "wide and sympathetic play to the defendants' views" (*War Within*, 233). Charles DeBenedetti, on the other hand, argues that "neither the trial nor the conviction of Spock, Coffin, Ferber, and Goodman, aroused much interest" (*American Ordeal*, 222). Both of Spock's biographers devoted an entire chapter to the trial but largely recapitulate Mitford's view of the event (Bloom, *Dr. Spock*, and Maier, *Dr. Spock*). The trial receives very brief mention in Zaroulis and Sullivan, *Who Spoke Up?* (see p. 173), and briefer mention in Unger, *Movement* (see p. 192). Even though many observers interpreted the Spock trial as a personal clash between Lyndon Johnson and Spock (a former supporter of the president), Melvin Small (*Johnson, Nixon, and the Doves*) writes nothing about the trial in his book about the impact of the antiwar movement on the Johnson and Nixon administrations. Likewise, the following syntheses and national narratives of the period also ignore the trial completely: Powers, *Vietnam*; Wittner, *Rebels against War*; Matusow, *Unraveling of America*; Miller, *Democracy Is in the Streets*; Gitlin, *Sixties*; Blum, *Years of Discord*; Farber, *Age of Great Dreams*; Small, *Covering Dissent*; Burner, *Making Peace with the 60s*; Terry Anderson, *Movement and the Sixties*; and Terry Anderson, *Sixties*.

31. Dellinger, *From Yale to Jail*, 342–43; Dellinger, *More Power Than We Know*, 106, 230–31; Kunstler, *My Life as a Radical Lawyer*, 22.

32. For a fuller account and analysis of the Spock trial, see Foley, "Confronting the Johnson Administration at War."

33. Mitford, *Trial of Dr. Spock*, 76–77; Wells, *War Within*, 232–33.

34. Joseph Sax, "The Trial," *Michigan Daily*, June 4, 1968, reprinted in Resist Newsletter No. 13, July 1968, 4, Box 28, BSP; Mitford, *Trial of Dr. Spock*, 76–77; Ferber interview, June 16, 1998.

35. Mitford, *Trial of Dr. Spock*, 78–84; Ferber interview, June 16, 1998; Coffin interview.

36. See records of *U.S. v. Coffin et al.*, CR-68-1, CFDCR; Ferber interview, June 16, 1998; and Mitford, *Trial of Dr. Spock*, 82.

37. Croce, "Boston Happening," 602; Wall interview.

38. *Meet the Press* transcripts, February 28, 1968; Ferber speech, January 11, 1968, and Spock speech, April 22, 1968, Spock FBI Files; Mitford, *Trial of Dr. Spock*, 169; "Courthouse's Squeaky Wheels of Justice Recalled," *Boston Globe*, August 23, 1998, B4.

39. Mitford, *Trial of Dr. Spock*, 91.

40. Ibid., 97–99.

41. See transcripts of *U.S. v. Coffin et al.*, CR-68-1, CFDCR; Mitford, *Trial of Dr. Spock*, 96–134; Daniel Lang, "The Trial of Dr. Spock," *The New Yorker*, September 7, 1968, 48.

42. "Closing Argument to the Jury by Mr. Wall," *U.S. v. Coffin et al.*, CR-68-1, transcript of trial, vol. 18, 93, 96, 98–100.

43. *U.S. v. Coffin et al.*, CR-68-1, transcript of trial; "Coffin Outlines Protest Goals," *Boston Globe*, May 31, 1968, evening edition, 6; Mitford, *Trial of Dr. Spock*, 139.

44. *U.S. v. Coffin et al.*, CR-68-1, transcript of trial.

45. Coffin interview.

46. Wall interview.

47. Lang, "Trial of Dr. Spock," 53.

48. "Dr. Spock, on Stand, Says He Saw Viet as Disaster," *Boston Globe*, June 10, 1968, evening edition, 1, 24; "Spock, Testifying First Time, Calls War Illegal," *NYT*, June 11, 1968, 10; see also Mitford, *Trial of Dr. Spock*, 170–75.

49. Zaroulis and Sullivan, *Who Spoke Up?*, 173; see also Matthews, "Spock Trial Was a Timid Affair," *Harvard Summer News*, July 12, 1968, 1, 4, which said, "[T]he proceedings were slowly paced and made little splash in the news after the first few days." In *Trial of Dr. Spock* (204), Mitford says, "Nationwide, newspaper coverage of the trial had been slim." On the press and the Vietnam War, see Wyatt, *Paper Soldiers*. On the press and the antiwar movement, see Small, *Covering Dissent*, and Gitlin, *Whole World Is Watching*.

50. *U.S. v. Coffin et al.*, CR-68-1, transcript of trial, vol. 18, 108–9, 113, 118.

51. *U.S. v. Coffin et al.*, CR-68-1, transcript of trial; Mitford, *Trial of Dr. Spock*, 182–84.

52. "Spock, 3 Others Guilty; 1 Acquitted," *Boston Globe*, June 15, 1968, 1; "Mistaken Identity for Raskin?" ibid., 3; Mitford, *Trial of Dr. Spock*, 196–206; Clark interviews, January 6, 1998, and April 29, 1998; Wall interview; "Spock, 3 Others Sentenced to 2 Years," *Boston Globe*, evening edition, 1, 3; Mitford, *Trial of Dr. Spock*, 208–9.

CHAPTER NINE

1. "Resistance and the Panthers," *Resistance*, undated (c. August 15, 1968), 7, RCP.

2. "Hippies Draw Fines for Defying Curfew," *Boston Globe*, July 22, 1968, evening edition, 3; "Judge Chastises, Penalizes Hippies," ibid., July 23, 1968, 1.

3. "Resistance and the Panthers."

4. Ferber and Lynd, *Resistance*, 224–25.

5. Shapiro interview; Larry Berren et al., "The Resistor," unpublished paper, undated (c. July 1968), MFP.

6. Jim Oestereich, "The Black Panthers, P.F.P., and the Movement," *Resistance*, undated (c. August 15, 1968), 7, RCP.

7. Berren et al., "Resistor"; Oestereich, "Black Panthers, P.F.P., and the Movement."

8. Joel Kugelmass, "Electoral Politics: The Art of Retaining Power," *Resistance*, undated (c. August 15, 1968), 5, RCP.

9. Hunt interview.

10. "Proposed Basic Theory, Strategy and Organization for the New England Resistance," paper presented at NER general membership meeting, October 18, 1968, BTP.

11. Dan Tilton, "Socialism and Human Freedom," *Resistance*, October 1968, 8, RCP.

12. Terry Anderson, *Movement and the Sixties*, 202.

13. "Multi-Issue," *Resistance*, undated (c. August 15, 1968), 2, RCP.

14. New England Resistance letter re: the Free School, undated (c. early July 1968), MFP; Mary Fenstermacher, "Transcendence: NER Free School," *Resistance*, undated (c. August 15, 1968), 8, RCP; Joel Kugelmass, "Free School," *Boston Free Press*, undated (c. July 11, 1968), 12, RCP; Olene and Dan Tilton interview.

15. Wright interview; Hector interview; Rossinow, *Politics of Authenticity*, 249; Neil Robertson, "Hippies and the New Left," *Resistance*, undated (c. August 15, 1968), 6, RCP.

16. Gitlin, *Sixties*, 238–41; "Up against the Wall, Mother Fucker," *Boston Free Press*, 8th edition, undated (c. August 1, 1968), 7, AJP.

17. Harris interview by Navias, October 27, 1994, ASCA Oral History Project; Thorne, "Resisting the Draft," 83; Robertson interview, August 7, 1998; Shapiro interview.

18. "CARS Mechanics," newsletter no. 2, undated (c. July 20, 1968), BTP. Indeed, the issue of complacency regarding the war faced most peace organizations as they entered the summer of 1968; Lyndon Johnson's announcement that he would not seek reelection created in many Americans a false sense that the war's end would come soon.

19. "Concord-Summer, 1968," newsletter, undated (c. June 1968), BTP.

20. Starr interview; "Concord Area Resistance Summer Activities," in "Concord-Summer, 1968," BTP; "CARS Mechanics," vol. 1, no. 4, undated (c. July 1968), BTP.

21. "CARS Mechanics," vol. 1, no. 4, BTP; "CARS Mechanics," vol. 1, no. 5, undated (c. September 1968), BTP; Starr interview.

22. Starr interview; "CARS Mechanics," vol. 1, nos. 2, 4, and 5, BTP.

23. "The Resistance: Audacious System to Beat the System," *Boston Globe*, July 2, 1968; NER Newsletter, January 1969, MFP; Arlook interview.

24. NER Newsletters, January 1969 and February–March 1969, MFP; Arlook interview.

25. Arlook interview; Robertson interview, August 24, 1997.

26. The image of antiwar protesters spitting on returning veterans has recently been challenged persuasively in Jerry Lembcke, *Spitting Image*. Lembcke, a Vietnam veteran and a sociologist at the College of the Holy Cross argues that not one single instance of an antiwar protester spitting on a veteran has ever been convincingly documented.

27. See Appy, *Working-Class War*, 223–24, 298–99, 301–6.

28. Resist Newsletters Nos. 14 and 15, July 29, 1968, and August 27, 1968, Series 2, Box 28, BSP; "Support Your American Way of Life," *WIN*, October 1, 1968, 11, AJP.

29. Nan Stone, "GI Support Speech," undated, Stone Papers, copy in author's files.

30. Stone, "GI Support Speech." For an insightful discussion of the various factors contributing to GI resentment of antiwar protesters, see Appy, *Working-Class War*, 299–306.

31. For a fuller description and analysis of the sanctuaries in Boston, see Foley, "Sanctuary!"

32. Harvard Divinity School Press Release, September 22, 1968, MFP.

33. Ibid.; NER press release, September 22, 1968, MFP.

34. "Marine Seeks Sanctuary at Harvard Divinity," *Boston Globe*, September 23, 1968, 1; "Harvard Silent on Sanctuary," ibid., September 24, 1968, 1; "Marine Explains Why He Dropped Out," ibid., September 24, 1968, 7.

35. "Marine Explains Why He Dropped Out," 7.

36. "Marine Seeks Sanctuary at Harvard Divinity," 1; Harvard Divinity School Press Release, September 22, 1968, MFP.

37. "Military Seize AWOL Marine in Harvard Divinity Chapel," *Boston Globe*, September 24, 1968, evening edition, 1; "Police Arrest Olimpieri, Who Condemns Students," *Harvard Crimson*, September 25, 1968, 1.

38. "Sanctuary Marine Says He's All Wrong," *Boston Globe*, September 25, 1968, 1.

39. "Police Arrest Olimpieri," 1. Despite several attempts to contact him through his family, I have been unable to locate Paul Olimpieri to get his side of the story.

40. "Marsh Chapel Held as Draft Sanctuary," *BU News*, October 2, 1968, 3, 9; "20 Sympathizers Protect AWOL Soldier in Sanctuary at B.U.," *Boston Globe*, October 2, 1968, evening edition, 5.

41. "Marsh Chapel Held as Draft Sanctuary," 3, 9.

42. "20 Sympathizers Protect AWOL Soldier in Sanctuary at B.U.," 5; "Marsh Chapel Held as Draft Sanctuary," 13, 9; "Marine Recants Statements Made during BU Sanctuary," *Boston Globe*, October 5, 1968, 21.

43. "Marine Recants Statements Made during BU Sanctuary," 21.

44. Thorne interview.

45. "Marsh Chapel Held as Draft Sanctuary," 3, 9; "20 Sympathizers Protect AWOL Soldier in Sanctuary at B.U.," 5; "B.U. Sanctuary Continues for Soldier," *Boston Globe*, October 3, 1968, 3; "500 Keep B.U. Vigil Awaiting GI Arrest," *Boston Globe*, October 4, 1968, evening edition, 2; Zinn interview.

46. "Asked for a Warrant, They Just Stepped over Me," *BU News*, October 9, 1968, 3, 8; "AWOL Soldier Seized at BU," *Boston Globe*, October 7, 1968, 3.

47. Alex Jack, "The Politics of Confrontation," *BU News*, October 9, 1968, A2–A3.

48. "Cultural Revolution at School of Theology," *Up against the Cross*, no. 1 (November 1968), AJP; Jack interview; "Kroll, AWOL GI of BU Sanctuary, Gets 3 Months Hard Labor," *Old Mole*, November 5, 1968, 3.

49. "It Had Salami and Donuts, but Spirit Sustained Chapel," *BU News*, October 9, 1968, A4; "A Sense of Responsibility," Resist Newsletter No. 18, October 28, 1968, 2, MZP.

50. Nelkin, *University and Military Research*, 20; 1969 statistics cited in Heineman, *Campus Wars*, 13.

51. Michael Klare, ed., *University-Military Complex: A Directory and Related Documents* (New York: North American Congress on Latin America, 1969), 13; Steve Shalom Papers (copy in author's files); Nelkin, *University and Military Research*, 48.

52. Noam Chomsky, "The Cold War and the University," in Chomsky et al.,

Cold War and the University, 181; Shalom interview; Chomsky interview; Kampf interview.

53. "Students Guard GI at MIT," *Boston Globe*, October 30, 1968, 47; "12 Days of Sanctuary at MIT," Resist Newsletter, December 2, 1968, 1, RSP; Shapiro interview.

54. Members of the MIT Resistance probably would not have met with much success if they *had* organized the sanctuary in the beautiful but very small chapel on campus. Designed in 1955 by the eminent architect Eero Saarinen, the Kresge Chapel is located not far from the student center but could have housed fewer than 100 people comfortably.

55. "12 Days of Sanctuary at MIT," 1; Shapiro interview.

56. "Statement of Jack M. O'Connor," undated (c. October 29, 1968), RSP; Resist Newsletter, December 20, 1968, 8, Box 28, BSP.

57. "12 Days of Sanctuary at MIT," 1; "Sala Sanctuary Established," *The Tech* (MIT), November 1, 1968, 1; Bill Berry, "Am I a Slave?" *Old Mole*, November 5, 1968, 5; Shapiro interview; Kampf interview.

58. "12 Days of Sanctuary at MIT," 1; "O'Connor's Sanctuary Ends," *The Tech*, November 8, 1968, 1; "Six-Day MIT Sanctuary Ends Quietly without Bust," *Harvard Crimson*, November 4, 1968, 1; Shapiro interview.

59. "Sanctuary Terminated by Arrest," *The Tech*, November 12, 1968, 1; Neil Robertson, "The Politics of Sanctuary," November 1968, 8, RCP; O'Connor sentence described in "Up against the *Wall Street Journal*," April 16, 1969, 15, RSP; Shapiro interview.

60. Chomsky interview; Berry, "Am I a Slave?" 5.

61. NER Newsletters, January 1969, February–March 1969, MFP. The Brandeis sanctuary for Sp/4 John Rollins, AWOL from Ft. Clayton, Panama, began on December 4 and lasted two weeks. On December 19, Rollins and the sanctuary community dissolved the sanctuary and went to Ft. Devens to distribute leaflets to GIs. Military police arrested Rollins there.

62. NER Newsletters, January 1969, February–March 1969, MFP; Stone interview, October 8, 1997; Kugelmass interview; Shapiro interview. In some ways, the Resistance began duplicating the Boston Draft Resistance Group's GI outreach program; the BDRG, for example, had been distributing *Vietnam GI* at bus stations since the summer of 1968.

63. Kugelmass interview; Stone interview, October 8, 1997; Tiltons interview; Robertson interview, August 7, 1998.

64. Stone interview, October 8, 1997; Kugelmass interview.

65. "A Year of Support," SUPPORT Newsletter, August 1969, 1, MZP; Zigmond interview.

66. Zigmond interview.

67. Ibid.

68. "A Guide for Indictees and Counselors," SUPPORT leaflet, March 1969, 2, MZP; "Draft Refusal Indictments Coming," *Old Mole*, September 12–22, 1969, 17; "Thirty-Six Men Indicted Since August," SUPPORT Newsletter, November 25, 1968, 1, MZP; "A Year of Support," ibid., August 1969, 1–2.

69. "Draft Refusal Indictments Coming," 17; "Year of Support," 2, MZP; Zigmond interview.

70. "Local Support Efforts," SUPPORT Newsletter, December 2, 1968, 2, MZP; Mr. & Mrs. William F. Curry letter to Michael Zigmond, January 20, 1970, MZP.

71. Wall interview.

72. Thorne, "Resisting the Draft," 124; Ferber and Lynd, *Resistance*, 282; written comment, Respondent no. 42, 1997 Boston Draft Resistance Survey, author's files; Clennon interview, June 12, 1997; written comment, Respondent no. 31, 1997 Boston Draft Resistance Survey, author's files.

73. Clennon interview, June 12, 1997; Etscovitz interview.

74. A good summary of the chronology of the *Oestereich* case is given in Arant, "Government Use of the Draft," 147–71.

75. *Oestereich v. Selective Service*, 393 U.S. at 237.

76. Flynn, *Louis B. Hershey*, 267.

77. Oestereich interview; "Oestereich Decision," SUPPORT Newsletter, January 16, 1969, MZP.

78. *Gutknecht v. U.S.*, 393 U.S. 295.

79. *Breen v. Selective Service Board No. 16*, 393 U.S. 460.

80. Sisson interview; *U.S. v. Sisson*, 294 F. Supp. 511.

81. *U.S. v. Sisson*, 294 F. Supp. 511. In some ways, Wyzanski's decision echoed an earlier Supreme Court decision in the case of *U.S. v. Seeger*, 380 U.S. 163 (1965), in which the court held that Seeger, an atheist, could not be denied conscientious objector status because he did not belong to one of the religious groups outlined in the Selective Service law. Wyzanski's decision differed from the *Seeger* decision in that it allowed for *selective* conscientious objection; that is, a registrant could decide which wars to fight in and which not to.

82. Of the thirty men who refused induction who completed the 1997 survey, eighteen were not prosecuted. Three of the remaining men prosecuted were acquitted, and the cases of the other four men were dismissed.

83. Statistics cited in Baskir and Strauss, *Chance and Circumstance*, 69.

84. O'Brien interview; Hicks interview; "Ex-Cons Talk!" *Avatar*, no. 20, March 1–13, 1968, 7; Gaylin, *In the Service of Their Country*, 25–28.

85. David Stoppelman interview; Hicks interview; Gaylin, *In the Service of Their Country*, 330.

86. Hicks interview; "Ex-Cons Talk!" 7.

87. Brustein interview; Hicks interview; Phillips interview.

88. Brustein interview; Hicks interview.

89. Hicks interview; Brustein interview. For a more complete analysis of war resisters' prison experiences, see Gaylin, *In the Service of Their Country*.

90. Michael Ferber letter to supporters, August 1968, MFP; NER Newsletter, January 1969, MFP.

91. Thorne, "Resisting the Draft"; Kurland Lagos interview; Stone interview, March 28, 1997; Robertson interview, August 7, 1998.

EPILOGUE

1. Zaroulis and Sullivan, *Who Spoke Up?*, 269, 271–72; see also DeBenedetti, *American Ordeal*, 255, 257, for a similar assessment.

2. Nixon, *No More Vietnams*, 102, 125. In addition to reforming and ending the draft, the Nixon administration used the CIA illegally and the FBI unethically in infiltrating the antiwar movement with the aim of destroying it. See Flynn, *Draft*, 237, and Churchill and Vander Wall, *COINTELPRO Papers*.

3. Flynn, *Draft*, 243.

4. Donald Rumsfeld to Peter Flanigan, November 25, 1968, WHCF, FG 216, SSS, Box 1, NPM; HR Haldeman to Peter Flanigan, April 28, 1969, WHCF, FG 216, SSS, Box 1, NPM; John Campbell memo to Egil Krogh, September 18, 1969, WHSF, Krogh, Box 57, "Youth" folder, 1 of 5, NPM.

5. Peter Flanigan to Arthur Burns and John Ehrlichman, April 26, 1969, WHCF, FG 216, SSS, Box 1, NPM; see also Flynn, *Draft*, 239, and Moynihan to Nixon, August 19, 1969, WHSF, Klein, Box 5, NPM. Some members of the Nixon administration were concerned that the draft lottery rollout would *feed* the protests. One aide wrote, "Let's appraise the initial reactions of students to our program before we risk the lives of members of the Administration by sending them on to campuses to explain it. This could be very dangerous" (Tod Hullin to Egil Krogh, September 17, 1969, WHSF, Krogh, Box 57, "Youth" folder, 1 of 5, NPM).

6. 120 of 185 (64.9 percent) survey respondents said they "remained active in antiwar movement" immediately after the draft resistance movement ended. In addition, 142 of 184 (77.2 percent) activists said that they were at least "somewhat involved" in "other Vietnam antiwar movement activities" (see Table A.25). It follows that at least two-thirds of the former draft resistance community remained active in protesting against the war.

7. Williams actually carried out her first draft board raid in June 1968, during the Spock trial, at Boston's Customs House with Frank Femia, another CNVA member, aided by John Phillips. Phillips later achieved further renown as a member of the so-called Chicago 15, when he joined Philip Berrigan in a massive nighttime raid of Chicago's Selective Service offices. Williams served a year and a half in prison and Phillips spent two and a half years in prison for their actions.

8. Zaroulis and Sullivan, *Who Spoke Up?*, 315.

9. Respondent no. 71, 1997 Boston Draft Resistance Survey.

10. DuBois interview, June 11, 1997; Field interview; Katz interview; Kurland Lagos interview; Stone interview, March 28, 1997; Thorne interview.

11. Arlook interview; Robertson interview, August 24, 1997.

12. Eight (4.3 percent) out of 185 respondents said .they joined PL after their resistance days (1997 Boston Draft Resistance Survey).

13. Marston interview; Von Rosenvinge interview.

14. Thirty-two (31 percent) of 103 anarchists, socialists, and communists among the population now consider themselves liberal Democrats.

15. The mean for each level of involvement was calculated only for the causes and social movements listed in Table A.24, save the Moral Majority and Christian Coalition (which, between them, attracted only one person from this group). The

mean for "very involved" is 9.67; for "moderately involved," 15.86; and for "somewhat involved," 33.24.

16. Respondent no. 56, 1997 Boston Draft Resistance Survey.

17. Respondent no. 164; ibid.; Jupin interview; Respondent no. 126, 1997 Boston Draft Resistance Survey.

18. Respondent no. 33, ibid.

19. Respondent no. 79, ibid.

20. Respondent no. 83, ibid.

21. Respondent no. 99, ibid.

22. Kohn, *Jailed for Peace*, 142; Baskir and Strauss, *Chance and Circumstance*, 67.

23. Flynn, *Draft*, 181, 236.

24. A January 1969 Gallup Poll found that 62 percent of Americans thought the draft should continue after the Vietnam War ended and that only 32 percent favored the idea of an all-volunteer force (Flynn, *Draft*, 237).

25. Martin Anderson to John Ehrlichman, "Decision Memorandum on All-Volunteer Force and Draft Reform," March 31, 1970, WHCF: SMOF, Anderson, Box 37, "Task Force," NPM; Anderson to John Erhlichman, July 13, 1970, ibid.

26. 150 (87.7 percent) of 171 respondents disagreed. Only four agreed strongly (1997 Boston Draft Resistance Survey).

27. Respondent nos. 1, 19, 40, 53, 61, 73, 82, 93, 121, 132, 144, 146, 151, 155, 157, 160, 169, 178, ibid.

28. Powers, *Vietnam*, xv; Garfinkle, *Telltale Hearts*.

29. Respondent no. 19, 1997 Boston Draft Resistance Survey; Respondent no. 59, ibid.

30. Chomsky interview.

31. Venn interview; Mungo, *Beyond the Revolution*; Stoppelman interview; Von Rosenvinge interview.

32. Oestereich interview; Bishop interview; Respondent no. 60, 1997 Boston Draft Resistance Survey.

33. Penney Kurland Lagos, e-mail to author, February 25, 1999; Bischoff interview.

BIBLIOGRAPHY

MANUSCRIPT COLLECTIONS

Arlington Street Church Archives. Arlington Street Church, Boston, Mass.

William Bischoff Papers. Personal collection.

Fred Bird Papers. Personal collection.

The Reverend Jack Bishop Papers. Personal collection.

New England Committee for Non-Violent Action Papers. Swarthmore College
   Peace Collection, Swarthmore, Pa.
      Boston Folder

The Reverend John Boyles Papers. Personal collection.

Robert Chalfen Papers. Personal collection.

Michael Colpitts Papers. Personal collection.

Michael Ferber Papers. Personal collection.

Charles S. Fisher Papers. Personal collection
   (now deposited at Swarthmore College).

Richard Hughes Papers. Personal collection.

James D. Hunt Papers. Personal collection.

Alex Jack Papers. Personal collection.

Lyndon Baines Johnson Presidential Library, Austin, Tex.
   Joseph Califano Papers
   Warren Christopher Papers
   Ramsey Clark Papers
   Clark Clifford Papers
   Tom Johnson's Meeting Notes (used by permission)
   John W. Macy Jr. Papers
   Meeting Notes File
   National Security—Defense Files
   White House Central Files

Howard Marston Jr. Papers. Personal collection.

Richard Nixon Presidential Materials. National Archives, College Park, Md.
   National Security Council Files
   White House Central Files
         Commission on All-Volunteer Armed Forces
         Department of Defense
         National Security–Defense
         Selective Service System
         Staff Member and Office Files
               Martin Anderson Papers

White House Special Files
  Staff Member and Office Files
    John Erhlichman Papers
    Peter M. Flanigan Papers
    H. R. Haldeman Papers
    Herbert Klein Papers
    Egil Krogh Jr. Papers
James Oestereich Papers. Personal collection.
David Satz Papers. Personal collection.
Robert Shapiro Papers. Personal collection.
Benjamin Spock FBI Files. Author's files.
Benjamin Spock Papers. Bird Library, Syracuse University, Syracuse, N.Y.
Nan Stone Papers. Personal collection.
Barrie Thorne Papers, 1967–early 1970s, Michigan State University Library, East Lansing, Mich.
Michael Zigmond Papers. Personal collection.

ORAL HISTORY INTERVIEWS CONDUCTED BY AUTHOR

Anonymous Female #1, October 9, 1997.
Ira Arlook, August 12, 1998, by telephone.
William Bischoff, January 5, 1998.
Rev. John Bishop, December 11, 1997.
Rick Bogel, August 22, 2001, by telephone.
Robert Bruen, August 13, 1997.
Daniel Brustein, December 30, 1997, by telephone.
Noam Chomsky, May 20, 1997.
Ramsey Clark, January 6, 1998; April 29, 1998, by telephone.
David Clennon, June 12, 1997; June 17, 1998, by telephone.
William Clusin, June 17, 1997.
Rev. William Sloane Coffin Jr., August 28, 1997.
Michael Colpitts, April 6, 1997.
William Dowling, August 2, 2001.
Ellen DuBois, June 11, 1997; November 27, 2000, by telephone.
Roxanne Dunbar-Ortiz, October 15, 1997, by telephone.
Lawrence Etscovitz, August 12, 1997.
Janine Fay, December 1, 2000, by telephone.
Michael Ferber, February 10, 1997; April 21, 1998; June 16, 1998.
Connie Field, June 17, 1997.
Mark Gerzon, July 18, 1997, by telephone.
Alexandra (a.k.a. Sasha) Harmon, October 14, 1997, by telephone.
Harold Hector, April 9, 1997.
Hilde Hein, September 18, 1998.
Gary Hicks, December 7, 1997.
G. Robert Hohler, December 11, 1997.
Richard Hughes, January 7, 1998.

William Hunt, October 31, 1997, by telephone.

Alex Jack, March 21, 1997.

Rev. J. Michael Jupin, December 28, 1997, by telephone.

Louis Kampf, September 10, 1998.

Sue Katz, March 2, 1999, by telephone.

Joel Kugelmass, June 16, 1997.

Penney Kurland Lagos, February 21, 1999, by telephone.

Paul Lauter, June 12, 1998.

Howard Marston Jr. and Deborah Jelmberg, December 13, 1997.

Bliss Matteson, August 29, 1997.

Allegra May, August 12, 1997.

John McDonough, June 3, 1998, by telephone.

Rev. Jack Mendelsohn, December 19, 1997.

Ray Mungo, June 13, 1997.

David O'Brien, July 3, 2001.

James Oestereich, December 20, 1997, by telephone.

John Phillips, August 29, 1997, by telephone.

Rosemary Poole, December 4, 2000, by telephone.

Hilary Putnam, December 18, 1997.

Neil Robertson, August 24, 1997; December 22, 1997, by telephone; August 7, 1998,
    by telephone.

Lawrence Rossini, September 5, 1997.

Peter Schenck, December 2, 2000, by telephone.

Steve Shalom, May 18, 1997.

Robert Shapiro, August 13, 1997.

John Sisson, July 13, 1998.

Susan Starr, August 4, 1997.

Nan Stone, March 28, 1997; October 8, 1997, by telephone.

David Stoppelman, December 8, 1997.

Barrie Thorne, October 28, 1997, by telephone.

Daniel and Olene Tilton, June 16, 1997.

John Van de Kamp, June 9, 1998, by telephone.

Christopher Venn, June 12, 1997.

Jannik von Rosenvinge, October 8, 1997, by telephone.

John Wall, June 26, 1998.

Xenia (née Suzanne) Williams, August 28, 1997.

Timothy Wright, August 25, 1997.

Michael and Naomi Zigmond, December 29, 1997.

Howard Zinn, July 6, 1998.

UNRECORDED TELEPHONE CONVERSATIONS WITH AUTHOR

Kathy Bower, July 27, 1998.

Ramsey Clark, March 13, 1996.

Joan Dehmlow, September 16, 1998.

Jean Kirkland, September 11, 1998.
Stanley Moss, February 24, 1998.
Edward Risden Jr., July 24, 1998.

OTHER ORAL HISTORY SOURCES

Arlington Street Church Oral History Project, Boston, Mass.
    W. Edward Harris. Interview by Eugene Navias, October 27, 1994.
    Jack Mendelsohn. Interview by Ann Friend, February 29, 1992.
    Karl Dan Sorensen. Interview by Carolyn Harrigan, December 1, 1993.
    George Whitehouse. Interview by Joan Goodwin, May 16, 1994
Lyndon Johnson Presidential Library, Austin, Tex.
    Lewis Hershey. Interview by Harry B. Middleton, December 15, 1970.
    Joseph Califano. Interviewed by Michael Gillette, January 5, 1988. Personal
       Papers of Joseph Califano, Box 131

NEWSPAPERS

Avatar, Boston, Mass., various issues, 1967–68
Boston Globe, Boston, Mass., 1965–69
Boston Herald Traveler, Boston, Mass., 1965–69
Boston Record American, Boston, Mass., 1965–69
Broadside and Free Press, Boston, Mass., various issues, 1968–69
BU (Boston University) News, Boston, Mass., 1966–69
Harvard Crimson, Cambridge, Mass., 1966–69
New York Times, New York, N.Y., 1965–69
The Old Mole, Boston, Mass., various issues, 1968–69
The Resistance, Boston, Mass., various issues, 1968–69
The Tech (MIT), Cambridge, Mass., fall 1968

CASE FILES, U.S. DISTRICT COURT RECORDS, NATIONAL ARCHIVES, WALTHAM, MASS.

United States v. William Sloane Coffin, Jr., Michael Ferber, Mitchell Goodman, Marcus Raskin, and Benjamin Spock.
United States v. Peter Crews.
United States v. Gary Hicks.
United States v. Howard Marston, Jr.
United States v. David O'Brien.
United States v. John J. Phillips.
United States v. Eugene Povirk.
United States v. David Reed.
United States v. John Heffron Sisson, Jr.
United States v. David Stoppelman.
United States v. Robert Talmanson.

UNITED STATES SUPREME COURT OPINIONS

Timothy Breen v. Selective Service Board No. 16, Bridgeport, Connecticut, et al., 393
    U.S. 460 (1969).

Gutknecht v. United States, 393 U.S. 295 (1969).

James Oestereich v. Selective Service Board No. 11, Cheyenne, Wyoming, et al., 393 U.S. 234 (1968).

United States v. David O'Brien, 391 U.S. 367 (1968).

United States v. Daniel Seeger, 380 U.S. 163 (1965).

BOOKS AND ARTICLES

Alonso, Harriet Hyman. *Peace as a Women's Issue: A History of the U.S. Movement for World Peace and Women's Rights*. Syracuse: Syracuse University Press, 1993.

Anderson, Martin, ed. *The Military Draft: Selected Readings on Conscription*. Stanford, Calif.: Hoover Institution Press, 1982.

Anderson, Terry H. *The Movement and the Sixties: Protest in America from Greensboro to Wounded Knee*. New York: Oxford University Press, 1995.

——. *The Sixties*. New York: Longman, 1999.

Appy, Christian. "Give Peace Activism a Chance." *Reviews in American History* 23 (March 1995): 137–43.

——. *Working-Class War: American Combat Soldiers in Vietnam*. Chapel Hill: University of North Carolina Press, 1993.

Arant, Morgan David, Jr. "Government Use of the Draft to Silence Dissent to War: A Case of Punitive Reclassification." *Peace & Change* 17 (April 1992): 147–71.

Avorn, Jerry L., et al. *Up against the Ivy Wall: A History of the Columbia Crisis*. New York: Atheneum, 1969.

Baskir, Lawrence M., and William A. Strauss. *Chance and Circumstance: The Draft, the War and the Vietnam Generation*. New York: Knopf, 1978.

Bellow, Saul. *Dangling Man*. New York: Vanguard, 1944; New York: Penguin, 1996.

Bloom, Alexander, and Wini Breines. *Takin' It to the Streets: A Sixties Reader*. New York: Oxford University Press, 1995.

Bloom, Lynn Z. *Doctor Spock: Biography of a Conservative Radical*. Indianapolis: Bobbs-Merrill, 1972.

Blum, John Morton. *Years of Discord: American Politics and Society, 1961–1974*. New York: Norton, 1991.

Booth, Heather, Evi Goldfield, and Sue Munaker. *Toward a Radical Movement*. Boston: New England Free Press, 1968.

Breines, Wini. *Community and Organization in the New Left, 1962–1968: The Great Refusal*. New Brunswick: Rutgers University Press, 1989.

Buhle, Paul, et al. *The Encyclopedia of the American Left*. Chicago: University of Illinois Press, 1992.

Burner, David. *Making Peace with the 60s*. Princeton: Princeton University Press, 1996.

Burns, Stewart. *Social Movements of the 1960s: Searching for Democracy*. New York: Twayne, 1990.

Buzzanco, Robert. *Masters of War: Military Dissent and Politics in the Vietnam Era*. New York: Cambridge University Press, 1996.

——. *Vietnam and the Transformation of American Life*. Boston: Blackwell, 1999.

Cagan, Leslie. "Women and the Anti-Draft Movement." *Radical America*
(September/October 1980): 9–11.

Califano, Joseph. *The Triumph and Tragedy of Lyndon Johnson*. New York: Simon
and Schuster, 1991.

Camus, Albert. *The Stranger*. Translated by Matthew Ward. New York: Vintage,
1989.

Capps, Walter H. *The Unfinished War: Vietnam and the American Conscience*.
Boston: Beacon Press, 1982.

Carroll, James. *An American Requiem: God, My Father, and the War That Divided
Us*. Boston: Houghton Mifflin, 1996.

Caute, David. *The Year of the Barricades: A Journey through 1968*. New York:
Harper & Row, 1988.

Cavallo, Dominick. *A Fiction of the Past: The Sixties in American History*. New York:
St. Martin's Press, 1999.

Chambers, John Whiteclay, II. *To Raise an Army: The Draft Comes to Modern
America*. New York: Free Press, 1987.

Chapman, Bruce K. *The Wrong Man in Uniform: Our Unfair and Obsolete Draft and
How We Can Replace It*. New York: Trident Press, 1967.

Chomsky, Noam. *American Power and the New Mandarins*. New York: Pantheon,
1967.

———. *The Trials of the Resistance*. New York: New York Review, 1970.

Chomsky, Noam, et al. *The Cold War and the University: Toward an Intellectual
History of the Postwar Years*. New York: New Press, 1997.

Churchill, Ward, and Jim Vander Wall. *The COINTELPRO Papers: Documents from
the FBI's Secret Wars against Domestic Dissent*. Boston: South End Press, 1990.

Coffin, William Sloane. *Once to Every Man: A Memoir*. New York: Atheneum, 1977.

Coffin, William Sloane, and Morris I. Liebman. *Civil Disobedience: Aid or Hindrance
to Justice?* Washington, D.C.: American Enterprise Institute for Public Policy
Research, 1972.

Collier, Peter, and David Horowitz. *Destructive Generation: Second Thoughts about
the 60s*. New York: Summit Books, 1989.

Cooper, Sandi. *Patriotic Pacifism: Waging War on War in Europe, 1815–1914*. New
York: Oxford University Press, 1991.

Cortright, David. *Soldiers in Revolt: The American Military Today*. Garden City,
N.Y.: Anchor/Doubleday, 1975.

Crow, Barbara A., ed. *Radical Feminism: A Documentary Reader*. New York: New
York University Press, 2000.

Dallek, Robert. *Flawed Giant: Lyndon Johnson and His Times, 1961–1973*. New York:
Oxford University Press, 1998.

Davis, Flora. *Moving the Mountain: The Women's Movement in America Since 1960*.
New York: Simon & Schuster, 1992.

Davis, James W., Jr., and Kenneth M. Dolbeare. *Little Groups of Neighbors: The
Selective Service System*. Chicago: Markham, 1968.

DeBenedetti, Charles. *An American Ordeal: The Antiwar Movement of the Vietnam
Era*. Syracuse: Syracuse University Press, 1990.

——. "A CIA Analysis of the Anti–Vietnam War Movement: October 1967." *Peace & Change* 9, no. 1 (Spring 1983): 31–41.

DeGroot, Gerard J. "The Limits of Moral Protest and Participatory Democracy: The Vietnam Day Committee." *Pacific Historical Review* (1995): 95–119.

——. *Vietnam: A Noble Cause? America and the Vietnam War*. Essex, Eng.: Longman, 2000.

Dellinger, David. *More Power Than We Know: The People's Movement Toward Democracy*. Garden City, N.Y.: Anchor Press, 1975.

——. *From Yale to Jail: The Life Story of a Moral Dissenter*. New York: Pantheon, 1993.

Dickerson, James. *North to Canada: Men and Women against the Vietnam War*. Westport, Conn.: Praeger, 1999.

Donner, Frank J. *The Age of Surveillance: The Aims and Methods of America's Political Intelligence System*. New York: Knopf, 1980.

Dowd, Douglas. "The Strength and Limitations of Resistance." In *Witness of the Berrigans*, edited by Stephen Halpert. Garden City, N.Y.: Doubleday, 1972.

Duffet, John, ed. *Against the Crime of Silence: The Proceedings of the International War Crimes Tribunal*. New York: Simon and Schuster, 1968.

DuPlessis, Rachel Blau, and Ann Snitow. *The Feminist Memoir Project: Voices from Women's Liberation*. New York: Three Rivers Press, 1998.

Echols, Alice. *Daring to Be Bad: Radical Feminism in America, 1967–1975*. Minneapolis: University of Minnesota Press, 1989.

Elliff, John T. *Crime, Dissent, and the Attorney General: The Justice Department in the 1960s*. Beverly Hills: Sage, 1971.

Emerson, Gloria. *Winners and Losers*. New York: Penguin, 1976.

Evans, Sara. *Personal Politics: The Roots of Women's Liberation in the Civil Rights Movement and the New Left*. New York: Knopf, 1979.

Fallows, James. "What Did You Do in the Class War, Daddy?" *The Washington Monthly*, October 1975. Reprinted in Walter Capps, ed., *The Vietnam Reader*. New York: Routledge, 1991.

Farber, David. *The Age of Great Dreams: America in the 1960s*. New York: Hill and Wang, 1994.

——. *Chicago '68*. Chicago: University of Chicago Press, 1988.

Farrell, James J. *The Spirit of the Sixties: The Making of Postwar Radicalism*. New York: Routledge, 1997.

Ferber, Michael, and Staughton Lynd. *The Resistance*. Boston: Beacon Press, 1971.

Fisher, Charles S. "Midwives to History: The Boston Draft Resistance Group." Unpublished manuscript, 1971.

Flynn, George Q. *The Draft, 1940–1973*. Lawrence: University Press of Kansas, 1993.

——. *Lewis B. Hershey: Mr. Selective Service*. Chapel Hill: University of North Carolina Press, 1985.

Foley, Michael S. "Confronting the Johnson Administration at War: The Trial of Dr. Spock and Use of the Courts to Effect Political Change." *Peace & Change* (January 2003).

——. "The 'Point of Ultimate Indignity' or a 'Beloved Community?': The Draft

Resistance Movement and New Left Gender Dynamics." In *The New Left Revisited*, edited by Paul Buhle and John McMillian. Philadelphia: Temple University Press, 2003.

——. "Sanctuary!: A Bridge between Civilian and GI Protest against the Vietnam War." In *The Blackwell Companion to the Vietnam War*, edited by Robert Buzzanco and Marilyn Young. Boston: Blackwell, 2002.

Foner, Eric. *The Story of American Freedom*. New York: Norton, 1998.

Fraser, Ronald, ed. *1968: A Student Generation in Revolt*. New York: Pantheon, 1988.

Friedland, Michael B. *Lift up Your Voice Like a Trumpet*. Chapel Hill: University of North Carolina Press, 1998.

Gallup, George H. *The Gallup Poll: Public Opinion, 1935–1971*. Vol. 3. New York: Random House, 1972.

Garfinkle, Adam. *Telltale Hearts: The Origins and Impact of the Vietnam Antiwar Movement*. New York: St. Martin's, 1995.

Garrow, David J. *Bearing the Cross: Martin Luther King Jr. and the Southern Christian Leadership Conference*. New York: Vintage, 1986.

Gaylin, Willard. *In the Service of Their Country: War Resisters in Prison*. New York: Viking, 1970.

Gettleman, Marvin, et al., eds. *Vietnam and America: A Documented History*. New York: Grove Press, 1995.

Gitlin, Todd. *The Sixties: Years of Hope, Days of Rage*. New York: Bantam, 1987.

——. *The Twilight of Common Dreams: Why America is Wracked by Culture Wars*. New York: Henry Holt, 1995.

——. *The Whole World Is Watching: Mass Media in the Making and Unmaking of the New Left*. Berkeley: University of California Press, 1980.

Goldman, Eric. *The Tragedy of Lyndon Johnson*. New York: Knopf, 1969.

Goodman, Mitchell, ed. *The Movement toward a New America: The Beginnings of a Long Revolution*. New York: Knopf, 1970.

Goodwin, Richard. *Remembering America: A Voice from the Sixties*. Boston: Little, Brown, 1988.

Gottlieb, Sherry Gershon. *Hell No, We Won't Go!: Resisting the Draft during the Vietnam War*. New York: Viking, 1991.

Goulding, Phil G. *Confirm or Deny: Informing the People on National Security*. New York: Harper & Row, 1970.

Gray, Francine du Plessix. *Divine Disobedience: Profiles in Catholic Radicalism*. New York: Vintage, 1971.

Hagan, John. *Northern Passage: American Vietnam War Resisters in Canada*. Cambridge: Harvard University Press, 2001.

Haig-Brown, Alan. *Hell No, We Won't Go: Vietnam Draft Resisters in Canada*. Vancouver: Raincoast Books, 1996.

Hall, Mitchell K. *Because of Their Faith: CALCAV and Religious Opposition to the Vietnam War*. New York: Columbia University Press, 1990.

Halstead, Fred. *Out Now! A Participant's Account of the American Movement against the Vietnam War*, 2nd ed. New York: Pathfinder, 1991.

Harris, David. *Dreams Die Hard: Three Men's Journey through the Sixties*. New York: St. Martin's, 1982.

———. *Our War: What We Did in Vietnam and What it Did to Us*. New York: Random House, 1996.

Hauser, Thomas. *Muhammad Ali: His Life and Times*. New York: Touchstone, 1991.

Heath, G. Lewis. *Mutiny Does Not Happen Lightly: The Literature of the American Resistance to the Vietnam War*. Metuchen, N.J.: Scarecrow, 1976.

Heineman, Kenneth J. *Campus Wars: The Peace Movement at American State Universities in the Vietnam Era*. New York: New York University Press, 1993.

Herman, Edward S., and Noam Chomsky. *Manufacturing Consent: The Political Economy of the Mass Media*. New York: Pantheon, 1988.

Herring, George. *America's Longest War*, 3rd ed. New York: McGraw-Hill, 1996.

Hershberger, Mary. *Traveling to Vietnam: American Peace Activists and the War*. Syracuse: Syracuse University Press, 1998.

Hoopes, Townsend. *The Limits of Intervention*. New York: McKay, 1969.

Horowitz, Irving. *The Struggle is the Message: The Organization and Ideology of the Anti-War Movement*. Berkeley: Glendessary Press, 1972.

Howe, Daniel Walker. *The Unitarian Conscience: Harvard Moral Philosophy, 1805–1861*. Middletown, Conn.: Wesleyan University Press, 1988.

Hunt, Andrew. *The Turning: A History of Vietnam Veterans against the War*. New York: Columbia University Press, 1999.

Irons, Peter. *The Courage of Their Convictions: Sixteen Americans Who Fought Their Way to the Supreme Court*. New York: Free Press, 1988.

Isaacs, Arnold R. *Vietnam Shadows: The War, Its Ghosts, and Its Legacy*. Baltimore: Johns Hopkins University Press, 1997.

Isaacson, Walter, and Evan Thomas. *The Wise Men: Six Friends and the World They Made*. New York: Simon and Schuster, 1986.

Isserman, Maurice. *If I Had a Hammer: The Death of the Old Left and the Birth of the New Left*. Champaign-Urbana: University of Illinois Press, 1987.

Isserman, Maurice, and Michael Kazin. *America Divided: The Civil War of the 1960s*. New York: Oxford University Press, 2000.

Jack, Homer. *The Gandhi Reader*. Bloomington: Indiana University Press, 1956.

———. *Homer's Odyssey: My Quest for Peace and Justice*. Becket, Mass.: One Peaceful World, 1996.

Jeffreys-Jones, Rhodri. *Peace Now!: American Society and the Ending of the Vietnam War*. New Haven: Yale University Press, 1999.

Johnson, Barry. "Seminarian in 'The Resistance.'" *Christian Century* 85 (January 3, 1968): 15–17.

Karnow, Stanley. *Vietnam: A History*. New York: Viking, 1983.

Katz, Milton S. *Ban the Bomb: A History of SANE, the Committee for a Sane Nuclear Policy, 1957–1985*. New York: Greenwood, 1986.

Keniston, Kenneth. *Young Radicals: Notes on Committed Youth*. New York: Harcourt, Brace, 1968.

Kohn, Stephen M. *Jailed for Peace: The History of American Draft Law Violators, 1658–1985*. New York: Praeger, 1987.

Kolko, Gabriel. *The Anatomy of a War: Vietnam, the United States, and the Modern Historical Experience*. New York: Pantheon, 1985.

Kunstler, William. *My Life as a Radical Lawyer*. New York: Birch Lane Press, 1994.

Kutler, Stanley. *The Encyclopedia of the Vietnam War*. New York: Macmillan, 1996.

Levy, Peter B. *The New Left and Labor in the 1960s*. Chicago: University of Illinois Press, 1994.

Lembcke, Jerry. *The Spitting Image: Myth, Memory, and the Legacy of Vietnam*. New York: New York University Press, 1998.

Lipset, Seymour Martin. *Rebellion in the University*. Boston: Little, Brown, 1972.

Liston, Robert. *Greeting: You Are Hereby Ordered for Induction . . . the Draft in America*. New York: McGraw-Hill, 1970.

Long, Priscilla, ed. *The New Left: A Collection of Essays*. Boston: Extending Horizons, 1969.

Lynd, Alice. *We Won't Go: Personal Accounts of War Objectors*. Boston: Beacon Press, 1968.

Lynn, Conrad. *How to Stay Out of the Army: A Guide to Your Rights under the Draft Law*. New York: Monthly Review Press, 1968.

Lyons, Paul. *Class of '66: Living in Suburban Middle America*. Philadelphia: Temple University Press, 1994.

——. *New Left, New Right, and the Legacy of the Sixties*. Philadelphia: Temple University Press, 1996.

——. "Toward a Revised Story of the Homecoming of Vietnam Veterans." *Peace & Change* 23 (April 1998): 193–200.

Lyttle, Bradford. *The Chicago Anti-Vietnam War Movement*. Chicago: Midwest Pacifist Center, 1988.

MacPherson, Myra. *Long Time Passing: Vietnam and the Haunted Generation*. New York: Doubleday, 1984.

Maier, Thomas. *Dr. Spock: An American Life*. New York: Harcourt, Brace, 1998.

Mailer, Norman. *The Armies of the Night*. New York: Signet, 1968.

Malbin, Michael. "Conscription, the Constitution and the Framers, An Historical Analysis." 40 *Fordham Law Review* 805 (1972).

Maraniss, David. *First in His Class: A Biography of Bill Clinton*. New York: Simon and Schuster, 1995.

Marcuse, Herbert. *One-Dimensional Man*. 2nd ed. Boston: Beacon Press, 1991.

Marqusee, Mike. *Redemption Song: Muhammad Ali and the Spirit of the Sixties*. London: Verso, 1999.

Matusow, Allen J. *The Unraveling of America: A History of Liberalism in the 1960s*. New York: Harper & Row, 1984.

McAdam, Doug. *Freedom Summer*. New York: Oxford University Press, 1988.

McDougall, Marion Gleason. *Fugitive Slaves*. Boston: Ginn & Co., 1891; New York: Bergman, 1967.

McNamara, Robert. *In Retrospect: The Tragedy and Lessons of Vietnam*. New York: Times Books, 1995.

Melman, Seymour. *In the Name of America*. Annandale, Va: Turnpike Press, 1968.

Menashe, Louis, and Ronald Radosh, eds. *Teach-ins U.S.A.: Reports, Opinions, Documents*. New York: Praeger, 1967.

Miller, James. *Democracy Is in the Streets: From Port Huron to the Siege of Chicago*. New York: Touchstone, 1987.

Miller, Melissa, and Philip Shenk. *The Path of Most Resistance*. Scottdale, Pa.: Herald Press, 1982.

Mitford, Jessica. *The Trial of Dr. Spock*. New York: Knopf, 1969.

Morgan, Edward P. *The 60s Experience: Hard Lessons about Modern America*. Philadelphia: Temple University Press, 1991.

——. "From Virtual Community to Virtual History: Mass Media and the American Antiwar Movement of the 1960s." *Radical History Review* 78 (Fall 2000).

Moser, Richard. *The New Winter Soldiers: GI and Veteran Dissent during the Vietnam Era*. New Brunswick: Rutgers University Press, 1996.

Moskos, Charles C., and John Whiteclay Chambers II, eds. *The New Conscientious Objection: From Sacred to Secular Resistance*. New York: Oxford University Press, 1993.

Moss, George Donelson. *Vietnam: An American Ordeal*, 2nd ed. New York: Prentice-Hall, 1994.

Mungo, Ray. *Beyond the Revolution: My Life and Times Since Famous Long Ago*. Chicago: Contemporary, 1990.

——. *Famous Long Ago: My Life and Hard Times With Liberation News Service*. Boston: Beacon Press, 1970; New York: Citadel Underground, 1990.

Nash, Gary. *The Urban Crucible: Social Change, Political Consciousness, and the Origins of the American Revolution*. Cambridge: Harvard University Press, 1979.

Nelkin, Dorothy. *The University and Military Research: Moral Politics at M.I.T.* Ithaca: Cornell University Press, 1972.

Nixon, Richard M. *No More Vietnams*. New York: Arbor House, 1985.

O'Sullivan, John. *The Draft and Its Enemies: A Documentary History*. Urbana: University of Illinois Press, 1974.

Peck, Abe. *Uncovering the Sixties: The Life and Times of the Underground Press*. New York: Pantheon, 1985.

Phillips, Donald E. *Student Protest: An Analysis of the Issues and Speeches*. New York: University Press of America, 1985.

Polner, Murray, and Jim O'Grady. *Disarmed and Dangerous: The Radical Lives and Times of Daniel and Philip Berrigan*. New York: Basic Books, 1997.

Powers, Thomas. *Vietnam: The War at Home*. New York: Grossman, 1973; Boston: G. K. Hall and Company, 1984.

Raskin, Marcus, and Bernard B. Fall. *The Vietnam Reader: Articles and Documents on American Foreign Policy and the Vietnam Crisis*. New York: Random House, 1965.

Remnick, David. *King of the World: Muhammad Ali and the Rise of an American Hero*. New York: Random House, 1998.

Robbins, Mary Susannah. *Against the Vietnam War: Writings by Activists*. Syracuse: Syracuse University Press, 1999.

Rorabaugh, W. J. *Berkeley at War: The 1960s*. New York: Oxford University Press, 1989.

Rossinow, Douglas C. *The Politics of Authenticity: Liberalism, Christianity, and the New Left in America*. New York: Columbia University Press, 1998.

Rusk, Dean. *As I Saw It*. New York: Norton, 1990.

Sale, Kirkpatrick. *SDS*. New York: Vintage, 1974.

Schalk, David F. *War and the Ivory Tower: Algeria and Vietnam*. New York: Oxford University Press, 1994.

Schulzinger, Robert D. *A Time for War: The United States and Vietnam, 1941–1975*. New York: Oxford University Press, 1997.

Seidenberg, Willa, and William Short. *A Matter of Conscience: GI Resistance during the Vietnam War*. Andover, Mass.: Addison Gallery of Art, 1992.

Simons, Donald. *I Refuse: Memories of a Vietnam War Objector*. Trenton: Broken Rifle Press, 1992.

Shafer, D. Michael. "The Vietnam-Era Draft: Who Went, Who Didn't, and Why It Matters." In *The Legacy: The Vietnam War in the American Imagination*, edited by D. Michael Shafer. Boston: Beacon Press, 1990.

Small, Melvin. *Covering Dissent: The Media and the Anti-Vietnam War Movement*. New Brunswick: Rutgers University Press, 1994.

———. "The Impact of the Antiwar Movement on Lyndon Johnson, 1965–1968: A Preliminary Report." *Peace & Change* 10 (Spring 1984).

———. *Johnson, Nixon, and the Doves*. New Brunswick: Rutgers University Press, 1988.

Small, Melvin, and William D. Hoover, eds. *Give Peace a Chance: Exploring the Vietnam Antiwar Movement*. Syracuse: Syracuse University Press, 1992.

Smith, Christian. *Resisting Reagan: The U.S. Central America Peace Movement*. Chicago: University of Chicago Press, 1996.

Southern Conference Educational Fund. "An Enemy of the People: How the Draft Is Used to Stop Movements for Social Change." Louisville, Ky.: SCEF, 1968.

Stewart, James Brewer. *Holy Warriors: The Abolitionists and American Slavery*. New York: Hill and Wang, 1976.

Surrey, David S. *Choice of Conscience: Vietnam Era Military and Draft Resisters in Canada*. New York: Praeger, 1982.

Swerdlow, Amy. *Women Strike for Peace: Traditional Motherhood and Radical Politics in the 1960s*. Chicago: University of Chicago Press, 1993.

Tatum, Arlo. *Guide to the Draft*. Boston: Beacon Press, 1970.

———, ed. *Handbook for Conscientious Objectors*. Philadelphia: CCCO, 1970.

Thoreau, Henry David. "On the Duty of Civil Disobedience." In *Walden and Civil Disobedience*. New York: Signet, 1980.

Thorne, Barrie. "Gender Imagery and Issues of War and Peace: The Case of the Draft Movement in the 1960s." In *The Role of Women in Peace and Conflict Resolution*, edited by Dorothy McGuigan. Ann Arbor: University of Michigan Center for Continuing Education of Women, 1977.

———. "Protest and the Problem of Credibility: Uses of Knowledge and Risk-Taking in the Draft Resistance Movement of the 1960s." *Social Problems* (December 1975).

——. "Women in the Draft Resistance Movement: A Case Study of Sex Roles and Social Movements." *Sex Roles* 1, no. 2 (1975): 179–95.

Tischler, Barbara, ed. *Sights on the Sixties*. New Brunswick: Rutgers University Press, 1992.

Tollefson, James W. *The Strength Not to Fight: An Oral History of Conscientious Objectors of the Vietnam War*. Boston: Little, Brown, 1993.

Tomes, Robert R. *Apocalypse Then: American Intellectuals and the Vietnam War, 1954–1975*. New York: New York University Press, 1998.

Tracy, James. *Direct Action: Radical Pacifism from the Union Eight to the Chicago Seven*. Chicago: University of Chicago Press, 1996.

Turner, Fred. *Echoes of Combat: The Vietnam War in American Memory*. New York: Doubleday, 1996.

Tyler, Alice Felt. *Freedom's Ferment: Phases of American Social History from the Colonial Period to the Outbreak of the Civil War*. Minneapolis: University of Minnesota Press, 1944; New York: Harper, 1962.

Unger, Irwin. *The Movement: A History of the American New Left, 1959–1972*. New York: Dodd, Mead & Co., 1974.

"U.S. Draft Policy and Its Impact." *Congressional Quarterly*. Washington, D.C., 1968.

U.S. National Advisory Commission on Selective Service. *In Pursuit of Equity: Who Serves When Not All Serve?* Washington, D.C.: GPO, 1967.

U.S. Selective Service System. *Annual Reports*. Washington, D.C.: GPO, 1964–76.

Useem, Michael. *Conscription, Protest, and Social Conflict: The Life and Death of a Draft Resistance Movement*. New York: Wiley, 1973.

Vogelgesang, Sandy. *The Long Dark Night of the Soul: The American Intellectual Left and the Vietnam War*. New York: Harper & Row, 1974.

Walzer, Michael. "Democracy and the Conscript." *Dissent* (January/February 1966).

Washington, James M. *A Testament of Hope: The Essential Writings and Speeches of Martin Luther King, Jr*. San Francisco: Harper Collins, 1986.

Wells, Tom. *The War Within: America's Battle over Vietnam*. Berkeley: University of California Press, 1994.

Westby, David L., and Richard G. Braungart. "Class and Politics in the Family Backgrounds of Student Political Activists." *American Sociological Review* 31 (October 1966): 690–92.

Williams, Roger Neville. *The New Exiles: American War Resisters in Canada*. New York: Liveright Publishers, 1971.

Witcover, Jules. *The Year the Dream Died: Revisiting 1968 in America*. New York: Warner Books, 1997.

Wittner, Lawrence S. *Rebels against War: The American Peace Movement, 1933–1983*. Philadelphia: Temple University Press, 1984.

Wyatt, Clarence. *Paper Soldiers: The American Press and the Vietnam War*. New York: Norton, 1993.

Young, Marilyn. *The Vietnam Wars*. New York: Harper, 1991.

Zaroulis, Nancy, and Gerald Sullivan. *Who Spoke Up? American Protest against the War in Vietnam, 1963–1975*. Garden City, N.Y.: Doubleday, 1984.

Zinn, Howard. *A People's History of the United States*. Revised and updated ed. New York: Harper Collins, 1995.

——. *You Can't Be Neutral on a Moving Train: A Personal History of Our Times*. Boston: Beacon Press, 1994.

DISSERTATIONS AND THESES

Haasl, Tekla Louise. " 'I Want to Knock Down the World': A Study of Radical Feminism and Cell 16." M.A. thesis, University of New Hampshire, 1988.

Hensley, William E. "The Vietnam Anti-War Movement: History and Criticism." Ph.D. diss., University of Oregon, 1979.

Katz, Neil H. "Radical Pacifism and the Contemporary American Peace Movement: The Committee for Non-Violent Action, 1957–1967." Ph.D. diss., University of Maryland, 1974.

Thorne, Barrie. "Resisting the Draft: An Ethnography of the Draft Resistance Movement." Ph.D. diss., Brandeis University, 1971.

INDEX

306–7, 334–35, 340; role of "adult" supporters in, 5, 94–96, 163–64, 192–97, 234–35, 238–39; in American memory, 6–9, 13, 129; critics of, 8–9, 13–14, 97, 98–99, 115, 117–18, 133, 168, 169–77; and civil rights movement precedent, 9, 14, 124; strategy of, 9, 25, 78–79, 126, 193, 272, 277; impact on antiwar movement, 14; impact on Johnson administration, 14, 134, 257–59, 263, 345–46; and Omega symbol, 15, 143; as act of good citizenship, 25, 171, 247, 248, 250; other historical antecedents, 26–27, 114, 174; students with deferments, 78; emphasis on community, 100–104, 142–43; and counterculture, 129, 253–54, 297–98, 303–5; and organizing difficulties, 141–43; supporters' demographics and backgrounds, 177–79; experience of gay men in, 184; reacts to Johnson's decision to forgo reelection run, 261–62; as part of international student movement, 270–72; revolutionary rhetoric of, 272, 273–75, 296–97, 298, 300, 302; shifting strategies of, 277–81, 294–95, 296–98, 299, 300–322 passim; and sanctuary for GIs, 277–81, 308–22, 335; clashes with police, 279–80; expands into suburbs, 305–8; and high school outreach, 307–8; and GI outreach, 308–22, 335; impact on Nixon administration, 338–39, 344; continued activism of participants, 339–43

Draft resisters: thirty-year reunion, 3–6; apply for conscientious objector status, 4; sexism of, 5, 181–91; compared to draft "dodgers," 7, 12–13, 24, 143; motives, 14, 42–45, 102–6, 107, 116, 120, 126–28, 132, 171, 238–39, 248–49, 250, 254; face violence, 19–21, 34, 40, 198–99, 245, 332;

prosecution of, 42–45; critique of Selective Service System, 43–45, 78; critique of Vietnam War, 43–46, 76–78, 170; anxiety over draft card turn-in, 99–100, 127–28; respond to critics, 104, 170, demographics and backgrounds, 116, 122–24, 129–30; draft classifications of, 122; reclassified punitively, 157, 326; ignored by local board, 158–59, 326; reaction of parents, 160–67, 243, 244–46; reaction of employers, 163, 168–77; refuse induction, 240–51, 253–55, 326; views of GIs, 309–10; apply for or accept new draft cards, 326–27; imprisoned, 331–34; post-draft resistance activism, 339–43; reflect on their resistance, 341–48

Draper, Theodore, 193
Drew, Bill, 162
Dubček, Alexander, 270
DuBois, Ellen, 183, 185, 189
Dunbar, Roxanne, 185, 190
Dutschke, Rudi, 270
Dylan, Bob, 129

Earth Opera, 277
Educational Cooperative, 195
Egleson, Nick, 72, 94, 104, 115; speech on Boston Common, 98–99
Eisenhower, Dwight, 292
El Salvador: U.S. intervention in, 341, 346
Emerson College, 29
Etscovitz, Larry, 3–4, 127, 327

Fallows, James, 12
Fay, Janine, 188–89
Federal Bureau of Investigation (FBI), 21, 41, 120, 125, 133–35, 136, 145–46, 148, 179, 198, 288; interviews draft resisters' parents, 138, 140, 161, 251; interviews draft resisters, 138–41, 143–44, 159
Feeney, Paul, 42

(SDS), 32, 51–53, 64, 72, 79, 179, 188, 189, 191, 195, 335, 340; origins, 57; and support of draft resistance, 57–58; and Vietnam Summer, 63; and intellectual influence on New England Resistance, 85, 273; criticism of draft resistance, 87–89
SUPPORT, 299, 323–25, 329, 335
Supreme Court, U.S., 15, 328–30
Sweeney, Dennis, 77

Talmanson, Robert, 80, 275–80, 281, 286
Taylor, Maxwell, 258
Taylor, Telford, 285
Temple, Larry, 151
Tent City protest, 269
Thich Tri Quang, 81
Thoreau, Henry David, 13, 19, 26; cited by draft resisters, 43–44, 114
Thorne, Barrie, 74, 314–15
Tilton, Dan, 85, 280, 302
Truman, Harry S., 36

Ultra-Resistance, 181, 340
U.S. Servicemen's Fund, 339
Ustinov, Peter, 101, 115, 248

Vance, Cyrus, 259
Van de Kamp, John, 133–34, 136, 155, 230
Van Ocur, Sander, 108, 114, 120
Venn, Christopher, 139–41, 165, 347
Veterans for Peace, 100
Vietnam Summer, 62–63, 71, 72, 79, 124, 179
Vietnam Veterans Against the War, 45, 277
Vietnam War, 31–32, 38; escalation of, 38; civilian targets hit, 45, 53, 84, 94–95, 100, 337; debate over origins, 53; fought by working class, 55–56; Geneva Accords, 94, 144, 292; as perceived by draft resisters and supporters, 94–95, 105, 125–26, 170–71,

228–29, 251, 254, 292; My Lai massacre, 251; Tet Offensive, 256, 257, 259, 346; GI casualties, 271, 337; Paris Peace Accords, 337; expands into Cambodia, 337, 344
Volpe, John A., 30, 118
Von Rosenvinge, Jannik, 242–43, 341, 347

Wall, John: prosecutes draft resisters, 42–45, 286, 325; and Boston Five indictments, 228, 230; and non-prosecution of resisters, 252; and trial of Boston Five, 285–86, 288–94
Wallace, George, 317
Walzer, Michael, 78, 193
Warnke, Paul, 259
Warren, Earl, 281
War Resisters' League, 33
Waskow, Arthur, 94, 133–34, 294
Weatherman (a.k.a. the Weathermen), 129, 189, 340
Westmoreland, William, 256, 257, 345–46
"We Won't Go" pledges, 49, 57, 61, 64, 94; Resistance critique of, 77
Wheeler, Earle, 146, 256
White, Byron, 248
White, Kevin, 298
Wicker, Tom, 90
Williams, George Hunston, 94, 106–7, 115, 120, 125
Williams, Suzanne, 20–21, 34, 41, 340
Wilson, Harold, 45
Wilson, Woodrow, 36
Winget, Bob, 313
Wise Men, 258–60
Wolcott, Richard, 237
Women: in draft resistance movement. See Boston Draft Resistance Group; Draft resistance movement; New England Resistance; Resist
Workshop in Nonviolence (WIN), 33